'The argument for the influence of love on medieval church architecture is exceptional in its originality, scope and development. Given his premises, the argument from theology is of such importance that it is sure to force a rethinking of the influences on medieval church building, while suggesting modern application as well.

The discussion of the churches reflects an unusually proficient grasp of the architectural issues. Lewis makes a strong case for understanding Gothic churches as expressions of vernacular architecture—something that historicist focus on developing styles has mostly misunderstood. This book will make a major contribution to the emerging field which one might call theology and the built environment.'

William Dyrness, Professor of Theology and Culture,
Fuller Theological Seminary, USA

The Architecture of Medieval Churches

The Architecture of Medieval Churches investigates the impact of affective theology on architecture and artefacts, focusing on the Middle Ages as a period of high achievement of this synthesis. It explores aspects of medieval church and cathedral architecture in relation to the contemporary metaphysics and theology, which articulated an integrated theocentric culture, architecture, and art. Three modes of attention: comprehension, instruction, and contemplation, informed the builders' intuition and intention. The book's central premise reasons that love for God was the critical force in the creation of vernacular church architecture, using a selection of medieval writings to provide a unique critique of the genius of architecture and art during this period. An interdisciplinary study between architecture, theology, and philosophy, it will appeal to academics and researchers in these fields.

John A. H. Lewis holds Bachelor and Master of Architecture degrees from the University of Auckland, and a PhD (Theology) from the University of Otago, New Zealand. He is a member of the New Zealand Institute of Architects, and practised as an architect for thirty years before concentrating as an independent scholar on medieval studies in architecture, theology, and Dante Alighieri.

Routledge Research in Architecture

The *Routledge Research in Architecture* series provides the reader with the latest scholarship in the field of architecture. The series publishes research from across the globe and covers areas as diverse as architectural history and theory, technology, digital architecture, structures, materials, details, design, monographs of architects, interior design and much more. By making these studies available to the worldwide academic community, the series aims to promote quality architectural research.

For a full list of titles, please visit: https://www.routledge.com/Routledge-Research-in-Architecture/book-series/RRARCH

Architectural Colossi and the Human Body
Buildings and Metaphors
Charalampos Politakis

From Doxiadis' Theory to Pikionis' Work
Reflections of Antiquity in Modern Architecture
Kostas Tsiambaos

Thermal Comfort in Hot Dry Climates
Traditional Dwellings in Iran
Ahmadreza Foruzanmehr

Architecture and the Body, Science and Culture
Kim Sexton

The Ideal of Total Environmental Control
Knud Lonberg-Holm, Buckminster Fuller, and the SSA
Suzanne Strum

The Architecture of Medieval Churches
Theology of Love in Practice
John A. H. Lewis

https://www.routledge.com/architecture/series/RRARCH

The Architecture of Medieval Churches
Theology of Love in Practice

John A. H. Lewis

LONDON AND NEW YORK

First published 2018
by Routledge
2 Park Square, Milton Park, Abingdon, Oxon, OX14 4RN

and by Routledge
711 Third Avenue, New York, NY 10017

Routledge is an imprint of the Taylor & Francis Group, an informa business

© 2018 John A. H. Lewis

The right of John A. H. Lewis to be identified as author of this work has been asserted by him in accordance with sections 77 and 78 of the Copyright, Designs and Patents Act 1988.

All rights reserved. No part of this book may be reprinted or reproduced or utilised in any form or by any electronic, mechanical, or other means, now known or hereafter invented, including photocopying and recording, or in any information storage or retrieval system, without permission in writing from the publishers.

Trademark notice: Product or corporate names may be trademarks or registered trademarks, and are used only for identification and explanation without intent to infringe.

British Library Cataloguing-in-Publication Data
A catalogue record for this book is available from the British Library

Library of Congress Cataloging-in-Publication Data
Names: Lewis, John, Ph.D., author.
Title: The architecture of medieval churches : theology of love in practice / John Lewis.
Description: New York : Routledge, 2018. | Series: Routledge research in architecture | Outgrowth of the author's thesis (Ph. D.—University of Otago) under the title: Influence on medieval church architecture of love for God: a theological approach. | Includes bibliographical references and index.
Identifiers: LCCN 2017024081| ISBN 9781138636200 (hardback) | ISBN 9781315206110 (ebook)
Subjects: LCSH: Church architecture—Europe. | Architecture, Medieval—Themes, motives. | Symbolism in architecture. | Love—Religious aspects—Christianity.
Classification: LCC NA5453 .L49 2018 | DDC 726.5—dc23
LC record available at https://lccn.loc.gov/2017024081

ISBN: 978-1-138-63620-0 (hbk)
ISBN: 978-1-315-20611-0 (ebk)

Typeset in Sabon
by Swales & Willis Ltd, Exeter, Devon, UK

Printed in the United Kingdom
by Henry Ling Limited

Contents

List of figures ix
Acknowledgements xii
Permissions and credits xiv
List of abbreviations xvi
Foreword xvii

1 Introduction 1
  A view of medieval churches 1
  Sources and searching 5
  Deductive methodology 7
  Reading theology 11
  Rethinking architecture 15
  Connections and integrity 19

2 The mind in love 27
  Perceptions of love 27
  Progression in love 31
  Measure, form, inclination 36
  Love in the Trinity 47
  Implications of incarnation 51
  Love as hierarch and worker 53

3 The mirror of comprehension: the trivium 63
  The logical arts 63
  Personifications. The scope of the mind 66
  Philology. The spirit of understanding 70
  Grammar 72
  Dialectic 80
  Rhetoric 90

viii   Contents

4   **The mirror of instruction: the quadrivium**   112
The mathematical arts 112
Computus model 116
Arithmetic 118
Music 124
Geometry 133
Astronomy 143

5   **The mirror of contemplation: life in nature**   157
In love with things 157
The Source, Support and End 159
The Creator of earthly nature 162
Reflection of nature in architecture 166
Mind and hand of an artificer 175
Angelic contemplation 179
Visualisation 183
Representation 188
Operatio 193

6   **Building in love**   201
Consideration 201
Judgement 204
Intuition 208
Incarnation and nature 214
Intention 220
Trinity and integration 225
Junction between heaven and earth 230

Bibliography   237
  Primary sources 237
  Secondary sources 242
Index   249
  Scripture references 261

Figures

All photographs of churches are by the Author, taken between 1995 and 2005.

Cover: Prenzlau, Germany. Cathedral church of St Mary. East end.

1.1	Morienval, France. Notre-Dame abbey church. Nave, view east.	10
1.2	Coutances, France. Cathedral church of Notre-Dame. South-west tower.	18
2.1	Amiens, France. Cathedral church of St-Firmin. West porch bas-relief.	39
2.2	Psalter of Isobel of France. Initial letter of Psalm 27. (Cambridge, Fitzwilliam Museum, fol. 26r.)	43
2.3	Lucca, Italy. Church of San Frediano. East front mosaic.	45
2.4	The Trinity. Psalter frontispiece. (London, British Library, Harley MS 603, fol. 1.)	49
2.5	'Operatio'. Medallion from Stavelot Abbey retable. Kunstgewerbemuseum, Berlin. (bpk/Kunstgewerbemuseum, SMB/Hans-Joachim Bartsch.)	54
3.1	Laon, France. Cathedral church of Notre-Dame. North transept rose window.	69
3.2	Coutances, France. Cathedral church of Notre-Dame. West front.	74
3.3	Magdeburg, Germany. Cathedral church of St Maurice and St Catherine. West front detail.	76
3.4	Wrocław, Poland. Church of St-Mary-on-the-Sands. Nave and aisle.	77
3.5	Moissac, France. St-Pierre Abbey church. Chapel detail.	79
3.6	Southwell, England. Minster of St Mary. Nave arcade.	85
3.7	Southwell, England. Cathedral church of St Mary. Choir arcade.	86

x *Figures*

3.8	Girona, Spain. Cathedral church of Santa Maria. Nave and choir.	88
3.9	Troyes, France. Church of St-Urbain. West front.	94
3.10	Troyes, France. Church of St-Urbain. East end.	95
3.11	Toulouse, France. Les Jacobins church. The tower on the north side.	98
3.12	Salisbury, England. Cathedral church of St Mary. West front.	105
3.13	Peterborough, England. Cathedral church of St Peter. West front.	106
4.1	Lincoln, England. Cathedral of St Mary. Chapter house.	115
4.2	Wells, England. Cathedral church of St Andrew. Chapter house.	119
4.3	Laon, France. Cathedral church of Notre-Dame. Central crossing.	121
4.4	Winchester, England. Hospital chapel St Cross.	128
4.5	Beverley, England. Minster church of St John Evangelist.	129
4.6	Mantes, France. Cathedral church of Notre-Dame. Interior of choir.	131
4.7	Soest, Germany. Collegiate church of St Patroclus. West tower.	135
4.8	Le Mans, France. Cathedral church of St-Julien. East chevet.	137
4.9	Milan, Italy. Cathedral church of Santa Maria Maggiore. Nave roof and crossing tower.	142
4.10	Metz, France. Cathedral church of St-Étienne. Choir triforium detail.	145
4.11	Wrocław, Poland. Church of SS. Dorothy, Stanislaus and Wenceslaus. Nave and choir.	148
4.12	Laon, France. Cathedral church of Notre-Dame. West front.	149
5.1	Angoulême, France. Cathedral church of St-Pierre.	161
5.2	Florence, Italy. San Miniato al Monte church. Interior.	165
5.3	Bristol, England. Cathedral church of the Holy Trinity. Interior.	168
5.4	Gloucester, England. Cathedral church of the Holy Trinity. Choir clerestory and vault.	170
5.5	St-Lizier, France. Cathedral church of St-Lizier. Nave vault, decoration.	173
5.6	Canon Table drawing. (Paris, Bibliothèque Nationale, MS Lat.9383, Evangeliar, fol. 2ᵛ.)	174

5.7	Lincoln, England. Cathedral church of St Mary. West front.	177
5.8	Lincoln, England. Cathedral church of St Mary. Nave and choir from west end.	177
5.9	Regensburg, Germany. Cathedral church of St Peter. South transept detail.	185
5.10	Brioude, France. Church of St-Julien. Sanctuary vault fresco.	187
5.11	Frontispiece of the *Bible historiée* of Jean de Papeleu. (Paris, Bibliothèque Nationale, Bibliothèque de l'Arsénal, MS 5059, fol. 1.)	188
5.12	Mantes, France. Cathedral church of Notre-Dame. West front.	192
6.1	St-Savin-sur-Gartempe, France. Church of St-Savin. West tower.	202
6.2	Hereford, England. Cathedral church of St Mary. North transept.	208
6.3	Coutances, France. Cathedral church of Notre-Dame. Ambulatory.	209
6.4	Vignogoul, France. Cistercian abbey church. Apse.	215
6.5	St-Bertrand-de-Comminges, France. Church of Ste. Marie. Apse clerestory.	217
6.6	Manuscript illumination. (London, The British Library, MS Yates Thompson 26.)	222

Acknowledgements

For their involvement and guidance in the doctoral dissertation, and subsequently, I especially thank:

> Dr James Ginther, Professor of Medieval Theology, Department of Theological Studies, Saint Louis University.
>
> Dr Murray Rae, Professor of Theology, Department of Theology and Religious Studies, University of Otago.
>
> Dr Mervyn Duffy, Dean of Studies, Good Shepherd Theological College, Auckland.

For encouragement, critique and support at different stages I am grateful to:

> Mr David Burt, Lawyer (retired) and Theologian, Auckland.
>
> Dr Ivor Davidson, Professor of Systematic and Historical Theology, University of St Andrews.
>
> Dr Allan Doig, Fellow and Chaplain, Lady Margaret Hall, Oxford.
>
> Dr William Dyrness, Professor of Theology & Culture, Fuller Theological Seminary, Los Angeles.
>
> Dr Stephanie Hollis, Emeritus Professor of English and Director of the Centre for Medieval and Early Modern European Studies, University of Auckland.
>
> Dr Brian Horne, Senior Lecturer (retired), Department of Theology and Religious Studies, King's College, London.
>
> Dr Bernard McGinn, Professor Emeritus, University of Chicago, Divinity School.
>
> Ms Karen Mackesy, Graphic Designer, Auckland.

Dr Estelle Maré, Emeritus Professor of Art and Architectural History, University of South Africa, Pretoria.

Dr John Morton, Emeritus Professor of Zoology, University of Auckland.

Mr Anthony Watkins, Senior Lecturer (retired), School of Architecture, Planning and Property, University of Auckland.

Dr Michael Wright, Senior Lecturer, and Research Fellow, English Department, University of Auckland.

Permissions and credits

Permission has been generously granted for the use of excerpts from published works as follows:

Excerpts from *Pseudo-Dionysius: The Complete Works*, translated by Colm Lubheid. Copyright © 1987 Colm Lubheid, Paulist Press, Inc., New York/Mahwah, NJ. Reprinted by permission of Paulist Press, Inc. www.paulistpress.com.

From Saint Augustine, *The immortality of the soul; The magnitude of the soul; On music*, FC 4. Copyright © 1947, republished with permission of Catholic University of America Press (CUA); permission conveyed through Copyright Clearance Center, Inc.

Martianus Capella and the Seven Liberal Arts, Vol. II: The Marriage of Philology and Mercury, trans. W. H. Stahl, R. Johnson and E. L. Burge. Copyright © 1977, New York, NY: Columbia University Press.

Bernard of Clairvaux on the Song of Songs, Volume I. For Liturgical Press reference 978-0-8790-7704-4 (CF004). Copyright 1971 Cistercian Publications, Inc. © 2008 Order of Saint Benedict, Collegeville, Minnesota. Used with permission.

Bernard of Clairvaux on the Song of Songs, Volume II. For Liturgical Press reference 978-0-8790-7707-5 (CF007). Copyright 1976 Cistercian Publications, Inc. © 2008 Order of Saint Benedict, Collegeville, Minnesota. Used with permission.

William of St Thierry, The Golden Epistle. For Liturgical Press reference 978-0-8790-7712-9 (CF012). Copyright 1971 Cistercian Publications, Inc. © 2008 Order of Saint Benedict, Collegeville, Minnesota. Used with permission.

On Charity, St Thomas Aquinas, trans Lottie H. Kendzierski. ISBN 9780874622102. Copyright © 1960, Milwaukee, WI: Marquette University Press. Reprinted by permission of the publisher. All rights reserved. www.marquette.edu/mupress

Three Medieval Rhetorical Arts, ed. James J. Murphy (Geoffrey of Vinsauf, *Poetria nova*, trans, Jane Baltzell Kopp), Berkeley, CA: University of California Press. Copyright © 1971 James J. Murphy.

The Seven Liberal Arts in the Middle Ages, ed. David L. Wagner. Copyright © 1983, Bloomington, IN: Indiana University Press. Reprinted with permission of Indiana University Press.

Faith Wallis, 'Images of Order in the Medieval Computus,' in *Ideas of Order in the Middle Ages*, ed. Warren Ginsberg, Binghamton: CEMERS (ACTA v. 15), 1990, 45–68.

Robert Jan van Pelt, 'Philo of Alexandria and the Architecture of the Cosmos.' *AA Files* No. 4, 1983. AA Publications, London. Courtesy of Architectural Association, London.

Auctores Britannici Medii Aevi, VI(2), Robert Grosseteste, *On the Six Days of Creation. A Translation of the Hexaëmeron* by C. F. J. Martin. ©The British Academy 1996. Used with permission.

Permission has been generously granted for the reproduction of artefacts and manuscript images as follows:

'Operatio'. Medallion from former Stavelot retable. Kunstgewerbemuseum, Berlin. Copyright © bpk-Bildegentur. Reproduced with permission.

Initial letter of Psalm 27. From the Psalter of Isobel of France, fol. 26r. Reproduction by permission of the Syndics of The Fitzwilliam Museum, Cambridge.

Canon Table. Paris, Bibliothèque Nationale, MS Lat.9383, Evangeliar, fol. 2^v. Reproduced with permission of Bibliothèque Nationale de France.

From the *Bible historiée* of Jean de Papeleu. Paris, Bibliothèque de l'Arsénal, MS 5059, fol. 1. Reproduced with permission of Bibliothèque Nationale de France.

The Trinity. From an Anglo-Saxon Psalter. London, British Library, Harley MS 603, fol. 1. Image in Public Domain.

Monk and Angel building. Illumination. London. The British Library, Yates Thompson MS 26. Image in Public Domain.

Abbreviations

ABMA   Auctores Britannici medii aevi (for The British Academy)
ACW   Ancient Christian Writers Series
AV   Authorised Version (King James Version, 1611)
CCCM   Corpus Christianorum Continuatio Mediaevalis
CCSL   Corpus Christianorum, Series Latina
CCT   Corpus Christianorum in Translation
CF   Cistercian Fathers Series
CS   Cistercian Studies Series
CWS   Classics of Western Spirituality Series
FC   Fathers of the Church Series
LCC   The Library of Christian Classics
MPTT   Mediaeval Philosophical Texts in Translation
MST   Mediaeval Sources in Translation
SBO   *Sancti Bernardi Opera*
TTH   Translated Texts for Historians
VTT   Victorine Texts in Translation

Old and New Testament quotations are from the Revised Standard Version, and Deutero-canonical (Apocrypha) quotations are from the Authorized Version, unless stated otherwise.

Foreword

Approaching an understanding of medieval architecture has always raised vexed questions, beginning with the word 'medieval' itself: between what ages? It was the central section of a tripartite view of history presented by Leonardo Bruni who revived the ideals of antiquity in the early fifteenth century, and was used by classicising Humanists to distinguish themselves and the new learning from the dark days since the fall of Roman civilisation to Gothic barbarism in 410 and the Sack of Rome. To the Renaissance mind, the 'Gothic' represented all that was irrational and fanciful in the arts, including architecture, as though civilisation was just rousing itself from a thousand-year bout of madness. Such caricature could only be seriously entertained by the most dedicated classicising humanist, but what did the astonishing technical and artistic achievements of medieval architecture mean within their own contemporary context? That, of course, is not a simple, nor even a single, question.

Petrarch saw Italy about to emerge from a 'Lethean sleep' of a dark age; in sixteenth-century France, the architect Philibert de l'Orme was more positive about Gothic vaulting which he called 'voutes de la mode & façon Françoise'; Christopher Wren in seventeenth-century England considered it to be a 'Saracen style' imported via Spain; in the eighteenth, Goethe called it German architecture, quintessentially resolved in the Cathedral at Strasbourg. For A. N. W. Pugin in the nineteenth century, it embodied religious and moral qualities which needed to be revived, and rational qualities that produced coherent style. John Ruskin and William Morris saw the Gothic Style in social terms and the expression and manual trace of the craftsman. Viollet-le-Duc believed the style was the result of consummate technical development in Gothic Rationalism. That technical approach amazingly reached its apogee in Antoni Gaudì's Sagrada Familia in Barcelona where it was overlaid with a complex symbolism.

In twentieth-century criticism, Emile Mâle took a didactic iconographic approach to the Gothic. His aim was to recover the complex meanings of the imagery of the church: 'The pathetic name of *Biblia pauperum* given by printers of the fifteenth century to one of their earliest books, might well have been given to the church', he wrote in the Preface to

The Gothic Image. On the other hand, Otto von Simson, in the Preface to *The Gothic Cathedral: Origins of Gothic Architecture and the Medieval Concept of Order*, maintained that:

> The Cathedral, as we shall see, was designed as an image, and was meant to be understood as one. It remains, nevertheless, quite true that ecclesiastical architecture represents the reality of which it is symbol or image in a manner that differs radically from that of painting or sculpture. Architecture is not the image of objects that our eye may encounter in nature; it has no content that we could distinguish from architectural style.

In *Gothic Architecture and Scholasticism*, Erwin Panofsky compared the methodology of the *summa* of the Parisian Scholastics with the visual dialectic of the contemporary architects of the Isle de France as a way of thinking that was generative of both *summa* and church. The English scholarly tradition is not at all the same in its approach, preferring to stick to historical and stylistic developments within their intellectual context.

When considering what buildings, or indeed any objects, mean, the broader context within which they were made and used is going to be of great importance. For medieval architecture, surely theology is of overriding importance and many, but by no means all, of the approaches just mentioned, take theology into account at least to some extent. However, few if any tackle the theological context head-on, though some explore biblical and theological narratives as Mâle does, or theological methodology as Panofsky. This book by John Lewis takes on that immense task, seeking to unravel the web through which theology might give rise to an architecture. How might theological content become embodied in a building? We shall see as this book unfolds.

Allan Doig,
Lady Margaret Hall, Oxford
15 May 2017

1 Introduction

A view of medieval churches

In portraying the battle to save the soul of Notting Hill—to save the identity of the city—G. K. Chesterton set it in a medieval time-warp. It was not, however, merely romantic medievalism. In the silent darkness at the close of the story a philosophising voice says, 'And in the darkest of the books of God there is written a truth that is also a riddle. It is of the new things that men tire—of fashions and proposals and improvements and change. It is the old things that startle and intoxicate. It is the old things that are young.'[1] The medieval architecture of churches and cathedrals which we still see can startle our minds and intoxicate our senses, and all the more as our world's obsession with 'fashion and proposals' hides a tiredness and temporariness affecting deepest human potentialities. The final dialogue in Chesterton's novel is heard by no one but the reader: it may be the same with this book, but it is warranted if here is 'written a truth'. We may see it participating in all truth—but it will only talk of certain matters.

Achievements in medieval church architecture and medieval theology alike had extraordinary power and enduring value. The theology may be a less immediately accessible field than the architecture, for while it is text-based the writings seem like dark books in our century. Architectural history has had little real engagement with it. This study tries to discern whether much of the power and value in the architecture can be elucidated through the minds that constructed the theology, and whether the theology was at some or many levels embodied in the buildings. It investigates the mental influence and creative impulses in the spiritual regimen, and draws from the parallel culture of learning and arts a context for the architecture. It thus seeks to understand central ideas directing somehow the makers of churches in the Middle Ages.

According to academic norms this is an interdisciplinary study, and because of established demarcations the connections in the subject may seem strained. But to medieval thinkers of profound ideas and makers of manifold things the opposite was rather the case: there was a sensed unity and coherence linking all that exists. If valid in the Middle Ages, it might have value for today to attempt to give an account of such noetic and spiritual awareness and pervasive, even unconscious, integration: this, hopefully, is an open possibility.

Although remote in time from their construction, very many churches are in the present time still used and loved. They evoke a sense that somehow these places locate us between two great preoccupations—architecture and theology. The underlying locus is deeply Christocentric thought. Architects now might admire medieval church architecture but are unlikely to venture very far into medieval learning, while those charged with the care of the churches tend to find archaeological aspects more pressing than theological ones. Architectural historians in such a rich field of study, though presumably having an awareness of theological subjects, do not follow far the ramifications of a spiritual focus in architecture. But when we are open to a convincing power and integrity in the works themselves the natural questions are: how were such extraordinary churches made? why were they made thus? Difficult as those questions may be, harder ones remain: what meaning do the works carry? how do they express it? We should not be surprised to find that the questions as to the making and the enquiry into the meaning have one underlying answer. We may come to see that that which held a central place in theology had a key role in the conception and art of making of these buildings.

Aside from architecture and theology, building and religion are two most fundamental activities in a culture (unless there be a wholly secular society). In the Middle Ages, while there was so much religion, vigorous theology was not impeded and the culture owned it, to the extent that the theology carried essentials of the culture quite *explicitly*. It can therefore effectively lead interdisciplinary enquiry. It was a dominant tenet that everything be connected to God by every person—and in community—coming to love him *first*; and this will be adduced from many written sources. The evidence will show that connecting 'everything' to God included the arts and, implicitly, architecture, which things were to be in fact means to the end of loving and magnifying God. The insight that embraces both architecture and theology, and becomes the key signifier of meaning, is that from conception to completion the buildings may properly be understood as works of love towards God, as material things pointing to spiritual.

To give attention to love as a central theme in the mentality may seem too oblique to the appreciation of architecture. But a starting point is that theocentric love could regard everything created and made as part of a universally integrating order. In the light of this emphasis, we will consider how it might have been intrinsic in the architecture and art. We will see love as central because it was reiterated in intellectual, affective, and mystical modes of theology as being indispensable in human attitudes and acts. A radical appraisal then of the architecture of abbey churches, cathedral churches, and parish churches will connect motivation, processes of making, and the buildings and art works produced, with this almost indefinable element.

The coincidence of developments in architecture and theology in the twelfth and thirteenth centuries brings this into sharpest focus. Both became highly articulate. Love for God was reiterated by theologians; and devotion may have operated with fervour in architects and builders of churches. Our first purpose is achieved if we can deduce that love for God was an effective motivating factor—without having to prove that this was the sole factor. Motivations are seldom single, as the theology of love well recognised; nor did it reckon human works to be perfectible. At that time theology and church building held primary places and their works were vast; and because of their diverse modes—one dealing with ideas and texts, the other with arts and phenomena—we have to be prepared to find evidence of connections quite dispersed and fragmentary. The problems inherent in this will be discussed shortly, but some boundaries of the topic and limits to research can be delineated.

It might be thought that use of theological evidence by itself entails a too simplistic theory of derivation. The hypothesis in turn may seem more idealistic than application to the material phenomena can support. Günther Binding, appraising a medieval text which employs a building metaphor, writes, 'These comments make it clear to us that theological ideas were not the prime mover in the design of Gothic cathedrals. [They] were a conceptual aid [. . .] but did not determine form.'[2] He allows that 'theoretical' theology reveals meaning but disallows any instrumental role of note. Such a view provokes the need for extensive and closer scrutiny of sources.

There were, of course, complex conditions underlying the construction of medieval churches; societal aspects such as patronage, and political and religious forces. There may seem to be a legitimate demand for exhaustive treatment of all surrounding issues, but even if that were possible it would, because of the special claims of theological love, only bear out theology's contention that love operates on or from a superior level, ultimately beyond contradiction or negation. We will not give attention to evidently contrary or equally prevalent features of medieval society, for instance profane love, or religious practices such as a regard for images which later reformers considered idolatrous. Such aspects are emphasised by some with the effect of detracting from spiritual influences shaping the works of ecclesiastical art and architecture, and diverting the focus away from positive substantive matters. Despite human deficiencies the main attitude of medieval theologians in treating human love for God is affirmatory, and we must resist being deflected from seeing its full ramifications. Also it should become apparent that distinctions between, or the emphases of, scholastic theology and monastic theology are not very relevant to our subject, although their milieu deserves to be taken into account. As to the role of liturgy in the architecture it warrants more particular treatment than this study can give.[3]

From the twelfth to the mid-fourteenth century both architecture and theology in Latin Europe produced extraordinary work which was innovative and prolific. The roots of the achievements in both endeavours are

4 *Introduction*

earlier, a continuum indeed from the start of the Christian era; there are also fine later achievements. Where evidence across the whole time span can be treated for its acuity rather than historically, it need not be precluded. Thus the time-frame for theological and intellectual sources can accommodate two strands of evidence: (a) earlier and contemporary written sources which might have been drawn upon by, or have indirectly influenced, the architects and builders; (b) literary evidence from contemporary and late medieval sources which might articulate or explain the architectural work which was being produced. The time-frame for the architecture for which the case is being made likewise extends to earlier works which may cast light on the matter. Later examples also are important, in order to accommodate the length of building projects, recognising too that 'development' was not necessarily linear or consistently 'progressive'. From the much studied high period in France and England we should allow a time lag of half a century and more to include the full achievements in the north and east of Europe.

The useful methodologies are not those of architectural history; rather they will be the detection of the critical elements of architecture—motivations, concepts, design processes, skills, and judgements, as pertaining in the time. In architectural history much valuable research is available, which we need not attempt to extend in those terms; we utilise it where it is relevant to our purposes. Because premises will be drawn from the contemporary theology, the study is not a historicist demonstration nor tied to a methodology in which stylistic developments and distinctions are core matters.[4] It will seek a reading of architecture more precisely in the light of the theology and learning, and will enjoy the variety and eccentricities of the phenomena both local and of Europe-wide diffusion, apart from the matter of styles. It is outside its scope to define or explain distinctions of Romanesque and Gothic, or of regional styles and 'schools', taking the view that architecture is not essentially about style. The confusing term Late Gothic is generally avoided lest it be assumed to refer to examples which show a decline of inner motivation and loss of authentic meaning preceding the classical Renaissance. The picture of decline and loss, or transition, is not simple as to time or geography, and we will not attempt to trace it here. More relevant is a discussion of the buildings as vernacular architecture. Robert Jan van Pelt notes that architectural historicism cannot deal with the phenomenon of vernacular building, which is 'architecture without history', because of the way historicism reads architecture.[5]

A problem may be perceived in that the study spans across two broad fields and more than two centuries with a single unifying idea—it is a narrative on a rather large scale. Yet the topic of love itself, the thrust of the theology, and the phenomenon of the architecture, all justify a constructive theory which recognises the regard of absolute values and ideal order in that quite highly integrated culture. The account, derived from the twofold material, has to be proportionate to the phenomenon. That derivation gives access to a valid view of the architecture which post-modern perceptions of the works apart from any perspective of intentionality, would be closed against. Madeline Caviness pertinently sketches the narratives of historicism and post-modernism, but without reference to the intellectual and theological context.[6] The synthesis of a motivating idea in no way overlooks the multifaceted complexity of the subject; rather it finds its warrant and outworking in that rich material.

Sources and searching

The main handicap to critical study of medieval architecture is the lack of contemporary texts—there are no treatises dedicated to the subject as there are in the fields of grammar, poetry, music, optics, astronomy, and others. Edward Farley, seeking sources on the subject of beauty, writes, 'While architecture, sculpture, music and words profoundly shaped medieval Christendom [...] medieval thinkers produced no overall theory of the arts.'[7] There are a few brief references to architecture in didactic works, and hints in dedicatory sermons and the like. Some accounts of building achievements, which will be discussed, give more expansive insights, such as Henry of Avranches' poetic praise of Lincoln cathedral, and, most famously, Abbot Suger's writings on the abbey of St-Denis. One work, the Sketchbook of Villard de Honnecourt, is much scrutinised by scholars to extract possible clues to a medieval architectural and aesthetic understanding; but it is a collection of annotated drawings and diagrams, not a written theory or exposition of architecture.[8] Late in the Middle Ages masons' lodgebooks were produced and some have survived, but they divulge little more than descriptions and details of the concerns and craft of masonry.[9] The earliest treatises on architecture to emerge when the Middle Ages were being overtaken by the classical Renaissance were those by Antonio di Piero Averlino, who was known as Filarete (*c*.1400–69),[10] and by Leon Battista Alberti (1404–72).[11]

Throughout the Middle Ages there had been considerable use made of building imagery in theological and diverse secular works. The Bible had provided an authoritative source for symbolic and prototypical buildings—the Mosaic tabernacle,[12] Solomon's temple,[13] Ezekiel's visionary temple,[14] St John's vision and description of the New Jerusalem[15]—and other constructions, notably Noah's ark.[16] Of more secular origins, figurative buildings such as the Tower of Wisdom and the Castle of Virtue were widely and variously employed, instructive in theology or morals. Though they do not pretend to address the art of architecture, the metaphorical associations deserve attention.

We have to go back to *De architectura* of Vitruvius (*c*.75–*c*.15BC) for any systematic text.[17] This was transmitted and commented upon in the fourth century by Faventinus, but interest in it in the Middle Ages was probably confined to geometrical and structural applications.[18] With curiosity and a sense of disappointment we learn from the *Confessions* of

Augustine (354–430) that at the age of about twenty-seven he wrote a book called *Beauty and Proportion*, which he lost.[19] Evidently he later began to write treatises on each of the liberal arts and intended to include architecture, but did not get that far.[20] We can suppose that, as in his *De musica*, he would have connected the subject with theology, and that it would have influenced medieval architecture. What the effect might have been is beyond speculation. We may, however, speculate to some purpose on just why it is that between Faventinus (or Augustine's project) and Filarete there is no known treatise on architecture, no architectural theory such as we might consider a proportionate account of the extraordinary building achievements. We may note here that this is not inconsistent with the nature of a vernacular phenomenon.

Thus a search for texts on architecture or representational arts produces little material for useful deductions. In the light of this and the relative opaqueness of theological texts it is unsurprising that in architectural research even where there is some underpinning of theological content it is rather uncritically inferred from a stock of truncated texts in currency. Arguments are constructed inductively, and conclusions are tenuous. The field has been largely left to architectural history, which has been the dominant kind of research in the twentieth century; certainly it is indispensable. For all that, in the uncertain and avoided territory between theology as it was written and architecture as it was built in the Middle Ages there have been fragmentary studies.

This search in the works of medieval learning will be quite eclectic. It is needless to identify particular sources here: they will appear throughout. The exploration first works toward a medieval understanding of the subject of love for God, the primacy and prominence of it, the principles formulated around it, and the potential in it to be a source of human response and action. Chapter 2 treats this, not exhaustively but economically, to pick up the ramifications which relate to our topic. An awareness of the scope of pragmatic applications will develop. Given the theological parameters drawn, the force of evidence adduced in following chapters can be judged. In texts of theology, philosophy, philology, and science (termed 'natural theology') there are descriptions and analyses of human motivation and inspiration, sometimes explicitly attributed to love, in other cases connected by inference.

The topics of learning and knowledge are then looked at for the reflections they offer, as mirrors, of love itself. We can gain insight into the working of the medieval mind, and be brought closer to seeing particular operations in the work of any artificer and artist by examining indications in the curriculum of medieval learning, starting with the foundational arts of the Trivium. Related studies have seldom considered this standard curriculum and conceptual framework, but the task here is to appreciate the powers of conceptualisation and expression of medieval minds as authentically as possible. Thus Chapter 3 lays bases of *comprehension*, in which texts provide indications that at a primary level a person's faculties of intellect were directed and sharpened, or at least disciplined; and the very exercise of these philological skills provides examples of the processes of visualisation, memory, imagination, and 'creativity'.

The second part of the liberal arts was the Quadrivium, in which a person was inducted into the arts called mathematical, for they involved measurement and structure of things. So Chapter 4 looks into the mirror of *instruction* in which these skills of the mind, conversant with the mysteries of magnitude and multitude, movement and time, reflected the divine intelligence. Claims were made in the texts, explicitly and obliquely, that in learner and adept love for God was a vital ingredient in the mind's development. The liberal arts were prerequisite disciplines to equip one for grasping higher knowledge.

The field of knowledge was all phenomena in their extrinsic nature and intrinsic nature. This was predicated on the nature of God, and his works of creation seen and unseen, material and spiritual. Nature open and admired in the mind and imagination of artificers and artists was a source of understanding through *contemplation*, treated in Chapter 5. Divine love was understood to be contemplated by angels. Believing and imitating this artificers and their work could be raised to a higher level of insight and meaning. The application of this is another stage in the demonstration. Attention is on the significance of artefacts participating in the natural and spiritual worlds.

The evidence produced in those chapters shows that it was so much a matter of love by which a skilful maker worked. While further evidence is accumulated, Chapter 6 makes explicit application, specifically the outworking in the architecture of churches. Pertinent connections are highlighted and the integration of the theology and architecture is articulated. In conclusion, as well as summing up the demonstration, some aspects which emerge are posited as important for a fresh appreciation of medieval architecture, while the integrity of that architecture may commend such theological verities for serious consideration by our culture in its works.

Deductive methodology

In the absence of significant contemporary written treatises on architecture, the method is to examine whether a central tenet of Christian theology treated with much emphasis in medieval texts, namely love due to God, might be found to inform somehow the architecture of churches, whether the process or product or both.

The method is to work *from* the theology and textual sources outwards *to* the architecture and the artefacts; from the informing general principles to the particular instances and evidences. In the overall framework the argument is deductive, not inductive. Specifically, the rationale is to read what medieval theologians (and philosophers, scientists, and poets) wrote concerning human thought and motivations, especially behind the works of artificers, and to give full weight to what they wrote—thus where they said that love is vitally important, to believe that they meant it. For it is *their* theology that must govern our enquiry. In academic disciplines (such as architectural history) dealing with artefacts, there is commonly an assumption that an inductive argument is required. But in this enquiry influence, intention, and meaning in the architecture is deduced from assertions in the primary theological and associated literary sources, not adduced from the physical artefacts, the buildings. In regard to them it is a matter of recognising that what the theology asserted is in some way signified. This is a necessary approach to medieval art and architecture—differing from a knowledge of art and architectural *history*.

For deductive argument the theology provides the essential frame of reference. Connections between things spiritual and things material are found expressed in the writings. The nature of connections we will consider shortly; but one that is methodologically important because it is an 'instrument for reasoning', has the form of a syllogism; it is deductive, and makes a new affirmation. Thus between two entities arises something which is *ipso facto* defined by the two—and is constituted a third entity. It is a triadic model, with the 'new' thing being that which is the union of the two, yet distinguishable from them. Thus in the liberal arts learning and art are related, revealing the nature of things made. A broad intellectual method and frame of reference is provided for architecture. With due attention it can even engage *us* in the exercise of comprehension and instruction somewhat as understood by medieval minds. Then the plan is to see how concepts concerning the nature of things are related to, or reflected in, human artifices which become integrated into nature—an ontological frame of reference. Ideally an achievable part of the method will echo original theological insights, in contemplation seeing specific applications in architecture. Two gradually emergent strands of architectural praxis, namely *judgement* and *intuition*, help to crystallise the connections. In the end we perceive theology in the architecture, the common referent being love.

We will not contend that love ordered to God, or any other spiritual motive, is the sole influence of significant meaning or greatness in the buildings. That caveat however prompts us to treat the theology broadly and eclectically to discover what is able to be deduced from it—the kind of evidence to look for in the buildings, significant congruence between the theology of love and the artefacts. The merit of the deductive argument is that if the theology and learning address sufficiently the subject and offer a substantial rationale, then a survey of the artefacts becomes essentially an exercise in recognising the theological and intellectual dialectic where it is conspicuous in the works. Our powers of recognition will improve, with an increase of our grasp of the language of the architecture.

The weaving of each strand of evidence may be quite complex, and an example, treated as simply as possible, will help here to crystallise the approach. We read in a sermon of Bernard of Clairvaux (1090/1–1153), written around 1136, that the glory that belongs to God is not to be usurped by anyone or anything. That is a theological truth. Bernard gives a tiny illustration:

> Who would believe the wall if it said it produced the ray of light that falls on it through the window?'[21]

He says, 'my bodily senses may tell me that and no more.' The wall appears glorious, but it is reflected light, the wall simply being responsive. The mind sees that it is not the wall—it sees the use of the window. The window's role is suggestive—it is there for a purpose. Wall, window, the sky too, are part of the connectedness of all things; all convey the glory of the light, but they do not produce it. Bernard straightway transposes the aesthetic appreciation of a building feature to a religious appreciation:

> I become aware that what makes [the saints] appear praiseworthy and admirable really belongs to another, and I praise God in his saints. [...] By his own nature invisible and inaccessible, he becomes somehow visible and a source of wonder in the lives of those who love him.[22]

The saints are to be admired, but only for their being connected to God, participating in him, reflecting *his* glory. In them his glory is 'somehow visible'; and the operative condition is given—'those who love him.' Neither picture, of building or saints, makes any explicit reference to a church; nevertheless in both Bernard teaches this: that love for God in a subject is a condition in which the glory is exhibited, and that a reflection or a ministration as in an artefact has a power to show God's glory.

For another text we can go to a passage in which a contemporary of Bernard, Honorius of Autun (1080–1156), wrote of a church, a little before 1130. He would have seen contemporary churches such as Autun cathedral (consecrated 1132) or Morienval Abbey. We can visualise it in his description:

> The transparent windows which keep out the weather and let in the light, are the Doctors who resist the storms of heresies and pour in the light of the Church's teaching. The glass in the windows, through which pass the rays of light, is the mind of the doctors, seeing heavenly things as in a glass darkly.[23]

Here the subject seems to be less theological than Bernard's picture; more ecclesiastical. Yet what Bernard had to say quite generally, is all here more specifically; it does apply. What he said about the saints must underlie what is said here of the doctors in particular; here are 'the lives of those who love him'. However, the picture and its metaphors is ecclesiological too; now it refers to a church. The simple window in Bernard's image is in Honorius the transmitter of spiritual light and vision. Here is the downward-working power of light itself, both solar and spiritual; with a whole retinue of metaphysical associations.

We have not gone beyond the written texts, except to posit a likely context for Honorius's picture. If we allow the full import of Bernard's theological point—God's glory is displayed in those who love him—and taking his wall and window trope as a suggestive bridge, we can make a valid inference that Honorius's ecclesiological picture is predicated on love for God. When we come to contemplate a physical church, what can we deduce from such texts? Theologically, that what transmits or displays the light and glory of God does so because of love for him; ideally, that light and beauty in a church can represent the glory; formally, that a *church* illuminated by bright windows embodies, in a measure, that love.

Figure 1.1 Morienval, France. Notre-Dame abbey church. Nave, view east. *c.*1122–30.

Experientially, we should go into the nave of St-Lazare, Autun, or Notre-Dame, Morienval, of the twelfth century, with the discrete clerestory windows, small but brilliant. The south windows illuminate the north wall in the way that Bernard had seen, perhaps even here at Morienval abbey (Figure 1.1). We would comprehend the architectural language of the walls, windows, and light. We would be instructed in the work itself that this was made in love. We would contemplate the relation of love between God and people. We would be illuminated by an inkling of the glory of God.

The example shows how we can work (albeit with many variations) from texts: (1) where theology generates or allows associations between love for God and material things, artefacts, and culture; (2) where a text illustrates a relevant strand of theology using a figure, image, or symbol referring to an artefact, sensory experience, making process, or tectonic concept; (3) where a text refers to or connects with some aspect of a church in concept, form, or function. From this material can be deduced, in some aspect or another, the power of love to work in an artificer or inform the artefact. Such a reading of texts directs engagement with and appreciation of the physical object, which is evidence and demonstration, large or small, of the making process.

Reading theology

How is medieval theology to be approached for these purposes? This study is predicated on the theology as indeed theocentric, and the mentality and culture likewise. In its driving force there was a vital centredness on God. The mind connected all things to God, philosophy and science were handmaidens of theology, and self-awareness did not become self-centredness. Accordingly culture was notionally the *cultus* in the original sense of 'the worship'. The community's works were referred to God, and were done in fealty and charity. This mentality translated spiritual vision into material places and forms, epitomised in monasteries and churches. Order and unity running through everything was expressed in so many ways. Order signified the divine law, moral and natural, thereby legitimising hierarchies in which all things took their places and participated. While this describes features ideally and the reality was always imperfect and sin-tainted, at its best it was so coherent that its centrality was unchallenged even though intellectual ideas evolved and new horizons inspired greater achievements.

Quite apart from any Hellenistic bearing on New Testament writings themselves, there was a significant influence of Greek philosophy, particularly of Plato (428–347BC), on the intellectual method of early Christian theology. It was transmitted through Plotinus (*c.* 204–270) and Porphyry (233–*c.* 300), the most prominent Neoplatonists. The prolific patristic theologian Augustine of Hippo was well acquainted with Platonist philosophers; however in his theology he in no way made them authoritatively superior to Scripture. Pseudo-Dionysius (fifth–sixth century) was a Neoplatonist Christian writer whose mystical theology was rather independent of patristic thought.[24]

12 *Introduction*

His and Augustine's works were two seminal early sources for medieval theology; their notions are germane to this study. Athanasius, Origen, and Boethius are also consulted. Here is an underlying meshing of theology and philosophy, generating a matrix of ideas in the later culture and in its architecture. Modern appraisals of the evolution of culture in the high Middle Ages generally give the influence of philosophy and metaphysics more prominence than theology. Philosophy-led theology is open to the objection that it does not give Scripture-based medieval theology its due, or credit it with radical perceptions and applications.

In architectural history Otto von Simson comes close to opening up the implications of a more rigorous theology. His exposition of the symbolism and anagogical meaning of the church architecture is well supported and convincing, but is capable of a further level of insight. Abbot Suger (*c*. 1081–1151) rebuilt the abbey church of St-Denis, the new choir being consecrated in 1144. Von Simson says, 'In his writings, then, Suger appears, and wished to be understood, as an architect who *built* theology'.[25] Probing the intention he says, 'Suger wished to express [the thought that] the great enterprise that is about to be undertaken requires an inner disposition, a state of grace, on the part of the builder'.[26] Then von Simson observes, 'Hence the church cannot be completed without the assistance of grace, which illuminates the builder's intellect as well as his moral and artistic powers'.[27] Here surely is an important statement of a condition of building which deserves theological amplification. He goes so far as to adduce support from Augustine who, in a sermon for the dedication of a church, wrote:

> How will God reward those who build for Him with so much piety, joy, and devotion? He will build them, as living stones, into his spiritual edifice toward which those direct themselves who are informed by faith, solidified by hope, and united by charity.[28]

Here was something about the frame of mind and state of heart of the makers of a church; and, while these qualities are important for the 'spiritual edifice', it raises the question: What part did these qualities play in the material edifice? Von Simson reverts, however, to his erudite account of symbolism, aesthetics, and style. Reiterating the question concerning the place of theology in this study, we could find other notable scholarly critiques of medieval architecture similarly touching on theology and pointing to theology, but in the end not engaging with it or indicating how it can be modelled.[29] Whereas these leave the issue, the following chapters will continue and probe the texts closely.

Von Simson emphasises Pseudo-Dionysian light metaphysics. Other studies see sacred geometry and mystical theology as key interpreters of Gothic cathedrals and abbey churches. Approaching the subject thus, Titus Burckhardt reckons the architects and masons to have been guided by esoteric wisdom and spirituality. He adduces from a truncated theology explanations of symbolism, imagery, and intention in the works; this is detached from moral and affective theology which might address motives and evaluate means and ends.[30] Christian Platonism, especially Platonic geometry, is expressly espoused by Nigel Hiscock in his extremely meticulous investigations of its theory and applications.[31] He meshes this with the wide repertoire of metaphysical ideas and Christian symbolism. His method is in the first place deductive—but his fundamental sources are Platonist and Neoplatonist philosophy, rather than theology. That is not to diminish his conclusions, for it may help towards a reading of the buildings as objects. But it does not help to deduce a significance of the buildings as directed by dialectical and ultimately moral theology.[32] If it can be done, the above-mentioned approaches need to be confirmed and extended according proper weight to the *theology* of the time, comprehensive, integrated, and often complex.

To illustrate a way that theology works in this study let us take a text from theology. It is in the Wisdom of Solomon: 'Thou hast ordered all things in measure and number and weight'.[33] In patristic writers and throughout the Middle Ages this text was noted in contexts from astronomy to affective theology. From it commentators unfolded the nature of being and phenomena, causal connections, and creaturely relations to the Creator. Modern historiography has given it considerable attention, but it is cited most often as an epigram, and interpreted with, at best, tangential reference to theology. The application of its *schema* of order requires care, lest it be transposed too narrowly in art to symbolism, for instance, or in mathematics to arcane mysticism. In our purview we will see it running through many fields of medieval thought, frequently in the context of the making of things. We will examine its context and see how that was paralleled or modelled in various applications. Its proximate context is expansive: 'The whole world before thee is as a little grain of the balance [. . .]. For thou lovest all the things that are, and abhorest nothing which thou hast made [. . .] O Lord, thou lover of souls'.[34]

Augustine will serve to illustrate this. In one place he predicated measure, number, and weight (*mensura, numerus, pondus*), on a new ontological triad, *modus, forma, ordo*, compressed thus: 'From [God] derives every mode of being, every species, every order, all measure, number, and weight'.[35] Here he was connecting all contingent things to the Source through three principles, each of which applies to all things, for stability and distinction as well as order. He was concerned to show this application— in a case enquiring into *the cause of the greatness* of the Roman Empire— that, while God's providence dispensed and 'ordered' all things thus, there are conditions of human will and necessity. In another place he cites the text on 'number, weight and measure' to conclude a discussion of the *perfection* of the number six, insisting that the theory of number is not to be lightly regarded.[36] He had distinguished two ways of knowing: 'For there is a wide difference between knowing something in the cause of its creation, and knowing it as it is in itself. [. . .] —the difference between the knowledge of the art and the knowledge of the works of that art'.[37] Angels know in the first way; humans ordinarily in the second. The digression on the perfection of the number six was to show the theory of number as an example of knowledge which knows the constitution of a thing. Thus the perfection of six can be known in the same way as the greatness of the Empire, if one can know a thing *in the cause of its creation*, knowing the art by which God made all things by order, weight and measure—whence perfection and greatness. Again Augustine used the text, not in relation to knowledge, but in the context of the will by which a person adheres to, or turns away from, the Creator: 'Do not hesitate to attribute to God as its maker every thing which you see has measure, number and order. [...] Wherever measure, number and order are found, there is perfect form'.[38] One has to grasp the weight he was giving to the imperative—*attribute all this to God, unhesitatingly*. He concluded this, urging, 'long for him with burning charity'. John Scottus Eriugena (*c.* 810–*c.* 877) cited this in his discussion of free will. In everything created by God is seen 'perfect form'. All humans have the gift of being able to choose or misuse every good thing—such as bodily forms and beauty perceived in things. They would use gifts rightly 'if they referred them back to the praise of the creator'.[39] In all this no building or architectural subject is mentioned, yet the theology directs, indeed requires, manifold pragmatic applications.

For another illustration of the way in which a work of similarly broad range is to be treated theologically—not left to literary criticism—we can take a short work from the thirteenth century, *Le Château d'amour*, by Robert Grosseteste (1175–1253), written possibly before 1235, perhaps for the Oxford Franciscan convent.[40] Here was an eminent theologian writing in the French vernacular, and it is a highly compressed telling of Christian doctrine of the world's beginning, middle and end, as the Latin prologue states: *De principio creacionis mundi, de medio et fine*. What has it to do with the building of cathedrals? Nothing directly, but several things indirectly. The one obvious yet dubious association is that it employs an architectural figure, a castle—not a cathedral. Another point might tenuously relate the central image of Mary, who is the castle, to the widespread dedication of churches to Notre Dame in step with thirteenth-century Marian devotion.[41] The castle is Mary, a fortress with towers, and within is a vacant throne, awaiting the incarnate God. On the outside it is painted in three stories, green, blue and red; within it is shining white, all perfection and beauty. It tells us nothing directly about church architecture, and even its symbolism does not offer explicit correspondences, but when we attend to the theological import we learn that there is an all-governing truth, that of love, which maybe has wider bearing. Following a précis of his plan Grosseteste's application starts to become apparent: 'Later, I will tell you the circumstances for it is good to recall this in order to love God more dearly'.[42] This is a key purpose, and we can observe through the overt subject the *role* and work of love. Incidentally, the literary plan comprehending and compressing all things into small compass seems to parallel the 'contraction' of God into the castle of the Virgin, which also seems to parallel the cathedral's comprehensive but finite form.

The model of love is enriched even further—the maker forming his work 'after himself' and giving himself, setting the scene for the picturing of the Incarnation. Responsive love is enjoined. Now the figure of the castle, Mary, is unfolded: 'this is the castle of love, of solace and of succour'.[43] In multiplied images its beauty and perfection is emphasised; with the exclamation that the Lord God loves this place. The upper part of the castle is painted more crimson than the rose, and seems aflame: 'This is holy charity with which she is aglow, set aflame by the fire of love to serve her Creator'. As the Son unfolds his redeeming work, he says, 'You need think of nothing more than loving God and your neighbour'—the line we will see reiterated consistently in medieval theology. Grosseteste, further, says that while the spirit of charity always loves humility, this does not preclude a person from having property, castles and woods of great size: 'he can, provided he lives humbly, uprightly and in charity. For the Lord God holds nothing dearer than perfect love from one's whole heart'.[44] The presentation of these several aspects of divine love and love returned to God are typical of what we will see in many other contexts. Here too we get a good sense of the culture of a spiritual mind, the invention of a rich *schema*, and the place of an architectural image. The difference in type between castle and church is inconsequential and subordinate to the central significance of *love*. Modelling theology in such a way to so attend to the matter of love is applicable and necessary in the deductive method, and is consistent with the emphasis of theocentricity in medieval thought.

Rethinking architecture

To see whether and how church architecture significantly involved theological concerns is complicated; for theology does not verbalise it as we might think it should if there were some connection. Nevertheless, contemporary writings of particular use will be those touching on the making process—from memory and visualisation to intention and operation. How far these applied in architecture will be considered. In contemporary texts, even in those not ostensibly theological, theocentricity is the substratum, and appeal to the role of love was common, often as a pragmatic summation. In theological and other sources we will also find pertinent concepts (such as the ordering of all things by measure, number and weight) which admit extension to applications in architecture and building, which they informed and in which they were embodied.

If we can engage with theology as suggested above, a question is whether it would have been the influence of *theology itself* concerning the nature and role of love which, consciously or sub-consciously, affected the architecture, or does our reading of the theology simply explain that *love itself*,

16 *Introduction*

unmediated, would have been operating in the architecture or building process? The evidence will suggest that it was both. We will want to scrutinise texts in order to understand the architecture so far as we can in both aspects. Both ways are deductive. It is obvious that, more than has hitherto been allowed, medieval architecture should be seen and known through the eyes and minds of the makers.

Carroll Westfall critiques our ways of thinking about the form and content of artefacts, stating first that, 'Current orthodoxy in the practice, theory, history and criticism of architecture prizes form over content and uses formal qualities as the route to knowing about content'.[45] In spite of the obfuscations of postmodern architectural theory this still seems to apply in practice. Looking back, he says that from the nineteenth century there persists 'the imputation of meaning on the basis of formal qualities'—

> Foremost among these were those of style, culture, the symbolic form investigated through iconographic and iconological analysis, and various semiological approaches of more recent invention. These provide surrogates for what used to be understood as the intrinsic content of objects or events. They are alike in that each belongs to its own world and not to the object or event. Because this is so, whatever content is imputed to the object or event must remain extrinsic to it in a way that the intrinsic content of the earlier world did not.[46]

What then was the way in which intrinsic content was *in* a medieval church? To answer that we have to know what was the imputed content; but what is imputed will not be accessed inductively from the artefacts. What then does a reading of a church do? It is not satisfied with the extrinsic form alone, but learning (from medieval writers themselves) the intrinsic content to look for, it is enabled to recognise manifestations of meaning in the artefacts. Where the work is good it will be because the extrinsic reflects with some clarity the intrinsic—a congruity between form and content.[47] Thus the reader is enabled to judge the thing in itself, as nearly as possible in accord with the judgement of the mind of the maker. The more the deductive process extends to such informed recognition and empathetic judgement the more secure it will be against subjectivity.[48]

The question whether products of creative work can themselves offer evidence of an influence and operation of love presents problems; nevertheless it is incumbent on us to examine this in the works themselves. Can we find the thinking or the love expressed? In poetry, a poet impelled by love, could (like Dante) expatiate on love itself. In representational art there was an almost explicit expressive voice and language; it could get close to conveying a theme such as love or justice by recognisable associations and understood symbols. We will see that there was close integration of representational and semiotic art with the building in its form, fabric and detail. So art may help to show associations of theology and architecture. Common outward features in works of imagination and invention cannot be undeserving of notice, nor be so opaque to us if we spend time with the texts and artefacts. One guide is to be conversant in the arts of comprehension, instruction and contemplation. It requires a balance of approaching an artefact with certain questions, yet being open and able to receive what it has to say, if it has power to communicate the maker's idea. The questions 'what idea?' and 'by what power?' are particularised as one is in and around an actual building. The ideation and power can be incorporated here only imperfectly through visual images, and contact with artefacts is necessary to assimilate the non-verbal language; yet the present buildings give but stripped indications of their original state.

In studying buildings we commonly give more attention to an architect's use of imagination and invention than to the use of judgement. We must be alert to all these aspects of the making process. Because the latter is often not considered, comment here may be useful. In theology there is a discourse between judgement and love. Judgement involves deciding what is truly good; for love wills the good.[49] There follows a compelling line of discovery: in studying an artefact we can see that there are levels of invention and composition in which the maker has had choices and made decisions—from large matters to minute, important ones and repetitive ones, with much interconnection. Diversity and ingenuity must be given due weight—aspects sometimes underestimated in historical comparisons searching for beginnings and derivations. Then it brings us close to a maker's thoughts when we detect ways in which judgement has been exercised.

As an example, consider first the west towers of Coutances cathedral (Figure 1.2; Figure 3.2). Whatever precedents there may be, they could not have been built without a mind judging, importantly, at what height to terminate the vertical elements in which so much of the conceptual vision is vested, and deciding how extremely to demonstrate it; how to effect the transition to the spire, and how to integrate the corner stair tower. Throughout the cathedral judgement and decision-making has been exercised uniquely, and the result is different from every other cathedral.

The imagination must also have compassed the central tower, whether there must be one, its height, a spire which must have been considered, and its relation to the west towers. It is harder to believe that *no* thoughts of the significance of vertical ascension were in mind, than that they were. The mind must ruminate, invention might outstrip experience, imagination overcome pusillanimity, motivation of love demand high aspiration—then, with all that weighed, judgement would be made. These are things which it expresses; and the single-mindedness, the composing of complexities, the effort under such inspiration, the integration between spiritual aspiration and the material—all point to intrinsic content at the highest level of insight and commitment. In this the contemporary theology claimed that the highest level of vision and action is love for God.

As mentioned, our reading of buildings is problematic because of their present state. Particularly, the original extent, kind, and effect of decoration

18 *Introduction*

Figure 1.2 Coutances, France. Cathedral church of Notre-Dame. The south-west tower of the west front (from south). Built mid-thirteenth century.

is always a matter of uncertainty, but we realise that it was integral and may try to visualise it. For instance, countless niches once holding sculpted figures are vacant and much of the intent is thus lost. Evidently these would have been brightly painted, as also significant parts, at least, of the exterior. In brick church exteriors much of the patterning still conveys original intent. Often interior surfaces were plastered and painted with decorative motifs, the effect still preserved especially in numerous small churches. For us the hazards of uncertainty are an impediment to an inductive critical method, while it reinforces the soundness of the deductive method.

Connections and integrity

The great pre-Renaissance cathedral and abbey churches comprise a class of buildings which actually eludes satisfactory explanation by aesthetic appreciation or architectural history alone. In modern critiques affective theology has been largely passed over; it has not been pursued to show that Godward love had any real bearing on or connection to the architecture. The lack of full engagement with or sufficient explanation of such a radical question as the motivations of medieval church builders, and the matters that stem from that, has left a gap which calls for a careful connection of medieval theology and architecture. We will scarcely find explicit directives to artificers or architects which would show connections and explain the power and significance of building achievements. Nor would we obtain more sure causal links by conjecture from the artefacts—an inductive method does not give much assurance of that. A deductive method makes connections differently, of various kinds, and not tied to historicist conceptions. Westfall posits what he calls a history of origins, which,

> works with the same material, but it is radically different from the histories of ends, beginnings or the middle. It is not linear [...] and it does not take the beginning or the end of the thing to be inexorably linked to its later or earlier form.[50]

It is that the precursors of an artefact do not necessarily govern its form, nor is the artefact always explained by an earlier form. He thinks thus:

> The intent here is to rebuild our understanding of the world in a way that recognizes the atemporality of types, or whatever we might call the part of the intrinsic content that interests us, and the temporality of the instances which bear the extrinsic content. [...] In this world architecture is not hitched to the march of time. Instead, it is connected with what is true about architecture.[51]

To build such understanding intrinsic content must be purposely modelled, and joined to the extrinsic, the phenomenal; it thus speaks of the architecture. Notwithstanding the limited expression in texts, we will find wide-ranging allusions to intention and meaning (intrinsic content). We will see that the maker's mind was in the built architecture even as a poet's mind is inseparable from the poetry itself. Specifically we deal with the truth (atemporal type) that the makers' love is inseparable from the architecture, embodied in the buildings, and expressed in the work (extrinsic content). This involves actual valid connections. The first task is to discover these made in the theology.

The mirror (*speculum*) was much used in the Middle Ages as a hermeneutic mode of connection between one matter and another, of different orders, but having an inherent correspondence, sharing a common image. The connection is not required to be logically proved, but is to be seen by the mind being attentive and receptive (through the eye, it may be). The figure was favoured for its multivalency: a visible thing or an accessible truth could reflect many things invisible and arcane with great veracity. In this figure there are two aspects to consider: first, the form and properties of the mirror—many things could be a mirror; second, the subject which was looked at in the mirror—the thing or matter that it was turned towards in order to reflect it to the viewer. Emulating *The Major Mirror* of Vincent of Beauvais (d. 1264), Émile Mâle applied this to pictorial and sculptural representations in Gothic cathedrals.[52] By it Mâle indicated their didactic and contemplative purpose, how they reinforced the teaching of schools and monasteries and inspired devotion. He saw the subjects conveyed in the cathedrals and churches which became mirrors of the mind and heart of the people. He articulated love for God in the many topics reflected in the buildings. Only in concluding his work he writes, 'Symbol of faith, the cathedral was also a symbol of love. [...] past and present are united in one and the same feeling of love. The cathedral was the city's consciousness'.[53] This summation is almost unexpected; for he had not been showing the theology informing the *architecture*.

Linguistic devices in dialectic and rhetoric, such as metaphor and simile, can elucidate connections between entities. They are transferable to other modes, notably pictorial, and, less obviously, architectural. Eriugena referred to images metaphorical (*translata*), 'which tend to come from three bases, namely likeness, contrariety, and difference'.[54] He defended metaphor as necessary for human understanding of what is knowledge in God: 'As if a transference could not be made from temporal things to eternal by some mode of similitude, or [...] by the most beauteous mode of contrariety'.[55] He asserted that such transferences are valid; and we will seek to apply this in physical instances later. In medieval thought a likeness (*similitudo*) firmly connected, in some particular respect, the appearance or form of the referee with the appearance or form of its referent.[56] As to images based on contrariety Eriugena said, 'So great is their power to express meaning that by a sort of privilege of their excellence they are rightly called by the Greeks *entimemata*, that is, concepts of the mind'.[57] In the connecting power of these devices there is understanding of extrinsic form and access to intrinsic content.

In deductive reasoning an *inference* is drawn from a premiss about something which is implied therein. When there is a single premiss an immediate inference can be made. For example, Augustine wrote: 'When we see a body and its image begins to exist in our soul, it is not the body that impresses the image in our soul'. So immediately he draws the inference: 'It is the soul itself that produces it with wonderful swiftness within itself'.[58] If we should add to Augustine's one premiss a second: 'The physical body is incapable of effecting such a thing', the inference is mediate—it is a syllogism. The conclusion about the soul producing an image connects in a new way the soul and the image.

A key kind of connection in medieval ideation was *conjunction*, the joining of things, and it lent itself to articulation, verbal or visual. It was effectively a syllogistic demonstration, but the point of it was the discovery of a link defined in terms of the entities which it joined. Ramon Llull (1232–1316) integrated categories of things with complex webs of conjunctions forming patterns which he diagrammatised. 'Lull, however, claimed that his Art was more than a logic; it was a way of finding out and "demonstrating" truth in all departments of knowledge.'[59]

In places the study draws *parallels*. It may be objected that these do not constitute proper connections; but what to us is a mere parallel was probably an intuitive understanding of like things signifying a great deal. The parallel is of interest because it has an informative purpose. If a correspondence signifies something in common there is a unitive element. A clear example, showing also the instructive purpose, is where William of St-Thierry (c. 1080–1148) says, 'For the cell (*cella*) and heaven (*celum*) are akin to one another'. He uses the linguistic parallel to intimate greater associations:

> For when heavenly pursuits are continually practiced in the cell, heaven is brought into close proximity to the cell by the reality which underlies them both alike, by the loving devotion common to both, and by the similarity of the effects they produce.[60]

It is not easy for modern minds to read the architecture as it ordered and joined a multitude of things on many levels. Representational art sometimes assists in indicating interpretations in the buildings. There are many modes of connection. As linkages are found the buildings will be understood as works causally integrated, as exemplified in, say, a rose window. Here, apart from subjects depicted, is an abstract *architectural* construct of special prominence. The viewer knows it to convey spiritual ideas—as a mirror. As an architectural device, situated strategically exteriorly and interiorly, it is one thing viewed in two ways because extrinsic and intrinsic modes of understanding are inseparable—as with similitudes. Composed with judgement and intuition, it is both a logical figure and an invented pattern of correspondences, a matrix of linkages. In itself and in the whole church it signifies much. It is an epitome of the unity of material and immaterial things—abstractions of circle, centre, and rose; and corresponding realities called pleroma, union, love. In attentive relearning of the architecture it is almost axiomatic that in the connections and coherence with divine verities is its integrity.

The premiss being that in this period in Latin Europe there was coherence and rigorous integration in theology, philosophy, science and arts, it is not to imply inflexible thought or uniform works produced, but to contend for a high degree of connectedness. The architecture is not to be interpreted narrowly and prescriptively. More useful and convincing is the perception that medieval architecture was quite 'relaxed' as to interpretation, enjoying

22 Introduction

diverse meanings. As Paul Crossley points out, 'The meanings of medieval architecture were multi-layered inherently right from the start, as well as after the fact'.[61]

On the matter of the 'integration' of *our* understanding of cathedrals, Willibald Sauerländer gives a critique of influential twentieth-century theories, and identifies critical problems which we will consider directly or indirectly. He distils three 'kinds of possible integrations', and asks whether integration is possible: in *time*, of *performance*, of *context*. Summing up, he writes:

> If integration is taken to mean, once more, that all the different parts and images of the Gothic cathedral corresponded to a medieval concept of order, then one can only say that such a holistic assumption is not confirmed by the study of the different cathedrals, of their program, of their performance, and of their context. [...] Integration will be productive only if it makes our discourse on the Gothic cathedrals broader and more enlightened, if it opens doors and leaves the old dream of the holistic cathedral alone.[62]

Has the view posited so far, then, been too comprehensive? The 'dream of the holistic cathedral' is epitomised in the drawing by Viollet-le-Duc of an ideal cathedral.[63] Sauerländer's observation of great variety and non-conformity in design is correct, and his concern is aimed at conventional stylistic analysis and synthesis. Here our study will be entirely non-prescriptive, and barely even descriptive of buildings. Rather, the discourse will be broadened and illuminated by re-opening the door which secularism closed. In the medieval milieu the question would be: What integration in God? or perhaps, 'into God'. Bringing this question in even alters what is meant by 'order' or demanded of 'integration'. Brief observations on Sauerländer's questions will help to secure their relevance to our work.

Integration in time (of programme)

Discussing the twelfth-century rebuilding of the façade and choir of St-Denis, he warns concerning a view of that programme as 'integrated into the meaningful continuity of history', that, 'this diachronic perspective could easily become no less dangerous a trap than the earlier vision of Saint-Denis as a revolutionary building' (the synchronic perspective).[64] Programmes imply a closed concept of time:

> This dialectic between possible intention and evident result seems to me to lie at the heart of the hermeneutic crux of our present discourse on Gothic.[...] We should operate with an open concept of time transcending the bias of either the synchronic or the diachronic perspective.[65]

Medieval theology itself guides our own thinking to 'an open concept of time', which in application spans building programmes. Thomas Aquinas (1225?–74) said, 'There is a proportion between the created intellect and understanding God [. . .] as of matter to form, or cause to effect'.[66] It is a remarkable rendering of that proportion. And, following this, in its vision of God the created intellect *sees* 'at once and at a glance'. Further, 'The intellectual soul is created *on the border line between eternity and time*'.[67] Intention can be concerned with eternity, and when this is admitted the dialectical perspective changes. So when Abbot Suger expressed his intention for St-Denis abbey church in terms of the vision of heaven, the hermeneutic crux here is to believe him. The building and liturgy was to be a material connection with a transcendent dwelling-place, and a temporal drawing of the present to the eternal.[68]

Integration of performance

On this Sauerländer writes: 'The integration of liturgy into our reading and mapping of Gothic cathedrals is certainly overdue. The building without the performance is but a piece of abstract architectural styling'.[69] However, integration of the liturgy and architecture of the Middle Ages would seem to suggest, ideally, an unselfconscious participation scarcely open to us; the attempt would have to transcend an artificial view of performance as a liturgical 'styling'. But the *theology* of the liturgy informed medieval performance and the building of the church, giving access to a unifying view. It will help us to avoid 'styling' to see that what we call 'space' was chiefly significant as 'place'; places imply and unify performance. We will treat 'performance' more widely as the process of making places, integrating the operations of love.

Integration of context

Sauerländer says that the shape and programme of cathedrals was affected by their 'outside' context 'more profoundly than we previously thought'. So too of the 'inside' context. On the context of civic, political, royal, and such interests, he questions: 'is the program an image of consensus and order in medieval Christian society?'[70] The two contexts inevitably were mixed, even if they seem mutually exclusive. Here we can address the context of spiritual imperatives, the pragmatic context of affective theology. Adverse contextual factors too often obscure the constructive ones, thus restricting the context instead of more widely integrating it.

In the same collection of essays Bernard McGinn, noting the unsatisfactory 'invocation of theological ideas' by respected earlier twentieth-century art historians, directs a challenge to theological historians: 'This dialogue challenges the historical theologian to say whether he or she can provide the

24 *Introduction*

art-historical investigator with a set of tools for a more complete—and more proper?—grasp of the meaning of these buildings'.[71] That is warrant for the deductive method, understanding the minds of the makers, using the tools of textual sources to explain the works as directly as possible. McGinn again:

> If the critical claim I have made in this essay is true—namely, that a theological mentality was all-pervasive in the world of the cathedral-builders and that it informed their sensibilities and hence their design commissions—I, or any historical theologian, must be prepared to examine monumental buildings in search of signs of theology, whether conscious or unconscious.[72]

The parameters for the search are thus set out. It will be carried forward in several aspects: theology informing architecture; embodied in it; architecture expressing theology; pointers towards architectural judgement. It will find integration at an even more over-arching level in links between human makers and the divine Exemplar. For where there is a theocentric inclination, there is always a higher level to which the integration of contingent things can be taken. In theology *love for God* has a constitutional claim to such efficacy. The implications of this vital level and interpretative power must not be neglected. We will be 'in search of signs of theology, whether conscious or unconscious'. That is a wide scope, but astutely stated. A comment by Chesterton at the end of his study of Thomas Aquinas is also astute: 'In short, [Thomas] belonged to an age of intellectual unconsciousness, to an age of intellectual innocence, which was very intellectual'.[73] That bears pondering, and we may come to see that it also applied in architecture.

A simple check should confirm our central theme: it is no surprise if artists and artisans *love* what they make. Then the connection between the activity and the worth of the thing made must be not far away—the love informs the thing itself. Even on a human level, creativity implies a process deeply linking creator and artefact.

Notes

1 Chesterton (1904), p. 194.
2 Binding (2002), p. 48. He cites Amalarius of Metz, *Liber Officialis*, written in 823, where his text followed that of Bede quoted on p. 224 below.
3 For background of the monastic context see Leclercq (1982). For a study of liturgy and architecture see Doig (2008).
4 A significant treatment of history is in Morrison (1990). It does not directly address architecture, though Chapters 2 and 3 suggest applications.
5 Van Pelt and Westfall (1993), p. 29.
6 See Caviness (1995).
7 Farley (2001), p. 20.
8 See Villard, ed. Bowrie (1959). See further pp. 140–1 below.
9 Refer, for instance, to Shelby (1977). See Hiscock (1999), pp. 184–7.
10 See Filarete, trans. Spencer (1965).

Introduction   25

11 See Alberti, trans. Leoni (1755) facsimile.
12 Exodus 26. See Bede, trans. Holder (1994).
13 2 Chronicles 3. See Bede, trans. Connolly (1995).
14 Ezekiel 40–42.
15 Revelation 21.10–22.5.
16 Genesis 6.14–22. See Hugh of St-Victor, trans. Religious of C.M.S.V. (1962).
17 Vitruvius, trans. Morgan (1914). Von Simson (1962), p. 30, comments briefly and details secondary sources.
18 See Faventinus, trans. Plommer (1973).
19 Intimated in *Confessiones*, 4.13, 4.15.
20 See Wagner (ed.) (1983), p. 20.
21 Bernard, *Sermones*, 13.5, trans. Walsh and Edmonds (1971–80), CF 4, p. 92.
22 Ibid., 13.6, p. 92.
23 Honorius, *De gemmae animae*, 30, trans. Mortet (1972), in Harvey, p. 226. Note that this does not mention figural representations; the windows and glass are themselves the metaphors.
24 For a valuable appraisal see Hou (2008).
25 Von Simson (1962), p. 133. (Von Simson's emphasis.)
26 Ibid., p. 127. This is referring to Suger's *De consecratione*.
27 Ibid., p. 128.
28 Augustine, *Sermo* 337. Cited by von Simson (1962), p. 130.
29 For instance: Frankl (2000), especially p. 264, pp. 295–9. Also Mâle (1961), pp. 392–9.
30 See Burckhardt (1995).
31 See Hiscock (1999) and (2007), passim.
32 On this see Hiscock (1999), pp. 18–19; pp. 132–3.
33 Wisdom 11.20.
34 Wisdom 11.22, 24, 26.
35 Augustine, *De civitate Dei*, 5.11, Bettenson (1972), p. 196. For an instance of the reception of this in the thirteenth century, see Bonaventure, *Itinerarium mentis in Deum*, 1.11. For commentary see Spargo (1953), pp. 124–5.
36 Augustine, *De civitate Dei*, 11.30, Bettenson (1972), p. 465.
37 Ibid., 11.29, p. 464.
38 Augustine, *De libero arbitrio* 2, 20, 54, trans. Burleigh (1953), p. 169. The Wisdom text is not infrequently cited in variant forms.
39 Eriugena, *De divina praedestinatione*, 7.3, trans. Brennan (1998), p. 46.
40 Grosseteste, *Le Château d'amour*, trans. Mackie (2003), pp. 151–79.
41 See Whitehead (2003), pp. 93–9. Whitehead offers this association, referring also to 'newly contrived images of the coronation of the Virgin [which] accentuate this trend' (p. 94). The association may be closer—that the church *was* Notre Dame, the trope adopted by Henry Adams (1913).
42 Mackie (2003), p. 161.
43 Ibid., p. 166.
44 Ibid., p. 171. Grosseteste, who became Bishop of Lincoln, might well have believed this as a sound argument for, and condition for, the Church's building and possessing great cathedrals.
45 Van Pelt and Westfall (1993), p. 49.
46 Ibid., p. 50.
47 See my notes on the form-content dialectic in Lewis (2007), particularly p. 79, p. 85.
48 See Watson (1997), Chapter 3, 'Literal Sense, Authorial Intention, Objective Interpretation: In Defence of Some Unfashionable Concepts,' pp. 95–124. This defence of authorial intention in Scripture is very applicable to texts of medieval learning, with fundamental parallels in all the arts.

26 Introduction

49 See Aristotle, *Nicomachean Ethics*, 1.1; Thomas Aquinas, *Summa theologica*, 2a 1a, q.8, a.1, a; and q.9.
50 Van Pelt and Westfall (1993), p. 54.
51 Ibid., p. 55.
52 The plan of Vincent's *Speculum maius* had four parts: *naturale, doctrinale, morale*, and *historale*, though unfortunately the *Speculum morale* was not written. Mâle (1961), pp. 23–26, discusses Vincent's work.
53 Mâle (1961), p. 398.
54 Eriugena, *De divina praedestinatione*, 9.2, trans. Brennan (1998), p. 60.
55 Ibid., p. 72.
56 An extended use of similitude, 'likeness', $d^e m\hat{u}wth$, is in Ezekiel 1, 8 and 10. It is the same Hebrew word used in Genesis 1.26, 'Let us make man in our image, after our likeness'. For discussion of medieval views of *similitudo* see Turner (1995), pp. 145–9. A good examination of its use, and of symbolism, is in Dronke (1997), pp. 4–5.
57 Eriugena, *De divina praedestinatione*, 9.3, trans. Brennan (1998), pp. 60–1.
58 *De Genesi ad litteram*, 12.16, 33, cited by Maurer (1982), p. 10.
59 Yates (1982), p. 11. This is discussed on pp. 225–26 below.
60 William of St-Thierry, *Epistola ad fratres de Monte-Dei*, 1.32, trans. Theodore Berkeley (1976), p. 21.
61 Crossley (1988), p. 117.
62 Sauerländer (1995), p. 15.
63 In *Dictionnaire raisonné de l'architecture française du XI au XVI siècle* (Paris: Banc & Morel, 1854–68); the drawing is reproduced in Ward (1986), p. 64.
64 Sauerländer (1995), p. 10. Sauerländer reinforces Westfall's approach to history discussed above.
65 Ibid., p. 11.
66 Thomas Aquinas, *Summa contra gentiles*, 3.54.13, trans. Pegis (1975), p. 476.
67 Ibid., 3.61.5, pp. 476–7. The predicate is cited from Aristotle, *De causis*, 2.
68 See Suger, *Liber de rebus in administratione sua gestis*, 31, trans. Panofsky (1979), p. 54.
69 Sauerländer (1995), p. 13.
70 Ibid., p. 15.
71 McGinn (1995), p. 43.
72 Ibid., p. 51.
73 Chesterton (1933), p. 234.

2 The mind in love

Perceptions of love

What might it be that makes a building 'come to life'? And what if it comes alive? Aristotle speculated on the apparent paradox that benefactors love their beneficiaries more than the beneficiaries love their benefactors. He says, 'This is just what happens in the crafts too. Every craftsman loves the work of his own hands more than it would love him if it came to life. [. . .] Loving is a sort of acting'.[1] It is the same truth that humans are loved by their Maker more than they ever love him. Yet, the Introduction asserted, love moved minds to respond and to act upon things. In medieval theology and aetiology it entailed practical performance, which will be evidenced in our study. Furthermore, the architectural subjects seem to embody life infused by an effectual power such as is intrinsic in love—though it is difficult to see this from our vantage point. We will be in a better position if we start from the theology.

Concerning love in a person—no more than a stone can throw itself into the air can one act in love as from an intrinsic principle; and if a stone were to have such a projective power in itself, it would have to have another nature given to it. This is an illustration which Thomas used, to show that charity in humans is created by God: what 'exceeds the entire capabilities of human nature' comes from a new nature 'perfecting the will, so that such an action would proceed from an intrinsic principle'.[2] Then, unless we are instrumental or efficient only, 'there must be a certain habit of charity created in us, which is the formal principle of the act of love'.[3] This chapter initiates integration in these terms: A new nature of love for God, governed by a perfected will, would be the intrinsic principle operating in the action of an artificer. Then there would be a sort of 'habit of charity' in the making, the 'formal principle'. The inspiration and integrity in the act of love toward the work would give to the work itself 'another nature' and overcome the inertia of the stone, in Thomas's metaphor.

If charity is implanted and increased by God we may surely look to theology to find explained the inner working of this in human experience. Augustine exclaimed in his *Confessions*, 'How could I expect that the

28 *The mind in love*

Platonist books would ever teach me charity?' The knowledge so gained had only bred self-conceit.[4] He says, 'For was I not without charity, which builds its edifice on the firm foundation of humility, that is, on Jesus Christ?'[5] Such is the basic image of love's activity in building. To give the theocentricity of medieval theology full weight is to recognise the specific place it gives to love, love for *God*. Love being altruistic we may expect theology to indicate manifold outworkings of it; and may hope to find some mention of, or connections to, creative work; yet on that there is reticence. But love of God is the main topic of many treatises, and is reiterated in a majority of others, having a key place even where we might assume it to be of marginal relevance. The theological works are prolific and this study must be limited to relevant aspects of their treatment of love.[6]

Much was affirmed for the monastic community as the mode of God-centred corporate life. For the moment we can observe that there was little in theory to distinguish the individual experience of love from the corporate. There was no necessary difference between what applied to one monk or nun and what applied to the monastery, nor between Christians in the secular world and in the Church. As in personal experience, in community the exercise of love suffered tensions too—always scope for its curative power to be proved. In monastic acts of devotion paradoxes of the presence and absence of God, of nearness and remoteness, of spiritual light and obscurity, inevitably persisted. All this characterised a world of experience for theology to speak to. Such dichotomies were referred back to fundamentals and spanned by greater glories. We find theology performing this function, and hear it repeatedly affirming love as the vital and highest element.

We need evidence in medieval texts to show, first, that they established the ideal centrality and efficacy of pragmatic responsive love for God by people and communities; and, second, specific to our purpose, that they asserted or implied the importance of this in relation to the work of an artificer sufficiently clearly and often enough to admit some plausible deductions. The first point is dealt with mainly in this chapter, with a hermeneutic framework and theological examples which facilitate the direction of the study. The second strand of evidence is traced through the following three chapters, with cumulative application.

In looking for evidence of the first matter—love for God in medieval theology—we will necessarily refer back to important early contributions to Christian doctrine such as those of Origen, Augustine, Pseudo-Dionysius and Boethius.[7] But, recognising the much debated aspect of neo-platonism in early influences, a brief starting point in two twentieth-century authors is useful.

Denys Turner, in *Eros and Allegory*, analyses the transmission of *eros* from Plato (the *Symposium* in particular) through Plotinus and Proclus, Christianised by Pseudo-Dionysius and Origen, and translated by Eriugena. He gauges its incorporation in both scholastic theology and monastic Biblical exposition. In the frequent treatment of the Song of Songs, he sees the appeal of *eros* as a twofold model of the love of God expressing itself, and the return of love by creatures. The neo-platonic theology was to hand and, 'the concept of love as a "yearning" or "longing"—as an *amor-desiderium*, or, in Greek, *eros*—exactly expressed what they wanted by way of a language of love'.[8] The *direct* influence of neo-platonism on monastic theology, Turner says, was normally slight; and in his study of Song of Songs exegesis he asks 'Why Eros?'[9] He himself employs the word *eros* almost exclusively, and emphasises a Pseudo-Dionysian slant in most medieval Song commentaries; yet in discussing the terminology of love he also seems to provide good materials for a non-Dionysian doctrinal exposition of love both moral and mystical. Turner explains the metaphysical paradoxes which *eros* answers to, some of which we will discuss later. It is not to say that the Latin vocabulary was not similarly expressive. In Latin *passio*, the exuberant and ecstatic quality of *excessus*, accentuates the idea of being taken out of oneself—a strand in the medieval milieu to be taken into account.

There are opposing views regarding *eros*; but to show that they can be harmonised, or to see that they have been, would be a difficult and unnecessary digression here. Josef Pieper in *Love and Inspiration* sets out the situation thus:

> Quite often we discover that even where we cannot fully accept Plato's literal statements, we find that they capture and express an aspect of reality which might otherwise have remained hidden from us. Nevertheless, there are enough instances where our own viewpoint cannot easily—sometimes cannot possibly—be reconciled with Plato's. This is especially so in regard to the doctrine of Eros. [...] There remains, for example, the question of whether the kind of love which is first kindled by sensuous beauty is *the* basic form of love altogether. Is not what the Christian calls *caritas* and *agapé*, and which he considers love's highest manifestation, something altogether different, [...] not only different from Eros but opposed to it?[10]

Pieper maintains that while considering such a writer as Plato, Christian theology has its own ultimate positions. To disregard or suppress those does not aid fruitful insight. His approach is to distinguish where the real difficulties lie to enable us to address the things that matter, rather than things which, it seems, were not contentious in the Middle Ages. In this he counterbalances Turner's emphasis on *eros*. He also says,

> Still another much-discussed divergence between the Platonic conception of love and our own doctrine proves, on closer examination, to be inconsequential. Plato's concept of Eros, it is said, refers, basically, to self-love, to egotistic seeking for enrichment and fulfillment, whereas the Christian concept of *caritas-agapé*, on the contrary, is of a renunciatory, unselfish, giving love. To contrast the two kinds of love in this manner is a dreadful simplification.'[11]

While Pieper takes the other Dialogues into account, commenting on the *Phaedrus* he points out from its internal structure that, 'Plato is therefore not beginning afresh at the bottom and constructing a comprehensive doctrine of love'.[12] This warns us against undue dissection which may kill the real insight of an author—even as Turner says of Bernard of Clairvaux: 'We have the impression that such questions, whether purely semantic or more substantive, did not much matter: *amor* is for him a term of multiple possibilities'.[13] Going back to Origen (*c.* 183–253) we read in his Prologue to *The Song of Songs Commentary*:

> It makes no difference whether we speak of having a passion for God, or of loving Him; and I do not think one could be blamed if one called God Passionate Love (*Amorem*), just as John calls Him Charity (*Caritatem*). [...] We wanted to distinguish more clearly and carefully between the nature of passionate love and that of charity. [...] At the same time we ought to understand also that it is impossible for human nature not to be always feeling the passion of love for something.[14]

So openness to every elusive 'aspect of reality', admission of human incapacity for full knowledge, and acceptance of the strictures of language especially in spiritual things, may enable us to move on to some more encompassing view. Before leaving Pieper's handling of the Platonic-Christian debate we may note his comments on *passio*:

> But *amor* is *passio*; it is stirred by an actual encounter. This is not to say that intellectual and spiritual love is a mere 'unfolding' of *amor*. Instead, Thomas Aquinas would undoubtedly say that *dilectio* and *caritas* can regulate, purify, and heal the *passio amoris*.[15]

This vocabulary is illustrated in the Latin Vulgate of 405 (possibly in the original Italic version) where in the Song of Songs Jerome used the three words *amor*, *dilectio* and *caritas* signally. The word generally used is *dilectio* which tends to emphasise freely given devotion. The only use of *amor*, the intense emotion, is in the plaintive 'I am sick of love', *amore langueo*.[16] The use of *caritate*, just three times, is interesting for it is more definitive of the essential operations of love. First, *Introduxit me*, 'he set love in order over me'; under the banner of virtue, in the banqueting house—this was its *locus*.[17] Then, the royal couch 'was in the midst wrought with love', or, love covers (*constravit*) the middle (*media*)—it was the experiential *situs* in the world.[18] At the end, with the image of the flashing flame of *dilectum*, 'many waters cannot quench love'— it is the supernatural *momentum* as of irresistible grace.[19] While *amor* may express the human emotional situation, the dialectical force of the Song is in *caritate*, love's voluntary choices; and its *locus*, *situs*, and *momentum* is the spiritual trajectory. This merely indicates the nuanced language used as a primary heuristic tool, and a teacher would tease out meanings for the edification of the learner's love for God.

The purview of the subject so far ranges over a long historical period, and the question will be asked in what ways the theology and perceptions of love of God changed and developed. For our limited purposes it is sufficient to recognise a remarkable consistency and continuity of the perceived, albeit nuanced, character of love over this long period; and love of God all this time was a central preoccupation. Jean Leclerq asserts:

> There is, then, in this exegetical tradition, not uniformity but unity, fidelity to sources and freedom of the spirit. The monastic authors were able to adapt formulas inherited from antiquity to certain requirements of their observance; there was no need for them to indulge in innovation.[20]

Progression in love

A distinctive feature of medieval theology, taught and applied in schools and monasteries, was analysis of love for God according to stages or degrees of development toward perfection. It was so from the beginning of Christianity. The Biblical formula essentially followed throughout the Middle Ages in the Latin West was that the object of one's love was God first, then one's neighbour, and the neighbour *as oneself*—this was deemed to presuppose a proper love of oneself, which considerably complicated the matter. As Augustine enunciated it:

> God, our Master, teaches two chief precepts: that is, love of God and love of neighbour. In these precepts a man finds three things which he is to love: God, himself, and his neighbour; for a man who loves God does not err in loving himself.[21]

This threefold love is what has to be ordered, underlying all situations and societal conditions as it does. Origen, addressing the first two precepts, drew attention to the source in God, but also the basis of order in unspoiled creation: 'The charity of God is always directed towards God, from whom also it takes its origin, and looks back towards the neighbour, with whom it is in kinship as being similarly created in incorruption'.[22]

Aelred of Rievaulx (1110–67) characterised the three distinct loves as the three sabbaths: the seventh day is the spiritual sabbath of the love of self; the seventh year is the kind of sabbath attained in love of others; the fiftieth year is the perfect sabbath of love of God. The essential idea is that of the sabbath being the time of everything being found in true order, the condition of rest and peace. He presents the twofold commandment: 'Yet if you diligently examine these two commandments, you discover that three things must be loved: yourself, your neighbor, and God'. He goes on to show that the three are marvellously bound together: 'None of them can be possessed without all. And when one wavers they all diminish'.[23] These three are engendered, nourished, fanned, and perfected by one another. In the sabbath of love of self, Aelred pictures a person withdrawing from all exterior distractions to look within himself, where he finds nothing disordered, everything harmonious—'the entire throng of his thoughts, words, and deeds'. On this sabbath the servile works and interests in the world cease; 'the shameful fire of concupiscence is not lighted and the burdens of the passions are not carried'.[24]

As to the primary duty, Bernard of Clairvaux, in *On Loving God* (c. 1126), detailed four degrees of love of a person towards God, one's progress from self-centredness to God-centredness. There has to be a starting point: it is the natural affection, *amor*. The call to the heart and mind is to love God; any failure is in the will, and the body is not blamed. But the orientation in which one loves oneself for one's own sake stands over against the first commandment, and is hardly a degree of love towards God. In the second degree is the dawning recognition that one's very self is to be for God, and that the love of others is also to be brought under the same principle. In the third degree one loves God for who he is, 'Thereupon His goodness once realised draws us to love Him unselfishly, yet more than our own need impels us to love Him selfishly'.[25] The fourth degree is that wherein 'Man loves himself for the sake of God'.[26] Bernard was not sure that it can be attained in this life, but it is the ideal. 'The body and all the good things which belong to the body will be loved only for the sake of the soul, the soul for the sake of God, and God alone for Himself.'[27]

At this point the actuality of the body is sharply drawn in a perhaps surprising sequence. As Bernard traverses the lower stages of the soul's progress he scarcely mentions issues concerning the physical body. When he is most occupied with the highest possible attainment of love and vision of God, he makes his listeners most aware of the body. Not a body sinful, but under the inclusiveness of, 'How will God be all in all, if something human survives in man? No doubt, the substance remains, though under another form [forma], another glory, another power'.[28] The body is changed in this key respect that it comes under the ordering of the spirit: 'Hence it is in a spiritual and immortal body, calm and pleasant, subject to the spirit in everything, that the soul hopes to attain the fourth degree of love, or, rather, to be possessed by it'.[29] It must be ordered by a cognitive, stable, 'intention of the will'.[30]

There is a turning point in the regard for the value of the physical. Bernard speaks of the body 'availing' something to the soul that loves God, in its glorified state even as in its former mortal state: 'Nor is it any marvel if the body, now of glory, seems to bring something to the spirit, since it is granted that, even when infirm and mortal, it was of no small avail to it'.[31] In this congenial doctrine the body of glory bringing 'something to the spirit' has a role overflowing to physical things—becoming bodies of glory also. The love which transfigures thereby connects the physical and spiritual. Just how the body, or the physical, may bring something to the spirit we will see.

Three modes delineated by William of St-Thierry in his Epistle to the Brothers of Monte-Dei (c. 1145) deal with one coming into relation with

God; each is defined by the quality of love. The first he calls the 'animal man', which we will turn to shortly. Second is the 'rational man', in which love begins to form. Then there is the 'spiritual man' in which love is perfected. He does not denigrate the animal or the rational, but crucially shows a person's will as having various objects: 'now God and the interior life, now the body and external things relating to the body'.[32] Here is a progression, in which, as natural symbolism, it begins and ends with spatial imagery:

> When the will mounts on high, like fire going up to its proper place, that is to say when it unites with truth and tends to higher things it is 'love' [*amor*]. When it is fed with the milk of grace in order to make progress it is 'dilection' [*dilectio*]; when it lays hold of its object and keeps it in its grasp and has enjoyment of it, it is 'charity' [*caritas*], it is unity of spirit, it is God. For God is charity [*caritas*]. But in these matters a man is only beginning when he arrives at the end, for they do not admit of full perfection in this life.[33]

William says '*when* the will' because this is the sharp point of distinction between the rational and spiritual: the rational mind may wander in its close attention and adherence to God. The spiritual state is constant. He says the spiritual man has this likeness to God: 'the inability to will anything else'.[34] The spiritual man examines his desire for God,

> not only in accordance with reason's judgement but also following the mind's inclination, so that the will is now something more than will: love, dilection, charity and unity of spirit. [...] But 'unity of spirit' with God for the man who has his heart raised on high is the term of the will's progress toward God.[35]

The notion of the 'animal man' has this interest for us that it refers to the form of life of the body dominated by the senses. In the account of this stage we need not follow nuances of meaning of the several words for love; and while William sees only the senses engrossed in physical things, this is part of the condition of human life and is not ignored. For the soul of the *rational* man easily becomes drawn into the life of the senses, taking pleasure in and loving those things. However, even as it becomes detached from them it nevertheless is able to make use of them in a particular way.

> When it enters into itself again and finds itself unable to take with it into its spiritual nature the bodies to which it has become attached by the strong glue of love and habit, it fashions for itself representations of them and with these holds friendly converse there.[36]

The rational soul, converting the perceptions of physical things, *fashions representations* to give to the spiritual man for higher use. It is such higher use that justifies and sanctifies the sensory experience. The animal man, rightly orientated, is refined in this way: 'Turned to God this animal state becomes holy simplicity'.[37] Attention is directed to the will offering itself in simplicity 'to its maker to be formed'. Far from passing over the material objects of sensory preoccupation William carefully shows them to be part of the pattern and hierarchy of love.

A person, making progress towards God, is enabled to employ material things: 'On the borders of animality and reason the kind Creator has left, in the nature of the human soul intelligence and inventiveness, and in inventiveness, skill'.[38] And a little later, picking up the thread: 'Hence derive in the realms of literature, art and architecture [. . .] so many branches of learning, so many kinds of professions, precisions in scientific research'.[39] Still further, 'Let inventiveness adapt the body to its purpose, let skill bring nature into shape, and let intelligence make the mind not elated but a ready learner'.[40] We can register in the progression real connections between the operations of love and the practical works and arts of an inspired artificer, which 'hence derive' from the gifts of the kind Creator.

Yet another treatment of progression in love is Richard of St-Victor's *On the Four Degrees of Violent Love* (c. 1170). The title has the word *caritas*, but as indicated by the term *violentae* it is with the passion which might be attributed to *eros*. In passing it is worth observing that the successive stages are accordingly shown under two conditions: positively when the object of a person's desire is God truly; but negatively when the object is merely some created thing. We will look at the former, which should prevail in monastic life—Richard does give it this *locus*. He applies it to singular inward experience: 'an inward flight to heaven and union with the divine'. Andrew Kraebel makes this kinetic connection: 'The structure of Richard's treatise is suggestive of a movement from extra-claustral life to life within the cloister, and finally to the contemplative experience that was to be the aim of such a life'.[41] Might a similar application be plausible, namely, that the structure of the four degrees might be sensed in the progression through the church: the nave, crossing, sanctuary, ambulatory? Such a correspondence, notional at least in affective terms, may be more evident after an outline of the degrees.

The first degree Richard calls 'wounding love', based on the text 'I have been wounded by love'; its effect is to pierce the mind with the sting of love, so that it can think of nothing else. There may be short breaks, but 'the boiling fire returns more intensely, and it enkindles the already-shattered mind more sharply and burns it more vehemently'. The love relentlessly pursues the mind. His psychology runs true to common experience: 'And so often receding and always returning greater than it had been, little by little this fire softens the mind. [. . .] It occupies the mind with the constant memory of itself, hems the mind in entirely'.[42] The nave is like the approach of the preoccupied mind.

The second degree binds the mind: Richard pictures a soldier who, when wounded, may yet escape, but when captured is bound and imprisoned. This degree, he says, does not allow any regression:

The mind in love 35

> One who is in the grip of this second degree of violent love cannot cut free from that one, internal, preoccupying concern, no matter what he does or where he turns. [...] If it cannot be overcome by any feelings, it is the highest, and if it clings inseparably, it is perpetual. [...] You see how much further the vastness of this utter preeminence may yet grow from this point, so that, although it is already the highest, it can also be unique.[43]

The spatial and kinetic features could find an architectural embodiment in the central crossing of a church, where the arrested horizontal *situs* and the insistent vertical axis intersect.

In the third degree the mind excludes every emotion towards any thing other than its object or which serves its loved object. This produces its own practical dilemma:

> The second degree envelops his thoughts; this third one dissolves his actions as well. [...] In this third degree the excess of love (*amoris*) is similar to languor. [...] And so in this state, the mind remains as it were immobile, and it cannot move itself anywhere through thought or action unless its desire draws it there or its emotion impels it.[44]

Richard describes the inadequacy of the mind in this situation: though it here holds everything, everything is not enough for it; though everything is under its rule, still its desire is not satisfied. 'See how boundless is the space into which desire can extend itself even after it has come through the third degree.'[45] It is as though the mind pictures itself prostrate in the sanctuary of divine love.

The mind in the fourth degree of violent love is boiling with insatiable desire: 'it knows no limit to its growth, for it has exceeded the limits of human possibility'.[46] It is jealous love, allowing no amelioration for the mind, nor is there any remedy. The exploration of this love still essentially concerns the powers and working of the mind. In the *Paradiso*, Dante is conducted by Beatrice until in the last ascent his intense sight of her merges into an intense glimpse of God. It is violent love in the mind. He speaks of *la mente innamorata*; he says his mind was in love, yearning after his Lady, even as she was directing him:

> And in this heaven there is no other Where
> than in the Divine Mind, wherein both move
> the Love that turns and Power that sheds the sphere.[47]

Richard, at the close of *Benjamin Major*, writes of the alienation of the mind, being carried away outside of itself. This process, which is both rigorous and relaxed, is effective for the renewing of the mind, and then has practical outcomes. The spur and the power are in the divine Mind.

But having treated the four degrees Richard says, 'Let us go deeper still, and let us speak more plainly', and traverses the progression again. He now offers a series of epigrammatic summations, such as, '[the mind] enters into the first through meditation; it ascends into the second through contemplation; in the third it is introduced into jubilation; and in the fourth it goes forth out of compassion.'[48] At the end he explains at some length this notion of the fourth degree. He applies St Paul's words specifically to this degree: 'Love endures all things, believes all things, hopes for all things, and sustains all things' (I Corinthians 13.7). He sees a person, as if in madness, rejecting his own life for the sake of the saving of others; even presumptively interposing himself between God's fires and some other's ruin, 'imposing a limit to necessity'.[49]

> And so in the first degree [...] the mind returns to itself, in the second it ascends toward God, in the third it crosses into God, and in the fourth it descends beneath itself. In the first and second it is lifted up; in the third and fourth it is transfigured. In the first it ascends toward itself, in the second it transcends itself, in the third it is conformed to the brightness of God, and in the fourth it is conformed to the humility of Christ.[50]

To continue the notion of the progression of the mind in love resonating with the spatial progression of the church, the ambit of this fourth degree might be likened to the less lofty ambulatory surrounding the sanctuary, girding it—diminished from the glory, but with a sense of radiating it even as it lies between the sanctuary and the world.

Spiritual progress was a preoccupation, yet work in the material world could accompany it. Personal and communal application may be evident in diverse results. Ascesis could stimulate rather than stultify new and expressive building work. In which case, rather than seeing the marvellous architecture as a contradiction—the physical distracting from the spiritual—we might deduce that on each level the passion and energy expressed minds intensely occupied and enamoured, striving for invisible realities, the potential for perfection.

Measure, form, inclination

While practical teaching of progression in love had a special place in the claustral life, in the scholastic forum many theological and philosophical matters devolving on love were perennial topics. An epigrammatic text often referred to can provide useful direction. In Chapter 1 use of the text Wisdom 11.20 was illustrated by two instances from Augustine. In one he said that all measure, number and weight derives from God; in the other that every thing in its measure, number and order is attributable to God the creative artist. The multiple yet related applications of this triadic formula can focus questions about essential attributes and operations of love. The point that God as creator and exemplar is the subject of this text we will return to later. However, we can note that the terminology was also often restated by medieval writers as *measure, form and inclination*.

At the apogee of scholastic theology, Thomas's *On Charity* (one of the *Quaestiones Disputata, c.* 1269–72) is a distillation of the subject of love for study by the proficient. Among the thirteen Articles are:

> Whether the object to be loved out of charity is a rational nature? (Article 7)
>
> Whether charity is the form of the virtues? (Article 3)
>
> Whether there is some order in charity? (Article 9)[51]

Throughout all the Articles but focussed in these he explains his doctrine of charity with frequent use of the concepts of measure, form and inclination—every inclination toward order with the proper end in view. It is not without application as, for instance, when Thomas refers to the productive works of wisdom and love. Arising from this we will see relevant correspondences when we turn to the subjects of architecture and arts and posit possible connections.

In this section we will draw especially on writings of Augustine and Thomas. Both emphasised the centrality of love, the eight centuries' span not essentially altering the doctrine. In an essay comparing them, Jacques Maritain writes:

> St. Augustine [...] employs the order of charity; however copiously he may philosophize, it is in love that he instructs [...]. St. Thomas employs the order of intelligence—setting it to work by means of love, and in order to exhale love, but carrying out its work in the pure atmosphere of objective demands.[52]

In this overview Maritain places love of God as the central and vital motive in the methods of both. The common emphasis was on the constraining impulse in will and mind to love God above all things, and to love things 'in God' and 'on account of God', *propter Deum*. If perhaps the doctrine, rooted largely in Augustine and reiterated in medieval theology, imbued the sub-consciousness of twelfth- and thirteenth-century architects, it would have comprised at least an important part of an intellectual context for architectural practise. If the theorists said that love was worked out according to measure, number and order an architect and an artificer might have there a starting point in their work. Also, the theology which was being written by such as Thomas, Grosseteste and Bonaventure at the same time as much cathedral building, may carefully be read for signs that it articulated the same motivation and activity, being a parallel participation in the culture, not necessarily explicit. Whether noetic or affective there would be priority in the *content* of the theology; and the ratiocination—the *structure* and *process* of reasoning—would follow. In *Gothic Architecture and Scholasticism* Erwin Panofsky perceived ratiocination itself as a model, but without relating it to an architect's motivation.[53] Despite criticisms, his work, novel compared with architectural history of its time, is not invalidated, and deserves re-evaluation. We must give close attention to the driving content of love in theology; and understand the mechanics, its structures and processes.

Measure

Love is often praised as being measureless, particularly in respect of an ideal object—say, Dante's love of Beatrice, and Beatrice drawing out his love of God. Yet common experience is that a question in probably every love, sooner or later, is how far must, or can, love go? In one place Thomas asks, 'Whether in loving God we ought to observe any limit [*modus*]?' But as to the nature of 'measure', or limit, he explains: 'The goodness of a measure which has definition of itself is better than the goodness of a measured object which has its definition from another'.[54] A defining character and imperative of love was being envisaged, and we can see this from common experience. Love is a measure, not a thing measured. The distinction is amplified by Thomas:

> A limit [*modus*] implies a certain fixity of measurement [...]. It belongs essentially to the measure, for a measure of itself fixes and limits other things [...]. Hence in the measure there can be nothing indeterminate, while the object measured is indeterminate unless it come up to the measure, or exceed it or fall short of it.[55]

So love is a yardstick, exact and indefective, a measure defining everything to which it is applied. An apt illustration is St John in his vision measuring the Temple. The subject is explicit: an angel has provided the measuring-rod and specifies what is to be measured—only the inviolable dedicated things. The parts outside those limits are not compliant subjects of measure.

> Then I was given a measuring rod like a staff, and I was told: "Rise and measure the temple of God and the altar and those who worship there, but do not measure the court outside the temple; leave that out".[56]

Zechariah and Ezekiel had recorded such visions of an interpreter with a measuring rod. Zechariah saw the measuring as signifying Jerusalem at peace expanded without walls, the Lord declaring '*I* will be to her a wall of fire round about, and the glory within her'.[57] Ezekiel's vision is first of the indefinables of the spiritual realm; only in the end he sees every part of

The mind in love 39

Figure 2.1 Amiens, France. Cathedral church of St-Firmin. West porch bas-relief. Above: Ezekiel ponders the wheel within a wheel; below: the Lord enters the Temple. 1230–36.

the temple precisely defined and measured; and then the Lord of glory enters.[58] The formal cause, and final cause is God (Figure 2.1).

Article 7 at the centre of Thomas's questions *On Charity* poses a question which might strike us as unprofitably recondite: 'Whether the object to be loved out of charity is a rational nature?' His argument runs thus, that charity takes as its proper objects of love such things as are related somehow to the good of divine beatitude as their true end; and that charity can wish that for them. That they be related *somehow* is answered pivotally: 'Since only intellectual nature was begotten to enjoy the good of eternal beatitude, then only intellectual nature is to be loved out of charity [. . .]'.[59] This provides one basis of measured, proportionate and perfectible charity. If this leap is surprising it is immediately addressed, Thomas stating that it was for this reason that Augustine distinguished four objects to be loved in charity as things can have eternal beatitude in various ways. These we saw in Bernard's sermons. Thomas casts them in terms of his question of the *rational* measure: First, God, who has eternal beatitude through his own essence, and is therefore the root of beatitude. Second, oneself, one that loves, a rational creature sharing in beatitude through participation in God. Third, one's neighbour, a rational creature as an associate in the participation of beatitude. Those three obviously agree with the first and second Commandments. The fourth we might think does not measure up, but he says, 'There is something else to which it pertains to have an eternal beatitude, but only through a certain return, viz., our body which is glorified through a redundance of glory from the soul to itself'.[60] The body can participate if it is informed by this redounding from the rational nature of the soul, and it occurs as it keeps to 'the measure of virtue'.[61] It is a consistent note which we will find again, that the body, having its glory from the rational soul, is to be loved and cherished.

Thus the rationale of charity is according to the measure of charity, the measure of rational nature, and measured goodness in things. As to this last Augustine found the measure of the worth of a thing to be in its conception, its origin, saying, 'Yet its value for us lies not in itself but in the creative art that made it: it is our seeing that it was worth the making that makes us approve it as made'.[62] This attributes the real measure to God acting in perfect freedom.

Medieval logicality characteristically searched for the limits of things. Yet love theologically is not limited. God is to be loved in an exceptional way, as Bernard said in the opening sentence of *On Loving God*: 'You want me to tell you why God is to be loved and how much. I answer, the reason for loving God is God Himself; and the measure of love due to Him is immeasurable love'.[63] In his *Summa theologica* Thomas cited Bernard: 'God is the cause of our loving God; the measure is to love Him without measure'.[64] St Paul used the figure of *measure* in the body of Christ attaining its full status in unity: 'according to the effectual working in the measure of every part, [which] makes increase of the body unto the edifying of itself in love'.[65] Bernard, commenting on this, observed that, 'it is its virtue that increases, not its substance. Even its glory is increased. [. . .] Eventually it becomes "a holy temple in the Lord"'.[66] Throughout there was a measure, in the whole a quality of virtue, a glory, a unity, a building up, love being *in media*. We may detect these 'measures' in the architecture which took the building of great churches to the limits, as if there were none.

Form

Plato's theory of Forms was interpreted in the early Christian period by the Platonists, especially Plotinus, Porphyry and Calcidius, and their mediated ideas of form were largely influential. Aspects Gerard Watson points to are transcendence, the dichotomy of two worlds, the form known through the senses (species), and imagination (of an artist or artificer, in particular).[67] We can usefully follow this résumé.

First, the aspect of transcendence. We saw that Augustine evidently associated number, the second subject of the Wisdom text, with form (*forma*). If the relation is obscure to us the reason is probably the transcendence. In his treatise *On Free Will* number is the proximate subject of twenty-four paragraphs,[68] and he argued that it is beyond the grasp of the senses: 'When I consider in my mind the unchangeable science of numbers and the recondite sanctuary or region or [. . .] realm and abode of numbers, I find myself far removed from the corporeal sphere'.[69] He considered how it may be linked with wisdom, adapting Wisdom 8.1: 'Perhaps it is called number from its potency to reach from end to end, and is properly called wisdom because it graciously orders all things'.[70] Augustine understood that the reaching for truth must go beyond immediate visible things to the integrity of the eternal in which all things enjoy being—to contemplate all things held together in that form.

The dichotomy of two realms—absolute changeless realities, and relative mutable things—was strong in medieval mentality, yet the transcendent-immanent polarity signified that there are relations, juxtapositions and oppositions between these orders. We notice it in the medieval regard of form expressed in characteristic ways in art employing a *duality* motif. The dichotomy is between the form conceived in the mind, an ideal, a model—and the material world furnished with known and made things.

Concerning the *species* known through the senses, Watson cites Augustine, the point of interest being that he mandates the perceptive mind of an artist to grasp the form:

> Calcidius comments that here Plato wants to give us an idea of 'the second *species* which comes into being when the artist conceives in his mind the outlines of the work that is to come, and, with the likeness of this fixed within him, on its model shapes what he has started on'.[71]

Concerning the imagination, to Augustine this too devolves on the conspicuous power of number: 'Whatever delights you in corporeal objects [. . .] you may see is governed by number, and when you ask how that is so, you will return to your mind within'.[72] This evidently supplies the matter which the imagining mind extends and expands, not aimlessly but seeing form. The dichotomous mode of apprehension of material and spiritual realities brings in the artificer.

All these aspects are involved in everything in the world having 'forms because they have number'; and this occupies the mind of the maker:

> They exist only in so far as they have number. The artificers of all corporeal forms work by number and regulate their operations thereby. In working they move their hands and tools until that which is fashioned in the outer world, being referred to the inner light of number, receives such perfection as is possible, and, being reported on by the senses, pleases the internal judge who beholds the supernal ideal numbers. [...] But rise above even the mind of the artificer to behold the eternal realm of number.[73]

Thus Augustine combined the ideas of number and form, and we can detect the notion that underlies both, namely rationality. Augustine proceeded to recommend the role of perceptible form in the apprehension of God. More than that, the role of the artificer is, through the form, to draw the viewer to 'affection' for the maker—explicitly, love for God himself:

> An artificer somehow suggests to the spectator of his work [...] to let his eye so scan the form of the material thing made that he may remember with affection him who made it. Those who love thy creatures in place of thee are like men who [...] miss the meaning.[74]

In the illuminated initial of Psalm 27, 'Dominus illuminatio mea', the device of upper and lower scenes, heavenly and earthly, is the duality visibly rendered as a *translatus* (Figure 2.2). It is to God that the lower things are being referred. The eye must interpret the triangular diagram, scan the form and count the number; and marvel at the integration. It is a similitude of God, and the artist's *imagination* has caught the transcendent reference of the psalm: 'That I may dwell in the house of the Lord [. . .], to behold the beauty of the Lord, and to inquire in his temple'. The lamps represent the *form* of light, known to sense. Sixteen is a number of perfection, indeed a 'number of love', as we will see. The form that is *seen*, then, is the immanent part of the duality. The monks and nuns in the lower scene adore the Light in symbol. Above, the king adores the Lord in direct vision.

The first Article of *On Charity* asks whether charity is something created in the soul, and Thomas repeatedly refers to 'form' and 'power' to show the implanted and gifted nature of charity. This is in the soul, to flow out as responsive love. When he sees a certain 'habit of charity' created in us by the Spirit, he makes it 'the formal principle of the act of love'.[75]

Figure 2.2 Psalter of Isobel of France. Illuminated initial letter of Psalm 27. Wavy lines indicate heavenly subjects and location. 1265–70. (Cambridge, Fitzwilliam Museum, fol. 26r.)

> The Holy Spirit, Who is Uncreated Charity, exists in man who has created charity [...]. He disposes all things sweetly [*suaviter*], because to all things He gives forms and powers inclining them to that [to] which He Himself moves them.[76]

The Spirit is discerned as he who induces in a person the 'superadded' likeness to God according to charity, the formal principle. Thomas also draws attention to the similitude that rational man has to God in that he is intellectual, and created in the image of God. So, put another way, God created without any efficient medium; but, although he did not need to, he created with a formal medium:

> He acts mediately in order that He might preserve order in things. But if we speak of a formal medium, it is clear that as the agent is more perfect, so much more will he induce a form. For an imperfect agent does not induce a form but only a disposition to the form.[77]

44   *The mind in love*

To speak of virtues extends the matter. In Article 3 the question was, 'Whether charity is the form of the virtues?' Thomas affirms that, 'charity is the form, the mover, and the root of the virtues'.[78] He affirms that it is the common form; also the exemplary form; and in its form and according to it things are produced:

> Charity, considered as an act, not only is regarded as an exemplar, but also as a virtue which moves and causes. But the exemplar does not cause without producing that which is made in imitation of it, because it produces it in existence.[79]

This discussion has in view actual achievements. Love causes things to be produced in a certain way. The virtue of an artificer's love is thus embedded in a work, implying that love is its form too. Adjunct to this is the imagination drawing upon the exemplar. Watson observes an earlier concept in theologians influenced by Platonist philosophy: 'The artist, according to Calcidius, has a vision like that of God looking at the Forms'.[80] But in our study we see the more pragmatic recognition of form deriving from the activity of virtue, and inhering in a work.

Inclination

William of St-Thierry referred to the inclination of the mind, and the spirit's progress in love. Thomas wrote of, 'natural inclinations which can be discerned in things that are done naturally, without deliberation'.[81] Frequently he addressed the *inclination* of each individual towards their desired end, and of all things according to their natures—'as can be seen in heavy and light objects'.[82] In Wisdom 11.20 inclination is connected with *weight*. Article 1, referred to above, has 'forms and powers inclining [all things] to that to which He Himself moves them'.[83] This is in the nature of theocentric love:

> The love of charity is a certain inclination infused in rational nature for the purpose of tending toward God. Therefore according as it is necessary for one to tend toward God, thus is he inclined out of charity.[84]

Love for God impels the soul toward him, the imagination toward his dwelling-place. Thomas also firmly connected inclination with the ordering of love. The Song of Songs was a fruitful vehicle by which theologians addressed the tensions felt in every age as paradoxes: having and not-having; presence and absence; proximity and distance; progress and relapse; temporality and eternity.[85] The language of love is of longing for fulfilment.

Commenting on the text, 'Draw me after you',[86] Bernard pictured the Church: 'her eyes followed the ascent of her Bridegroom into heaven, filled with desire to follow him and be assumed with him into glory'.[87] It is curious

The mind in love 45

Figure 2.3 Lucca, Italy. Church of San Frediano. East front mosaic. The Disciples at the Ascension and Christ in Session. 13th C.

that the Song, so readily pictured in sermons, was seldom a subject in art which depicted almost every significant story in Scripture. But the theme (albeit not from the Song) was stunningly presented in the dual scene on the façade of San Frediano at Lucca (Figure 2.3). The front faces east (whether intentional or adventitious) contrary to the orientation of almost every church; and such is the *gravitas* of the great elevated scene of Ascension and Session that this suggests the reason—that the longing of Christ's lovers should be drawn up to him in the glory of the sun ascending on the church. In any case, by contrast, the weight of experience was expressed by Bernard thus:

> The contemplation of sublime truths can be achieved only little by little and in weariness of spirit; one is certainly not free to follow the Bridegroom wherever he goes. [...] Even the bride herself may repeat out of her distress: "Draw me after you; for a perishable body presses down the soul, and this tent of clay weighs down the active mind".[88]

A more objective psychology of inclination was earlier explored by Eriugena in his *Treatise on Divine Predestination*. Having treated at length the matter of every person's free choice, he related it to time and space, and to potential. He reasoned that, 'the natural motion of the human substance, by which clearly it first turned towards the knowledge and love of its God and then towards itself', has its superior cause in the Creator.

> What prevents us from referring all right motions of our mind to our creator who [...] moves our created spirit through time without place, and moves our bodies through time and place? Into our nature too he introduced a cause by which we could ourselves move freely, reasonably, voluntarily, towards the pursuit of those ends to which it had been intended that we should attain. [...] How much more should we praise him for our own substance which he so endowed that it should of its own motion cleave to its creator.[89]

In nature a thing was reckoned to tend toward its end according to an inclination implanted in it; and similarly a rational soul should tend toward God by the inclination of love infused into it. This was indeed a basis of the psychology of love. On the other hand, theologians were well aware of complex dichotomies, distractions and burdens on the soul. Thomas saw that,

> For those who will tend toward God as to an end, what is especially needed is that there be divine help; secondly, that there be some self-help; and thirdly, that there be cooperation with fellow-men. And in this we see a gradation [...]. Our body and those things which are necessary for the body also help us tend towards God, but only instrumentally.[90]

In the help obtained from others toward the goal, 'there also arises a factor of propinquity'. Then, as the body too assists, even as an instrument, he says, 'Finally, we ought to love our body'.[91] This is a balanced theology which brings in material things as playing their part. We see a gradation, all with a view to the end of loving God. In this life love needs to be ordered in its inclination even while it still lacks propinquity. Then, while saying, 'the charity of this life is in imitation of the charity of heaven', he foresees the state where inclination and ordering is no longer a question: 'Those who are in heaven are joined to their final end, and therefore their love is regulated solely by that end; thus there is no order of charity in them, except that which is concerned with their nearness to God'.[92] In heaven inclination terminates in vision. For that the powers of sight have to be strengthened, and the movements of love have to be ordered.

These are things brought in under Aquinas's question in *On Love*, Article 9: 'Whether there is some order in charity?' Order is highly prominent in medieval thought, and pivotal in the subject of love for God. Thomas commenced his answer citing (as Augustine had) the text, 'The king brought me into the house of wine, he set in order charity in me'.[93] His assertion is unequivocal: 'According to every opinion or authority on Scripture, such order must, without doubt, be designated to charity so that God is loved above all things, both in regard to affection and to the effect of love'.[94] When he concludes this section he links in a person's other loves of manifold things, that they all be part of the order: 'Other lawful and noble loves which arise from other causes are also able to be ordered to charity'.[95] It is necessary to see the role of order in the connections between love for God and things done or made, for these depend upon the condition of the soul in their inclining and in their virtue.

The devout Franciscan Spiritual, Jacopone da Todi (*c.* 1236–1306), is a witness from within the monastic system. Penitence leading to conversion, and dealing with fears of death and punishment, had been a long and deep process. Then he entered with intense fervour into a sustained experience of the love of Christ. His poetry expresses love suffusing all creation, reconciliation of oppositions, ecstasies of mystical union. Yet in one *Lauda* Christ stops him, saying,

> Restrain this love [*amore*], you who love me; there is no virtue without order. Since you so press to find me that your mind is renewed with the virtue of loving me, I wish that you call your love [*caritate*] to order. [...] Everything which I have created has been made with number and proportion, and they are all ordered to their purposes and keep their quality in this order, and even more the love [*caritate*] if it is kept in nature's order.[96] Hence, how have you been driven mad, o soul, through your heat? You have burst out of order and not restrained your fervour.[97]

Christ's appeal is to his own creatorial pattern, explaining that love itself—created indeed by him—was made and ordered with number, proportion and inclination. It was a practical appeal to 'nature's order', and that will have wider applications in our subject.

Love in the Trinity

We have seen something of the paradigm of love in human affective relation to God. Reflection on the duality device of depiction noted earlier may notice in the link an inkling of a triadic form—that between a person and God is charity itself. The understanding of human love as potentially 'in God' was engendered by the perception of love within the Deity. Returning to Augustine's *The Trinity* we read:

> Embrace the love that is God: through love embrace God. He is the very love that links together in holy bond all good angels and all God's servants, and unites them and us to one another and in obedience to himself. [...]
>
> But now you will say: "Charity indeed I see [...]. But my vision of charity is not a vision of the Trinity". Well, let me try to make you see that it is.[98]

Augustine reasons from the two-fold Commandment and from St John's Epistle. The imperative to love God first is inseparably linked with the necessity to love our neighbour as ourselves. He points out the *pattern*— love connecting and uniting things and persons, everywhere. Four times he enjoins us to love the pattern: we love the 'everlasting fixity and changelessness' of it; seeing its operation 'stirs us somehow to love it'; love of it engenders love for the lives of others; there 'stirs in us towards the same pattern a more burning charity'.[99] This is part of a close discussion of the pattern which is trinity. On the same pattern Augustine showed that the mind, its knowledge, and its love, constitute a trinity, teasing out the relations, their wholeness and perfections.[100]

> Love is the activity of a lover, and it has a certain object. There, then, we have three things: the lover, that which is loved, and love. Love itself is nothing but a kind of life which couples together or seeks to couple some two entities, the lover and the loved.[101]

Regarding the Trinity he shows that here is the essence of love and the perfect pattern. Mutuality-and-exchange is perfect. He has given the identifications: Spirit is 'that mutual charity whereby the Father and the Son love one another'.[102] Augustine concluded that the Spirit is most fitly named Charity. The intrinsic nature and operation of love is displayed and patterned.

All this underlies twelfth-century thought. Bernard spoke of the congruity of the Trinity in unity in this way: it is in nothing other than the Trinity that the very essence of love is. In *On Loving God* he wrote:

> What in that supreme and blessed Trinity preserves that supreme and ineffable Unity, save charity? It is law, then, and charity the law of the Lord, which in a certain way holds together the Trinity in Unity, and binds it in the bond of peace. [Charity is] that divine substance; which is neither new nor strange, for John says: *God is love*. Charity is then rightly called both God and the gift of God.[103]

It is in the context of a discussion of oneness with God which a person can know, that William of St-Thierry identified the bond as in the divine Trinity; again, the Holy Spirit, who is love:

The mind in love 49

It is called unity of spirit not only because the Holy Spirit brings it about or inclines a man's spirit to it, but because it is the Holy Spirit himself, the God who is Charity. He who is the Love of Father and Son, their Unity, Sweetness, Good, Kiss, Embrace and whatever else they can have in common in that supreme unity of truth and truth of unity, becomes for man in regard to God in the manner appropriate to him what he is for the Son in regard to the Father or for the Father in regard to the Son through unity of substance.[104]

Love in the Trinity, we might say, is the subject of a frontispiece of an Anglo-Saxon Psalter (Figure 2.4). Unity and love are signified in the two principal

Figure 2.4 The Trinity. Psalter frontispiece (detail). The Holy Spirit is symbolised as the Dove. Christ Church Cathedral Priory, Canterbury, *c*. 1020. (London, British Library, Harley MS 603, fol. 1.)

figures and the dove, and by the superb vesica both enclosing and divulging the scene. The essential subject is the intimacy of the Father and the Son, with the Spirit, the dove, symbolising the divine kiss, the love. Inspiration for this image may have come from an earlier Song of Songs commentary; we can certainly find the spiritual signification in twelfth-century works, such as the *Brevis commentatio* of William of St-Thierry, written around 1124:

> Now there is a sort of "turning" of the Father towards the Son and of the Son towards the Father [...]. And this "turning towards" is in a kiss and embrace. The kiss is a mutual recognition, the embrace a mutual love [...]. And so the kiss and the embrace of Father and Son is the holy Spirit who proceeds from them both, the love of the Father for the Son and of the Son for the Father.[105]

Nor is application lacking, for William said that a person's spirit is inclined to this same unity, and that, in an appropriate way, the Spirit 'becomes for man in regard to God' what the Spirit is within the Trinity. He also said *we* are 'touched by the kiss when we are filled with love and knowledge'.[106] In the Psalter illustration the vesica seems to sequester the Trinity—and there *within* the love of God is held the world. William provides this application: 'The soul in its happiness finds itself standing midway in the Embrace and the Kiss of Father and Son'.[107]

Even in terms they used of the divine Trinity, so these twelfth-century theologians expressed the union of a person and God, not as a duality but a trinity. It is a logical and experimental truth that where there are two connected things there is *ipso facto* a third entity, distinct yet inseparable, having definitive relations to the two. The unitive entity we have seen is the *love* between lover and beloved. The theology sanctions the triadic love as a similitude of the divine Trinity. There is pattern and law in the definition. The law of love is the union of lover and beloved. The law in the beloved is the return of love to the lover. Between the three identities is equality. Then the same pattern is between creature and Creator.

Here was a model shown in Christian revelation, not received from Hebrew or Greek thought. The intuitively understood figure of the equilateral triangle doubles to model essential correspondences. It is visualised without base or axis for it depends on no space-time relations.

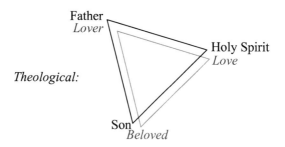

The mind in love 51

If warrant for the triangular diagram as a form analogy of the Trinity is needed, we find it where Bonaventure (1221–74) commented on the Genesis text in which the Trinity says, 'Let us make man in our image and likeness'.[108] The application as he explained it is specific:

> 'Image' is a sharing in the determination by shape (*in distinctione figurali*), in the manner of a triangle, in which there are three apices and three lines; just in the same way there are three powers any one of which has a relation with any other, and so too with the three Persons; thus a power or a person has the character of an apex, whereas a relation of a procession (*emanatio*) has the character of a line.[109]

This description is of an abstract figure capable of universal application. In these terms Bonaventure expressed the image of a person 'sharing in' this triadic form; it is their constitution. It is not just a model; it is the actuality. Wherever it is identified, the entities or persons, and median acts or powers, are all linked. Attention is drawn to the relations; they are lines flowing out and returning. A plausible transfer is that the graphic lines represent *acts* of love.

Love in the Trinity is a recurring theme expressed both as being and acting. In the powers and acts of love Grosseteste characterised the divine Persons as 'remembering, understanding and loving'. He offered this as one of a number of illustrations of the Trinity:

> The begetting memory and the understanding that is begotten reflect on each other a mutual and connecting love. And this is an illustration of the Trinity that is closer to it than any of the others which have been given.[110]

Often the triad was posited as 'memory, understanding and will', for instance by Augustine who suggested, in this regard, that, 'If indeed any Person in the Trinity is to be termed specially the will of God, the name is applicable rather, like charity, to the Holy Spirit. For charity is strictly a form of willing'.[111] These and countless explications of theology emphasise not a passive, detached God, but the One who is generative, dynamic and active in will and love. In terms of the illustrations referred to, the Trinity is not only in the Persons (the *apices*) but in the Processions (the lines); the nouns and verbs of love.

Implications of incarnation

From its beginning Christian theology has framed human nature by the initiatives of the Trinity in Creation and Incarnation. The first was known only as a sketch, but pregnant with meaning. The second was the demonstration of divine intention which was witnessed and wondered at—God in

52 The mind in love

human flesh. However little understood the mysteries of divine creation and incarnation still operate. In medieval theology the place of the Incarnation is reported by James Ginther:

> Grosseteste asserts that the whole Christ is the subject matter of the discipline of theology. [...] It encompasses the Trinity, the Incarnation, the Church and all creation. [...] He argues for four fundamental features of the subject. First it is a unified subject, where the Incarnation is the 'glue' of the discipline.[112]

In relation to our topic there are two aspects particularly important because they provide key connections: the peculiar privilege of humanity in the way in which it is connected to God, and the power of sensible things to turn the human mind to God. Athanasius (298–373), explaining the necessity for the incarnation of Christ, wrote:

> The Word of God, in His great love took to Himself a body and moved as Man among men, meeting their senses, so to speak, half way. He became Himself an object for the senses, so that those who were seeking God in sensible things might apprehend the Father through the works which He, the Word of God, did in the body.[113]

Incarnation does mean an actual embodiment, and involvement in time and place. By extraordinary identification the senses even become Christocentric, as the soul grasps the love demonstrated by its Maker—and if so then the material objects of attention take on their own significations.

As to the mode of the divine incarnation, Athanasius makes explicit what reflection must show could not be otherwise—that it was on the initiative and by the design and act of God solely. A number of times he calls God 'the Artificer'. He also makes the point thus: 'He takes to Himself for instrument a part of the whole, namely a human body, and enters into that'.[114] He rejects an objection that 'the Greeks' might raise, that God could have instructed and saved mankind by 'mere signification of His will'; the case demanded an active intervention and identification.

> For that reason, therefore, He was made man, and used the body as His human instrument. If this were not the fitting way, and He willed to use an instrument at all, how otherwise was the Word to come?[115]

Thus it is of the essence of incarnation that it come forth from the maker alone, and that the material thing is instrument of the new form. This is instructive if we are to find meaning in medieval church architecture in the light of the Incarnation. For the works become instruments, meeting the human senses and mind as sacramental, expressing the Word manifest in flesh. The whole building becomes a 'signum', a sign, of the active love of God remaking disordered nature.

The Incarnation was a matter of deep theological examination; and Thomas Aquinas framed this basic question: 'Whether it was necessary for the restoration of the human race that the Word of God should become incarnate?'[116] In our time a reader might ask how this question is relevant to our subject. Its relevance is in the reconstitution of things out of chaos, and because it has to do with the infusion of love. How it can be seen and followed—this and more will be in Chapter 6. Furthermore, restoration involves, for our need, an instrument capable of giving a person a new nature (recalling the beginning of this chapter). Thomas went on to show how the Incarnation was necessary to our having a remedy for the disorders of sin, so to be able to love God in return.

Again, the purpose of the Incarnation was expressed by Hugh of St-Victor in an elaborately worked image—the ark of salvation.[117] In a brief essay titled 'What Truly Should be Loved?' he, like Thomas, called it the work of restoration:

> Consider the two works of God, namely the work of creation and the work of restoration [...] the work of restoration is the Incarnation of the Word and all things that, from the beginning of the world up to the end, either preceded to foretell it, or will follow to confirm it.[118]

Notice how Hugh compressed Christ's Incarnation and the participation of 'all things' in it, at the same time predicating full restoration from beginning to end on the Incarnation. In his treatise *On the Sacraments* he extended his thought thus: '[. . .] the creation of the world with all its elements [. . .]; the Incarnation of the Word with all his sacraments'.[119] If Hugh's statement is accurate such a work as a church could be both an incarnation to 'follow to confirm' the divine Incarnation, and a work of restoration. Even thus was a material church sacramental, a visible word, infused with love.

Love as hierarch and worker

In Chapter 1 we discussed a passage in which Augustine said that high knowledge of a thing in the very cause of its creation is reached through *knowing the art* by which God made all things by measurement, number and order. In the reading of that formula we learned that love operated in the art. Then in the aspects of the Trinity we have begun to see both the primacy of love and the relations and acts of love. Medieval exegesis of the Genesis account of creation was prominent especially in *Hexaëmeron* commentaries; and the theme of God as Cause and Creator of all things, and humans in his image, was applied as God the Exemplar for artificers as makers of things, albeit so inferior. God was sometimes called Artist, Artificer and Architect; thus the great worker to be emulated, endowing the human mimetic roles with transcendent significance. Many texts insist that God created all things in love for those things, and through love flowing from his own being. Whether or not there was conscious imitation by

54 *The mind in love*

human artificers, the grounding of this insight particularly in the Trinity and the Incarnation reveals important perceptions about the relativities and operations of love.

It would be a digression at this point to compare Greek philosophical thought and Christian doctrine of the act of creation, but it may be useful to cite Grosseteste on the meaning of the beginning (*principium*) of creation.[120] He rebuts the theory of three origins posited by Plato and the two by Aristotle. He said that, 'Plato was wrong, too, in his positing of Ideas: he claimed that the Idea was an exemplar distinct from God, which God looked into in making the world'. Grosseteste's objection was to any proposition that God created *in principium* from any other than 'attributes [which] belong to God alone'.[121] So God the Creator is himself the Exemplar, and himself the Love by which he created. In a discussion of Thomas's sympathy with neo-platonic theory of 'creative diffusion', Fran O'Rourke comments that he radically extended Dionysius' definition of love as a unitive power,

Figure 2.5 'Operatio'. A medallion from the Stavelot Abbey retable. The work of love personified as an angel. Mosan enamel, 14 cm o.a. dia., *c.* 1150. (bpk/Kunstgewerbemuseum, SMB/Hans-Joachim Bartsch.)

to God's love as 'also an originative and creative power': 'Divine love, therefore, is distinct from human love: for God to love is to cause the beloved to be. Divine love operates in the profound manner of a production: 'love is capable for producing', *habet efficaciam ad producendum*.[122]

In considering the Trinity there is a particular point in the *operation* of love. In the Exemplar is the efficient cause, the actual work, the compulsion and operation of love. Flowing from this is a hierarchy of operation. A medallion of the Stavelot retable depicts an angel as a divine worker, even representing God's operation in the world[123] (Figure 2.5). The left hand holds the orb as a holy thing; the right hand on the breast surely signifies the love in the work, *operatio*. Bernard, in a sermon addressing his monks, said: '[Your angels] are all spirits whose work is service'.[124] The medallion was so placed in the retable as to honour the Bishop Remaclus, worker and servant. A point to pursue is that humans might emulate God as workers each in their place as operatives of love.[125] Grosseteste in one place cites Basil (*c.* 330–79) verbatim:

> [God] gave us the power of being in his likeness, and left us to be the workers of this likeness in act [...] so that we might not be like statues made by the artist that lie there pointlessly [...]. For when you see a statue carefully made in the form of its original, you do not praise the statue: you admire the artist.[126]

God the artist is admired, even loved, when he is seen reflected in people displaying his likeness, which is when humans act, work, labour and make things in love. It flows from a perception of love as the Cause in all causes.

Thomas gave a basis for this in aetiological terms. In his treatise on Creation, the 'perfection' of a thing made is predicated on the cause and the model; perfect likeness must be the aim:

> It is according to the form of the effect pre-existing in the agent that the effect attains likeness to the agent, for an agent produces its like with respect to the form by which it acts. [...] The perfection of the universe of creatures consists in its likeness to God, just as the perfection of any effect whatever consists in its likeness to its efficient cause.[127]

In the subsequent treatise on Providence, the same thinking is extended to focus on the image which is to represent (*repraesentet*) the original; to which end it has likeness to it:

> All creatures are images of the first agent, namely God, since *the agent produces its like*. Now the perfection of an image consists in representing the original by a likeness to it, for this is why an image is made. Therefore all things exist for the purpose of acquiring a likeness to God, as for their last end.[128]

This theology persistently makes the application that the creature, the likeness, must be ordered to the Creator, the Exemplar; it is in line with the inclination and ordering which we have considered.

The notion of hierarchy which permeates much medieval thought is inherent in work as in love. Hierarchy is such a prominent concept in the writings of Pseudo-Dionysius.[129] Andrew Louth observes that, 'Denys does not really regard hierarchy as something imposed on "us" and independent of "us": rather it *consists* of us'.[130] The perception is commonly missed, that hierarchy itself does not define or sum what a relationship amounts to. Thomas makes a distinction: 'Charity does not recognize a hierarchy of the lover to the loved because it unites the two. It does, however, recognize the hierarchy of two objects to be loved'.[131] When a person's attention to each and every different thing brings it into relation to God, all will have, within the person's love, proper places in relation to one another.

Love is the primary practical art of moving all things under it to the desired end. Love is a worker mandated to be form-giving, as an architect brings together building elements and the form into which they are to be built. Love works as a hierarch and as a master-builder. Thomas, describing the moving power of charity, used such an illustration:

> Every higher act or power is said to move a lower act or power, so that the act of the lower is ordered to the end of the higher. For example, a house-builder commands a stone-mason so that the act of the stone-mason is ordered to the form of the house, which is the end of the builder.[132]

The principle of the working of a hierarchy had been clearly stated by Pseudo-Dionysius. Here he expresses its work in terms of love: 'Love moves those, whom it unites, to a mutual relationship: it turns the inferior to the superior to be perfected thereby; and moves the superior to watch over the inferior'.[133] This has important application in the matter of judgement. The whole schema of Dante Alighieri (1265–1321) in the *Commedia* is based on hierarchies. In *Paradiso*'s heaven of the Seraphim, signifying Love, he explains the working of love through all the orders below:

> These orders all gaze upward, and downward
>   have such conquering might that toward God
>   all are drawn and all draw.[134]

Dante acknowledges the derivation from Dionysius in the lines immediately following. Incidentally we may draw attention to the highest inspiration of Dante's exposition, its comprehensiveness, his skill, and achievement; and draw parallels with the great cathedrals, even to all the extensive and intensive theology informing both.

Hierarchy and order in monastic and scholastic culture were for a purpose. The ordering of love, Godward and towards others, requires obedience and practise, which in the end supersedes such debates as whether *eros* underlies or usurps *agape*, or how far neo-platonism influenced Christian thought. In terms which sharpen the actual application Ineke van 't Spijker writes:

> Far from being left to its own psychological devices, religious *experientia* is subject to the process of composition, including both *cogitatio* and *affectus*. As well as *homo interior*, the word 'composing' and its equivalents, or *forma* and its derivatives, can be found in the texts. They refer to the background of monastic pedagogy, and give access to an important element of how interiority is conceived. The canon or monk composes his (inner) life, making it into a work of art.[135]

In this chapter's brief account the characteristic medieval noetic treatment of the subject has been prominent, but interwoven with a theology more mystical, as to be expected in the matter of love. In scholastic learning as well as in monastic discourse there was desire to know divine truth. Grosseteste, who wrote on the science of light, particularly as a medium in which things in their very nature were apprehended, related it to the mind's seeing, which is then impelled to desire, as in love:

> In the same way as 'light' is understood to mean the knowledge of the truth, with regard to the glance [*aspectus*] of the mind, in just that way it is understood as the love of the known truth in the desire [*affectus*] of the mind.[136]

William of St-Thierry in his *Epistola* wrote of *aspectus* and *affectus*. The *aspectus* he characterised as the gaze that wonders and loves: it is when the soul, 'looks upward [*suscipit et miratur*], and affects [*affectat*] what is above it, and the devout image hastens to adhere to its similitude [*similitudini*]'.[137] Van 't Spijker shows that he described ever growing intensity: from imagining, to looking, to affecting, to adhering, to inhering. She teases out the nuances of *affectus*—how it works with God's illuminating grace; and with the instrument of imagination, so far as it goes; and then the unity of adhering and inhering—all with the emphasis William laid on love for God.[138] The discussion of the 'process of composition' in the 'background of monastic pedagogy' of the interior experience, can surely be extended to the corporate experience, in the art of the liturgy, and its locus in the church: all the elements and operations are paralleled.

An example of the 'mystical' strand of theology can be drawn from Ramon Llull. The imagery is spatial and luminous:

> Love lit up the cloud placed between the lover and the beloved, and made it as bright and shining as the moon by night, the morning star at dawn, the sun by day, and understanding in the will. And it is through this shining cloud that the lover and beloved speak to each other.[139]

58 *The mind in love*

This 'cloud' medium proportions *aspectus* and *affectus* in and to each—understanding and will are here. The cloud is a presence, 'placed', clear as light, representing love, sustaining the very converse between lover and beloved. Here brilliantly is the axiomatic trinitary form. We may see the same form in the medieval churches; operating even as this mediate cloud.

In summary, love is the condition in which all work should be somehow composed and done. The salient points are: that medieval authors consistently reiterated the real causes and effects of love; that theology taught a due integration of and love for the physical nature of things; that the material-spiritual dichotomy is answered by the form of love—effected in trinity and incarnation; that love is mandated to be form-giving; and that it is the primary and practical art of hierarch and worker relating all things above and below to a perfectible end. Love itself, applied and understood with these features, justifies the reading of intention, motivation and meaning in all the tectonic arts.

Notes

1. Aristotle, *Ethics*, 1167b34-35; 1168a19, trans. Thomson (1955), p. 299; Rousselot (2001), p. 111.
2. Thomas Aquinas, *De caritate*, a.1, ad., trans. Kendzierski (1960), p. 21.
3. Ibid., p. 22.
4. Augustine, *Confessiones*, 7.20, trans. Pine-Coffin (1961), p. 154.
5. Ibid. He alludes to I Corinthians 8.1: 'Knowledge puffs up, but love builds up'.
6. The following are indicative of twelfth and thirteenth-century works having this central theme: Aelred of Rievaulx, *De speculo caritatis*; Bernard of Clairvaux, *De diligendo Deo*, *Sermones super Cantica canticorum*; Bonaventure, *De triplici via, seu incendium amoris*; Robert Grosseteste, *Le chateau d'amour*; Hugh of St-Victor, *De substantia dilectionis*; Ramon Llull, *Librum amici et amati*; Richard of St-Victor *De quatuor gradibus violentae caritatis*; Thomas Aquinas, *De caritate*, *De Trinitate*; William of St-Thierry, *De caritate*.
7. In particular: Origen, *Cantica canticorum*; Augustine, *De libero arbitrio* and *Enchiridion*; Pseudo-Dionysius, *De mystica theologia* and *De caelesti hierarchia*; Boethius, *De consolatione philosophiae*.
8. Turner (1995), p. 20.
9. Ibid., the title of Chapter 1 (pp. 25–43).
10. Pieper (1965), pp. 91–92.
11. Ibid., p. 96.
12. Ibid., p. 93.
13. Turner (1995), p. 78.
14. Origen, *Cantica canticorum*, trans. Lawson (1957), pp. 35–36.
15. Pieper (1965), p. 94. See further, Thomas Aquinas, *Summa theologica*, 2a 2ae, q.25, a.5.
16. Song of Songs (Vulgate), 2.5, 5.8. Or, 'I am wounded by love'.
17. Ibid., 2.4.

18 Ibid., 3.10.
19 Ibid., 8.7.
20 Leclercq (1982), pp. 112–13.
21 *De civitate Dei*, 19.14, trans. Dyson (1998), p. 941.
22 Origen, *Cantica canticorum*, Prologue, trans. Lawson (1957), p. 34.
23 Aelred of Rievaulx, *De speculo caritatis*, 3.2.3, trans. Connor (1990), p. 222.
24 Ibid., 3.3.6. p. 225.
25 Bernard of Clairvaux, *De diligendo Deo*, 9.26, trans. van Allen (1959), p. 45.
26 Ibid., 10, trans. Stiegman (1995), p. 29.
27 Bernard of Clairvaux, *Epistola 11, Ad Cartusiensis*, 11.7, trans. Eales (1904), p. 172.
28 Bernard of Clairvaux, *De diligendo Deo*, 10.28, trans. Stiegman (1995), p. 30.
29 Ibid., 10.29, p. 31.
30 Ibid., Emero Stiegman in his Commentary, p. 124.
31 Bernard of Clairvaux, *De diligendo Deo*, 11.30, trans. Gardner (1916), p. 109. C.f. II Corinthians 4.7.
32 William of St-Thierry, *Epistola*, 2.234, trans. Berkeley (1976), p. 87.
33 Ibid., 2.10, p. 88. Ineke van 't Spijker (2004), Chapter 5, gives a thorough account of William's theology and psychology of love in the *homo interior*. For her commentary on this passage see pp. 192–5.
34 Ibid., 2.262, p. 95.
35 Ibid., 2.256–7, p. 94.
36 Ibid., 1.46, p. 27.
37 Ibid., 1.49. p. 28. In two footnotes Berkeley relates bodily experience with its limitations to the consequences of original sin, so rather diverting attention from William's discussion which does not have that in view.
38 Ibid., 1.55, p. 31.
39 Ibid., 1.59. p. 32.
40 Ibid., 1.69. p. 35.
41 Kraebel (2011), pp. 266, 269.
42 Richard of St-Victor, *De quatuor gradibus*, trans. Kraebel in *On Love*, ed. Feiss (2011), p. 277.
43 Ibid., 8, 9, p. 278.
44 Ibid., 11, 12, pp. 279–80.
45 Ibid., 13, p. 280.
46 Ibid., 14, p. 280.
47 Dante, *Paradiso* 27, 109–11, trans. Anderson (1932), p. 552.
48 Richard of St-Victor, *De quatuor gradibus* 29, trans. Kraebel, in *On Love*, ed. Feiss (2011), p. 287.
49 Ibid., 46, p. 295.
50 Ibid., 47, p. 296.
51 Thomas Aquinas, *De caritate*, trans. Kendzierski (1960): Article 7, pp. 58–65; Article 3, pp. 33–9; Article 9, pp. 74–80. I treat them in this order to follow the subjects in the Wisdom text.
52 Maritain (1934), p. 200.
53 A short critique of Panofsky's hypothesis is in Price (1992), pp. 138–41.
54 Thomas Aquinas, *Summa theologica*, q.27, a.6, ad.1, trans. Crehan (1964), p. 291.
55 Ibid., 2a 2ae, q.27, a.6, ad., p. 290.
56 Revelation 11.1, 2.
57 Zechariah 2.1–5.
58 Ezekiel, chapters 40–43.

60 *The mind in love*

59 Thomas Aquinas, *De caritate*, a.7, ad., trans. Kendzierski (1960), p. 61. See also Thomas Aquinas, *Summa contra gentiles*, 3, 53.5; 54.9.
60 Ibid., a.7, ad., p. 62. See further, Augustine, *De doctrina christiana*, ed. Martin (1962), 1. 23. Augustine treats the first three objects of love in some detail in *De vera religione*, 46.86–48.93, trans. Burleigh (1953), pp. 269–73.
61 Ibid., a.7, ad.14, p. 64. The 'measure of virtue' is a topic for a separate study.
62 Augustine, *De Trinitate*, 8, 5.3, trans. Burnaby (1955), p. 43.
63 Bernard of Clairvaux, *De diligendo Deo*, 1.1, trans. van Allen (1959), p. 16.
64 Thomas Aquinas, *Summa theologica*, 2a 2ae, q.27, a6, ad., trans. Dominican Fathers (1915–28), vol. 9, p. 366. William of St-Thierry wrote, in *De natura et dignitate amoris*, 2: 'Love is due to God only, and for no other reason than God Himself.' trans. Webb and Walker (1956), p. 14.
65 Ephesians 4.13, 16 (AV).
66 Bernard of Clairvaux, *Cantica canticorum*, 27.10, trans. Walsh and Edmonds (1971–80), II, p. 83.
67 Watson (1986).
68 Augustine, *De libero arbitrio*, 2, 8.22–17.45.
69 Ibid., 11.30., trans. Burleigh (1953), p. 154.
70 Ibid.
71 Watson (1986), p. 41. Calcidius first translated the *Timaeus* into Latin, with a commentary, in *c*. 321.
72 Augustine, *De libero arbitrio*, 2, 16.41, trans. Burleigh, p. 161.
73 Ibid., 2, 16.42, pp. 161–2.
74 Ibid., 2, 16.43, p. 162. Compare Hebrews 3.3–4: 'The builder of a house has more honour than the house. For every house is built by some one, but the builder of all things is God'.
75 See p. 37 above.
76 Thomas Aquinas, *De caritate*, a.1, ad., trans. Kendzierski (1960), p. 22.
77 Ibid., a.1, ad.13; ad.14, p. 24.
78 Ibid., a.3, ad., p. 35.
79 Ibid., a.3, ad.8, p. 37.
80 Watson (1986), p. 41.
81 *Quodlibetum* 1, a.8, trans. Vincelette, in Rousselot (2001), p. 88.
82 Thomas Aquinas, *De caritate*, a.9, ad., trans. Kendzierski (1960), p. 76. Also, a.7: 'for man to tend towards his beatitude'.
83 Ibid., a.1, ad., p. 22.
84 Ibid., a.9, ad., p. 76.
85 Turner (1995) in the bibliography has an extensive list of medieval expositions.
86 Song of Songs 1.4.
87 Bernard of Clairvaux, *Cantica canticorum*, 21.1, trans. Walsh and Edmonds (1971–80), II, p. 3.
88 Ibid., p. 4.
89 Eriugena, *De divina praedestinatione*, 8.7., trans. Brennan (1998), p. 55.
90 Thomas Aquinas, *De caritate*, a.9, ad., trans. Kendzierski (1960), p. 77.
91 Ibid., a.9, ad.12, p. 79.
92 Ibid.
93 Song of Songs 2.4. Refer p. 30 above.
94 Thomas Aquinas, *De caritate*, a.9, ad., trans. Kendzierski (1960), p. 76.
95 Ibid., p. 77.
96 This second predicate is lines 159–60 from text in Peck: 'e molto più ancora caritate /sè ordenata nella sua natura', trans. Barbara Askam.
97 Jacopone da Todi, *Laude* 88, 147–62, trans. Peck (1980), p. 179.
98 Augustine, *De Trinitate*, 8, 12.8, trans. Burnaby (1955), p. 52.

The mind in love 61

99 Ibid., 8, 13.9, p. 54.
100 Ibid., 9, 4.4, p. 60. That the triad comprises entities is clear in 9, 8.5.
101 Ibid., 8, 14.10, p. 54.
102 Ibid., 15, 27.17, p. 157.
103 Bernard of Clairvaux, *De diligendo Deo*, 12.35, trans. Gardner (1916), p. 121. Gardner treats this passage fully in his Notes, pp. 168–73.
104 William of St-Thierry, *Epistola*, 2.263, trans. Berkeley (1976), pp. 95–6.
105 William of St-Thierry, *Brevis commentatio*, 12, trans. Turner (1995), p. 283. The same meaning is in Alan of Lille (d. 1202) in *Elucidatio*, trans. Turner (1995): 'It is [the Holy Spirit] who unites Father and Son, for his is the love of them both, their embrace and their kiss' (p. 295). Similarly in Thomas of Perseigne (d. c. 1190) in his *Commentarium in Cantica canticorum*, 1.5, trans. Turner (1995): '[. . .] the Father who kisses, the Son who is kissed, and the kiss itself, the Holy Spirit' (p. 313).
106 William of St-Thierry, *Brevis commentatio*, 12, trans. Turner (1995), p. 284.
107 William of St-Thierry, *Epistola*, 2.263, trans. Berkeley (1976), p. 96.
108 Genesis 1.26.
109 Bonaventure, *In Sententiarum* 2, 16, a.2, q.3, r., cited and trans. Turner (1995), p. 146.
110 Grosseteste, *Hexaëmeron*, 8, 4.12, trans. Martin (1996), p. 228. See further in 8, 5.1.
111 Augustine, *De Trinitate*, 15, 38–9 (20), trans. Burnaby (1955), pp. 167–8.
112 Ginther (2003), pp. 249–50.
113 Athanasius, *De incarnatione Verbi Dei*, 15, trans. Religious of C.S.M.V. (1944), p. 43.
114 Ibid., 43, p. 79.
115 Ibid., 44, p. 80.
116 Thomas Aquinas, *Summa theologica*, 3, q.1, a.2. p.7.
117 Hugh treated the 'ark' image fully in *De arca Noe morali*. See my article, 'History and Everlastingness in Hugh of St Victor's Figures of Noah's Ark', Lewis (2003).
118 Hugh of St-Victor, *Quid vere diligendum est*, 3.7. trans. Butterfield (2011), p. 180.
119 Hugh of St-Victor, *De sacramentis*, trans. Defarrari (1951), p. 174.
120 Grosseteste, *Hexaëmeron*, 1, 10.1, trans. Martin (1996), p. 63. Here Grosseteste examines the significations of *principium*.
121 Ibid., 1, 9.1, p. 61. Grosseteste claims the support of Ambrose, Jerome, Bede, and 'other sacred writers', and contests the Hellenists' views, naming Anaximander, Thales of Miletus, Diogenes, and others.
122 Fran O'Rourke (1992), p. 232.
123 The retable is destroyed but is recorded by a drawing in the Archives de l'état, Liège, a reproduction of which is in Kessler (2004), Figure 19, p. 63.
124 Bernard of Clairvaux, *Cantica canticorum*, 7.4, trans. Walsh and Edmonds (1971–80), I, p. 41.
125 This theme is continued on p. 194 below.
126 Basil, *Hexaëmeron*, 10.16–17, in Grosseteste, *Hexaëmeron*, 8, 8.1, trans. Martin (1996), p. 234.
127 Thomas Aquinas, *Summa contra gentiles*, 2, 46.5, trans. Anderson (1975), pp. 140–1.
128 Ibid., 3, 19.4, trans. Pegis (1975), p. 439. The clause in italics cites Aristotle, *De generatione et corruptione*, I, 7 (324a 1).
129 See Hou (2008), pp. 256–7.
130 Louth (1989), p. 132.
131 Thomas Aquinas, *De caritate*, a.9, ad.3, trans. Kendzierski (1960), p. 78.

62 The mind in love

132 Ibid., a.3, ad., p. 36.
133 Pseudo-Dionysius, *De divinus nominibus*, 4.2. and 4.12. See Luibheid (1987), pp. 72, 81.
134 *Paradiso* 28.127–29, trans. Wicksteed (1899). In *Convivio* 2.6 Dante specified in detail the theological-hierarchical structure of *Paradiso*.
135 Van 't Spijker (2004), p. 9. Van 't Spijker elucidates the medieval meanings of the Latin terms. Brief pointers are: '*Cogitatio* is thinking, but framed within an elaborate network of mental activities. Words like *affectus, affectio, afficere, sentire, sensus* refer to what we call emotion, feeling and perception, but their usage points to a different perception of emotional life than ours' (p. 5).
136 Grosseteste, *Hexaëmeron*, 2.9.2, trans. Martin (1996), p. 96.
137 William of St-Thierry, *Epistola*, 2.209, trans. van 't Spijker (2004), p. 203.
138 See van 't Spijker (2004), pp. 198–208 in particular.
139 Llull, *Liber amici et amati*, verse 123, trans. Bonner (1993), p. 205.

3 The mirror of comprehension
The trivium

The logical arts

Throughout the Middle Ages, with various shifts in emphasis, the liberal arts provided skills central in learning. Often in diverse texts we notice the arts bringing in connections to theology to affirm love as a condition or referee. The task now is to take this regimen of the mental culture to see how it worked and its bearing on architecture.

The structure and content of learning to a fair degree indicates the preoccupations and goals of the culture. As suited the content, the form of the curriculum was conceptual and pragmatic, and whether in monastery, cathedral school or university it reflected the discipline and determination to access the meaning of all things by *cogitatio*. As to content it should be appreciated that *this* field of concern for truth was distinguished from the truth disclosed by nature below it, and the truths to be lived on the moral plane above it. In the middle was the truth to be learned, the mind skilled in comprehension and informed by instruction accordingly. Our application of this is to seek correspondences with aspects of the architecture, in both formal structure and content. Accordingly we might discern the *cogitatio* and *affectus* flowing in medieval art and architecture, including the centuries before the Gothic. Karl Morrison, in an essay examining the vital role of the liberal arts in Christian culture, goes back to Augustine to bear this out:

> Christian remedies for the emptiness of the pagan arts, and of incentives for studying them, began with theories about mental process [...]. In the passage from the most fleeting event—a physical sensation—to the most general predicate, the mind therefore imitated and recapitulated natural order. It progressed by natural sympathy with and imitation of the objects of knowledge, an affinity that reminded the Fathers of love.[1]

From mere sensations to mental concepts a logical power drew out knowledge, and to real purpose. Morrison's referring to love is not merely casual, for he later writes:

[Augustine] remained convinced that, necessary as they were for ordered social life, the arts were not autonomous, self-justifying techniques, but rather that each practitioner bent them to serve the object of his love. As we have seen art and love intersected. The Christian doctrine of conversion called for a redirection of love away from associations in the physical world to those in the spiritual, and the arts were important as means toward bringing about, explaining, and understanding the emotional displacements that ensued.[2]

So the liberal arts, creative arts, love of the work, and love for God were interconnected. The seven liberal arts, directed by love, gave access to and insight into 'objects of knowledge'. The arts of the trivium—grammar, dialectic and rhetoric—equipped the mind with language, logic and persuasive power. We will see that these skills had equivalent operations in art and architecture. The four arts comprising the quadrivium—arithmetic, music, geometry and astronomy—were skills by which the mind was instructed in laws and principles governing phenomena.

In antiquity nine liberal arts had been delineated by Varro (126–27BC). They included architecture and medicine; but Martianus Capella (*c.* 400–39) eliminated these.[3] The exclusion of architecture from the liberal arts is surely a factor in the lack of treatises on the subject. Then too, a real difficulty of architecture is that its own language is non-verbal and is notoriously difficult to translate, teach and analyse. The buildings must largely speak for themselves in a language, and about things, which must be assimilated; but strategically the liberal arts furnish a framework of comprehension and instruction even in architecture. Aristotle considered the relation between words and things in *De interpretatione*, on which Boethius (*c.* 480–524) commented: 'Words signify, not things, but thoughts (*intellectus*). Thoughts must be carefully distinguished from images (*imaginationes*). Truth and falsehood belong to thoughts and not images'.[4] This, as a commencement, is a useful view of the field of logic. The logical arts, language-based, were a mirror of the mind, for comprehending meaning wherever it is to be found. Yet for the mind to express itself Thomas Aquinas thought of the skill it needs, not only linguistic but in all modes of communication and representation:

> What could not be perfectly represented by one thing might be, in more perfect fashion, represented by a variety of things in different ways. For instance, when a man sees that his mental conception cannot be expressed adequately by one spoken word, he multiplies his words in various ways, to express his mental conception through a variety of means.[5]

Pertinent to the trivium arts, clearly in the works of Augustine, as of St Paul, there was from Christianity's beginning a high regard for the powers of the mind and skills of understanding. Even as he completed the view of the City in the *City of God*, Augustine marvelled that, surviving all the twisting of nature and declension from God, there are divine gifts in humans:

> There are all the important arts discovered and developed by human genius [...]. Consider the multitudinous variety of the means of information and persuasion, among which the spoken and written word has the first place; the enjoyment afforded to the mind by the trappings of eloquence and the rich diversity of poetry.[6]

Augustine enumerated all seven liberal arts as well as the four cardinal virtues. Learning was to be for enrichment in this life, for fulfilment in the City.

From the Genesis account of God and Adam naming all things made, to twelfth-century chronicles of the baffling multitude of things in nature, the world was comprehended in language of description, speculation and recitation. The sheer multitude of things and thoughts required endless effort in discerning the real and true. The scope widens to unfold the arts of comprehension being transferred to, and employed in, constructive works. The multiplicity is paralleled in tectonic arts, and immense labour was invested in things of importance and meaning. In Chartres cathedral's north porch alone there are said to be over seven hundred carved figures, all significant.[7] It reflected the understanding of a providential rational plan and humans ordered within it. So situated, the intellect strove for integration and comprehension.

Learning was not an end in itself. The arts were not for comprehension only but for reflection too. So Hugh of St-Victor (1096–1142) in *Didascalicon* (*On the Study of Reading*) regarded the arts as having philosophy as their *modus operandi* towards knowing the divine mind. While he subsumed all fields of activity and modes of working under that direction he distinguished arts of making from disciplines of mind:

> That can be called art which takes shape in some material medium and is brought out in it through manipulation of that material, as is the case in architecture; while that is called a discipline which takes shape in thought and is brought forth in it through reasoning alone, as is the case in logic.[8]

This quasi-definition of art emphasises the primacy of the material medium and preoccupation with the 'bringing out' of shape by 'manipulation'; which may be obvious, but should not be lost sight of. For in this rare mention of architecture it does not suggest a purpose to create or mould 'space', nor that shape is capricious or arbitrary. The juxtaposition of architecture and logic Hugh obviously takes to be apt—the arts employing both the medium of the material, and the medium of the mind. Each involves comprehension. To give some architectural context: Hugh would have been aware, and quite likely have seen, the abbey churches of St-Germer-de-Fly and St-Denis, and the cathedral of Sens, being built.[9] It is hard to suppose that he would not have reflected on the inherent connections between theocentric intention, the discipline of thought, and the arts that could so 'bring out shape' in material.

To begin to comprehend meaning required the precision and power of language to be engaged through the study of grammar. No less it required discovery and judgment through rigorous thought, the skilful use of dialectic. Yet these would fall short of their purpose were there no persuasion of the mind by the appeal of rhetoric. Meaning, or truth, is not in narrow ideas; the trivium arts have expansive, comprehensive roles. Correspondences appear in the ideas, language and operations between, for instance, linguistics and architecture, and between logic and aesthetics. Ideas flow from participation in things in which are found likenesses to things of a different order. The abstraction of ideas in the mind, and their architectonic construction, enables the communication of meaning and truth behind all images. The architecture and visual arts have the impress of ratiocination of extraordinary power, scope and integrity, which warrants some emphasis in order to increase our appreciation of the force of the three comprehension skills.

Personifications. The scope of the mind

Pictorial and sculptural presentations of personifications and allegories were age-old devices to express the preoccupations of mind and spirit in things corporeal and material. In Gothic sculpture, frescos and paintings there are numerous portrayals of the liberal arts, personified almost invariably as women; yet they do not appear as muses but as symbols of the mind's skills. Take away personifications and symbolic persons and such elaborate visual allegories are hardly possible.

The early recognised literary model for the personification of the arts was Martianus Capella's *The Marriage of Philology and Mercury*, in which the union of eloquence (Mercury) and learning (Philology) corresponds to the wedded disciplines of the trivium and quadrivium. The seven, characterised as beautiful women, each present an oration describing their art, in an ascending order corresponding to the planetary heavens. In the marriage ceremony the lower powers of nature and the physical world have been eclipsed by the uplifting and deifying power of the empyrean realm. Thus, Philology 'paid reverence to the presiding deities of the world of pure understanding, and to their ministers, to whom the powers of the sensible world owe veneration'.[10] In other words, the arts, availing in things spiritual, raise each person from the mundane, sensuous world, and connect them to the unseen intelligible world. In the pithy conclusion Martianus restates the book's idea—of this contrast yet connectedness—and caricatures his own art which has intentional and apt correspondence to vernacular language.

> Our garrulous Satire has heaped learned doctrines upon unlearned, and crammed sacred matters into secular; she has commingled gods and the Muses, and has had uncouth figures prating in a rustic fiction about the encyclopedic arts.[11]

Later medieval authors similarly praised the liberal arts, conscious of mundane and superior worlds and the acknowledged priority of the intellectual and spiritual; always they were intent on ordering the complexity and richness. In the twelfth century Alan of Lille (*c.* 1128–1202) in *Anticlaudianus* used personification in an allegory of Philosophy who, mounting in quest of God, needs a special chariot. This the seven Liberal Arts are able to construct, and five horses which are harnessed are the five senses. The senses have their vital role for the arts, but are purposeless if undisciplined.

Transposed into sculpture, the arts are given an important place in the twelfth-century right portal of the west front of Chartres cathedral. In the tympanum Mary is seated. In the surrounding archivolts are women personifying the seven liberal arts. Below those of the trivium, Grammar, Dialectic and Rhetoric, are their Classical originators or exponents: Priscian (or Donatus), Aristotle and Cicero; likewise with the other arts.[12] Mary, bearing Christ upon her lap, is 'herself the *sedes sapientiae* chosen by God as his throne. Around these images of the mystery of the Incarnation are placed the wisdom and learning of this world'.[13] By this juxtaposition the arts of learning are subordinate yet prerequisite in the exposition of this and the subsequent theological subjects.

In the north porch, of the mid-thirteenth century, the scope is expanded with historical subjects from the Old Testament. The beginning is in the central outer arch, at the left-hand springing. The archivolts depict Creation, Eden, Adam, and the Fall.[14] The frontal sequence then leads to the right-hand portal where the Liberal Arts are represented in the pedestals, while the archivolts depict the Seasons and the Zodiac. Crossing to the left-hand portal, the Cardinal Virtues are represented in the pedestals, upon which were types of the Active Life and the Contemplative Life, while the arch displays the scope of the Active and Contemplative Lives and the Heavenly Beatitudes.[15] The depth of the porch draws the viewer inward to the second sequence, finishing in the central tympanum which depicts the death, assumption and coronation of the Virgin. Here are schemes in which the liberal arts and the cardinal virtues are shown having a foundational place. The hermeneutic intention is borne out in the design. It is the language of an art expressing the mind behind the work; for ideas must find apt means of communication. Here an architectural grammar serves architectural dialectic set forth by architectural rhetoric. All is for the sake of the subject, expanding the mind in a rich *schema* of comprehension.

As we trace attributions of meaning behind the art to God, we grasp the entire work as ideation, speech and presentation of the divine mind. Eriugena had written of the participation of things in intelligible causes:

68 Comprehension: the trivium

'These ideas, existing in the mind of God, contain the substances of all things: man, for example, is most correctly defined as a certain intellectual notion eternally made in the divine mind'.[16] Tracing the 'idea' from Plato's *Timaeus*, and Porphyry, through Boethius, to Bernard of Chartres, John of Salisbury (*c.* 1118–1180) pondered the divine mind:

> The idea is [...] a sort of effect which subsists in the inner sanctuary of the divine mind, without needing any extrinsic cause. [...] The works of the divine mind are of two kinds. The first sort are created out of, or together with matter; the second are made out of and contained within the divine mind itself, without need of anything external. Thus the divine mind from the very beginning conceived the heavens in its understanding, nor did it need to employ any matter or form extrinsic to itself for this mental conception.[17]

This is illustrated by a dual figure in Chartres' north porch 'Creation' archivolt, interpreted plausibly as Adam as an idea in the mind of God.[18] The iconographical context and this subject could have come from Bernard of Chartres who was chancellor from *c.* 1119 to 1126 and prominent in establishing the logical arts there.

In the literary sources of such schemes the ideas, imagery and figures which ranged over all human culture and the natural world were found in proximity to, even partly expressing, what could be known of the mind of God. This was not an exclusive prerogative of verbal and literary communication, it belonged to art and architecture too. Thinkers addressing wide and profound themes pondered how the mind exercised itself; they perceived the power and richness of mental images. Even in the third century, the Roman philosopher Porphyry wrote: 'There cannot be a thought without an image; and the action of the intelligence in producing a thought from an image is compared to the colouring in of an outline drawing'.[19] Boethius' thoughts on imagination, where he claims a place for the visual sense, are explained by John Magee thus:

> *Imaginatio* shares with *sensus* the facts (a) that it is not what is signified by spoken sounds, and (b) that it is somehow distinct even from *primi intellectus*. *Imaginatio(nes)* is (are) the precondition for *intellectus*. Also like *sensus*, *imaginatio* is likened to the *primae figurae* laid down by painters; it is associated with the images or forms which come into the soul and is characterised as a visual rather than a linguistic medium.[20]

The scope of the imagination involves work to do in apprehending images and showing them to the thinking mind.

The window of a north transept is one of the pre-eminent places for a didactic statement on a great theme. In Laon cathedral's north transept,

Comprehension: the trivium 69

Figure 3.1 Laon, France. Cathedral church of Notre-Dame. North transept rose window. Lady Philosophy in the centre. The liberal arts in eight roundels (Medicine included), *c.* 1205.

in eight roundels of the great plate-tracery circle, the Liberal Arts are represented as noble women who love to reward, on a supra-sensual plane, those who love them (Figure 3.1). They surround Philosophy who is portrayed as she appeared to Boethius, as he recorded.[21] On the bottom hem is embroidered the Greek letter Pi, and on the top hem the Greek letter Theta. The letters stand for practical philosophy and speculative or contemplative philosophy. Here again is Mind expressing itself, the executor of the Wisdom of God ordering the whole, as a beginning of the sequence of comprehension, an explication of the architectural cathedral. Or, as the centre of a north transept window was often Mary's place, a transfer of meaning would have been easy in the medieval mind: Mary also represented Wisdom whom men of pure and humble mind love and seek.[22] Albertus Magnus (1193–1280) posed the question, 'Whether the Blessed Virgin possessed perfectly the seven liberal arts?' and answered it on the basis of the personifications and identifications:

I hold that she did, for it is written, "Wisdom hath built herself a house, and has set up her seven pillars". That house is the blessed Virgin; the seven columns are the seven liberal arts. Mary therefore had perfect mastery of science.[23]

That expressed the conviction that all knowledge accessible to human enquiry must be connected to and devoted to divinely revealed wisdom.

Philology. The spirit of understanding

The trivium and quadrivium, and philology, largely assumed the Word, the Spirit and Wisdom, which they could not subsume. The fresco by Andrea di Bonaiuto in the original Chapter House of Santa Maria Novella, Florence, is an exposition of this. According to Bargellini, the doctrinal scheme was by the prior Fra Zenobi de' Guasconi:

> [He] had in mind the *Summa Theologica* of St Thomas Aquinas, where the following words are to be found in the chapter entitled 'De Dono Sapientiae': 'Wisdom, by means of which, according to the divine laws, man is able to judge all things, is in us by virtue of the Holy Spirit'. Wisdom comes from the Holy Spirit which is symbolised in the gentlest and purest of creatures, the dove, flying in the fire of love.[24]

In that passage in the *Summa* Thomas said that in a particular field, 'for instance, architecture', to be wise in that genus is in knowing the highest cause in it. He referred to I Corinthians 3.10, 'As a wise architect I have laid the foundation'. In the fresco, in the arcade of niches, seated in consistory as it were, are the Arts personified. The arts of Theology and Law are on the left, complementing the seven Liberal Arts on the right (with the seven planetary Heavens signified in the gables). In the higher zone are historical Biblical representatives. In the lower sky are the four Cardinal Virtues portrayed as angelic persons; in the topmost heaven are the three Spiritual Virtues; the highest is Love, hovering over the scene. The focus is on Thomas, the philosopher-theologian—his open book bearing the verse, 'I desired Wisdom and it was granted me; I called on the Spirit of Wisdom and it came to me, and I have preferred it to kingdoms and thrones'.[25] The fresco is itself a philological work using visual grammar, dialectic and rhetoric. It shows the liberal arts adopted assiduously by the ecclesiastical world; and reciprocally the theological arts informed the culture.

Where in this scheme of learning and morals does architecture feature? It is the setting and framework for the philological exposition, doing with figures at a miniature and mural scale what cathedrals, such as on the west fronts at Salisbury, Wells and Exeter, did full size (Figure 3.12). The stalls for the Arts with gabled canopies are modelled on chapter house or choir stalls. The centre-piece, the great throne, follows a highly architectural convention—the same form, the same motifs, using the same language of signification, as cathedrals themselves. In its gable medallion, pivotal in the composition, is 'the half-figure of a young man with a halo; his right hand supports an open book and in his left hand is a mirror. The book is the symbol of learning, the mirror that of reflexion'.[26] It is the Mirror of Wisdom. Wisdom in architecture is to know its highest cause.

In Gothic development chapter houses were highly expressive designs embodying the wisdom and arts which the Church endorsed and used in monastic learning.

> The Chapter House of Santa Maria Novella was the parliament and the law court of the monastery, and constituted, so to speak, the brain and the conscience of the common religious life. It was therefore of great importance. After the church it was the place where the architecture was most severe and the decoration most significant. Everything aimed at recalling to the friars' minds ideas of spiritual elevation and disciplinary rigour, and reminding them of the lofty purposes of the life which they had all freely chosen.[27]

As a discrete centralised place a chapter house had a conceptual identity of concentrated purpose. Particularly in England chapter houses were often separate structures (Figure 4.1). The chapter house of Old St Paul's cathedral, London (begun in 1332), was set *within* the cloister garth which was an unusual location. It was a powerful association of ideas, of the gathering of minds in the light-filled centrally focussed place, yet environed in the cloister of generally individual spiritual exercise.[28] In many extant chapter houses we still see a perfect congruity in the canopied seats in which men took their places, like their models portrayed in arcaded walls, screens or windows. Chapter house, cloister, choir, chapels and cells were a matrix of intention, meditation, participation, communion, aspiration. In the buildings we will see associations of ideas and formal equivalences amounting to an architectural philology.

Cloisters embodied profound clarity, simplicity and concordance with purpose, the typical form being an arcaded quadrangle. Instead of interior focus, attention is drawn outwards to the open space. The garth is set apart from too-casual use and access by logical demarcations, a vocabulary of definition, an architectural dialectic of seclusion-openness, of proximity-distance, of centripetal implied movement, centrifugal actual movement. Appealing to the mind through the senses, the cloisters expressed an aspect of ideal religious life. Here was a relaxed rhythm, rather than the intense concentration expressed in the chapter house; both embodied the spirit of wisdom, but differently. It was a place for private reading, tuition, manuscript copying and illumination—the *scriptorium*. Mary Carruthers draws a literary interpretation from Richard de Fournival of Amiens (1201–*c*. 1260), who in his *Biblionomia* described the library in the simile of a cloister garden.

It is all arranged centrally around the liberal arts—'his organizing scheme an *ortulum* or "little garden". The books, classified according to divisions of the liberal arts are planted in beds or *areolae*'.[29]

A direct association of the liberal arts with the cloister was made by Peter of Celle (d. 1182):

> The cloister lies on the border of angelic purity and earthly contamination. If someone passes from the world like a Hebrew from Egypt and brings with him to the cloister some grains of uprightness borrowed from the neighbouring arts called liberal, he can use them without being judged a thief. For 'all wisdom is from the Lord God'.[30]

Then he stated that any teaching not contrary to faith can be 'married to' and transformed by spiritual wisdom. 'Thus grammar, dialectic, rhetoric, music, arithmetic, geometry and astronomy are seasoned by the strong salt of divine Scripture.' Further, Peter said that reaching the mind through the senses could be a strategic role of the cloister likened to the inner courtyard of the tabernacle. The novice dwells in-between the outer and inner worlds, 'located on the border of reason and sensation'.[31] It invites us to see associations of understanding in the trivium arts with sensory experience as of architecture. As to 'angelic purity' he said: 'Nothing in this discipline is disordered, nothing irksome, nothing irregular. Charity melts and unites all those spirits in the love of God and of each other'.[32]

Grammar

Grammar, introducing her matter in *The Marriage of Philology and Mercury*, said she had two duties: the active duty of reading and writing correctly; and the contemplative function of understanding and assessing—a duty shared with philosophers and critics.[33] While the latter wider purpose was accepted in antiquity, throughout the Middle Ages the view was reiterated that grammar is indeed directed toward highest objectives. Bernard of Chartres, a leading grammarian, regarded it as the basis of culture. That may seem to be claiming too much; or it may be regarded as merely stating the obvious. Much the same may be claimed (or simply obvious) in a critique of the grammar of architecture. Surely grammar is both logical and affective; and that the early and high Gothic churches are pleasing is partly due to their good visual grammar.

The arts of the trivium are intimately connected. Hugh of St-Victor called them 'linguistic logic'.[34] Grammar laid the linguistic foundation; dialectic and rhetoric built up rational logic. In Andrea di Bonaiuto's fresco Grammar is seated at the right-hand end, the beginning of the instructional sequence in praise of Wisdom. She indicates a narrow door, the discipline through which to reach the other arts. In such ways it has been portrayed—as demanding mental preparation, and as being the fundamental skill leading to things of greater significance. In the gable above Grammar is the Moon, the 'first heaven' in ascent above the Earth. Martianus Capella had ascribed the Moon to Grammar, describing it as 'a soft spherical body composed with the smoothness of dew from heaven, reflecting, like a gleaming mirror, the rays of light that fell upon it'.[35] In Dante's scheme of *Paradiso* the planetary heavens correspond to the Trivium and Quadrivium, with the Moon representing Grammar in the figure of a pearl. Thus grammar, and good language altogether, can mirror high intellectual light, and the mind of the holy community.

The primary materials of language—alphabet, vocabulary, identification of parts, number, and syntax of sentences—become serviceable and intelligible by association, arrangement, nuance and complexity. Simple elements take compound forms; everywhere meanings multiply and are recognised. Then there is an added affective power of expressiveness, the concern of art. All of this applies to architecture so obviously that *language* is scarcely a metaphor. With language is its concomitant grammar, the basis of comprehension. When John of Salisbury introduced the subject of grammar he noted the meaning of the Greek word *gramma*, namely, 'letter': grammar is 'literal'; adding that *gramma* means 'line': grammar is also 'linear'. He made the comparison:

> In augmenting size, the length of lines is fundamental, and, as it were, the basic dimension of plane surfaces and solids. So also this branch, which teaches language, is the first of the arts to assist those who are aspiring to increase in wisdom.[36]

Likewise line is in an elementary way grammar; the linear is grammatical. John saw that letters are visual symbols which silently represent sounds; and also, 'they stand for things, which they conduct into the mind through the windows of the eyes'.[37] It is reiterated in the articulated letters and lines of medieval art. The adjective *architectural* can properly apply in disciplines such as painting and sculpture to denote the formal organisation. With such an awareness, graphic architectural images and devices were prominent in all media throughout the Middle Ages. An apt example in manuscript illuminations is the canon tables produced from the fourth century onward.[38] The organising principles—the indexing and compartmentalising, the textual lists and serried arches, the writing and embellishing—make an integrated visual grammar. These tables of vertically exaggerated arcades ran to many pages producing virtually a 'building'. In the visual grammar of the St Alban's Bible (*c.* 1170) repetitive single arches in the upper register are bracketed in pairs, whereas the lower register's interlaced arches multiply the associations.[39] Even using the basic linguistic element of the arch, dialectic and rhetoric become quite complex, and there is much rhetorical freedom. Clearly this device is in the same idiom as blind arcades in churches, as, for instance, on the west front of Lincoln cathedral church of the early thirteenth century; yet we are hardly able to read the full intention (Figure 5.7).

74 *Comprehension: the trivium*

The main elements of building grammar, functional rather than stylistic, can be suggested. The letters and words are the building materials.[40] The range was limited, but in use the possibilities were infinite, as in writing and speech. Some of the materials' sensuous properties—density, texture, colour, transparency, resonance—we transfer to linguistic morphology. There is vocabulary by which parts are visually denominated: shafts, mouldings, cusps, crockets, a multitude of motifs. These are instances of the primary level of language. Each single, intentional word from the vocabulary of the master-mason or architect plays its effective part without demanding attention, not existing for its own sake, not gratuitous. Even if a piece of work seems unimportant it is not dispensable and must be done well.

Such elements comprise the grammar and, just as a child learns naturally to comprehend, so one naturally becomes conversant in the building

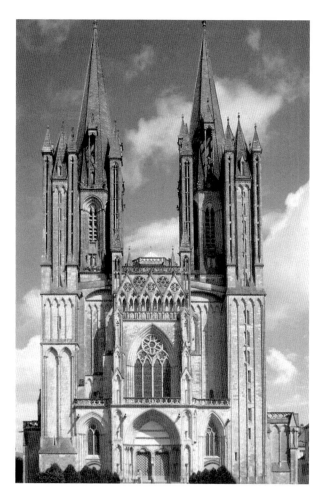

Figure 3.2 Coutances, France. Cathedral church of Notre-Dame. West front. Mid-13th C.

language. The building grammar has formal and structural references. With composition and complexity signification increases. Consistent use largely constructs the native idiom. Each part belongs ultimately to the complex knowledge of the society, and over all the endless variety in medieval churches is comprehended by a common language.

The west front of Coutances cathedral has great grammatical clarity, while, unlike many Gothic cathedrals, it does not display figural sculpture, except originally around the porch (Figure 3.2). It breaks away from repetitive arch designs ubiquitous in Romanesque language. Here the thin vertical shaft is the simple dominant word. At the next level of complexity, architecture's grammar works with its own syntax and figures. Clearly, as this example shows, medieval architects employed consciously such devices as linearity, repetition, rhythm, verticality, horizontality, and interplay of salience and regression as visually expressive of the notion and ideal in the mind; and these also work as abstract linguistic devices expressive of the structural imperatives of the design.

Building language plays its part in communicating meaning, and is always exploited and deployed in chosen ways by different cultures in different periods. Wilhelm Worringer investigated latent forces in Northern European visual art leading from early precedents, through Romanesque experiment, to new twelfth-century Gothic expression. He posited that on the basis of an elementary 'grammar of line, a particular linear language gradually developed'.[41] His argument is narrowly based, but his observations on the perception of line provide valid insights. Of line perceived as 'organic' he pointed out, 'For directly we admit a line to our consciousness at all, we unconsciously feel inwardly the process of its formation'.[42] This is doubtless applicable in both maker and viewer. Of line perceived as 'spiritual', the following also rings true, but probably depends on conscious attention in the maker more than the viewer:

> For here, too, we ascribe to the line as expression the sensation of the process of its execution felt afterwards at the moment of its apperception. And as the line appears to impose its expression upon us, we perceive it as something absolute, independent of us, and therefore we speak of a specific expression of the line.[43]

The visual use of *line* acquired to a pre-eminent degree the power of words; and to express transcendent things it was fashioned into a language. Its ability to concentrate, control and direct the mind—even as text does on a page—is in contrast to *surface*, which much more communicates and mediates material certainties to the body. By linear figures and patterns surface was broken up, even in Romanesque architecture. By concentration of line by multiplicity and intensified rhythm material could appear less solid, even less present. This evidently underlies the use of ubiquitous blind arcade and tracery devices, as on Magdeburg cathedral where the west face is almost a flat plane. Without the linear diagrams it would lack due expression (Figure 3.3). By deliberate choice the ascendency of vertical line over horizontal was an insistence that minds be directed to the things which are infinite, endless

76 *Comprehension: the trivium*

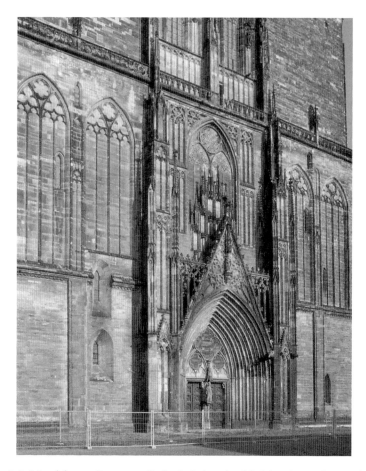

Figure 3.3 Magdeburg, Germany. Cathedral church of St Maurice and St Catherine. West front detail. Note the shallow relief. First half of 13th C.

and 'above'. All constructions of visual grammar could be used each in their proper way as artificers chose, with much experimentation, invention and licence. It was a rich distinctive grammar of outer and inner worlds.

At another level, in applications of some subtlety, the art of grammar was of greater power and scope of authorial intention than we now attribute to it. In Jeffrey Huntsman's analysis, a philosophical and *speculative* grammar, distinct from pedagogical grammar, developed in the thirteenth century:

> These philosophical grammars attempted to achieve a level of explanation that was not only adequate for all languages but ultimately applicable to the organization of the world in general. For this reason one type of philosophical grammar was called speculative grammar (from Latin *speculum* 'mirror'), for it attempted to mirror the structure of the universe.[44]

Comprehension: *the trivium* 77

Figure 3.4 Wrocław, Poland. Church of St Mary-on-the-Sands. Nave ribs (left) are stone; column mouldings and aisle ribs are brick. 1350-69.

He relates this to a grammarian's chief interest being in the formal causes and efficient causes in language. The formal cause would entail the mind behind the language (*logos*, 'meaning'), the definition of the matter (*eidos*, 'form'), and the figure of its appearance (*paradeigma*, 'model').[45] This is just as pertinent in architecture where the construct is comprehended, matter is given form, and the phenomenon is modelled.

Perhaps an indication of speculative grammar is in the variform vaultings where beyond structural purpose there was clearly an aspiration for metaphysical expression—the language itself being a mirror of the mind. Numerous examples in subsequent chapters show a logical and aesthetic grammar of vaulting which can scarcely be separated from the architectural

78 Comprehension: the trivium

dialectic and rhetoric. An example in Poland, the church of St-Mary-on-the-Sands, illustrates how comprehension is raised (Figure 3.4). The columns are without capitals giving uninterrupted ascent, and there is unity and coherence of expression. Yet the aisle vaults are curiously asymmetrical calling for analysis of the dialectic and rhetoric.

The raw material of construction was usually either carefully refined, or concealed, particularly in interiors. Stone masonry could be executed as ashlar work (perfectly sized, dressed and fitted). But an alternative device was the rendering of rough masonry, then adding a decorative painted overlay representing stone masonry. The actual stone is concealed, yet its ideal form reinterpreted consciously becomes the 'word' with greater power. It is used throughout Europe from Lübeck St Marienkirche on the Baltic to St-Lizier cathedral in the Pyrenees (Figure 5.5).

Analysing efficient cause in language Huntsman says the grammarians 'were expressly concerned to track the correspondence of the attributes of reality with those of thinking and those of language'.[46] To this end they studied the modes of language and thought in order to see congruous modes of existence and establish working connections:

> First, there was a level of actual existence, the *modus essendi*. Second, there was a level of mental existence, the *modus intelligendi*. Finally, there was a level of existence as an entity of language, the *modus significandi*. [...] The *modi intelligendi* were manners of understanding; the *modi significandi* were manners of signifying. [...] Mediating between these levels of potential or actual existence were the active modes of understanding and signifying, the *modus intelligendi activus* and the *modus significandi activus*. [47]

This would have equivalence in the architecture: in the appearance of any discrete part the *modus significandi activus* imparts the mediating, and thus enlightening, level of apprehension. A building or part of it may, in the way it appears, signify an actual existence at another level open to understanding. This aspect of building grammar worked in manifold ways. It is recognisable in the northern-European exterior use of plastered and painted panels contrasting with the fabric of brick masonry. At Prenzlau cathedral the device may give an impression of real openings in the fretted brickwork, potentially altering the signified form, albeit subtly in subconscious apprehension (Front cover image).

Recognising a medieval propensity to convey theological meaning through abstract devices, it is under the aegis of the logical arts that we can begin to discuss this sort of abstraction. With the interior décor of Moissac Abbey church as an illustration, we can observe the *modus intelligendi activus* of grammar working in theological discourse and architectural invention (Figure 3.5). It would be the more difficult to follow the lines of intention and patterns of meaning in the intricate forms

Comprehension: the trivium 79

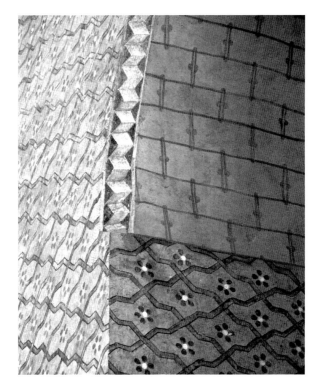

Figure 3.5 Moissac, France. St-Pierre Abbey church. A chapel recess in the nave. The whole interior is decorated in such patterns. Twelfth century.

of Gothic art if its distinctive *modus significandi activus* did not provide visual clues. Here is the device of masonry signified purposely, and 'theological' meaning shown in the linking motif on the perpends. In all design logic, in making figures, in using symbols, grammar is at work. It establishes definition (of the idea transposed into the medium), proportion (of the representation to the thing represented), and recognition (of the form of the figure or symbol).

The form of the Gothic arch, so distinguishable from the Romanesque and Renaissance round arches, became a constituent feature, a grammatical 'word'. Much might be said about it—its antecedents, generation, geometry, structural integrity, serviceability and economy; then its repetitions in arcades, extensions into vaults, and ubiquitous use in non-essential embellishment. So we allow that the pointed arch was a congruent 'word' with extraordinary importance in the design repertoire. Taken a degree further we see its power to address the intellect; we detect the presence of an idea, the *modus intelligendi*, which purports to associate man and God. The *modus significandi* indicates that the motif is a symbol *of something*. As a natural symbol the arch particularly relates to the human figure. It also represents an opening between two places, where the figure is held. The round arch could focus attention on the human head, more than a horizontal lintel could. But the pointed arch, often with cusps, reinforced the symbol with superior intimations. The apex implies an upward movement of aspiration. It is a sympathetic idea, in which a place set apart, the setting and framing, bestow holiness, affirmation and even affection. Such significations are in its form and line.

The Gothic renovators of the façade of Peterborough cathedral used the arch as an emphatic word with triple iteration, exceeding all its usual limits of expression (Figure 3.13). Structurally the arches are an over-statement and they do not relate logically to the body of the building or even the wall behind. The form is emphasised by multiplication of the arch mouldings, as purely *linear* as possible. The mode is architectural, not sculptural or pictorial. Functionality is replaced and transcended by the arch as a grammatical symbol. In the interiors of great churches the implications of just this one symbol, functional or not, are complex and subtle. For example, the importance (even in small churches) of the chancel arch indicates its communicative power. Defining the sanctuary from the body of the church it conveys *holiness*. Its strength and clarity suggest coherent *truth*. Then, recalling Thomas's trope of charity, which in its definition is its own measure, in 'the measure' of the arch we have an apt sign of *love*.[48] In such ways, as with verbal language, architectural vocabulary could express the values of the culture.

As we study illustrations of cathedrals which bring together features of grammar, their scale and power sometimes complicates the focus of any single idea, and it is worth considering that smaller churches can serve as primers of comprehension through their plain speech. And in seemingly simple dialectic and rhetoric they speak with purpose and power of the same things as the great churches. Now we have to recognise that the logical arts are inseparable; we cannot leave grammar isolated from dialectic and rhetoric.

Dialectic

The art of dialectic is for finding and clarifying meaning by rigorous judgement, commonly exercised in logical disputation. It provides the intellectual material which rhetoric can then present. In the Santa Maria Novella chapter house fresco Dialectic has the founder Aristotle at her feet, and the divinity Mercury, the second planet, above, as the cosmic influence. The swift messenger Mercury was associated either with dialectic or eloquence.[49] The shining ambiguous quicksilver was one of the seven metals known from antiquity, and its mercurial movement, dividing and combining of itself, and its ability to absorb gold and silver by amalgamation, were physical properties with apt associations.[50] The personifications and the physical symbols point up the agility of mind and discernment of spirit exercised by logic.

It has even greater point in the Gospel episode of the twelve-year-old Jesus with the doctors in the Temple.[51] The incarnate Word, the divine Mind, reasoned with men as never before. Medieval illustrators caught the scope and concentration of dialectic (and rhetoric) in the Queen Mary *Psalter* where he is shown perched on a pedestal; dialectic is signified by his hand gestures.[52] The place is filled by the participants and observers, a plenary place of thought and exchange. As so often in medieval art the subject is presented and integrated by the architecture of arches, towers and niches. Well-known sculptural instances are on the west screen front of Exeter cathedral, and the west wall of Reims cathedral's nave, both with lively ranks of persons, many evidently in dialogue.

Aristotle taught that for real comprehension it is incumbent on dialectic to establish the specific foundations of a particular science by beginning from a general ontological foundation. The logical art itself requires first things first, the laying of foundations. This element was still vital at the time of which Eleonore Stump writes:

> Scholastics in the latter half of the thirteenth century became increasingly concerned with two questions: (1) What are the *ultimate* criteria (rather than the simple formal criteria) for the validity of inferences?; and (2) What sort of things in the world can be the subjects of necessary and unchangeable premisses?[53]

Logic was structured in later medieval learning as an art of discovery, as Aristotle had treated it.[54] The dialectician was concerned with getting at the truth of things, reliably and convincingly. It was an amalgam of metaphysics and logic, in which dialectic ran everywhere touching material things too. John Marenbon draws attention to the breadth of application throughout the Middle Ages: 'Problems of logic fascinated the ablest minds, and logical distinctions influenced a host of other areas of knowledge—theology, rhetoric, poetic theory, grammar—in a way which has surprised, and sometimes appalled, later times'.[55] Might not this radical concern have also touched (even engendered) prodigious architecture, though the logic might baffle the viewer?

Dialectic is an intellectual activity in any field; thus when any work is using this art equivalences emerge. Taking a case which may be instructive for our subject—the problem of how universals are connected to objects really existing—Boethius reasoned that, even as the various members of a species bear a resemblance to one another which the mind perceives so that the likeness itself is considered in the mind and envisaged, even so the universals are gathered from the sensible objects as a matter of thought.[56] Connection on the level of dialectical reasoning working from a perceived sensible resemblance of things, could ensure reliable comprehension and discovery of the truth of a matter. At what level of consciousness *artificers* employed dialectical processes is difficult to discern. Somewhere there was a mind receiving a message, accepting, understanding, judging. So in architecture there must be a supposition of a mind at work, seeing what is, making associations, amalgamating. If there is a grammar as the basis of an architectural language, there is also an architectural dialectic.

In Mercury, the symbol of material influence, two aspects seem to provide a substantial basis for dialectical activity, namely, the agent itself, and the method of discovery of reality. The agent, the mind, envisaging essential principles, skilfully works to construct, with acute logic, the scheme of things that exist. The principles are radical, comprehended as in God. Such use of dialectic need not be—such use of the mind cannot be—confined to linguistics and philosophy; it ranges from technics to theology. Dialectic could anchor everything in ontological terms to truth, disclosing it to the artificer, who might not be able, or might not choose, to make it explicit for comprehension. Foundations, like thoughts, are of their nature hidden; but upon them depend sound superstructures. But Aristotle showed that dialectic, by articulating the argument, must establish an assertion which becomes the *specific* foundation, the knowledge and rationale pertaining to the art or science.[57] Without a medieval corpus of architectural theory, we have to reconstruct the logical connections between the architecture and the theology. Dialectic is more than a thesaurus of symbols, juxtaposition of images, or closed definitions: it produces a reasoned whole account out of many truth associations. That there must have been an understood dialectic of architecture with a theological foundation is a reasonable assumption to make.

That theological associations and principles were in currency for cathedral builders may be construed from various literary sources themselves. Honorius of Autun set out extensive correspondences which became quite conventional such as: 'This House [the material church] is set upon a stone foundation, and the Church [spiritual] is founded on the sure rock of Christ'.[58] Henry of Avranches (fl. 1220–40), anagogically in his *Metrical Life of Hugh of Lincoln*, treated the foundations and the earth as dialectically connected: 'The foundation is buried in the womb of the earth'. 'The foundation is the body.' 'The body belongs to the earth.'[59] In the last book of *Didascalicon*, Hugh of St-Victor set out the formal structure of instruction. In some detail he showed the levels of learning—history, allegory and tropology—to be analogous to the process of building: preparing foundations, laying the courses of base and superstructure, and the embellishment.[60] The foundation which is in the earth he calls the first foundation; it does not have very well-shaped and smoothly-fitted stones. He gives greatest attention to the second foundation built thereupon, and its function of providing an accurately set out base wall on which the fabric's walls are raised in a well-fitted and well-proportioned structure—a properly-reasoned dialectic:

> The fact that the first course of stones to be laid upon the foundation is placed flush with a taut cord—and these are the stones upon which the entire weight of the others rest and to which they are fitted—is not

without its meaning. All things rest upon the first foundation but are not fitted to it in every way. As to the latter foundation, everything else both rests upon it and is fitted to it.[61]

It is a matter of dialectic that there be attention to proportion, symmetry and balancing of masses, and this was necessary in ensuring stability. He goes on to describe the raising of the walls course by course, doctrine by doctrine, each based on the one below it, with concentration, nothing omitted:

> Here is the whole of divinity, this is that spiritual structure which is raised on high, built, as it were, with as many courses of stones as it contains mysteries. [...] See now, you have come to your study, you are about to construct the spiritual building. [...] You stretch out your cord, you line it up precisely, you place the square stones into the course, and, moving around the course, you lay the track, so to say, of the future walls. The taut cord shows the path of the true faith. The very bases of your spiritual structure are certain principles of the faith—principles which form your starting point.[62]

This represents dialectical consideration. In a chapter, 'Concerning the Theory of Argument', Hugh says that *invention* and *judgement* are integral parts of the discipline of dialectic, 'argumentative logic', and suggests that they are also integral parts of other disciplines, specifically rhetoric and, inferentially, design.[63] Of invention Hugh said that it, 'teaches the discovery of arguments and the drawing up of lines of argumentation'. Judgement he calls a science, it 'teaches the judging of such arguments and lines of argumentation'.[64]

Dialectic dealt with every kind of idea: in architecture dialectic worked at every level of ideation. To study the parallels we can use the most identifiable and transferable features of the logical art. John of Salisbury likewise considered that the broad scope of logic entailed the two activities, invention and judgement. They involve working with material, making inferences and connections, the emphasis being on the exercise of skill as by a craftsman: 'Logic not only reigns over invention and judgement, but also is skilled in division, definition, and argumentation. In short, it produces a [master] craftsman'.[65] When he contrasted dialectic with rhetoric it was to show that dialectic engrosses itself with the *thesis*, the proposition, ranging widely over questions, and bringing out succinct formulations to convince, not the crowd, but a single critical judge. It is concerned with definitions, the method of discovery, the discerning of a scheme. It sets up the thesis, mercurially it amalgamates the elements of the argument, and judges it. It clarifies the end task of joining of form and the material.

An application is in John of Salisbury's critique of the Aristotelian view that the universals are not ideas, forms, things, existing *as entities*. Universals, as ideas, forms, things, John argued, are existing as *abstractions*. This may be compared with the 'conceptualism' of Peter Abelard (1079–1142).[66]

One can look at the essences of things apart from their being composite with matter. Alternatively, by an investigative combining (or separating) process, one can look for a *composition*, but the difficulty John saw in this activity is how to maintain real objectivity which is important. He gives the abstracting process more weight, as being accurate and true to reality, saying in a simile that it constitutes 'the common factory of all the arts'.[67]

Chapter 5 will provide evidence in written sources of dialectic's abstractions in arts as they signify 'the essences of things' in nature. Exchange between nature and the comprehending mind took place in directed contemplation, or consideration.[68] At the point where he began to argue for the utility of the contemplative process John supplied a pertinent instance of abstraction dealing with the forms of certain things intrinsic in the art of architecture:

> That man on the other hand who thinks of a line or a surface apart from body, is simply with the eye of contemplation separating form from matter, for all that form cannot exist without matter. In this case, however, the understanding which separates does not conceive that form to be without matter—for that would be a composite understanding—but simply looks at the one without the other, for all that the one cannot exist without the other.[69]

By directed contemplation an architect could abstract the 'givens' (*assumere*) from which he aimed to produce, in his own terms, a construction (*complexio*), and its demonstration. By this he engaged with meaning and truth, with the idea not just with the material. That which he truly grasped he would try to make objectively manifest. Regarding things being objectively manifest Aristotle showed the use of prior and posterior representations: the general, unpredicated things are more naturally *prior*; the more particular, individual things are *posterior*. Knowledge of the first may need to be by the second being manifested and the connection made—the *posterior* path, commonly most accessible. Or the second more immediate things may be explained and grasped through understanding the first—but this *prior* path is more difficult and subtle. In the following example of the use of prior representation the key concern is what is 'more evident':

> The point is prior to, and in itself more evident than the line. The same may be said of the line relative to the plane surface, and of the plane surface with reference to the solid.[70]

John of Salisbury cited this and commented:

> Even though it is true that what is posterior is best defined by what is prior, and this is always more scientific, still, frequently, of necessity, and to provide subject matter within the ken of our senses, what is prior is actually explained by what is posterior. A point is thus said to be the end of a line; a line the edge of a surface; a surface, the side of a solid.[71]

Comprehension: the trivium 85

Figure 3.6 Southwell, England. Minster of St Mary. Norman nave. Arcades of aisles, tribune and clerestory. Nave begun 1108.

To see the posterior case, consider the proposition: *A point is said to be the end of a line; a line the edge of a surface; a surface, the side of a solid.* Take the nave arcade of Southwell minster (Figure 3.6). The 'points' at the springing of the arches are the capitals which take their shape and identity wholly from the terminating lines of the arches bearing down upon them, while the vertical lines of each short tribune pier end in a base planted plainly on the horizontal line at a 'point' made only with reference to intercepted and intercepting lines. The 'lines' of the arches, the frieze moulding, the tribune floor, and even those defining the short piers are all clearly edges of surfaces; that is their character. The surfaces of the spandrels, the column faces, and even the arch soffits, appear as the sides, the containment, of the solid mass. It is not surprising then that the judgement of eye and mind is affected by massiveness, for the definition, the scheme, has led to that.

86 *Comprehension: the trivium*

Figure 3.7 Southwell, England. Cathedral church of St Mary. Gothic choir arcades of aisle and clerestory (no tribune or triforium). Choir begun 1234.

For the prior case take the other proposition: *The point is prior to, and in itself more evident than the line. The same may be said of the line relative to the plane surface, and of the plane surface with reference to the solid.* The convenient illustration is the same minster's thirteenth-century choir (Figure 3.7). The points of arch springing and divergence, of vault springing and terminations, of apex of pointed arch, appear as primary identifications, sufficiently emphatic that the quite subtle arrangement of them is evident. The lines of arches and columns, and also now of vaulting, follow clear figures, and their business is more important than the surfaces. The plane surfaces are more like panels having their own definition and character, without reference to solid mass. Hence the whole is judged to have lightness, perspicuity and perceptible reference to the maker's precise ideation.

If we use John of Salisbury's case of the role of abstraction, dissociating form from matter 'by the keen blade of contemplative insight', we may refer again to the example we used in grammar—the pattern of imitative masonry (Figure 3.5). The device leads away from the direct sensory perception of the material, substitutes an ideal image to the eye, and presents the form to the mind. But in the pillar and vaults of the Wells chapter house dissociation of form from matter is achieved differently, by a keener abstraction, with great power (Figure 4.2). The material is not decorated, but intentionally, by superb workmanship, evidence of joints is absent, and natural surface texture refined. The pillar is made complex with such strong imposition of line as further suppresses association of the form with the material. A new concept is posited. Here high aspiration is understood, and a bodily lifting-up appears possible, even easy. Such examples emphasise the role of method and logic underlying the design process. We can suppose that this was for architects then much as it is still—that they seldom (or very incompletely) enunciate the real logic of their *schemata*.

Dialectic working on a much larger scale is well illustrated by the duality of towers characteristic of many west façades. The duality entails a balance and symmetry. There is necessarily a linking element, subordinate yet of central importance. Each of the three parts is dialectically connected to the other two, its form and identity justified by them. The topics (*loci*) from which designers drew their premises, the logic of divisions, invention, defining of order, judgement of stability, the coherence of form and matter, all come before considering eloquence. We should allow that the architects were versatile in grammar and logic, able to state matters both straightforward and complex. Remarkable diversity and originality are obvious as we compare the west fronts of Coutances cathedral (Figure 3.2), and Peterborough cathedral (Figure 3.13), and in the distinctiveness of every church, large and small. They caution us of the tendencies of narrow criticism tied to period classifications, stylistic conformity, and even geographical influences. Consideration of the works themselves should be a check to the supposition that the organising mind was beholden to any dominating fashion.

An architect does not work in a cultural and architectural vacuum, but will take premises (*assumere*) that are convenient and make propositions (*complexiones*) that are efficient, based on experience and what seems reasonable (*dispicere*).[72] But we are likely to make false assumptions from our distance in time if we suppose that the premises selected in any part of the design work, large or small, would have been ones we might think important. Their selection might seem odd, leading to inferences which we perhaps find irrelevant, or which escape us altogether. The mental *loci* are different.[73]

In the documented case of Girona cathedral church the major issue of the rebuilding of the Romanesque nave was stated in terms of design dialectic and explored with some dialectical rigour. The choir and chevet had been built in the first half of the fourteenth century with similarities to Barcelona and Narbonne, but the choir's height was less than 80 feet (like Barcelona's) while Narbonne's choir is 130 feet high. The question, in 1416, was whether the new nave should match the form of the choir with aisles, or have a single-span vault of the width of the choir and aisles together (Figure 3.8).

The latter was a bold proposition conceptually and structurally, and the Chapter called twelve architects separately from Catalonian cities, including Barcelona, and from Languedoc-Roussillon, including Narbonne. Three questions were asked: would a single-nave form be stable and enduring? Would the continuation of the triple-nave form be 'congruous' and 'sufficient' in height, or to what height should it be built 'to prevent mistake'?

Figure 3.8 Girona, Spain. Cathedral church of Santa Maria. Original choir and aisle built *c.* 1321–50. View from the new nave. Commenced in 1416.

And, 'What form or continuation [. . .] will be the most compatible and the best proportioned to the chevet?'[74] All affirmed the structural soundness of the single-vault proposal. On the second question, seven judged that a triple-nave arrangement of the new work would be congruous; and be 'beautiful' *if* the height were increased and an oculus incorporated above the centre arch—otherwise it would be congruous but insufficient. The others considered that a triple-nave scheme would not be congruous; they did not see simple replication, such a unison, as amounting to congruity; rather, they visualised a greater harmony, conceiving the old and the new *as a whole*. It could not be sufficient if it were 'mean' and 'dark', indeed some said 'deformed'. With varying degrees of disapproval these five regarded the raising of the height of the new centre nave alone as mere expediency. So, coming to the third question, they not only visualised a beauty and nobility in the great single-nave in itself, but that it did make a properly 'compatible' scheme, 'proportioned' to the chevet. One called it 'more reasonable, more brilliant'. Guillaume Boffy, the Girona architect, asserted it would be 'the most conformable to the choir'.[75] They saw that the clarity of the whole logical entity would be beautiful.

Thus the concept was scrutinised, clarified and judged. The use of measurement, geometry and harmony was signalled; but that would follow. The key decision principally relied on the art of dialectic. The new single nave was built with a height of 110 feet and span of 75 feet, giving a quite uncharacteristic expression—which is then a matter of rhetoric.

To place the art of dialectic, or logic, in a medieval philosophical, indeed theological, context we can look at a piece of eighth-century text. Since Augustine, logic, physics and ethics were the usual parts of philosophy, forming a world-view to complement theology. Ralph McInerny refers to a passage in *De dialectica* by Alcuin (732/5–804), which is in the form of a dialogue with Charlemagne:

> [Alcuin] 'For in these three classes of philosophy the Scriptures consist.'
> [Charlemagne] 'In what manner?'
> [Alcuin] 'For example, concerning physics they usually examine Genesis and Ecclesiastes; or concerning morals, Proverbs and all the sundry books; or concerning logic, for which our theologians lay their own claim, where but in the Song of Songs and in the holy Gospels.'[76]

Alcuin moved in a culture of learning where the Scriptures spoke to every concern of the human mind. But McInerny asks from the modern perspective:

> Where is logic to be found? Alcuin's answer boggles the mind. Logic is contained in the *Song of Songs*. [...] Is not logic, one of the liberal arts that are presupposed to the pursuit of wisdom, one of whose parts is logic, improbably located in the *Song of Songs*?[77]

90 *Comprehension: the trivium*

If we think about the Song of Songs, we may see that what Alcuin was reporting, as an accepted ascription after all, was remarkably instructive. Flowing from its poetic character, the Song makes great play on grammatical devices and subtle vocabulary—the language of love has always been trying to expand the boundaries of denomination and definition.[78] The protagonists in their respective parts exploit the possibilities of dialectic—the terms, arguments and propositions of love exercise affective or mystical reasoning. The rhetoric is a model of persuasion. Love is a theme to test the highest logic. The coupled ascription to the Gospels is also congruous in numerous ways: the clear words of Christ; the penetrating conversation, the perspicacious parables; the irresistible eloquence, all convey the divine logic of love. Ought not human logic aspire to reflect the divine? We might ask, how does this operate and appear in any art? The way in which Alcuin saw it as obtaining in Scripture indicates the way in which medieval thinkers could have seen it as obtaining in architecture. Thus, 'concerning logic'—for which medieval architects may lay their own claim—are not the churches, chapter houses and cloisters full of it? We may reasonably adduce the dialectic of love in them too.

Rhetoric

In the architectural application of the trivium we now consider the third skill and its pervasive role. Considering the west fronts of Coutances (Figure 3.2) and Mantes (Figure 5.12), or Troyes (Figure 3.9) and Peterborough (Figure 3.13), we see that with all their nuances of vocabulary and differences of logic, a viewer's comprehension largely depends on a common visual language. Mind and sight are alike impressionable, and the art to which they are most susceptible is rhetoric. In dialectic we noted the place of judgement, primarily as a private exercise. Martianus Capella said that in all aspects of rhetoric judgement is required.[79] In rhetoric it glosses similarities and differences, and seeks to attract and persuade. In his allegory Martianus praised Rhetoric's striking beauty and adornment in terms that were applied to rhetorical ornament: *lumen* (light), *figurae* (devices), *schemata* (figures), *colores* (colours), and *gemmae* (jewels).[80] Rhetoric issues an invitation or challenge to the viewer to judge. In the Chapter House in Florence, Rhetoric, left hand on hip in an attitude of challenge, unfurls with her right hand a scroll inscribed, 'With words of rainbow colours I impress when I speak'.[81] At her feet sits Cicero, the orator. In the gable medallion above is a figure symbolising the planet Venus. In rhetoric the trivium reached its highest jurisdiction—and was in the service of Love no less.

The five parts of rhetoric identified by Cicero (106–43BC) in *De inventione* were *inventio, dispositio, elocutio, memoria* and *pronuntiatio*, and this framework was followed through the Middle Ages. It will be useful to see that all these parts of linguistic rhetoric have parallels in architecture.

Martin Camargo traces historical shifts in emphasis and kinds of rhetoric: its original practical use in politics and judicial courts; how treatment of it by Cassiodorus (c. 475–568) focussing on *inventio* helped establish it and the trivium in monastic study; the Carolingian renaissance of learning stimulating interest in rhetoric; how from Boethius to many late-twelfth-century scholastics rhetoric became subservient to dialectic. Of its character in that period he says, 'At least until the mid-eleventh century, the dominant strain in rhetoric was technical rather than sophistical, forensic rather than epideictic [for display as in oratory], and inventional rather than stylistic'.[82] The contemporary Romanesque architecture also tended to exhibit technical, forensic and inventive qualities. If that first long era in the history of the trivium had reflections in art and architecture, so too the next developments had parallels in an emergent and mature Gothic. Around the beginning of the twelfth century there was a revival in the practical use of rhetoric in *ars dictaminis* (rhetorical skill particularly in the art of letter-writing) in the northern French cathedral schools where it was closely linked to grammar, and in Italy, notably at Bologna university.[83] Camargo writes that the Italian view was that,

> The French *dictatores* espoused a 'pagan' style characterized by frequent quotations from the *auctores*, unusual vocabulary, and highly figurative language. The Italians sought to simplify the language of *dictamen*, to replace the pagan *stilus supremus* with the Christian *sermo humilis*.[84]

From its apogee in the first half of the thirteenth century, the vitality of the *ars dictaminis* began to decline and it became largely a matter of imitation. Perhaps we can also recognise in Gothic buildings, in some contrast to the Romanesque, a proclivity towards more sophistical, oratorical and stylistic rhetoric. In such terms we can recognise general correlations between linguistic and architectural arts. As an aside, Camargo's description is interesting because it seems applicable to Italy's architecture of the time, which, as rather distinct from that of western and northern Europe, has often been treated as less than properly Gothic. Compared particularly with apparent French experimentation, aloofness, and 'high' expression, many Italian Gothic churches seem conservative, empathetic, even colloquial.

From the late twelfth century rhetoric became subdivided into three categories, the two beside *ars dictaminis* being *ars poetriae*, the art of verbal expression in poetry (more broadly, contrivance and composition); and *ars predicandi*, specifically, the art of preaching (more broadly, declaration). Around 1210 Geoffrey of Vinsauf wrote the *Poetria nova*, which will serve well now for a closer study of the Ciceronian five parts of rhetoric, from which to deduce applications in architecture.

Inventio

Cicero regarded *inventio* as a most essential part of rhetoric, using it to find out an argument suitable and plausible in a given case.[85] According to Martianus Capella in *De nuptiis* its use was more the making of an inventory and compiling of subject-matter.[86] While invention had such a role in dialectical logic, bringing in everything for consideration, in rhetoric it then had to see what strategic convincing use to make of the dialectical findings. Geoffrey deals with *inventio* immediately in his introduction and has advice for an author: 'Since the ensuing discussion [on *dispositio*] takes its own course from a plan, of primary importance is, from what boundary line the plan ought to run'.[87] It is the making of an inventory in the mind, and the generating of a plan, a scheme which will serve the rhetorical purpose, communicating the author's mind. The interior process is deliberate and conceptual; the construct is shaped as an archetype:

> If a man has a house to build, his impetuous hand does not rush into action. The measuring line of his mind first lays out the work, and he mentally outlines the successive steps in a definite order. The mind's hand shapes the entire house before the body's hand builds it. Its mode of being is archetypal before it is actual.[88]

The metaphors of *line* convey deliberation: the 'boundary line' indicates the givens and the context; the 'measuring line' of thought ensures soundness of concept and integrity of content. Geoffrey makes the *circle* a metaphor of attention and comprehension: 'Let the mind's interior compass first circle the whole extent of the material'. He has the image of *points* where the work is to start and end. He sums it: 'As a prudent workman, construct the whole fabric within the mind's citadel'; which he then calls 'the hidden chamber of the mind'.[89] It is incidental that he employs building imagery, yet he can do so because the applications he makes in poetry have clear correlates in architecture. More than that, as a description of indispensable preparation it is perceptive: the author constructs a whole virtual building, measuring and shaping, requiring his own mind to grasp it—*comprehendere*. It is in his whole consciousness, complying with, pliable under, his inner affection.[90] Surely this too can be applied in the preparation for the making of artefacts. The work of the 'mind's hand' deals with invention, complexity and clarity; inner rhetorical acts, with results such as in the Wells chapter house (Figure 4.2).

The work of the mind to comprehend and compass the church is witnessed in the rhetorical portrayals of bishops, abbots and patrons holding models of their churches—conventionally in the left hand close to the heart—not in pride, nor for self-glorification; rather, memorials that they built them in love. The device conflates the spiritual building and the material building. Thus in a window of Gloucester cathedral, St Peter, the proto-builder, symbolically holds the Church; and in St Maria im Kapitol, Cologne, is a bas-relief (*c.* 1280) of Mary bearing the Church on her left arm, her right hand on her breast, signifying affection. On the well-known tomb cover of Hugh of Libergier (d. 1263), architect of St-Nicaise abbey church in Reims, convention is changed and model and rod are reversed in his hands, the achievement of his work being in his right arm, while the symbol of his *auctoritas* and skill is across his heart. He is perfectly framed by a cusped arch. Study of the drawing of the St-Nicaise façade convinces us of Hugh's masterly use of *inventio*.[91]

The starting point for architectural rhetoric was where *inventio* brought in the real subject. Regarding the conjunction of architecture and theology, the measuring-line of theological and moral verities was the subject's measure; the archetype was the matter's true form; and the interior compass was the mind's intention and heart's inclination.

Dispositio

Dispositio, or arrangement, works with the structural order of grammar and the ratiocination of dialectic to achieve patent order: it is 'that which puts the matter in order'.[92] When the material is first ordered, then, writes Geoffrey of Vinsauf, 'let poetic art come forward to clothe the matter with words'.[93] So in *dispositio* the inner plan is articulated and takes shape. The process is the arranging of the matter, the balancing of parts. Geoffrey addresses the order in which the material is to be presented, praising the way the art can, by transpositions, alter the order from a 'natural' simple sequence to an artificial, more sophisticated, 'artistic' order. There is but one 'natural' sequence: any theme has a beginning, middle and end. This accords with the 'natural' rhetorical arrangement of a church as: an engaging west front, the nave being a narration, the crossing marking intervention, the choir expounding the mystery, the sanctuary intimating the splendour. Such disposition is usually able to be comprehended from the exterior, but becomes clear and intelligible interiorly. By 'artistic' reorderings the theme is fertile with varied associations. For instance, the splendour of the end, by being brought forward, lends its brightness to the whole. Thus, as Geoffrey said of poetry,

> The first peak of the work is not only luminous with light from the very end, but its glory is twofold: coming either from the end of the theme [...] or from the middle of it.[94]

In St-Urbain church, Troyes, the splendour of the east end is shown on the west façade in anticipatory beauty (Figures 3.9 and 3.10). It is a common enough arrangement—that the west front first presents such a considered statement of splendour that it must seem to vie with the choir's glory.

94 *Comprehension: the trivium*

Figure 3.9 Troyes, France. Church of St-Urbain. West front with geometrical and rectilinear screen tracery to porch and upper window. 13th C.

An earlier example is the rose windows at each end of Laon cathedral on the west-east axis. A rhetorical effect is that the rose of the west front has been explicitly transposed to the east rose, which it comes to prefigure (Figure 4.12).

Using another *dispositio* device some different superior matter may be placed in juxtaposition to plainer matter to develop rich associations:

> If the first part of the work aims at even greater splendor [...], let a well-chosen *sententia* incline in no respect to the particular, but rather raise its head higher, to something universal; and in its new splendor, let it not desire to remember the actual form of the material [...]. Let the *sententia* stand above the given theme, but glance straight at it; let it say nothing outright, but develop its thought therefrom.[95]

Comprehension: the trivium 95

Figure 3.10 Troyes, France. Church of St-Urbain. East end. The choir clerestory and triforium. Note the salient gables and lower screens. 13th C.

The traceries of St-Urbain seem to work in this way. It is an explanation and effect of oculi as at Girona cathedral (Figure 3.8); and of special attention given to gables as at Peterborough (Figure 3.13). Those distinctive parts say something on 'the given theme', or develop it. Also Geoffrey praises the arrangement of beginning with an *exemplum* to lend beauty and dignity. Many portals and porches may serve thus, as, for example, the blind tracery above the doors of St-Urbain, Troyes (Figure 3.9). A common device is an elevated centre-piece embedded in the west front where attention is focussed. At Coutances cathedral an exquisite traceried gallery is both a *sententia* and an *exemplum*, and Geoffrey's description seems entirely applicable (Figure 3.2).

96 Comprehension: the trivium

Along with *inventio*, this subject of *dispositio* brings us close to the crux of the artificer's working. The following description develops the metaphor of the mind's hand introduced in *inventio*:

> The mass of the subject matter, like a lump of wax, is at first resistant to handling; but if diligent application kindles the intellect, suddenly the material softens under this fire of the intellect and follows your hand wherever it leads, docile to anything. The 'hand' of the inner man leads, in order that it may either draw out or compress the material.[96]

At the beginning the 'lump' is like the earth 'without form, and void'. It is an inchoate mass of matter, void of meaning. It must be rightly disposed. The subject fully occupies the maker's attention. The kindled intellect is knowledge turned into intention, understanding what to do. It evokes the trope of 'Adam in the mind of God'. The inner 'hand' is the moulding power of the mind. The metaphor suggests this: to manipulate the material the hand has direct sensuous contact with it: there has to be intimacy between the mind and the material. The heart lovingly shapes the docile material. It reflects the original unique act: 'The Lord God formed man of dust from the ground'.[97] The hand is the intellect engaged in executing what the mind conceives. The hand's moulding of the material, arranging it, is necessary in effective rhetoric.

There is another aspect of *dispositio* which is paralleled in the rhetoric of architecture. To connect things, comparison, *collatio*, may use similes: they are signs which 'reveal the knot of joining'. Or comparison may use metaphors, and be covert,

> as if there were no comparison there, but rather some new transformation were being marvelously ingrafted [...] and it appears to be integral with your material, but it is not there either. Thus it fluctuates, as it were, between extrinsic and intrinsic, now here and now there, now near and now far; there is a difference and yet there is a similarity. [...] this is the form of subtle joining, the device in which the things joined come together and meet as if they were not contiguous; they are continuous, rather, as if the hand of art had not joined them, but rather the hand of Nature.[98]

The operation of a metaphor in a particular work aids comprehension of higher things. The key is not just in the subtlety but in the real *joining*. Architectural application may be at any scale. For example, in the configuration of towers and spires 'comparison' is invited—indeed is formally unavoidable—between tower and spire, for they are contiguous and joined, and they are connected in the sense of belonging together. The junction, as a rhetorical arrangement, may be a simile or a metaphor. At St-Savin-sur-Gartempe, by simile, the joining is a direct conjunction and connection of tower and spire, a clear contiguity (Figure 6.1). At St Patroclus, Soest, the connection is firmer, like a knot (Figure 4.7). But in the towers of Coutances cathedral the joint is subtle as tower merges into spire—a continuity rather than contiguity (Figure 1.2). What is the point of such rhetorical *collatio*? Was it for aesthetic pleasure or delight in invention? In rhetoric, simile and metaphor must be *of* something, the referent idea. This is the strength of medieval architecture. The power of metaphor is in a marvellous ingrafting or transformation being effected. In the case in point, it might be shown from the metaphor of the ark of the tabernacle in *Benjamin major* of Richard of St-Victor (d. 1173) how tower and spire may signify stages of contemplation, translocation from earth to heaven—but we will come to this in Chapter 6.

Elocutio

Elocutio in a broad sense was the province of utterance; more narrowly, it was 'style'. The *Rhetorica ad Herennium* was a writing of antiquity known from Jerome throughout the Middle Ages. Reckoned to be a sequel to Cicero's *De inventione*, it was studied chiefly from the late eleventh century. In this pseudo-Ciceronian work the scope of *elocutio* dealt principally with style and ornamentation:

> Its division of style into three levels—grand (*gravis*), middle (*mediocris*), and simple (*adtenuata*)—was extremely influential in the Middle Ages [...]. Most of book IV, however, has to do with means of lending distinction (*dignitas*) to style by rendering it ornate. This is accomplished through two kinds of figures (*exornationes*): figures of diction and figures of thought.[99]

Dignitas validated the simple and middle styles as well as the grand. Martianus Capella said, '[*Elocutio*] chooses words that are proper or figurative, invents new usages, and arranges words of traditional usage'.[100] Figures of diction and thought were meant to articulate and convey *ideas* appropriately. All were pleasing figures; they were the 'colour' of *elocutio*, the whole palate of possibilities. But figuration was not to be simply for its own sake. There is the hazard that eloquence of utterance is inclined to be very conspicuous, with a tendency to become superficial and overly influential. It can overwhelm the subject matter and meaning.

Romanesque architectural rhetoric was characterised by pictorial and ornamental use of figures and schemes in a way that lent richness and countered the austerity due particularly to massiveness. Gothic eloquence honed it to make the purpose expressive. Yet *style* came to acquire dominance over most other matters in the judgement of patrons, practitioners and critics, and medieval architecture has often been appraised with this bias. It might be identified as a clear symptom of the decline of the Gothic achievement.

Figure 3.11 Toulouse, France. Les Jacobins church. The tower (of red brick and white stone) is on the north side. The top of the east apse is in the foreground. Thirteenth century.

But when style is treated as but one part of rhetoric, itself just part of the trivium, there is discipline and truer balance. Geoffrey said that one must know what it is one wishes to say and the vital spirit of it—its inward colour—before devising the outward colour, adding pointedly: 'Unless the inward colour conforms to the outer, it is insulting to the intelligence'.[101]

Like the *Rhetorica ad Herennium*, the *Poetria nova* modelled levels of dignity of style; but always directed to the object of thought and meaning.

First, serious or rich matters are expressed with due weight by four rhetorical tropes which Geoffrey calls *transsumptio*, namely metaphor, allegory, antonomasia and onomatapoeia.[102] Their use requires particular skill, for they are suited to elevated subjects, and will be grasped best by the initiated. The important idea of *dignitas*, as applied to the conception and arrangement of a subject, had the role of locating it 'vertically', as it were, in relation to earthly and heavenly preoccupations.[103] The premiss is that at each level there are subjects of real meaning, explicit or oblique, which the figures render discernible. Thus figures of thought dealt with matters at high levels, and figures of diction supplied the beauty of appropriate 'clothing'. In the example of Les Jacobins church, Toulouse, the concept of the tower of ascending vision is expressed in its arrangement formally and the language of its design. There is clarity and richness of vernacular idiom not borrowed style (Figure 3.11). It also illustrates the next rank.

Second, in matters whose weight must be lightened somewhat to suit the hearer, the speaker or writer has recourse to six other figures, which include metonymy, synecdoche and hyperbole. There may be originality, but obscurity must be avoided. Having approved apt means to high ends Geoffrey warned against abstruse show, with advice for any discipline of an art:

> When you teach a craft, let your speech be that native to the craft; every craft delights in its own vocabulary. But let the craft's words be content with the craft's boundaries. [...] In its own house a speech may be its own man; in public, let it suit the public.[104]

A common device of communication of inner matter by lightening the weight of built form was in the storied arcading of wall elevations, an ascending (*ascensus*), with graceful style (*venustas*) covering what would otherwise seem bare. Such direct comprehensible eloquence is common in Romanesque and Gothic churches, with endless variation and delight in detail, such as in blind traceries. Eloquence must observe 'the craft's boundaries'. It does so on the west front of Magdeburg cathedral where blind tracery graces the wall surfaces extensively, and references the actual nave windows. In the whole scheme there is an effective hierarchy of elements (Figure 3.3). In the transept of Hereford cathedral the triforium arcade delights by its refined eloquence (Figure 6.2).

Third, introducing thirty-five plain figures, Geoffrey said, 'If your language is intended to be light and yet beautifully colored also, do away with all devices of dignity and use instead the plain [. . .]'. Later he said, 'Control the detail and conserve the meaning'.[105] Rhetorical colour works most convincingly by appearing as natural as possible, the art being to conceal art.

> Do not let [words] enter with unsightly mien; rather, see that there is both internal and external adornment. Let the hand of artistic skill provide colours of both kinds. Yet there are times when adornment consists in avoiding ornaments, except such as ordinary speech employs and colloquial use allows.[106]

This is the speech, albeit not ordinary, of St-Bertrand-de-Comminges, a single-nave church of restrained rhetoric (Figure 6.5). Within and without, the *elocutio* is intelligent and controlled. The simple form speaks of human empathy; the fenestration is clear and convincing; the harmony of wall and vault elements is faultless. It shows 'conserved' meaning.

As he closed this subject, Geoffrey explained how, by long reflection revolving and evolving the work, he himself polished his words. Such refinement is for the sake of imparting a comprehension of noble things: 'You will be able to discern beauty of form clearly in this mirror. [...] Let a triple judgement of mind and ear and usage decide the matter'.[107] From this analysis of linguistic *elocutio* it is not hard see a rhetorical counterpart in buildings. On the part of the viewer the architectural expression is a mirror of meaning. And the eloquence does not override the judgement of mind, eye and usage.

Memoria

Martianus Capella described *memoria* as 'the firm guardian of our matter and our diction'—that is, of *inventio* and *elocutio*. The guardianship should be well noted for, in respect of vernacular art, memory is important. Before going on to the art of delivery, Geoffrey interposed the strategic use of memory. First, one needs to find delight and be refreshed by what one drinks in from the place of memory. 'The little cell which remembers is a little chamber of pleasures.'[108] Second, the memory is most effectively exercised when attention is frequent but intermittent to avoid tedium. 'After a short delay has intervened, let another part be summoned up. [...] Two of the aforementioned memory cells will at last be associated, and well cemented, and use will glue them together.'[109] The active mind continually joins up more and more things. Third, as facilitator, recollection works via specific associations to draw upon things thought, seen or done. 'Places, times, shapes, or other similar cues are reliable roads for me which lead me back to the details I want.'[110] These are interior activities of apparently only private interest. Yet their role is as the constant supply line to rhetoric for the presenter. Where we noted Geoffrey referring *elocutio* to the 'judgement of mind and ear and usage' it was in its exterior effect.

Boncompagno da Signa (*c.* 1170–*c.* 1240) taught rhetoric at Bologna, and aimed to make it purposeful. He emphasised the imagination and art involved in memory, and offered three keys which work together: 'The first key is in the imagining of nature. The second is in the exercising of the mind. The third is in the working of the soul'.[111] Here Boncompagno's description of the interior movements of memory may seem merely wordy—or, followed carefully, it may be a useful analysis:

> In the case of the first, nature works through the means of extremes. In the second, progress is made from the parts to the extremes. In the third, completion of each of the two takes place. The soul works through contemplation, in order that the extremes may be brought back to the first,

that those in the middle may be united and may establish an entirety out of the extreme parts until it attains wholeness, in which natural memory is joined through energetic exercise with artificial memory.[112]

'Artificial memory' refers to the work of memory as a device. The use of machines (*machinae*), as devices for fabricating and lifting, were common in medieval building. Augustine had used this simile, writing, 'Knowledge should be used as though it were a kind of machine, by means of which the structure of charity rises up, which lasts forever [. . .]'.[113] He made knowledge serviceable in the building of a work of love. Also, Mary Carruthers writes:

> Gregory the Great, invoking the same figure, says that 'the machine of the mind is the energy of love' by which in this existence we are lifted on high. This 'machine' is contemplation, which can lift up the human soul. Implicit in this characterization, of course, is that 'contemplation' is also an inventive act, a 'construction.'[114]

Contemplation builds up the function of memory. Carruthers elucidates multiple medieval uses of memory such as: in its labyrinthine ways following patterns of coherence; in the visualising of places as a device for locating and retrieving experience; in the ordering, structuring, and use of visual mnemonics and cues. It is in relation to memory that she characterises the poet as a master-builder.[115]

Carruthers brings in application to sensuous things, saying, 'Language-produced and sense-produced memory is cognitively the same thing, made in the same way'.[116] If so, then physical artefacts such as buildings can have mnemonic functions akin to fictive images—and with similar power. She writes: 'To characterize such works as I have done is to insist that all medieval arts were conceived and perceived essentially as rhetoric, whether they took the forms of poems or paintings or buildings or music'.[117] The employing of mnemonic elements worked throughout buildings, a part of architectural rhetoric. Evidence is in the visual memory cues and schemes in frescoes and murals, architectural motifs and settings ubiquitous in manuscript illustrations, and in actual buildings in niches and aedicules which so strongly identify each place as a significant site.

Whereas Carruthers' focus is on the mnemonic power of the image, our study pursues the point made by Augustine and Gregory—that the energy *of love* works by memory to shape the metaphorical building. In *The Craft of Thought* Carruthers connects literary and fictional models to physical buildings, producing a sequence of ideas which carry numerous architectural references which become progressively more precisely embodied in actual buildings.[118] She treats the buildings as scenes or backgrounds, in which the processes of learning and practices of devotion can be illustrated.[119] We may go further to see that the buildings themselves witness that they were designed and made employing the repertoire of mnemonic and other significations, not least theological. There was all the thought and theological memory embedded in the buildings from smallest to largest scale, as has been the tenor of this study so far. Carruthers seems to undermine the theological substance when she writes of Suger's St-Denis abbey and Bernard's Clairvaux monastery:

> Both men used theological arguments and justifications for their programs, but they used them rhetorically—to invent and persuade. In other words, their theological ideas do not constitute a final explanation for what and how they built, but a rhetorically deployed strategy.'[120]

That seems to invert the authors' intended means and ends—it validates the rhetoric by eclipsing theological content so important to the authors. In rhetoric, as in dialectic, the subject matter was crucial and influential. The use of the mirror of comprehension was surely in order to see *what* is declared. Even thus an artist brings forth from what is within—and what is lacking within will be lacunae in his work.

In the whole person storing away or retrieving images brought in by the senses, or by the arts of comprehension and instruction, or by feelings tethered to happiness, memory must be so constructed that love for God conditions it. In memory embedded in the architecture (like cells or hewn stones joined together), in the way churches were arranged, and in the way they were 'read', love for God opened access to deepest reality. The full scope of memory ranged through the intricacy and vastness of the places, drawing souls towards comprehension of the divine Mind. When this was the case the rhetoric was fit for the divine subject.

Pronuntiatio

Our overview of the trivium concludes in seeing that in architecture the contemporary churches and great cathedrals were means of expression of things that mattered.[121] Rhetorical delivery of a subject requires skilful exercise of control, making some things 'pronounced' and others restrained, and every part expressive to serve its purpose. In speech it referred to the control of voice, movement and gesture; in other arts there were corresponding techniques of *pronuntiatio*. Martianus Capella wrote, 'The purpose of delivery is to win the goodwill of the listener, to persuade him to believe, and to inflame and move his spirit'.[122] Robert of Basevorn, in a treatise (*c.* 1322) on the subject-matter and methodology of preaching, made this point: 'Who will hesitate to say that wisdom and eloquence together move us more than either does by itself?'[123] The concern is that for subjects of intrinsic importance there must be appropriate and effective delivery. 'For it is meaning, and not spectacle, which delivery and expression are meant to enhance.'[124]

The figure by which *pronuntiatio* tries to present the inner matter itself Martianus called *diatyposis*: '*Diatyposis* is description or representation in which we express the very look and appearance of the people or things under discussion'.[125] By such means figures of thought and figures of diction require exact, true, correlation by the skill of the orator or painter who can so present the appearance that the hearer or viewer grasps the inner reality of the thing. The figure of thought has its own life and influence independent of variability in the diction and its devices. Extolling the exercise of many disciplines John of Salisbury said, 'by means of *diacrisis*, which we may translate as imagery or vivid representation, [. . .] the finished product somehow seemed the very image all the arts'.[126] He also termed this *oratio nitens*, 'the lustre of eloquence'.

Though we have scant sources in artists writing about their practice, we can see in their work evidence of the persistent ideal of a level of *pronuntiatio* which could vie with both the merely sensory and the purely mental apprehension of reality. Dante speculated that an artist's work might surpass Nature herself. He went further: it exceeded Nature's skill because it was a direct work, a visible word, of God.[127] The divine mind furnished this new medium of supra-mundane *pronuntiatio*. Many a medieval sculptor striving for eloquence might have dared to think his work could be so attributed and deemed precious for God's sake.

In Henry of Avranches' poem praising Lincoln cathedral, the church as a whole—in figures throughout its fabric, even in the eloquence of the stones—has a double refulgence. The visible material is made beautiful for the sake of the spiritual: the outer is to be the declaration of the inner:

> Thus the insentient stones enclose the mysteries of living stones, the fabric made with hands depicts the fabric of the spirit; just so the appearance of the church flashes out double, adorned in the twofold arrangement.[128]

The capturing of the dual reality is *diatyposis*: outward, conspicuous figures truly representing inward concealed figures. Henry's affirmations of a level of abstraction beyond literal images of painting and sculpture are of a grammar and dialectic which provide rhetoric with figures translatable into architectural forms. It is a clue to how the dual reality is captured that John's term *diakrisis* carries in the root *krisis* ideas of discernment, distinguishing and judgement.

A declaration requires reception in the hearer or viewer. Earlier we outlined the scope of the mind of the maker working in the linguistic arts; but at this point the mental experience of the recipient comes to the fore. Returning to Boethius' theory of signification expounded by Magee, a received image may be a *simplex intellectus*; however if it goes beyond that by *imaginatio*, 'the subject and the accident remain indistinct'.[129] For, unlike intellect, the imagination is unable to combine or separate things, to 'put

104 *Comprehension: the trivium*

things together'.[130] This *simplex intellectus* he equates to *intuitus*. It is not the metaphysical 'simple contact' which divine natures (the angels) have with truth. Rather, Magee says,

> Boethius' *primi (simplices) intellectus* are the *passiones animae* (closely tied to *imaginationes*) which grasp in a phenomenal (spatio-temporal) entity the form or the 'quiddity' that corresponds to the Idea or exemplar in the mind of God.[131]

To grasp at such a level what such a form or quiddity might be in time and space was the proper object of arts. But the problem of how what is signified is to be comprehended implicates the imagination of the recipient:

> Imagination receives the form of an object by translating the sense-perception into a confused picture or likeness that is completed by thought. This completion of the confused image is somehow to be understood in relation to a pronouncement that occurs within the soul.[132]

Magee analyses what goes on in this movement 'from a *res* to a *sensus* and *imaginatio*, then to an *intellectus* or pronouncement within the mind'. A kind of judgement in the recipient clarifies the imagination. The *intellectus* is like a go-between of the outer and inner *pronuntiatio*. Such an inner pronouncement, imparted through the rhetorical delivery, 'evidently unfolds and pours out the bright speech' to the soul.[133] He says, 'The result of this process is what Boethius refers to as *cogitabilis oratio*, an inner speech which "participates" in truth or falsity'.[134]

Pronuntiatio applied in visual arts and architecture as much as in oratory or poetry. In a passage concerning 'open visual display rhetoric' Dirk van den Berg discerns two kinds of pictorial image effect:

> Consider the extreme positions in this regard—the first of 'transparency' where the picture itself becomes 'invisible', being replaced by the illusion of the depicted object's 'real presence', the second of 'opaqueness' or 'non-transparency' where the supposedly 'non-representative' picture only shows its own means of pictorial design.[135]

The first kind can be illustrated in south-west England's cathedrals, where the west fronts as great screens display arrays of figural sculpture ordered in the architecture to be eloquent of the mind of the church (Figure 3.12). The second case seems applicable to the west front of Peterborough cathedral (Figure 3.13). It is 'opaque' in that, being 'non-representative', it rhetorically masks its meaning.

Outward beautiful eloquence accords with the architecture's extraordinary rhetorical power to announce, and induct one into, the inner spiritual experience. Even as one comes to comprehend, so one seems to

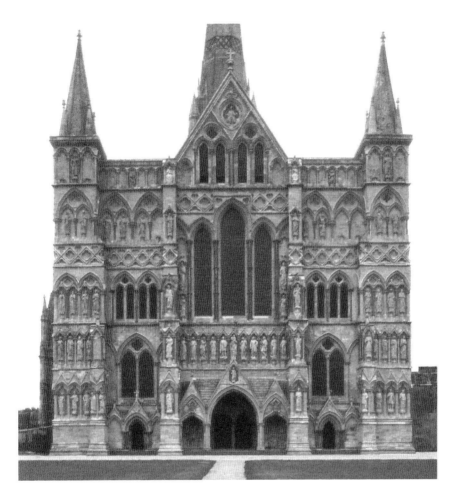

Figure 3.12 Salisbury, England. Cathedral church of St Mary. West front, a 'screen' to the church, 1220–60. The main spire (behind gable) is over the central crossing.

be comprehended by the building. The maker's delivery, the mode itself, and the effect in the recipient are interwoven. They are cognate in visual grammar, in formal dialectic, and in rhetoric—invention, disposition, eloquence, memory and delivery all clearly being employed.

Allegorically, the power of Rhetoric, the third liberal art, belonged to the third heaven, the sphere of Venus. Dante acknowledged Cicero and Boethius as the rhetoricians who had set him on the way of love for Lady Philosophy, the love of Wisdom.[136] In the *Convivio* he expressly associated rhetoric and love:

106 *Comprehension: the trivium*

> The heaven of Venus may be compared to rhetoric because of two special properties: the one is the brightness of her aspect [...], the other is her appearing now at morn and now at even. And these two properties characterise rhetoric; for rhetoric is the sweetest of all the other sciences, since this is what it chiefly aims at.[137]

The morning and evening appearances signify speaking and writing: they are the sweetness and intention in this sphere. Dante says that, 'the eyes of this lady are her demonstrations, the which, when turned upon the eyes of the intellect, enamour that soul which is free in its conditions'.[138]

Figure 3.13 Peterborough, England. Cathedral church of St Peter. West front, 1201–22, built across the original Romanesque façade. The 'Galilee porch' in the centre was added *c.* 1370.

What the recipient soul, free to exercise its powers, is given to perceive is the causes of 'the adornments of the miracles [. . .] which is what she demonstrates'.[139] It is consistent with Boethius' description of the inner pronouncement, the bright speech, that the enamouring—and the demonstration—is as immediate as a lover's look. The love returned by the recipient, in this allegory, is the study of the thing which enamours, the loving attention of the mind seeking to comprehend wonderful things. Glauco Cambron notes that,

> Love, as a god of curiosity, took the guise of study to become an *amor dei intellectualis* [...]. Of course *studium* originally meant zest, and Dante was reviving the secret history of a word in his apparently arbitrary equation.[140]

It is the equation between the passion of an enquiring intellect studying in all fields of knowledge or art, and the comprehension of the mind in love—in which its attention was captured to be free in the love of God. The relevance to art and architecture (in medieval church buildings) is in two main points: first, the rhetoric of the work may be seen to be a pronouncement pertaining to the divine mind; second, there is an inward effect of inspiration in the attentive recipient, whose mind is enamoured. Then the viewer understands that the eloquent work, the very artefact, is the result of its maker being 'in love', inspired by something of divine origin. The recipient becomes a participant in the comprehension of the artist; 'participation' was a notion deeply embedded in medieval thought and theology.

The trivium laid the foundation of learning in skills of comprehension. We have found in diverse textual sources that the linguistic, logical and locutional principles were given visual equivalence or associations. Thus we can deduce parallel applications to visual and tectonic arts. We will want to consider further how consciously they were employed. Language is used as a means to ends beyond its own art, with skill the greater according to the greatness of the ends. The trivium equipped one for instruction in the quadrivium; but we have noticed already that the ends were broader than mere acquisition of knowledge. Indeed the trivium arts were reckoned to have application on higher levels to theological issues, aiding access by both intellect and affections. Connections with love have clearly been asserted in the texts. As we appreciate in each building example the importance of architectural grammar, dialectic, and rhetoric embedded in the culture, proficiency in these arts facilitates our reading and judging artefacts in a medieval context. For us to be receptive to their operation and scope everywhere in a church, must lead to better comprehension of the architecture, and of connections with ideas that informed it, which will be traversed in the next two chapters.

108 Comprehension: the trivium

Notes

1. Morrison (1983), p. 40.
2. Ibid., p. 43.
3. See Martianus Capella, *De nuptiis*, trans. Stahl, Johnson and Burge (1977).
4. Boethius cited by Marenbon (1983), p. 32. For a pertinent review of art historiographical theory of visual images, see van den Berg (2004).
5. Thomas Aquinas, *Summa contra gentiles*, 3, 97.1, 2, trans. Bourke (1975), vol. 2, p. 66.
6. Augustine, *De civitate Dei*, 22.24, trans. Bettenson (1972), p. 1072.
7. Marriage (1909), p. 100.
8. Hugh of St-Victor, *Didascalicon*, 2.1, trans. Taylor (1961), p. 62.
9. The abbey of St-Victor was just south of Paris. These three churches in and near the Ile-de-France show early Gothic invention: St-Germer, built *c.* 1120–40; St-Denis, begun 1137 and finished *c.* 1144; Sens, begun *c.* 1135. See Gardner (1938), pp. 43–5.
10. Martianus Capella, *De nuptiis Philologiae et Mercurii*, 2.202, 2.203, trans. Stahl, Johnson and Burge (1977), p. 61. See **p. 147** below for the fuller passage.
11. Ibid., 9.998, trans. Stahl, Johnson and Burge (1977), p. 381. Compare Carruthers (1998), 'Art objects in medieval ekphrases [plain declarations] tend to be loquacious, even garrulous' (p. 223).
12. Marriage (1909) pp. 72–3, and Bony (1954), p. 30, interpret the Chartres archivolts.
13. Henderson (1968), p. 58. See also von Simson (1962), p. 153.
14. Likewise in the inner portal, with the Tree of Jesse in the archivolts, the origin is in the corresponding place. Abbot Suger described his window sequence at St-Denis as starting 'from that first one which begins [the series] with the *Tree of Jesse*'. See Suger, *De administratione*, 34, in Frisch (1971), p. 10.
15. See Marriage (1909), pp. 104; 108.
16. Eriugena, *De divisione naturae*, trans. Burch (1955), in Fremantle, p. 83.
17. John of Salisbury, *Metalogicon*, 4.35, trans. McGarry (1955), p. 260. Refer also to discussion by Marenbon (1983), pp. 145–7.
18. See Marriage (1909), p. 137.
19. Marenbon (1983), p. 32.
20. Magee (1989), p. 100. Chapter 4 title is '*Cogitabilis oratio*'.
21. Boethius, *De consolatione philosophiae*, 1, 1, trans. Watts (1969), p. 36.
22. See Cowan (1979), p. 82.
23. Cited by Adams (1913), rev. edn., p. 91. The Scripture text is Proverbs 9.1.
24. Bargellini (1954), p. 19. The passage cited is in *Summa theologica*, 2a 2ae, q.45, 1, a.
25. Wisdom of Solomon 7.7–8.
26. Bargellini (1954), p. 22.
27. Ibid., p. 10.
28. A history of the buildings is in Cook (1955). For the cloisters and chapter house see pp. 24; 42–4.
29. Carruthers (1998), pp. 273–4. On the function as scriptorium, see Christopher de Hamel (1994), pp. 82–3.
30. Peter of Celle, *De disciplina claustrali*, 5.4, trans. Hugh Feiss (1987), pp. 79–80.
31. Ibid., 12.2, p. 91.
32. Ibid., 9.1. pp. 87–8.
33. Martianus Capella, *De nuptiis*, 3.230. This has a radical bearing on judgement.
34. For instance in Hugh of St-Victor, *Didascalicon*, 2.28.
35. Martianus Capella, *De nuptiis*, 2.169, trans. Johnson (1977), p. 55.

36 John of Salisbury, *Metalogicon*, 1.13, trans. McGarry (1955), p. 38. Similar semantic explanation is found in Martianus Capella, *De nuptiis*, 3.229.
37 Ibid., p. 38.
38 For some examples see Weitzmann (1977), Plates 34, 35 (Rabbula), Plate 43 (London).
39 de Hamel (1994), p. 79, Plate 65 (St Albans).
40 Kessler (2004), Chapter 1, discusses materials, and cites an extensive literature, albeit in relation to medieval art not architecture.
41 Worringer (1964), p. 41.
42 Ibid., p. 43.
43 Ibid., pp. 44–5.
44 Huntsman (1983), 'Grammar', ed. Wagner, p. 64.
45 This might correspond to the divine 'Word', in theology, generating, upholding, and explaining all things.
46 Huntsman (1983), ed. Wagner, p. 80.
47 Ibid., pp. 82–3.
48 Refer **p. 38** above.
49 In Martianus Capella's *De nuptiis*, 2.172, see Stahl, Johnson and Burge (1977), p. 56. Mercury had been married to Eloquence before his marriage to Philology.
50 Dioscorides (315 BC) called it *hydrargyros*, 'liquid silver'. Pliny (23–79 AD) called it *argentum vivum*. Alchemists gave it the sign of the planet Mercury.
51 See Luke 2.41–52.
52 British Library, Royal MS 2B, VII, fol.151. Early fourteenth century. Another episode, the dialectic between Jesus and the woman of Samaria at Jacob's well (John 4.4–26), is depicted in a mural in the Slavonic Abbey cloisters, Prague.
53 Stump (1983), p. 130.
54 See Aristotle, *Sophistici Elenchi*, 183a37–40.
55 Marenbon (1983), p. 20.
56 Ibid., p. 31.
57 See Evans (1977), pp. 31–2.
58 *De gemmae animae*, 29, trans. Mortet, cited in Harvey (1972), p. 226. Harvey states that the treatise was written 1120–30.
59 Henry of Avranches, *Vita Sancti Hugonis*, 859, 919–20, ed. Dimock (1860), Also excerpt in Harvey (1972) pp. 237–8. See **p. 150** below for a fuller passage.
60 See Hugh of St-Victor, *Didascalicon*, 6.3, 6.4. The three parts evidently parallel the trivium.
61 *Didascalicon*, 6.4, trans. Taylor (1961), p. 140.
62 Ibid., p. 141.
63 Ibid., 2.30, p. 82.
64 Hugh of St-Victor, *Didascalicon*, 2.30, trans. Taylor (1961), p.81.
65 John of Salisbury, *Metalogicon*, 2.5, trans. McGarry (1955), p. 81.
66 See Poole (1932), 'Abailard found no difficulty in the *universalia ante rem* [. . .]; since universals might equally be conceived in relation to the mind of God as to our own' p. 120.
67 John of Salisbury, *Metalogicon*, 2.20, trans. McGarry (1955), p. 120.
68 See Bernard of Clairvaux's distinction, **p. 202** below.
69 John of Salisbury, *Metalogicon*, 2.20.86, trans. Hall (2013), p. 218.
70 Aristotle, *Topica*, 6. 4.141b. 6, *The Works of Aristotle Translated into English*, ed. W. D. Ross; in McGarry (1955), p. 136.
71 John of Salisbury, *Metalogicon*, 2.20, trans. McGarry (1955), p. 136.
72 Martianus Capella in *De nuptiis*, 4.328, introduces Dialectic with these features. The Greek *endoxon* has more exactly the sense of 'what seems reasonable'.

73 For my article considering the differences of perception, and the mental dialectic, see Lewis (2007), 'Medieval perception of space and place in the architecture of Gothic churches'.
74 See Frisch (1971), p. 149. The record was translated by George E. Street in, *Some Account of Gothic Architecture in Spain*.
75 Ibid., pp. 148–57.
76 Alcuin, *De dialectica*, Migne, *Patrologia latina* 101.952 (my trans.). See also McInerny (1983), p. 270, f.n. 29.
77 McInerny (1983), p. 256.
78 Refer **p. 30** above.
79 Martianus Capella, *De nuptiis*, 5.442. See, *Martianus Capella*, ed. Stahl, Johnson and Burge (1977), p. 162.
80 Ibid., 5.426, p.156, f.n.13.
81 Bargellini (1954), p. 26. The Latin text is '*Mulceo dum loquor varios induta colores*'.
82 Camargo (1983), p. 100.
83 Boncompagno da Signa was a leading teacher of *ars dictaminis* at Bologna, completing his *Rhetorica novissima* in 1235. See Boncompagno, trans. Gallagher (2002).
84 Camargo (1983), p. 110.
85 Cicero, *De inventione*, 1.7.9.
86 'Matter, or invention, is the prudent and searching collection of issues and arguments.' Martianus Capella, *De nuptiis*, 5.442, trans. Stahl, Johnson and Burge (1977), p. 162.
87 Geoffrey of Vinsauf, *Poetria nova*, 78–80, trans. Kopp (1971), p. 35. Geoffrey rather confusingly calls the first part of the next section *dispositio*, the beginning of his treatise.
88 Geoffrey of Vinsauf, *Poetria nova*, 43–7, trans. Nims (1967), pp. 16–17. Kopp (1971) translates 'the measuring line of his mind' as 'his heart's inward plumb line', p. 34.
89 Ibid., p. 17.
90 It seems pertinent to recall the process of the formation of the 'inner man', as described by van 't Spijker. See **p. 57** above.
91 The church, built c. 1230–63, has not survived, there is only an engraving of 1625.
92 Martianus Capella, *De nuptiis*, 5.442, trans. Stahl, Johnson and Burge (1977), p. 162.
93 Geoffrey of Vinsauf, *Poetria Nova*, 60–61, trans. Nims (1967), p. 17. The trope of 'clothing' is also used in *elocutio*.
94 Geoffrey of Vinsauf, *Poetria nova*, 118–19, trans. Kopp (1971), p. 37.
95 Ibid., 126–33, p. 37.
96 Ibid., 213–18, p. 41.
97 Genesis 2.7.
98 Geoffrey of Vinsauf, *Poetria nova*, 249–62, trans. Kopp (1971), p. 43.
99 Camargo (1983), p. 99.
100 Martianus Capella, *De nuptiis*, 5.442, trans. Stahl, Johnson and Burge (1977), p. 162.
101 Geoffrey of Vinsauf, *Poetria nova*, 741–2, trans. Kopp (1971), p. 60.
102 Ibid., pp. 60–7.
103 Hugh of St-Victor makes this explicit in a theological treatment of *dignitas* in *De arca Noe morali*, 4.18, 4.20.
104 Geoffrey of Vinsauf, *Poetria nova*, 1087–90, trans. Kopp (1971), p. 72. This has a bearing on a vernacular art.

105 Ibid., 1094–6, 1877, p. 100.
106 Ibid., 1881–4, trans Nims (1967), p. 84.
107 Ibid., 1945–8, p. 86.
108 Ibid., 1971, excerpt trans. Carruthers (1998), p. 117.
109 Ibid., 1997–2000, trans. Kopp (1971), p. 104.
110 Ibid., 2014–15, p. 105.
111 Boncompagno da Signa, *Rhetorica novissima*, 8.25, trans. Gallagher (2002), p. 117.
112 Ibid.
113 *Epistulae*, 55, 21.39.1–6, cited by Carruthers (1998), p. 23. Compare I Corinthians 8.1: 'Knowledge puffs up, love assuredly builds up' ('*Scientia inflat, caritas vero aedificat*').
114 Carruthers (1998), p. 23. The line of Gregory is from *Moralia in Job*, 6.37.58.
115 See Carruthers (1993), 'The Poet as Master-Builder'.
116 Ibid., p. 132.
117 Ibid., p. 223.
118 The architectural associations are paramount in Chapter 1 (pp. 7–24), and Chapter 5 (pp. 221–76).
119 See Carruthers (1998), pp. 254–76.
120 Ibid., p. 224.
121 See my full discussion of *pronuntiatio* in building rhetoric, in 'Presentation of verbal and visual images in the Middle Ages', Lewis (2005).
122 Martianus Capella, *De nuptiis*, 5.540, trans. Stahl, Johnson and Burge (1977), p. 204.
123 Robert of Basevorn, *Forma praedicandi*, 13, trans. Krul (1971), p. 131.
124 Martianus Capella, *De nuptiis*, 5.543, trans. Stahl, Johnson and Burge (1977), p. 205.
125 Ibid., 5.524, p. 197.
126 John of Salisbury, *Metalogicon*, 1.24.52, trans. Hall (2013), pp. 174–5.
127 See Dante Alighieri, *Purgatorio*, 10. 32–33; 94–96.
128 Henry of Avranches, *Vita Sancti Hugonis*, 946–49 (my translation) from text in Charles Garton (1986), pp. 58, 60. A prior passage is cited below, **p. 176**.
129 Magee (1989), p.112. Refer also **p. 68** above.
130 See Magee, ibid., p. 103.
131 Ibid., p. 113.
132 Ibid., p. 116.
133 Ibid. The text of Boethius is in *Commentarii in Librum Aristotelis*., 2.33.33. '[. . .] *scilicet explicat et effundit oratio nitens*.'
134 Ibid., p. 116.
135 van den Berg (2004), p. 171, f.n. 14.
136 Dante Alighieri, *Convivio*, 2.13, 15–17; 2.16, 1–9.
137 Ibid., 2.14, 110–19, trans. Wicksteed (1931), p. 117.
138 Ibid., 2.16, 28–30, p. 132.
139 Ibid., 2.16, 86–88, p. 134.
140 Cambron (1969), p. 11.

4 The mirror of instruction
The quadrivium

The mathematical arts

The power of the mind to form concepts cannot be judged simply by how complex or abstruse the material is which it has to work upon. Certainly the range of raw data available to the mind will partly steer the course of ratiocination; but a high power of conceptualisation can engage with limited 'factual' material and bring in acutely speculative matters. In terms of our topic, the best educated medieval minds, though completely without access to physical science as it has burgeoned since, nevertheless could work with valid philosophical concepts, albeit different. It cannot be supposed that such powers because different were inferior or misguided. The opposite may be attested by the end to which they were applied.

The liberal arts, comprehending and transmitting knowledge, give insight into the medieval intellectual milieu. The logical arts of the trivium were necessary for arrangement, integrity and clarity. The quadrivium arts—arithmetic, music, geometry, astronomy—were for the understanding and handling of phenomena. These disciplines were *mathematical*, purporting to 'number' all things. Bonaventure, observing the division of natural philosophy into physics proper, mathematics and metaphysics, said that mathematics, 'considers forms that can be abstracted in their pure intelligibility'.[1] It is a description to keep in mind in this chapter on the mathematical arts—they lie between physics and metaphysics, and have reference to both. Access may have been through intuition; but truths would be perceived as axiomatic.

Mathematics grasped the nature of the universe, to interpret its physical, rational, and even moral, clarity. Integrity and stability were seen as crucial. Some things were regarded as always stable, and everywhere the same; but things differing, apt to change, had to be accounted for. Plato's influence on medieval thought, albeit mediated, extended to mathematical arts.[2] In *Timaeus*, for apprehension of both the sensible world and the intelligible world, he attributed instructional value to the 'different' (concerning phenomena) and the 'same' (concerning ideation):

> Whenever reasoning that is true, whether about the different or about the same, takes place, being carried on without speech or sound in the self-moved, if it concerns the sensible world, and the circle of Different, running straight, reports it to the whole soul, then there arise opinions and beliefs that are sure and true: but if it concerns the world apprehended by reason, and the circle of Same, running smoothly, declares it, then the result must be apprehension and knowledge.[3]

Beside the different and same (phenomena and ideation), Graeco-Roman philosophy perceived many dichotomies—visible and invisible, material and spiritual, temporal and eternal, image and reality. Lacking apprehension of the invisible, spiritual, eternal and real, one only obtains knowledge (however 'sure and true') of the world of sensible things. The mathematical arts aimed at coherent knowledge having reference to superior things. Proclus (fl. 437–85) interpreted Plato and Euclid at the close of the Roman era, and in summing his theory of mathematics Dominic O'Meara writes:

> Mathematics thus promotes perfection in the life of discursive reasoning, but it also prepares the soul for a higher level of reasoning, that of theology or metaphysics, the practice of which prepares the soul in turn for access to a yet higher level [...] the life of divine Intellect.[4]

In the Christian era theology pursued the great synthesis of order on the inferior level and order on the superior. All things had meaning because of their connections to the foundations of the world, the providence of the Creator, and the realities of the spirit—conditions which imply arrangement, underlie stability, and ensure clarity. Such a state Augustine described as 'a universal commonwealth'.[5] The 'numbering' of all things denoted the law and power of the Creator in the entire cosmos, perfect and executive Wisdom. He saw this imitated in the rational mind engaging divine truths, to access knowledge translatable by a teacher or maker. Jesus quoted Isaiah when he said, 'It is written in the prophets, "And they shall be all taught of God"'.[6] Isaiah had pictured the preparation and process—foundations laid, walls, gates, pinnacles, being built in precious stones. Expounding St John's text, Grosseteste, in his *Hexaëmeron*, cited Augustine at length:

> We can call this same wisdom of the Father a reckoning, since according to Augustine this wisdom of the Father is number. [...] 'That power that reaches in might from beginning to end could perhaps be called number, while that which disposes all things in gentleness is now properly called wisdom. Both belong to one and the same wisdom, but wisdom gives a number to everything, even the lowest and last of things. For all bodies, even those at the ends of the universe, have their number.' [...]

Understanding things in this way I think we can correctly understand there to be a reckoning in Christ, since he 'reaches from beginning to end in might', giving numbers to all things and counting everything.[7]

Even with Wisdom and number thus connected we may wonder what bearing this kind of knowledge had upon the making of artefacts under an impulse of love for God. A philosophical percept, supported in common experience, is that order, permanence and beauty are desired by anyone who truly loves. If an artificer desires things 'disposed in gentleness', and has his mind well instructed, he can work with a high level of knowledge and insight. The intelligibility believed to run through everything can be apprehended and transmitted. Both ways, in intellectual grasp and in the media of making, there was 'a reckoning in Christ', where all connections are made. The actual 'commonwealth' was built as everything, including the work of artificers, was so fitted into it.

An example of the deductive method which we can follow shows the explicit role of instruction in directing the arts, different works connected by explicit deductions or derivations. Boethius, in *The Consolation of Philosophy*, gave a description of the seven liberal arts. It was the textual source for a later circular diagram interpreting the liberal arts schematically, inserted into an early-twelfth-century copy of his *On Music*, with a full descriptive text prescribing how the arts should be depicted. Then a late-twelfth-century drawing rendered this pictorially; a circle of architectural arcades for the personifications of the curriculum, with seven streams of wisdom flowing from Philosophy giving unlimited vitality to each art.[8] The trail leads to the north transept of Braine abbey church where, around 1203, this model of the arts was transposed to the architecture as a compendious wheel window.[9] As with the diagram and the picture, the explanation of the window is derived from the philosophy and theology. It could be read as an abstracted form of 'pure intelligibility'. Meaning now is located in the church (even intimated in the seven churches held in the centre); and a further abstraction and deduction may suggest application to the church itself.

Boethius, in the Proemium of *On Arithmetic*, outlined from number theory how things of unchangeable essence could be studied in the quadrivium, and be pursued in the sciences; they are found to have participation in bodies and, consequently, existence and mutability in nature, according to their variety. Multitude and magnitude he took as primary divisions in the theory of number, and subdivided each, thus making the four arts, 'by which the mind is able to ascend' to philosophy:

> Of these types, arithmetic considers that multitude which exists of itself as an integral whole; the measures of musical modulation understand that multitude which exists in relation to some other; geometry offers the notion of stable magnitude; the skill of astronomical discipline explains the science of moveable magnitude.[10]

Thomas Aquinas connected the quadrivium arts to the Wisdom text ('measure, number, weight' or 'measure, form, inclination'). He reasoned that, *inter alia*, everything actually existing possesses a form, and thus its matter is determined by form, so nothing can be infinite in essence. Clearly every natural body has a substantial form of determinate quantity. Similarly a mathematical body has to be actualised under some imagined form, and, 'since the form of quantity as such is figure, such a body must have some figure. [...] Figure is confined by a term or boundary'.[11] Magnitude is treated '*mathematically*, in which case we consider its quantity only, and *naturally*, in which case we consider its matter and form'. Magnitude pertains to geometry and astronomy. Multitude pertains to arithmetic and music. Altogether, the quadrivium dealing with specifics of figure and order, had a certain pragmatism, and material applications.

These aspects working in a material object are epitomised in English chapter houses. At Lincoln (Figure 4.1) the figure has *measure*, modular, exact; the multitude of parts are *numbered*, integrated, formalised; the magnitude of the whole has *weight*, order, inclination. Nothing is aimless, and all things are 'gathered together'. To Thomas order expressed a Christocentric rational plan. Not only does his reasoning employ the principles of mode of

Figure 4.1 Lincoln, England. Cathedral of St Mary. Chapter House from the east. Decagonal plan, with a central interior column. Built 1220.

116 Instruction: *the quadrivium*

being, of species, and of order, but it derives from affirmations concerning the Creator, addressing not only the origin of things but their ultimate end: 'And thus, the reason for the diversity of forms in things is derived from this end. Moreover, the reason for the order of things is derived from the diversity of forms'.[12] This leads into a discussion of *definitions* of things (numbers being signifiers); *gradations* (drawing together the last members of things in a higher class, with the first members of things in a lower class[13]); *operations*; diverse *proper ends* in things; *composition* of form and matter in things; *proportion* in composition; diverse *agent actions*; and diverse *properties and accidents*. All this, he says, comprises evidence of divine wisdom, providential and rational. While that engaged matters mathematical and metaphysical, it might in turn direct architectural reckoning, and on a superior level can be recognised as a theological discourse.

Computus model

In considering connections between the mathematical arts and theology, and potential implications for architecture, we find a model in the science of computus, which was 'a major vehicle for ideas about the metaphysical and religious dimensions of number in the early Middle Ages'—from the fifth-century computist Victorius of Aquitaine to the end of the twelfth century.[14] As a functional artifice it is exemplified by the Paschal table:

> In natural time, the cycles of the moon and the sun are incommensurate, but the computist, by ordering time into conventional units, can coordinate these two cycles to produce the Paschal table; he can literally measure the unmeasurable.[15]

A computist deals with unmeasurable concepts using time, place and number to bestow order. When discussing 'reason, and the guarantee of order' Faith Wallis cites Isidore of Seville (*c.* 570–636) who wrote:

> Using the science of numbers we have an ability to stand fast (*consistere*) to some degree, when through this science we tell the hours, when we discuss the course of the months or learn the span of the revolving year. Indeed through number we are taught so that we do not fall into confusion. Take number away, and everything lapses into ruin. Remove *computus* from the world, and blind ignorance will envelop everything [...].[16]

This is reminiscent of a passage by Augustine: 'Behold the heaven, the earth, the sea; all that is bright in them [. . .] all have forms because they have number. Take away number and they will be nothing [. . .]. For they exist only in so far as they have number'.[17] The point he makes is that the mind's appreciation of corporeal things (indeed of beauty) is in perceiving the operation of number; it validates the existence of every material object.

This provides a bridge to an architecture which 'measures the unmeasurable'. While it dealt particularly with numbering and time-reckoning, the methodology admits parallels with medieval architecture, as indicated where Wallis says: 'The corpus of medieval *computistica* is vast [. . .]. Much of it is anonymous, derivative, and "uncanonized" [. . .] an unstructured body of material which can freely be excerpted, interpolated, re-arranged, or adapted according to particular tastes and needs'.[18] Such freedom and non-conformity seems to characterise medieval church building—though it may frustrate comparative architectural history. Yet Wallis describes computus tables even as we might describe cathedrals—as 'images of order'. Both have to be understood *in their artefacts*, with no texts of systematic theory:

> *Computus* is not built up around a syllabus of canonized texts; in fact, it is not built around texts at all, but rather around tables. [...] In the final analysis, *computus* does not need treatises; it needs these two tables. Hence it is a science with a strong graphic orientation. It is also a science indissolubly wedded to the concrete manuscripts by which it is conveyed.[19]

In our study the equivalent of the computus manuscripts are the buildings, and the epistemology modelled can aid an epistemology of medieval architecture. We can also infer in Wallis's topic another stratum of knowledge in mathematical arts and in architecture:

> For all its façade of grimly practical technique, most of [computus] is neither practical nor a technique. Much of what transpires in those cryptic tables or unblinkingly didactic texts is, in fact, poetry, and poetry on a very serious subject. It is poetry about order.[20]

Architecture was an artifice by which to coordinate and encompass the incomprehensible house of God 'not made by hands'.[21] Thus while artificers refined the knowledge (*scientia*) and art (*ars*) of construction, most of what we might consider the design (or the poetry) was not driven by practical criteria nor restricted by technique. But even as the computus used tables, so there was a rule for each building, the great measure, the *ordinatio*, and a module, the specific *quantitas*.[22] Comprehending the scope and order, the artificer introduced and located everything.

> The computists stressed that this intellectualized art of measurement has universal application. Its methods and units could be used to measure anything; an atom, for instance, could be the smallest part of a physical body, or a number, or a word, or a unit of time.[23]

Wallis cites its use in grammar, music and geometry. The parallel aspect of this for us is the vastness and intricacy of cathedral architecture, where

118 *Instruction: the quadrivium*

everything is accommodated. Through instruction in its order a great deal was explained. The order to be grasped, however, was the poetic order intelligible only in the building. Wallis continues the analysis of the computus, suggesting for our subject a further insight into the 'reading' of a cathedral and hinting a yet closer affinity with medieval architecture. She explains the AEIOV lunar table of Abbo of Fleury (*c.* 945–1004):

> The clarity of [its] rows of letters is in sharp contrast to the extremely contorted procedure required to read it. What lies behind this extraordinary ingenuity, I believe, is the notion that visual patterning embodies the man-made order inherent in the *computus*; it echoes Bede's intuition that the calendar is a conceptual scheme of concrete and visible *places*.[24]

For all the clarity of visual patterning even in a complex cathedral there is an underlying knowledge not easily read: it pertains to the mathematical arts in just such a way as the computus did. By comparison theories of number symbolism, divine harmony, sacred geometry and cosmic mysticism seem to come from a desire to rationalise and impose meaning at a level on which the medieval mind was not working. Rather, the quadrivium arts enabled the mind to be complicit in a 'contorted procedure'. Although the computus was but an application of number theory it was dealing with the deep matter of the ordering of time and place; and its ingenuity was in the visual and graphic mode of conveying meaning. Although built on number the computus as a construction actually had a more imaginative than didactic purpose. Similar to its graphic ordering the entire, hardly comprehended, order of a cathedral provided in memory and imagination locational associations. A baffling complex in such a way could be a composition of significant places, even as the computus seemed to Bede. *Our* difficulty in understanding is no doubt largely because we are not literate monks in the seventh or twelfth-century world, and the cathedrals as they stand now are considerably changed, in milieu totally different. Their times and places and devotions were under the ideal of *regula*, stable and measured. 'Hence', says Wallis, 'many of the images of order associated with the medieval *computus* are specifically monastic images'.[25]

This brief outline of computus as model of aspects of architecture parallels what Panofsky did in *Gothic Architecture and Scholasticism* where scholastic epistemology is a model for the architecture. In both cases the further task has to be to weigh the causes and the content, seeing the philosophical and theological sources. In this chapter we seek valid connections between the quadrivium and those sources.

Arithmetic

Guy Beaujouan remarks that in non-scientific works of twelfth-century teachers: 'the store of mathematical knowledge displayed is very small, consisting chiefly of common-places'.[26] But we must consider that many definitions and formulations embodied valid *intuitive* percepts. For instance,

Instruction: the quadrivium

Boethius, to show arithmetically the primary nature of unity, works through a logical pattern of number sequence which is just below a threshold of obviousness but is easily seen once pointed out. He indeed explains that in numbers this is 'according to the natural arrangement of things'.[27] Reducing it to its limit, the terminal point in unity, he states what we know without thinking, that only *one* is not a middle term between two numbers—it has no number before it. But he has supplied a demonstration, to give it new clarity and significance. There is a subtlety in the idea which he then adds: that one, the primary unit, 'is rightly recognized as the generator of the total extended plurality of numbers'.[28] This too we recognise instinctively; but something deeper is brought to the threshold of consciousness: the profound truth of everything, even infinity, being 'generated' out of unity. In the ensuing treatment of numbers he refers to unity as the 'mother' to all numbers.[29] This illustrates two things: that *ratiocination* is often not so far from 'natural' intuitions as it might seem; and that the field of *ratio* often connects with ultimate truths and divine mystery.

Figure 4.2 Wells, England. Cathedral church of St Andrew. Octagonal chapter house. Central pillar with sixteen shafts of black polished Purbeck marble. Completed *c*. 1319.

Where number mathematics in various ways made reference to God, it should be noted that it was in a mental temper well removed from the esoteric and magical. Michael Masi emphasises the often bypassed distinction between mystical number theory and philosophical number theory 'which carries much more intellectual weight'. The latter depends on 'reasonably intelligible numerical relationships', with intellectual grasp being possible because of inherent order, albeit, 'an order that can be determined only by careful calculations'.[30] The degree to which mystical number symbolism was engaged by medieval designers seems to be conventional and often quite *ad hoc*. It is *philosophical* number theory that belongs in the quadrivium—and in architecture—as a mode of transmission of divine wisdom. An exemplar of such reckoning of number is the central column of the Wells chapter house (Figure 4.2). Rather than being a mere necessity, it is an expression of unity and plurality, the generation of parts and the integration of the whole.

Boethius tied his theory of number to ultimate reality in a way which resonated with medieval views of existence and order. He commenced *On Arithmetic* with an expectation that the primacy of number would be self-evident, not least in the creative mind:

> From the beginning, all things whatever which have been created may be seen by the nature of things to be formed by reason of numbers. Number was the principal exemplar in the mind of the creator. From it was derived the multiplicity of the four elements, from it were derived the changes of the seasons, from it the movement of the stars and the turning of the heavens. [...] The status of all things is founded on the binding together of numbers.[31]

It is the very way, and inexhaustible number of ways, in which numbers connect and are coherent, that makes number an 'exemplar' in which every member *is*, is unique, and none is missing or dispensable. Arithmetic is stable; in its patterns all numbers are bound together. According to Boethius, it is plain that number is 'composed of parts' which are dissimilar but adhere to each other with 'reasonable proportion'. 'They come forth from one source and are joined into one composition and harmony.'[32] Such a basis for arithmetic seems remote from any real function, yet reflection might admit it as a quite natural datum of consciousness, and a possible vantage point for expansive objectivity. Augustine said the laws were within us. To know that *one* is unity, the primary unit, the ultimate point, sharpens the intuition of the deity as monad, the One, the Alpha, the Omega. To know the unity as also the generator of all is to conceive everything as participating in the being of God as the source and sum of all.

In an early thirteenth-century drawing a scroll linking Lady Arithmetic to Boethius has the epigraph, 'Through me is known the virtue of all numbers'.[33] This *virtus*, excellence, power, was claimed for number's integrated multitude. A more complex demonstration of Boethius' number theory, something not simply grasped, is shown by a drawing which prefaces a probably

Instruction: the quadrivium 121

tenth-century gloss on his *On Arithmetic*. It is a planar diagram of a fundamental feature of number, namely evenness and oddness, patterned in number sequences based on 'natural order': the simple series of odd numbers are multipliers, and the even numbers that are 'born out of them' are multiplicands.[34] The pattern resolves into a diagram closely resembling the plan of a cruciform church having four apses extending from the central crossing. The numeric connections are demonstrations of symmetry and harmony. The whole pattern *shows* mathematical order, 'in imitation and agreement', and 'so the participation of this inborn property is recognized'.[35] The diagram is a construct where each number of an arithmetic demonstration is in place.

In such a cruciform church the square central crossing is the generator of the four principal parts, nave, choir and each transept arm, each proportioned to it. Laon cathedral illustrates the pattern with great clarity and

Figure 4.3 Laon, France. Cathedral church of Notre-Dame. View north-east from nave to choir, through the central crossing formed by the transept. Crossing tower above, *c.* 1160–1200.

resolution (Figure 4.3). These four parts connect directly to the sides of the crossing, and the aisles lead into and out of them; each is 'proportioned' to the crossing. It is emphasised where there is a semicircular apse and ambulatory (such as Soissons cathedral), which returns one aisle to the other, in a form resembling the arithmetic demonstration (without asserting derivation one of the other). The reading of the architectural arrangement is the same: the modes of order and participation, namely proportion and multiplicity, lead, as it were, naturally to symmetry and harmony. These qualities are apprehended particularly as one moves through the crossing itself; and here too the vertical axis intersects; here one is in the very matrix of numbers.

Arithmetic was to sharpen the mind to philosophical verities; and two attributions in number theory are of special interest here. The first is that certain numbers were called 'perfect'. In such a number the sum of its *aliquot* parts equals the number itself. An *aliquot* part is any number which can be divided into the number in question without remainder. Thus the *aliquot* parts of 8 are 1, 2 and 4. The sum of those numbers is 7. So 8 is not a perfect number. The first perfect number is 6, for 1+2+3 is 6 itself. In each rank of numbers there is only one perfect number: in tens, the number 28, in hundreds, 496, in thousands, 8,128, etcetera.[36] The adjective meant 'complete'; and the perception was also aesthetic. Yet more than that; it went back to the cause of things. Outlining perfect number theory and consulting Scripture, Augustine associated the perfection of six with a theological demonstration: God ordered his works in six days because that number explained their completion and perfection. He was clear that this was not imposed symbolism, repeating that, 'In this number God brought his works to complete perfection. Hence the theory of number is not to be lightly regarded'.[37] In architectural application Nigel Hiscock adduces documentary evidence of an intention to express perfection by six stages of a tower built at New Minster, Winchester, in the late tenth century.[38]

A second attribution giving specific qualities to a number, comes from William of Auberive, who published *De sacramentis numerorum* around 1164. Beaujouan comments:

> He introduced some concepts that were apparently new: if the sum of *aliquot* parts of a number was greater than that number, then the excess was called *fructus*; if the sum of the *aliquot* parts of two numbers was the same, this sum was called 'number of love'.[39]

In the first three decads are two such pairs, and thus two such 'numbers of love'. The first pair is 6 and 25, both of which have 6 as the sum of their *aliquot* parts. The second pair is 12 and 26, both of which have 16 as their sums. Thus 6, which we have seen is the first 'perfect number', has also this quality, 'love'. And 16 is a 'number of love': it is the first sum which is a *fructus*, and is also the sum of 10, the decad, plus the first perfect number, 6. Evidently William was seeking to establish philosophical number tropes of mathematical legitimacy. The notion of 'love', brought into number theory, meant concord at least—and could well mean charity. For instance, of interest here is Grosseteste's second attribution to the number two: 'So the two, in so far as it fractures unity, is the type of malevolence which retreats from unity. But in so far as it turns back to unity and unites the two, it is a type of concord and of two-fold love'.[40]

Hugh of St-Victor wrote: 'The power of number is this—that all things have been formed in its likeness'.[41] This asserts that abstract philosophical number is involved pragmatically in the forming of 'all things': its generative power and formal excellence are always in act. I doubt there are grounds for positing an invariable, conscious use of numerology in the work of architects; yet Hugh's assertion may equally apply in an often informal and *ad hoc* use of number—even as we saw in the grammar, dialectic and rhetoric of arches that the device of emphasis and enrichment of line augmented their logical and affective power, to an increase of knowledge, wisdom, affection.

Commonly in canon tables arches are used for visual ordering: the intention is clear, and the subject being communicated has precise content (Figure 5.6). We saw the operation of the logical arts in them; and we may consider an operation of the power of number. The mind conducts exercises in mental arithmetic to read the vertical lists arranged in colonnades with bracketing arches, the interlacing arches ingeniously connecting each tabular column with every other in a stable continuum. Number patterns lie just below the surface and work without conscious analysis. The whole is ordered (mnemonically and numerically) by the contiguity (*indistantia*) of discrete places, and the integrated pattern. Extensive examples, such as the St Alban's Bible canon tables (1170), closely parallel building applications such as the blind arcades of the west front of Castle Acre priory, Norfolk (*c.* 1100). The triforium of St Cross chapel, Winchester, is a smaller illustration (Figure 4.4). In both media the artist's mind is working on a level of visual, poetic, architecture. In the same way and with formal similarities, the interior elevations of Laon cathedral (Figure 4.3) and Beverley minster (Figure 4.5) seem to be as much arithmetical as geometrical, an architecture of 'integrated multitude'. The geometry is, of course, congruent, but without the repetitiveness and an almost compulsive visual counting there would be a diminished sense of significance and delight.

The perception of 'multitude' in a great church impresses with a powerful logic, and even suggests infinitude. In the course of discussing the infinity of God Thomas questioned whether infinite multitude in creation is possible. While philosophical, the point is pragmatic—multitude of operation does not just happen, but is generated by focussed work, an art, a movement, an instrument. This theory of work involves measure and limits—numbering:

> Furthermore, multitude in the world is created, and everything created is comprehended under some definite intention of the Creator; for no agent acts aimlessly. Hence everything created must be comprehended under a certain number.[42]

Thomas also questioned whether infinite magnitude is possible. The two questions are connected thus: 'the increase of a multitude follows upon the division of a magnitude'. This therefore brings in geometry as concerned with magnitude, making a connection of the two arts. The principle, in both arithmetic and geometry, is that by division there is a nisus towards particularisation of *matter*, whereas by addition there is a nisus towards completion of a *form*.[43] Aesthetically it is actually obvious—a difference of perception according to focus. But this number theory employs ratiocination; and the point of interest is that philosophical number could be related to matter and form. While the chevet of Le Mans cathedral will illustrate geometry, it also shows the arithmetic notion of *division* emphasising the materiality, and *addition* demonstrating its form (Figure 4.8).

The interior arcades of Southwell cathedral, considered under Dialectic, also illustrate Thomas's principle. In the early-twelfth-century nave arcades (Figure 3.6) there is relatively small use of division of mass and addition of parts to express matter and form, compared with the thirteenth-century choir (Figure 3.7), in which the lines and joints of individuation and articulation are expressed, indicating an 'arithmetical' fluency in Gothic architecture.

The particularly instructive feature emerging is how arithmetic as a discipline aided one's perceptions of the mode of existence of things; which could well extend to an artificer's thinking about the essence of his own work. We can hardly know how far artificers understood or simply followed the principles in practice. An artificer dealing with *number* and *dimension* (characteristic of the medieval idiom is the endless replication of elements and motifs) will find stable images of multitude and magnitude forming in his mind under his hand. Following Bonaventure's dictum that mathematics 'considers forms that can be abstracted in their pure intelligibility', we might sense a further level of perception: in the features of number an aesthetic may be discerned, accessible to the medieval mind. This can be more fully indicated in the subject of Music.

Music

In Arithmetic, number theory which involved and depended upon clear *ratio* could also be apprehended at a level just below conscious attention. The same applied significantly in music where participation in actual performance was important. We saw that it was a characteristic of computus to order number in vast intricate patterns of 'poetic' meaning, and music did the equivalent. For centuries it worked without the 'texts' of a visual score, until the abstraction of useful notation of accent and metre, particularly at Notre-Dame, Paris, in the mid-twelfth century.[44] Arithmetic characteristically dealt with stable, integrated multitude; music dealt with modulated multitude, the movement of sound, progression in *tempus*.

Augustine produced a theory of music in *On Music*. It deals with technical aspects of rhythm and metre, and with the power of number, known within the rational soul. Robert Taliaferro comments that Augustine avoids 'the consequent disorders arising from the irresponsible independence of music as a fine art', by treating it as a science and art of instruction.[45] It thus pertinently relates to our approach both in the correspondence in church architecture, and the performance of liturgical music within it. Throughout, Augustine tacitly connects the *ratio* of the soul with ratio in numbers, and accordingly, in the last chapter, it reaches to the ends of the universe—that is, infinity. But he begins with ratio 'which forces such an infinity back into some measure'; indeed, 'returning again and again to one, the beginning or principle of numbers'.[46] Yet such a dialectic is anchored in the reasoning of the mind and experience of the physical.

Before Book I of *On Music* ends, when the great harmony of the first three numbers is brought out, the affective power of this subject is introduced. In the dialogue, the disciple, instructed by his master in such great matters replies: 'I don't know why, but I admire and love this unity you commend'. Then he is shown the power which the number four has to order all things to the one, by 'any conjunction and connection': 'The unity you love can be effected in ordered things by that alone whose name in Greek is *analogía* and which some of our writers have called proportion'.[47] It is as in arithmetic—that numbers have a sovereignty in discursive reasoning, and aesthetic power. That a mere number has intrinsic relations to other numbers which generate real effects, such as unity and order, was a matter for contemplation. Naturalness yet strangeness of numerical relations both intimate and infinite was perceived; they were viewed as bound up in, and proportioned to, eternal and divine things. Here is Augustine explaining the 'most beautiful art of progression' through the interval from one to four:

> One and two are the beginnings and seeds, as it were, of numbers [that] three is made from; and this accounts for three numbers. And when they are brought together by proportion, the number four appears and comes to be, and is joined to them by rule, to become the final number of the measured progression we seek.[48]

Following that, the sum of the numbers one to four is ten, which is the 'first articulation' in the infinity of numbers, for the counting of multitude proceeds in decads. Books Two to Five treat metre and rhythm in all their forms, based on number theory.

But with Book Six the master wants his disciple to pass from corporeal things to incorporeal. The general subject is the discovery of six kinds of 'number' applicable to music, theoretical and technical. The first is *corporeal*: sound in its physical sounding. The others are all in the soul in one way or another. So the second is the *sensory* experience of the sound, in which the soul is 'reacting' by what he calls 'the affection of the ears'. The third is the production or *pronouncing* by the maker, making it harmonious, short or prolonged, so 'advancing' the sound; and the making being essentially

126 *Instruction: the quadrivium*

an act of the soul, it can be produced silently in the mind. The fourth is in the *memory*, where a sound may be present though the corporeal sound has passed, or where memory supplies sound even during a 'rest'.[49] All these interest us because we can detect parallels in dealing with architecture: the tangible-visible material of the fabric; the experience of the soul reacting with an affection of the eyes; the making of the artefact in the soul, developed in the mind, advanced, produced, pronounced; and memory locating visual experience in a continuum of places. Applied in a mathematical art all these can be seen as functions of number, pertaining in architecture as in music. Yet these aspects are hardly translated explicitly in buildings because they are indeed 'in the soul'. These progressions mirror the stages of experience of love for God, such as William of St-Thierry described in his *Epistle*.[50]

At this juncture Augustine says these four numberings are mortal, fading quickly or slowly. He finds a fifth sort, more excellent, in the activity of judgement: *judicial numbers*. This kind of judging ranges widely—universally—reckoning time-spans, intervals, multitude and motion.

> To each living thing in its proper kind and in its proportion with the universe is given a sense of places and times, so that even as its body is so much in proportion to the body of the universe whose part it is, and its age so much in proportion to the age of the universe whose part it is, so its sensing complies with the action it pursues in proportion to the movement of the universe whose part it is.[51]

He affirms that this proportionality is one of and for delight; and by it the soul can learn how places, times, and indeed bodies, are harmonised. Likewise the numbers of wisdom attune it to God. The disciple exclaims, 'The force and power of these judicial numbers moves me to the utmost'.[52] But direct judgement has practical limits: for instance it cannot assess musical metres or rhythms if the time span is extremely drawn out. Judgement delights in equality; favouring equal intervals, rejecting 'perturbed' ones; seeing symmetry in certain metrical feet, contriving it in others, and making up deficiency by the expedient of *rests* of placidity. However he detects that the sensuous delight of the soul is not scrupulous about slight deficiencies, finding that imperfect approximation of equality delights by its own inferior beauty.

There is a need more easily seen than met (or easily ignored) for superior appraisal, using number on yet another quite challenging level: It takes four chapters (9 to 12) for Augustine to unfold this vital matter.

> [We] are delighted through judicial numbers, and appraise it by still others, and in accordance with these more hidden numbers we bring another judgement on this delight, a kind of judgement on the judicial numbers.[53]

We can tease out the following. It is a matter of appraising whether the judgement of delight is true or not. Appraisal is carried out by reasoning. Reason cannot deal with the 'judicial numbers' under it without its own more powerful numbers. As to what such vital 'numbers' are, Augustine's answers are rather elliptical. It becomes clear that internal ordering of oneself is a pre-condition, almost as if one must become properly 'in proportion' to, in harmony with, the imperfect and perfect worlds. And delight again appears, like a lodestone, now more spiritually pure. 'So we are not troubled by lower, and take delight only in higher things. For delight is a kind of weight in the soul. Therefore, delight orders the soul.' This *weight* is evidently that inclination of love for God.[54] The higher things, like lodestars, are laws of equality, unity, and time that imitates eternity. 'So terrestrial things are subject to celestial, and their time circuits join together in harmonious succession for a poem of the universe.'[55]

We have to remember the original premiss of power in number, for now Augustine unfolds the matter of power. He says, 'these numbers are pre-eminent by virtue of the beauty of ratio'.[56] The double meaning of *ratio* is nowhere stronger than here. First he emphasises the analogy to arithmetical ratio. In connection with corporeal things these superior numbers give numbers on one level power to alter those below. The explanation is that 'advancing-numbers' by moving over 'reacting-numbers', and 'reacting-numbers' over 'sounding' ones, alter them and produce sensible beauty. As for memory moving over all those below, it produces 'phantasias'.[57] The beauty of ratio in phantasias is admitted, but it carries dangers and enticements for the soul which thinks that it is exercising understanding. So, overarching the mathematical use of ratio is a philosophical use of *ratio*, reason, in which spiritual judgement delights. 'With a restored delight in reason's numbers, our whole life is turned to God, giving numbers of health to the body, not taking pleasure from it.'[58]

We may attempt an architectural appreciation of 'advancing' and 'reacting' numbers, 'sounding' number, and the power of ratio. The triforium came to have a decidedly aesthetic importance. The example in St Cross, Winchester, is a measured display of visually light interlaced arches (Figure 4.4). The later Beverley minster elevation excites the senses and memory with a complex play of number (Figure 4.5). Both use such devices as Augustine defined to progress and retrogress, to advance and retreat in depth and height, to delight the mind with 'mathematical' ratio and 'philosophical' ratio. In Beverley minster 'phantasia' evokes admiration—even at the risk of distraction.

Lastly here, in Chapter 12, the disciple is to consider reflectively that memory also has *spiritual* movements in the mind's search for equality. This is 'nowhere in the spans of places and times'; not 'in the forms of bodies'; not 'by pure experiment; nor in intervals of times'. The master points to rhythmical and metrical *art*. It uses—possesses, he says—numbers which verses are made of. The verses pass away, even from memory; the

Figure 4.4 Winchester, England. Hospital chapel of St Cross. A late Romanesque cruciform church. North elevation of chancel. Begun 1160.

numbers remain, unchangeable in their equality, in fact eternal. That is what music as an art is about when the highest working of reason seeks the source and eternal order in God. Two points provide substantiation in concrete experience: that the verses are made by an artist whose art is inseparable from some affection of his mind; and that one who is unskilled (not an artist) can assay to understand, whereupon reason's numbers, impressed on his mind by art, engender affection.[59] The artist will be making the work according to the ratio of his art, because of the affection of his mind; and the auditor, responding of his own accord, will be moved in the affection of his mind by the ratio of the art. The connection between the artificer and the artefact is explicit: it is the ratio of the art working on the level of affection. Although Augustine expressly goes beyond art in order to explore the spiritual, the example he takes of rhythmical and metrical art models for all arts—including architecture—the 'spiritual' power of number.

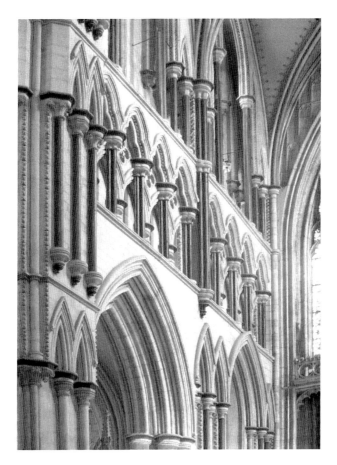

Figure 4.5 Beverley, England. Minster church of St John Evangelist. North elevation of choir. East end and transepts. Building begun *c*. 1220.

Augustine's theory of music persisted even in late medieval thinking. Bonaventure, for instance, asserted that its seven kinds of number are like steps by which one ascends 'from sensible things to the Maker of all things', and thence by ordered descent 'to the numerical forms of those things made by art'.[60] The *Mirror of Music* of Jacques de Liège (*c*. 1290), called by Kay Slocum 'the largest surviving medieval treatise on music', had its sources in Pythagoras, Pseudo-Dionysius, Augustine and Boethius.[61] She considers that Jacques was in the mainstream of music theory up to the early fourteenth century. Jacques had a philosophical and theological basis for his use of mathematics and number theory, much as we have been studying in early sources. Slocum shows his attention to number symbolism, but how far the music was intended to transmit such meaning is nevertheless difficult to clearly tell from music, and a like difficulty is in architecture. Greater tropes and greater power are in the abstraction of forms and the composition of forms, working at the limit of the maker's conscious intention and invention.

Slocum describes in some detail Jacques de Liège's theological awareness and motivation, concluding: 'The *Mirror* was an attempt at demonstrating the ways in which music, properly understood, should reflect the Divine Exemplar'.[62] It was Jacques' purpose that music in the church should reflect the eternal world in the sensible. So to compose according to principles such as ratio, consonance and proportion, the *musicus* needed 'the ability to judge intervals, modes, rhythms, and melodies according to a true understanding of the numerical properties of music'.[63] The fact that musical intervals are numerical ratios had led to aesthetic theory based on number. It was susceptible to judgement; and speculative reason was confirmed by empirical evidence. In this way praxis made actual connections between intellectual and sensuous apprehension of a kind we have not so far seen. Qualitative judgements as to unity, concord, perfection, could be made. Five intervals are found in the ratios of the first four numbers.[64] These are consonances, and the first three, being simply related to unity, were called multiples. Unison, 1:1, expressed such a unity as could hardly be thought of as a ratio, just as 'one' in arithmetic could hardly be called a number. Nevertheless Jacques included and stressed unison as the first consonance, basis of true equality.[65] The more closely ratios relate to unison, the more 'equality' and harmony is in the consonance. Such intervals, along with others judged to be dissonances, display an inner hierarchy; and Slocum asserts, 'this hierarchy had a philosophical dimension'.[66]

Regarding the *material* of sound, it is easy to see that compositions are made with pitch and harmony, and time and metre; that is, 'height' (altitude) and 'length' (amplitude). This is the two-dimensional make-up of music, in score as in sound.[67] Regarding musical *form*, composition unites consonant modal ratios in a time continuum. It has regard for time in proper metre and rhythm. In rhythm, *tempus perfectum* was based on the ternary numbers system (triples), which to Jacques showed the perfection of the Trinity in unity. *Tempus imperfectum* was based on division into two equal parts, giving duple metre which always, to infinity, is divisible and not reducible to unity, and the duality is always imperfect in relation to trinity. Yet more comprehensively, perfection in things is as form is actualised and is simple. Reduction to formal clarity brings the subject closer to the irreducible reality and idea.

> The arrangement of simplicity of form and of greater and greater actuality, is seen reduced to the order of perfection which is taken from the form. For anything which from part of a form tends to the more simple is by this tending to the actual and more perfect.[68]

Musical composition thus uses reduction to eliminate everything that cannot be turned to the particular musical idea. The particular idea is judged in its form and order, its structure; and the clearer the reduction the more acute a judgement will be.

Instruction: the quadrivium 131

Figure 4.6 Mantes, France. Cathedral church of Notre-Dame. East hemicycle from the choir. The church has no transepts. 1170–1230.

Such analysis can safely be applied to medieval church architecture. Extending the musical reference, the formal medium of the two dimensions, pitch and time, apply where altitude and amplitude are patterned, producing such visual harmony and metre as in Mantes cathedral (Figure 4.6). Here the power of reduction to formal clarity of the structure, to the whole unified intention, to precise pattern, dispensing with embellishment yet achieving delicacy, has been exercised on both the intellectual and sensuous levels. The following observations by Theodore Karp on music could have been made equally on architecture:

132 *Instruction: the quadrivium*

> [The patterns] furnish the strongest examples of the interpenetration of speculative thinking and artistic creativity during the High and late Middle Ages. [...] It is not necessary to know musical notation in order to verify [this] since it is possible merely to compare the visual patterns formed by the notation in order to ascertain the regularity. [...]
>
> Passages such as these reflect especially the growing desire for balance and symmetry, which are artistic values and not merely servants of number speculation. The balance and symmetry are clearly perceivable by the senses. But interest in rhythmic formulae increased steadily and gradually took on compositional values that appealed more and more to the mind and that were less readily perceptible by the senses.[69]

This appertains primarily to the mind of a maker, but would also be appreciable to participants or auditors.

In constructing an ascesis on contemplation, Richard of St-Victor shows how the soul advances through manifold and diverse affections. He describes it as the work of the divine Musician:

> Yet the Spirit of the Lord daily combines [the affections] little by little in His elect and skillfully forms them into one harmony and by the plucking of the instrument of His graces fits them together in a certain harmonious consonance like a learned harp player.[70]

He then marvels at the thought of the multitude of such souls all tuned by love to love with 'consonant concord'; concluding, 'That multiform grace of the divine Spirit does and sets in order all these things'.[71] At the end of the highest stage the state of spiritual harmony is attained. He draws the picture of Elisha the prophet to whom the external melody of a singer resonated with his memory and interior harmony, so causing his ascension.[72] An ecstasy catches up the mind. It is God's instruction. That is Richard's main point; yet the soul can prepare itself, become receptive to the divine music, by itself singing in his presence:

> So, because of such psalmody and spiritual harmony, the contemplative soul accustomed to spiritual contemplations begins [...] to suspend itself above the earth and all earthly things and to pass over completely to contemplation of celestial things by alienation of mind. Therefore, it is this, as we have said, that is effective for the renewing of the mind.[73]

Grover Zinn sees this as a commendation of liturgical chanting, for achieving spiritual harmony. 'In Richard's consciousness the paths of spiritual ascent and liturgical celebration cross in a new way.'[74]

Such theory and practice, theology and liturgy, indicates the heightened way they also crossed in the experiencing of architecture. This is to say that at highest levels of understanding the art of music was an interpreter;

with the architecture providing the setting—indeed it corresponded to and embodied the music. The participants in the Mass could see and read the score of the great building, the rhythmical elevation flowing from the west door to the retrochoir (Figure 5.8). The chant sounded through the arcades and storeys, each section of the Mass taking on aural correspondences with *loci* in its progress from the *Introit* to *Benedicamus Domino*: *Kyrie* in the nave, *Gloria* at the great crossing, *Gradual* at the ambo, *Alleluia* ascending from the choir, *Credo* before the throne, *Offertory* at the ascent, *Sanctus* in the sanctuary, *Agnus Dei* and *Communion* at the altar. The carrying of such music in the acoustics of the structure united the architecture and the liturgy in the judging mind. The progress of the soul fully involves the senses and the mind—both *ratio* and *intelligentia*. In music we have seen the connection between sensuous and intellectual apprehension. We have touched on aesthetics, and begun to explore the scope of judgement.

Geometry

The first three disciplines conceived the properties of number in this way: arithmetic generated one-dimensional linear abstractions; music composed in two-dimensional figures; geometry went further employing number as the basis of bodies in three dimensions. Like arithmetic and music it could be apprehended both mentally and sensibly. This seems straightforward theory which would relate to the forms of objects and arrangement of things. We can cite Hugh of St-Victor, who wrote: 'Geometry is the discipline treating immobile magnitude, and it is the contemplative delineation of forms, by which the limits of every object are shown'.[75] While the first clause (reiterating Boethius) sets the parameters, the second clause and the predicate is of great interest. The 'contemplative delineation of forms' implies a specific, and perhaps unusual, apprehension of the mind, apart from the eye, although visual sense brings objects to the mind's eye. Importantly, geometry was to instruct in the forms of things. We will treat it in this way.

An underlying idea of *form* which minds wished to apprehend is in Thomas's thought where he says, 'It is in accord with its form that a thing has being'.[76] Then, not only its existence but also its function follows the form:

> For, since everything acts in so far as it is actual [...], and since every being is actual through form, it is necessary for the operation of a thing to follow its form. Therefore if there are different forms, they must have different operations.[77]

In the modern epigram that 'form follows function' the form is that of the material object; but here the subject is the conceptual form as known in the mind. The function or functions will be foreseen and follow in the operation. But geometry is charged to perceive forms at the highest level.

134 *Instruction: the quadrivium*

For background we can start from Plato. In *Timaeus* he was quite pragmatic, teaching the elemental composition of things, and a mystical-symbolic purpose does not appear to have been his concern here. Indeed, what he called 'necessity' seems to amount to the pragmatism of the world of things. It is as the work of 'necessity' that the things that 'are becoming' (fire, earth, air and water) assume homogeneity, balance, proportion, measure, shape and number. Accordingly, after a description of primitive chaos, Plato ascribed to those four elemental 'solid bodies' definitive geometrical figures (tetrahedron, cube, octahedron and icosahedron) as the very atoms of their construction. A fifth, the ether, was necessary to make the cosmos. Its figure, the dodecahedron, approximates a spherical body, which contains all the others. Reducing the surfaces of solid bodies to the two basic constituent triangles (equilateral and isosceles), he postulated the derivation of the elements from these, appealing to 'likelihood and necessity'; adding that 'their more ultimate origins are known to god and to men whom god loves'.[78] In this rational organising scheme he enunciated the principle of union of two things by a third:

> It is not possible to combine two things properly without a third to act as a bond to hold them together. And the best bond is one that effects the closest unity between itself and the terms it is combining; and this is best done by a continued geometrical proportion.[79]

Germane to our subject we note that he says that by so coming into concord the universe has amity.[80] Plato's unity incidentally justifies the geometrical diagram produced in Chapter 2. Air and water he posited as the middle terms of solid geometry, proportioned to fire and earth, binding them together. Ordered to an eternal model their unity was 'geometrical'. His geometric images of bond and unity carry intimations of care, nurture, even love, for things brought into being. In such connections there was a kind of necessity like a law of love.

Martianus Capella began his allegory of the liberal arts with a hymn to the 'sacred principle of unity': 'You bind the warring seeds of the world with secret bonds and encourage the union of opposites by your sacred embrace'.[81] Where there is true order there will be unity. Regarding mathematical geometry a basic aspect evidently intrigued him—that geometry is well apprehended by sight, whereas arithmetic is accessed chiefly by intellect:

> [Geometry] is the linear and demonstrable knowledge drawn from this dust; begotten indeed from incorporealities, and fashioned into manifold perceptible shapes from a slight and scarcely comprehensible beginning, it is elevated even into the heavens.[82]

Martianus believed the range of Geometry included tracing generation from origin to end, and the coincidence of the visible and invisible, corporeal and incorporeal. The origin of a *demonstration* is a point, the beginning and

Figure 4.7 Soest, Germany. Collegiate church of St Patroclus. West tower. The transition from square tower to octagonal spire effectively uses planar and solid geometry. Corner turrets are as miniature towers. *c.* 1200.

begetter of knowledge. While the point, *punctum*, or mark, *signum* (*monad* in arithmetic, and *tone* in music) is unmeasurable, irreducible, it is identified in its *locus*. It may sometimes be the *focus* of the whole. Then the relation of the surface to the body of a solid object received his attention. Here the proximate beginning of a solid is the surface: 'Its extremities consist of surfaces, just as the extremities of surfaces consist of lines'.[83] In the tower of St Patroclus, Soest (Figure 4.7), we see points generating lines, lines defining surfaces, and surfaces bounding the body. The object is known by its surface. Martianus noted that the word for 'surface', *epiphaneia*, means 'a shining forth', or 'brightness'.[84] There is keen interest in being able to grasp the nature of this elusive boundary of a body. It is pertinent, for if that nature is not known aesthetic cognition is indeed superficial. Excepting transparent things, the physical vision is stopped at the *epiphaneia*, and to that boundary it draws the attention of the intellect which goes on to apprehend, if possible, the actual reality of the body. This definition of solid matter by visible surface was the body being geometrised in the medium of light. Taking place at the surface, the form, made intelligible by line, is joined with the sensuous. It sheds light on the medieval love of line and décor of surfaces—the making of epiphanies (Front Cover image; Figure 3.3).

The theme of geometry instructing the mind concerning the nature of things is treated by Augustine in *The Greatness of the Soul*. It connects things of material and spiritual orders, things as different as geometric bodies and the measure of the human soul.[85] He reasoned that the mind's eye mediates between the realities of soul and body by abstraction. And by abstraction bodies are reduced to geometrical diagrams, to assist the reasoning mind to apprehend the maker's intention. He instances seeing only length in the spider's thread even though it does have 'width and height'.[86] We noticed in arithmetic how Boethius appealed to truths of number which are obvious or lying just below the surface of ordinary recognition. We need to see where this procedure takes us.

Evaluating the first figures that can be made by straight lines, namely triangles and quadrilaterals, Augustine demonstrates that the equilateral triangle and the square are the most perfect, and the square more so than the equilateral triangle. The demonstration satisfies because one can see it with the mind's eye, and it concurs with natural judgement. Then he asks: 'Which figure has the more beautiful and striking proportions?'[87] This evaluation is a necessary part of the logical process. The answer lies in the greater 'equality' of parts that inheres in the square. It is demonstrated correctly, but, again, the equality has to be 'seen'. Of even greater perfection is the figure of the circle. Now he uses 'indivisibility' as the criterion of value, to show that just as a line (length) is less divisible than a figure (length and width), so a point, being absolutely indivisible, is the most excellent. The centre point regulates the circle's symmetry such as in rose and wheel windows. *Integritatem* in centred figures is patent, and geometrical perfection is never compromised in those architectural features.

Leaving figures, the third dimension, 'height', added to the others, makes bodies—corporeal entities which can be 'seen with the eyes of the body, in accordance with certain marvelous affinity of natures'.[88] But by the factor of height a body is constituted in a way that confers another power on the beholder to grasp it: 'I mean the dimension which makes it possible for the interior of a body to be an object of thought, or, if the body is transparent as glass, the object of sense perception'.[89] This is the power of thought concerning the abstract form of a material object. It is in the geometry of such a clear form of a French chevet as of St-Rémi abbey, or Le Mans cathedral (Figure 4.8). It is in the articulated logic of vaulting such as in the Church of St Dorothy, Wrocław (Figure 4.11). The *geometry* of line and figure is, strictly speaking, seen by the *mind's* eye alone, by the soul through its affinity with incorporealities. If skilful geometry and directed reason can

Figure 4.8 Le Mans, France. Cathedral church of St-Julien. East chevet. Note the dividing of each radiating buttress into two. Second half of the thirteenth century.

integrate physical dimensions with theocentric intention an extraordinary power may distinguish the architecture.

Geometry connected measures and forms; now attention to causal and contextual aspects seems necessary. In the first part of *Timaeus* Plato described the universe, model and copy, as the work of *reason*. He mentioned the good of divine boons and what intelligence has made of them, such as the invention of number, the notion of time, the principles of order and harmony. But the second part reckons with the power of *necessity*, the 'indeterminate cause', the irrational element, anomalous chaos. 'It was by subordination of necessity to reasonable persuasion that the universe was originally constituted as it is.'[90] So to the model and copy, Plato added an entity to accommodate the indeterminate cause influencing things which are 'coming to be'. Showing its character by calling it *receptacle*, and *winnowing basket*, he then named it *space*. In it and by it everything is accommodated and organised. After describing it to some degree, he admitted rational and practical objections:

138 Instruction: *the quadrivium*

> Space which is eternal and indestructible, which provides a position for everything that comes to be, and which is apprehended without the senses by a sort of spurious reasoning and is so hard to believe in—we look at it indeed in a kind of dream and say that everything that exists must be somewhere and occupy some space, and that what is nowhere in heaven or earth is nothing at all.[91]

Similar difficulties seem inherent in what we call 'architectural space'. The senses fail to find any information about it. How can one think and reason about 'space' if it is defined solely by reference to solid things? Plato concentrated on its function—as receptacle, nurse, mother (that in which things 'become'), winnowing basket; each is an image providing a position, a place, for everything. Space is occupied by things and exists for their sake.[92] There is a wide difference between Platonic and modern concepts of space. Modern theory has been enamoured with its concept of space, the seeds of which were sown in the Renaissance discoveries of pictorial and plastic space. But in medieval art and architecture visual qualities of *things* receive endless attention, and the focus is in the place where things have meaning, the medium in which they are organised. If we mention space it is safer to think of it as having this function. In considering the computus and the use of memory, we noted the functions of locational place. It was that that gave it credibility. Space was not void or something residual. If the term was used it referred to the three-dimensionality of place.[93] Accordingly significance accrues to every part, all comprise a whole, and all objects are integral with the architecture even by simple association.

Thomas Bradwardine (c. 1290–1349), in a scientific-philosophical treatise, *Speculative Geometry* (c. 1325–35), discussed the 'filling of place in planes', and the 'filling of place in solids'. Such is the province of three-dimensional geometry: 'To fill place [*replere locum*] is to take up one whole corporeal space [*spatium corporale*] that surrounds a point [*punctum*] at which three lines mutually intersect at right angles'.[94] Recognising the attention given to place may help us to perceive geometrical forms more as medieval architects saw them, better to grasp architectural definitions. One aspect is that the intrinsic importance of all *things*, in due order and plenary power, rendered objective space unimportant but required right geometrical arrangement and shaping of places for them to cohere and be coherent. An example is the great porch of Peterborough cathedral (Figure 3.13). The whole intention of the architecture, and the extraordinary transition from outside to inside, is in the composing geometry. Another percept is that place, exterior or interior, takes its identity and power most directly from 'the surface' of adjacent or most proximate parts of the surrounding fabric, this comprising the geometrical *locus*. Through familiarity it is easily taken for granted. Thus the apse and semi-dome of San Miniato, Florence, make the place for the altar, the focus being intensified by the semi-dome presenting the eternal Christ, the surface being an *epipheneia* indeed (Figure 5.2).

A geometry of place challenges the assumption that modern theory of architectural space can provide principles of appraisal of medieval churches. Our usual concepts cannot be a basis for inferences or inductive argument as to the designers' insights and intentions. The overarching necessity for order in all things was seen as flowing from their form and mode; but if we appraise this order according to post-medieval notions of physical space we find that properties and accidents, agent actions, operations, gradations, proportion, composition, cannot be predicated of *space* as they are of corporeal things, and of place.

Work by historians, such as Charles Radding and William Clark, and Stephen Croddy, perpetuates a doctrine that shaping of 'space' was a fundamental concern and technique in medieval architecture. In mid-twentieth-century studies Otto von Simson, in defining an aesthetic of light and structure, managed without invoking it; but Paul Frankl espoused a 'geometry of aesthetics' in line with the then rising emphasis on space in architectural theory. Comparing architecture and theology in parallel strands of learning and design disciplines, and at the level of cognitive processes, Radding and Clark assume, without pertinent deduction, that Gothic designers must have been somehow shaping space consciously and conceptually:

> Simply stated, the shift is away from thinking of design in terms of flat, undifferentiated planes of walls and ceilings toward discovering means of delineating the spatial units and volumes contained within buildings; indeed, it hardly overstates things to say that the articulation of spatial volumes was central to the architecture of the late eleventh and early twelfth centuries.[95]

They rightly point out the dubious value of style classifications, but posit instead a conscious spatial concept: 'Cutting across this enormous diversity of forms, however, is the modular conception of space developed in the first half of the eleventh century'.[96] But the attributed thinking and discovering is evidently inductive and not supported; nor is there warrant for the aesthetic and formal interpretations. Rather, the evidence is that things and places and functions were what mattered—the nature of the world, the human situation, physical and spiritual acts.

Croddy also imposes on the architecture notions of space: 'A building's spatial form is an abstraction analogous to the abstract forms of geometry'.[97] At first he has regard for building elements; but he goes on to posit that the abstraction of geometric shapes was the distinguishing preoccupation of Romanesque designers, and the modelling of space of Gothic designers who, 'created elements which encourage a sense of spatial flow while simultaneously emphasising the modelling capacities of light [. . .]. The difference in the components employed resulted in a difference in the manner in which space was structured'.[98] Whether a sense of spatial flow was of interest to medieval minds, or whether a structuring of space (by

140 *Instruction: the quadrivium*

flying buttresses, traceries, rib vaulting, or such elements) was conceived, is not demonstrated. Modern analyses of formal spatial qualities or of stylistic characteristics of medieval churches do not seem to connect to realities or ideas or theological meanings that engaged the makers' minds.

Search for meaning in medieval churches has sometimes focussed on 'sacred geometry', or 'platonic geometry'. Derivations from Classical sources made by Christian patristic writers and their successors seem to promise insights into meaning in the architecture. Nigel Hiscock supports this against a simply utilitarian geometry: 'Was geometry employed simply as a practical expedient for setting out work, as numerous studies have suggested? Or did its use also embrace the expression of the beliefs the architecture was erected to proclaim?'[99] With this object he studies symbolic and mystical applications of geometry.[100] Caution is, of course, necessary in any inductive approach. It is salutary to heed the general scope and role of geometry in the quadrivium. If it was reckoned that by geometry is the actualisation of form, that would be more primary than use in symbols. Beside which, symbolism in architecture ought not be attributed narrowly to geometrical constructions.

The great importance of physical shape in the structure of Gothic churches is cogently explained by Jacques Heyman. Geometry had key practical applications. The first concern had to be stability. He shows that work which has correct proportions (according to rules discovered empirically) will be stable 'at once, and ever after'. 'It is the shape of the structure that governs its stability.'[101] In the practical applications of setting-out, squaring, sizing and proportioning, there was a ruling power of knowledge, indispensable in the design and building process. Reducing matter to form, body to integumentum, and building to mathematical model, was a ruling passion in the mind. The great chevets of French cathedrals, such as Le Mans and Beauvais, show such geometry clearly and convincingly by their lasting performance (Figure 4.8). They show the reduction and rationalisation of the material to precisely what is required for the purpose, the purpose being grasped in the interior, the light and glory of the sacred place oblivious of the structure.

To focus on geometry's workings consider the setting out of the plan of a church. Assuming it was to be cruciform, Vitruvian principles of arrangement, eurythmy and symmetry as well as propriety (reflecting the purpose of the building) would generate the plan with greatest power where the transepts cross the longitudinal body.[102] Symmetry and economy would recommend that the crossing be a square. Boethius' principle of form might also operate: 'From squares and from figures longer by one side [rectangles] the idea of every form takes its being'.[103] From the Gothic period the sketchbook of Villard de Honnecourt (*c.* 1230) has survived and has been the subject of intense interpretation. In von Simson's view, 'he composed his model book in order to set forth what he considered the principles that underlie all artistic composition [. . .]. These principles are geometrical'.[104]

Yet arguably it is an eclectic memorandum of items, ideas and useful techniques, not explicitly demonstrating or systematically developing principles. One series of drawings is simply annotated: 'Here begins the method of representation as taught by the art of geometry, to facilitate work'.[105] Wayne Ewing is surely correct:

> When Villard speaks of 'the method of drawing as taught by the art of geometry' he indicates that the purpose of his labors in the Sketchbook is to make the work of his colleagues less difficult. This is not so much a theory, as a practical guide to drawing with the aid of plane figures. In fact it is not a theory at all.[106]

Yet in his influential work von Simson claimed that Villard,

> expounds not only the geometrical canons of Gothic architecture but also the Augustinian aesthetics of 'musical' proportions [...]. He is our earliest theoretical witness to the proportion 'according to true measure'; even more interesting, however, is one of his designs representing the ground plan of a Cistercian church drawn *ad quadratum*, i.e., the square bay of the side aisles is the basic unit or module from which all proportions of the plan are derived.[107]

While, in this diagram, the whole plan is based on squares, it is hard to see why, or even how, an architect would be concerned primarily with the size of the side aisles.[108] It is more logical and important to start with the square crossing, its ratio, magnitude and location, and so generate the four arms, the bay dimensions and the side aisles. In the crossing, of all places, the geometry must be unequivocal and stable. Here the whole form is focussed, here the very axes of the church are most intelligible.[109] A parallel to such things revolving in the mind of the architect, is in Hugh of St-Victor's careful, explicit procedure for beginning his drawing of the Ark with the square cubit in the centre, at the intersection of the axes of length, width and height.[110] Identifying the centre and heart of the ark he understood the geometry of generation. A medieval architect surely knew, with the form in his mind, that the geometry of divine domination of the heart was the place to begin.

In 1401, after a decade of debate over the setting-out geometry for the integrity and stability of Milan cathedral, the original concept of the Milanese workshop masters had to be reiterated. The crossing was to be marked by a great tower, with towers at its four corners (Figure 4.9). The anagogical plan was an abstract diagram of the conventional symbolic portrayal of the Lord in glory and the Tetramorph (Figure 5.10). This meaning was deemed to be the very rationale of the tower. The corner towers were conceived thus:

142 *Instruction: the quadrivium*

In the first place, to integrate aforesaid church and transept so that they corresponded to a rectangle according to the demands of geometry, but beyond this, for the strength and beauty of the crossing-tower. To be sure, as if a model for this, the Lord God is seated in Paradise in the center of the throne, and around the throne are the four Evangelists according to the Apocalypse, and these are the reasons why [the towers] were begun.[111]

Typically the crossing generates and marks the principal vertical axis. In the Milan evidence the design was to be an integration of earthly and heavenly geometry on three levels—practical, formal and representational. It is illustrated in many churches where, in the geometry of the crossing, symmetry is uncompromised, clarity is manifest and theocentric meaning is intensified. In geometry was a capacity to make the places intelligible, the form actual, and to mark spiritual connections.

Figure 4.9 Milan, Italy. Cathedral church of Santa Maria Maggiore. Nave roof. Central crossing tower on right, with one of four corner stair turrets. 1403–90.

Astronomy

The prominence of the theocentric world-view in the culture of the Middle Ages has been considered in various contexts. It is certainly important in the discipline of Astronomy.[112] The focus turns to the notion of hierarchy, to connections between earthly and heavenly reality, and mental and spiritual orientation. Early Christian neo-platonism established the nine angelic orders. The first seven related the planetary heavens to seven angelic orders usually thus: the Moon, Mercury and Venus are Angels, Archangels and Principalities; the Sun, Mars, Jupiter and Saturn are Powers, Virtues, Dominations and Thrones. The eighth and ninth heavens, the Fixed Stars and Primum Mobile, are the Cherubim and Seraphim.

In cosmology, the Moon, Mercury and Venus were correlated with the disciplines of the Trivium. Next, ascribed to the Sun was the generating power of number in Arithmetic; to Mars the judgement of multitude and motion producing Music; to Jupiter the pragmatism of stable magnitude in Geometry. Now in Saturn the 'thrones' of the steadfast yet perpetually moving cosmos preside over Astronomy, uplifting all the arts in noetic quest of the Deity. In Greek cosmology and through the Middle Ages it was reckoned that the cone of Earth's shadow reached to Venus. Thus the Trivium studies were subject to earthly limitations, whereas a person pursuing the Quadrivium curriculum was released to unlimited views of the nature of the universe.

Hugh of St-Victor in *The Vanity of the World*, and Dante in *Paradiso*, pictured their protagonists rising through the heavens, under tutelage of their guides, looking down and seeing the Earth, a paltry semblance; 'the little threshing-floor, that makes us so fierce'.[113] The most fierce deed, of cosmological impact, was the crucifixion of incarnate Love.

Pseudo-Dionysius divided the angelic orders into three triads, placing the Thrones in the highest hierarchy, below Cherubim and Seraphim.[114] By metonymy this collective title of heavenly beings, *thrones*, designates them a seat and sovereignty of the deity, exalted places signifying the immanent presence of God:

> The name of the most glorious and exalted Thrones denotes that which is exempt from and untainted by any base and earthly thing, and the supermundane ascent up the steep. For these have no part in that which is lowest, but dwell in fullest power [...] and receive the Divine Immanence above all passion and matter, and manifest God, being attentively open to divine participations.[115]

In *The Ecclesiastical Hierarchy* (*De divina hierarchia*), Pseudo-Dionysius transposed the idea of the heavenly hierarchy to the hierarchs in the Church. In so doing he meant to provide human nature a means of being lifted up to see that superior hierarchy which 'belongs to the domain of the conceptual and is something out of this world'.[116] This is, he says, by way of perceptible

144 Instruction: *the quadrivium*

images which the hierarchy itself could supply. Emulating this explicit transposition, there is logically nothing to preclude another transposition, from the ecclesiastical to an architectural hierarchy. This also would be modelled on the heavenly. The first transposition shows the mode of thought which could see hierarchies in everything; as Pseudo-Dionysius explicitly says, 'that hierarchy and *every hierarchy* [. . .] has one and the same power throughout all its hierarchical endeavor, namely the hierarch himself'.[117] At the end of the same passage he refers to 'Jesus, the source and perfection of every hierarchy'. The universe is Christocentric. So, as the cosmos and as the Church, the form of a great church is Christocentric. As the Thrones, so the *Cathedra*, literally the seat in the sanctuary—rising to the actual in heaven.

Saturn, the highest planet, was the beginning of the ascent to the Fixed Stars, where the cherubim were images particularly of divine wisdom. Above them the Primum Mobile gave measurement and movement to everything; here the seraphim were images of divine love. Astronomy which deals with 'moveable magnitude' derived its acuity and knowledge from those superior images. Above all was the Empyrean, the measureless and timeless place of bliss. Yet that was not all that could be said, and the physical order was still a complication.

Thomas argued for the Empyrean's existence from the state of glory which is both spiritual *and* corporeal: the glory must be in some *body* incorruptible and of lucid brilliance—'a physical place is assigned to contemplation, not on the basis of necessity, but of appropriateness, matching an outer clarity to the clarity within'.[118] Thomas said it could indeed be called place, *locus*, not because of esoteric isolation, but as appropriate to the dual glory in the encompassing hierarchy. In dichotomies such as corporeal-spiritual the whole person searches for *appropriate* connections. The connection significantly is in a place, and the contemplation knows two-fold clarity. It does not seem to press the insight too far to suppose the great clarity of a cathedral's interior was matching the inner clarity of the oblates (Figure 4.11). In the north transept rose window of Sens cathedral the metaphysical order is apparent and explicitly figured entirely as a display of angels focussed on God. In the range of vertical windows below the rose earthly holy scenes are displayed; and by the window's form they are integrated with the rose. Vertical and rotational movement is embodied in an image of corporeal and spiritual worlds connected. The realisation of clarity and glory of a physical place is when it is matched to spiritual clarity and glory. Surely in the cathedral church of Metz is the intent that the interior be full of light. So to deal with the bodily material, the stone is reduced, refined and refigured. The brilliant windows are partly foiled by traceries which fracture and recombine the light in patterns of refulgence (Figure 4.10).

In studying phenomena of magnitude and motion medieval scientists and theologians considered the principle that whatever undergoes movement is moved by another. If the perceived regulation of the movements of the heavenly spheres was hierarchical, it depended ultimately upon an

Figure 4.10 Metz, France. Cathedral church of St-Étienne. Choir triforium with inner traceries as a foil to outer window tracery. End of the fourteenth century.

'unmoved Mover'. So too astronomy taught appropriate connectedness: the lower to the higher and highest; even the elements of earthly, corruptible matter to the incorruptible fifth element, ether; and all to the divine Being. Further, on the sense of place, William Wallace, noting that the universe was regarded as a plenum, with no empty space, writes:

> The motion of bodies was reckoned not according to their traversal of space, but rather according to their change of place. Place itself was defined, following Aristotle, as the first immobile surface of the circumambient medium. A body changes its place by taking up a new position, or location in place, which is designated by the Latin term *ubi*. Apart from the simple location in place, it is also possible to specify the arrangement of the parts of a body with respect to place; this further specification gives rise to the category of situation, in Latin, *situs*.[119]

Wallace is stating the significance of *ubi* and *situs* in astronomy; but, taking the macrocosm as prototype of the microcosm, when the 'body' is earthly such percepts impinge on human experience in ways so intricate they can hardly be isolated. Given hierarchical connectedness, if these definitions apply to the experiencing of a building it becomes a model of the cosmos, and we can say two things. First: every place is a significant 'where' (*ubi*), because every movement incurs a change in dynamic relation to the building, not in vacant space. Second: a participant is incorporated into the place, related 'thus' (*situs*) to the building; one has an orientation, a posture, a gesture, in some sort of response to or experience of the place. Such focus of subconscious movement in devotions and ritual linked a person experientially to the universe, and to transcendent Love which moves all. Dante wrote of the Primum Mobile, 'This heaven has no other *where* but the Divine Mind, in which is kindled the love that turns it and the virtue which it rains down'.[120]

Astronomy provided the big-picture of all particular participations. Plato said that the father of the universe, wishing to make it a likeness of eternity, gave it 'an ever-flowing likeness moving according to number—that to which we have given the name Time'.[121] He also posited that the heavenly bodies were endowed with intelligence, 'set in the intelligence of the supreme to keep company with it'.[122] The cosmos reflected a divine mind with which its movements conformed. A powerful reality in astronomy is relativity of size, that is, scale. Everything mortals can have knowledge of is in the macrocosm and measured by it. It was not only organisational, it was also deemed beautiful, with elemental brightness, perfection of shape and noble purpose, displayed by each heavenly body. Each personified in classical cosmology as gods, they occupied a temple which is the universe. Interestingly, the macrocosm was conceptually bounded, contained by a surface. Plato's *Phaedrus* has the picture of the immortals standing on the outer surface of the universe:

> When they reach the summit of the arch, [they] go outside the vault and stand upon the back of the universe; standing there they are carried round by its revolution while they contemplate what lies outside the heavens.[123]

It is a powerful image of contemplation, from the vantage of all knowable experience, endeavouring to comprehend the incomprehensible. 'So the mind of a god, sustained as it is by pure intelligence and knowledge [. . .] is satisfied at last with the vision of reality.'[124] It is a matter for the mind. It also opens one to possession by love.[125]

The steps of instruction followed in the quadrivium are meant to conduct one to metaphysical realities, all the intelligibles. In Martianus Capella's allegory, Philology, having been immortalised so that she could marry the god Mercury, ascends to the place of the gods where the nuptials are to take place. The fitness of the match she had ascertained by study of numerology, and the ascent was marked by musical tones, completed as an octave of perfect harmony. Rising above the planets, the zodiac and Milky Way, she stood on the outer surface and periphery of heaven. Here again is the admission of some deeper dimension *outside* the boundary of the universe.

> [Philology] was aware that the god who was the father of such a work and so great a system had withdrawn even from the very acquaintance of the gods, for she knew that he had passed beyond the felicity that is itself beyond this world, and he rejoiced in an empyrean realm of pure understanding. On her knees beside the wall of the outer periphery, concentrating the whole attention of her mind, she prayed long in silence, [...] she paid reverence to [...] the entire universe contained by the depth of the infinite Father.[126]

It is a strong trope: the boundary of the universe is the extreme *locus* for created beings and intelligence. The question forms, what would one *do* or *say* there? The allegory poignantly describes Philology's situation (*situs*). One may find this trope in a cathedral. It was a characteristic achievement of Gothic churches. If the soul rises up to the height of the heavenly vault, may it pass right through the *integumentum* and on the periphery perceive that the world lies in the bosom of the Father? For a learnéd medieval mind acquainted with such metaphysics the imagination would be matched with extraordinary facility—experienced, for instance, in the ability to go out on the top of many of the towers, or perambulate on the roof of Milan cathedral's nave (Figure 4.9). Or, in the church of St Dorothy, Wrocław, if drawn into the intense light in the sanctuary, in the ultimate degree of *dignitatem* of the Holy of Holies—is anything really there? Is this the glory of the Lord? (Figure 4.11). This, in all churches, was the transcendence. When Philology turned toward the boundary of the cosmos the architecture that embellished it is described:

> There was the abode of Jove, which, astonishing in size, encompassed the periphery of the universe [...]. Moreover, it shone so brightly that one would think it made of silver. There glowed refulgent walls and a white-edged roof, and Jupiter was now sitting there with Juno and all the gods.[127]

There is a tradition of describing the universe and its parts under the metaphor of a building. What the archangel Uriel is claimed to have revealed to the patriarch Enoch, who was translated to heaven without seeing death, was such a vision. The Maccabean pseudonymous 'Enoch' (before 110BC) wrote in 'The Book of Astronomy':

> I saw six portals in which the sun rises, and six portals in which the sun sets: and the moon rises and sets in these portals, and the leaders of the stars and those whom they lead: six in the east and six in the west, and all following each other in accurately corresponding order: also many windows to the right and left of these portals.[128]

In a most useful study of Philo of Alexandria (*c.* 25BC–*c.* 45AD) Robert Jan van Pelt calls Philo's speculations that the ancient Jewish tabernacle

148 *Instruction: the quadrivium*

Figure 4.11 Wrocław, Poland. Church of SS. Dorothy, Stanislaus and Wenceslaus. The nave of the hall church. The brilliance of the sanctuary is from full-height apsidal windows. Begun 1351.

and temple signified the cosmic building, 'the first epistemological use of architecture'.[129] If so, it was a very influential concept; and by a double transfer of meaning it made a sacred building both a microcosm reflecting the macrocosm of the universe, and a macrocosm in relation to man's soul. Drawing to a conclusion, van Pelt writes:

> Because it legitimised architecture without constricting it, the concept of the cosmic tabernacle was a primary factor in the unique development of Christian church architecture. [...] Translating the archaic notion of the 'world building' into the abstract coordinates of an intellectual model, Philo laid the foundations of a religious architecture true to the spiritual conception of the temple taught by Christian theologians as well as the traditional motive of the cosmic temple.[130]

Instruction: *the quadrivium* 149

Figure 4.12 Laon, France. Cathedral church of Notre-Dame. West front. Two similar towers (not visible) are at the transepts. Completed scheme would have had seven towers. Built 1190–1205.

The multivalency of the model is apparent. Philo showed how the whole Judaic high-priestly vestment was a cosmic model, designed to exhibit God's wisdom. He saw in the breastplate, with its twelve gems, the Zodiac signifying universal order: 'Heaven and its contents are all framed and ordered on rational principles and proportions, for nothing there is irrational'.[131] These ancient sources show syntheses of cosmology, theology and architecture.

Under the trope of ordered magnitude in the quadrivium great churches can be characterised as architecture embodying knowledge by minds amazed by the infinite. A sense of the cosmos beyond the bodies of geometry, and of the magnitude of the cosmos of which a church was a part, is conveyed by Laon cathedral's towers where transcendence is in the scale and multiplicity of ascending aedicules (Figure 4.12). Then the mind is baffled by the feat of making it. Contemplation of the cosmos leads to the question, How was it made?

Around 1150 Bernardus Silvestris wrote *Cosmographia*, an allegory in two books. In the *Megacosmos*, Nature marshals primal matter, separates the four elements, sets the angelicals in nine orders, arranges the planets, and determines their movements. In the *Microcosmos*, Man is created through Nature and Urania (queen of the stars), by the instrumentality of Physis (natural science) and her daughters, Theory and Practice—that is, three kinds of speculative knowledge. Making Man, the microcosm, was enormously difficult. Physis re-examined the material she was using. She had to separate the elements and re-mingle them according to the design of the Creator, working with utmost care to respect their true nature. She remembered how the elements related to one another. She set the powers in balance, combined the parts, shaped them, and found that coherence duly appeared, until the fullness constituted the body:

> She gave a rounded shape to the head, which occupied the chief position, following the example of the firmament and the sphere of the heavens. She raised the head to the position of a temple or capitol for the body as a whole, making it stand out toward the heavens; for it was fitting that she so exalt the region of the head, where the divine quality of pure reason was to dwell.[132]

So Physis and her daughters made the microcosm with three principal parts: head, breast and loins—described as 'the three foundations of its life'. The allegory is very much about instrumentality, the speculation and reach of Astronomy even in the creative design process.

Henry of Avranches, surveying the whole of Lincoln cathedral, interpreted its three building elements similarly; not to be esoteric but to make plain the essential hierarchy of the earthly-heavenly church:

> Of the parts of the whole cathedral: The foundation is the body, the wall is the man, the roof is the spirit: the division of the church is thus threefold. The body has as its portion earth, the man has the clouds, the spirit has the stars.[133]

The human body was a metaphor for the church, and the integral harmony and interdependence of its parts is not to be missed. Here the church, under that figure, was connected to the universe, and as a mirror it reflected the cosmos; the whole interior gives a sense of this (Figure 5.8). The constructive process itself could draw on the concept of creation found in astronomy. In it the rationale of the cosmic context was working, and the numinous mode of love.

Empedocles (*c.* 440BC) was perhaps the first to posit the differentiation of matter into the four elements, which were able to be combined in many ways and varying proportions, as we have seen. The motive causes, however, he characterised as love and strife running ontologically through all things. William Guthrie comments:

They appear as natural forces exercising a purely physical attraction and repulsion. Strife, by whose influence each element tends to dissociate itself from the others, is at the same time a tendency of like to like, whereby every particle seeks to attach itself to others of the *same* element. Love is the force which mingles one element with *another* to create composite creatures. [...] When Love is supreme, the elements are fused together in a mass. When Strife has the victory, they exist in separate concentric layers—for the whole is conceived as spherical—with earth at the centre and fire at the circumference.[134]

Aristotle refuted this in *Metaphysics*; and Thomas commented, 'But as to the reason why this alternation takes place, so that at one time hate predominates and at another time love, [Empedocles] said nothing more than that it was naturally disposed to be so'.[135] Sayers' construction is that the general state was that 'the universe was held together in tension by discord among the elements; but that from time to time the motions of the heavens brought about a state of harmony (love)'.[136] Dante, employing Empedocles' theory, pictured Hell itself jeopardised by the harrowing by Christ:

> [...] the Universe, I thought,
> was thrilled with love, whereby there are who say
> The world was many a time to chaos brought.[137]

Such a mighty universal flux of love would signify the work of necessity being naturally, even consciously, subject to supra-natural fiat (as indeed in the coming of Christ). Everywhere the operation of love is to mingle diverse things to create composites; fusing them to invent coherent structures.

Augustine alluded to pre-Christian speculative philosophy when he took a lesson for humans from the composition of things and their capacities for love, using a metonymical formulation of earth, water, air and fire:

> If we were stones or waves or wind or flames or anything of that kind, we should, indeed, be without both sensation and life, but we should still not lack a kind of desire for our own proper place and order. For the weight of bodies is, as it were, their love, whether they are carried downwards by gravity or upwards by their lightness. For the body is carried by its weight wherever it is carried, just as the soul is carried by its love.[138]

That, in *City of God*, reminds us of the association, without symbolism, of magnitude and movement and the spiritual virtue of love in *Confessions*: 'A body inclines by its own weight towards the place that is fitting for it. [...] In my case, love is the weight by which I act'.[139] Love can hardly be radically involved in the making process and not be the motivation.

A number of links between architecture and love for God have been seen. They are via instruction and knowledge in matters pertinent to architecture being learned by the wholly attentive mind. Also, in astronomy the role of contemplation has been evident. Dante the poet organised *Paradiso* on the cosmology of the ten heavens. He has himself as protagonist growing in understanding through the seven planets (the trivium and quadrivium) until in the seventh he joins the contemplatives. Here the poet has the conventional figure of the ladder of contemplation, but it does not represent the mystical ascent; rather, the scaling of the heavens by the understanding, the intellect impelled by love. In the divine injunction, 'love the Lord your God with all your mind', the word is *dianoia*, literally 'a thinking through', or 'thinking over', 'a meditation', or 'deep thought'.[140]

The most essential feature of the quadrivium curriculum is surely the place given to the intellect, the disciplined, reasoning mind—always directed by love. Arithmetic trained the mind to perceive abstract principles in the patterns and relations of things, at conscious and subconscious levels of intelligibility. Music sharpened aesthetic perception and powers of noetic judgement, connecting sensuous and intellectual apprehension. Geometry equipped the visualising mind to define formal entities and configure bodies, aiming at useful applications. Astronomy advanced the understanding of hierarchy and movement, through perspective and contemplation conceiving the great orders of reality and divinity.

The quadrivium, then, had an unmatched role in focussing and connecting knowledge—making all things accessible to the intellect and unifying everything. Following this purpose we have construed connections with architecture. Connections also have been discovered by drawing on contemporary theological and metaphysical sources where ideas are associated as explicitly as we may ever find. This is material for making the deductive case that the architecture was informed by learning and theology. Integration of this kind modelled a scope of learning having a role and relevance largely lost to us. If there was any rift between intellect and affection, and between a person and God, the most necessary thing to do was to repair it. Instruction, knowledge, and all loves, were predicated on this integration. Experiencing medieval church architecture, insofar as we can, we need to grasp its intellectual context. But the high rationale in this architecture was the love which, ordered to God, could motivate the mind of a maker.

Notes

1 Bonaventure, *De reductione artium ad theologiam*, 4, trans. Healy (1955), Vol. 1, p. 27.
2 See Mueller (2005).
3 Plato, *Timaeus*, I, 37b–c, trans. Lee (1965), p. 50. Dialectic and rhetoric can be seen in the running to 'report' and 'declare'.
4 O'Meara (2005), p. 138.
5 Augustine, *De civitate Dei*, 11.22.

6 John 6.45. The Old Testament text is Isaiah 54.10–13.
7 Grosseteste, *Hexaëmeron*, Proemium, 57, trans. Martin (1996), p. 29. The commentary is on Ecclesiastes 8.16. C.f. Wisdom of Solomon, 8.1. Augustine is cited from *De libero arbitrio*, 2.123–25.
8 Herrad of Landsberg, *Hortus deliciarum*, f. 32. reproduced in Boethius, trans. Masi (1983), in *Boethian Number Theory*, fig. 1.
9 A full study of this window is by Caviness (1990).
10 Boethius, *De institutione arithmetica*, 1.1, trans. Masi (1983), pp. 72–73.
11 Thomas Aquinas, *Summa theologica*, 1a, q.7, a.3, a, pp. 57–58.
12 Thomas Aquinas, *Summa contra gentiles*, 3.97.2, 3, trans. Bourke (1975), vol. 2, p. 67.
13 This is a prominent motif in Pseudo-Dionysius; for instance in *De divinis nominibus*, 7.3.
14 See Wallis (2005), p. 183. Principal *numerus* theorists were Isidore of Seville (*Etymologiae*), Bede (*De temporum ratione*, 725), Abbo of Fleury (*Commentarius*) and Byrhtferth of Ramsey (*Enchiridion*, *c*. 1011). Wallis gives extensive bibliographical references.
15 Wallis (1990), p. 51. See Claudia Kren (1983), p. 231, for an outline of this issue.
16 Isidore, *Etymologiae*, 3, 4, trans. Wallis (1990), p. 47.
17 Augustine, *De libero arbitrio*, 16.42, trans. Burleigh (1953), p. 161.
18 Wallis (2005), p. 184.
19 Wallis (1990), p. 46.
20 Ibid., p. 47. Use of the word 'poetry' is validated as Wallis's essay develops.
21 Expressed variously in the New Testament, e.g. Acts 17.24, II Corinthians 5.1, Hebrews 9.11.
22 See Heyman (1995), pp. 141–42; also his discussion following on the Milan cathedral design, pp. 148–50.
23 Wallis (1990), p. 52.
24 Ibid., p. 54 (Wallis's emphasis).
25 Ibid., p. 58. Wallis sees the connection being made by Bede, by Byrhtferth, and notably in a twelfth-century Cirencester manuscript in which the table is integrated into the longitudinal section of a church.
26 Beaujouan (1982), p. 482.
27 Boethius, *De institutione arithmetica*, 1.7, trans. Masi (1983a), p. 78.
28 Ibid., 1.7, p. 79. Pseudo-Dionysius had expressed the connection between unity and number in *De divinis nominibus*, 5.6.
29 Ibid., 1.1, 1.14, 1.17 ('mother and creator').
30 Masi (1983b), 'Arithmetic', ed. Wagner, p. 149.
31 Boethius, *De institutione arithmetica*, 1.2, trans. Masi (1983a), p. 75.
32 Ibid., p. 76.
33 Munich, Staatsbibliothek, MS 2599, f.102v. '*Per me cunctorum scitur virtus numerorum*'; reproduced in Masi (1983a), *Boethian Number Theory*, fig. 3.
34 See Boethius, *De institutione arithmetica*, 1.11, trans. Masi (1983a), p. 86.
35 Ibid., pp. 87, 89.
36 Boethius' account is in *De institutione arithmetica*, 19 and 20.
37 Augustine, *De civitate Dei*, 11.30, trans. Bettenson (1972), p. 465. This theory and theology of the number six was repeated by Thomas Aquinas in *Summa theologica*, 1a, q.74, a.1.
38 See Hiscock (1999), p. 151.
39 Beaujouan (1982), p. 483.
40 Grosseteste, *Hexaëmeron*, 3.13.1, trans. Wright (2017).
41 Hugh of St-Victor, *Didascalicon*, 2.7, trans. Taylor (1961), p. 67.

154 *Instruction: the quadrivium*

42 Thomas, *Summa theologica*, 1a, q.7, a.4, ad., trans. Pegis (1948), p. 60. See also 1a, q.7, a.2, a, trans. Pegis (1948), p. 55.
43 In *Summa theologica*, 1a, q.7, a.3, ad.3, Thomas stated: 'By division of the whole we approach to matter, since parts are as matter; but by addition we approach to the whole which is as a form'.
44 See Harman (1973), pp. 40–54, for a general account of the development.
45 See Augustine, *De musica*, trans. Taliaferro (1947), p. 161.
46 Augustine, *De musica*, 1.11.19, trans. Taliaferro (1947), p. 195.
47 Ibid., p. 200.
48 Ibid., p. 202.
49 Ibid., 6.2.2 to 6.3.4; also 6.6.16. Thus the four kinds are: sounding-numbers, reacting-numbers, advancing-numbers, recalling-numbers.
50 William of St-Thierry, *Epistola*, trans. Berkeley (1976). See pp. 32–3 above.
51 Augustine, *De musica*, 6.7.19, trans. Taliaferro (1947), p. 343.
52 Ibid., 6.9.23, p. 348.
53 Ibid., p. 349.
54 As Augustine also wrote, 'My weight is my love'. *Confessiones*, 13.9, trans. Outler (1955), p. 304.
55 Augustine, *De musica*, 6.11.29, trans. Taliaferro (1947), p. 355.
56 Ibid., p. 356.
57 Ibid., 6.11.32, p. 357. Augustine here distinguishes 'phantasias' in the memory from 'phantasms', images made out of memories and likely to lead to error.
58 Ibid., 6.11.33, p. 358.
59 See Augustine, *De musica*, 6.12.35.
60 Bonaventure, *Itinerarium mentis ad Deum*, 2.10, trans. Boas (1953), p. 19. Bonaventure is specific: 'Augustine shows this in his book *De vera religione* and in the sixth book of *De Musica*'.
61 Slocum (1993), p. 11.
62 Ibid., p. 24.
63 Ibid., p. 15, p. 17; also p. 16.
64 i.e., 2:1 (octave), 3:1 (twelfth), 4:1 (double octave), 3:2 (fifth) and 4:3 (fourth).
65 See Jacques de Liège, *Speculum musicae*, 2.a.20. See Slocum (1993), p. 30, f.n. 27.
66 Slocum (1993), p. 21.
67 Boethius treated proportion vis-à-vis music in *De institutione arithmetica*, 2.40–54. The nature of arithmetical numbers was characterised as linear, one-dimensional; in geometry we can expect to see a three-dimensional make-up.
68 Jacques de Liège *Speculum musicae*, 4.84, text in Slocum (1993), p. 32, f.n. 38 (my translation).
69 Karp (1983) p. 186.
70 Richard of St-Victor, *Benjamin maior*, 5.24, trans. Zinn (1979), p. 257.
71 Ibid., p. 258.
72 Ibid., 6.17, p. 340. The incident of Elisha is in 2 Kings 3.15.
73 Ibid., 6.18, p. 342.
74 Introduction in *Richard of St. Victor*, Zinn (1979), p. 43.
75 Hugh of St-Victor, *Didascalicon*, 2.15, trans. Taylor (1961), p. 71.
76 Thomas Aquinas, *Summa contra gentiles*, 3, 97.4, trans. Bourke (1975), vol. 2, p. 68.
77 Ibid.
78 Plato, *Timaeus*, II, 53d, trans. Lee (1965), p. 72.
79 Ibid., I, 31b–c, p. 43.
80 Ibid., I, 31c.
81 Martianus Capella, *De nuptiis*, 1.1, trans. Stahl, Johnson and Burge (1977), p. 3. Johnson notes, 'The concept owes something to Empedocles' (f.n. 2).

82 Ibid., 6.706, trans. Stahl, Johnson and Burge (1977), p. 264. 'Drawn from this dust' alludes to the practice of drawing diagrams on a dusted ground.
83 Ibid., 6.721, p. 271.
84 Ibid., 6.708, p. 265.
85 Augustine addressed the question of the soul's magnitude with the aim of showing that the soul lacks corporeal quantity but 'yet is something great'.
86 Augustine, *De quantitate animae*, 6.10.
87 Ibid., 8.13, p. 74. This is the subject of his Chapters 8–10.
88 Ibid., 13. 22, p. 83. This refers back to his Chapters 4 and 5.
89 Ibid., 4.6, p. 65.
90 Plato, *Timaeus*, II, 48a, trans. Lee (1965), p. 65.
91 Ibid., II, 52a–b, p. 70.
92 See 'Medieval perception of space and place,' Lewis (2007), where I have described four ways in which *place* was constituted: conceptual, actualised, contracted and composed.
93 See Grosseteste in *Commentarius in octo libros Physicorum Aristotelis*, text in Dales (1957), p. 24: 'For nothing has a third dimension without a body. For place is always filled with space. [...] And since there are no dimensions without a body, it is impossible for a place be void of a body' (my translation).
94 Bradwardine, *Tractatus de continuo*, 4.3, trans. Molland (1989), p. 135.
95 Radding and Clark (1992), p. 12.
96 Ibid., p. 36.
97 Croddy (1999), p. 268.
98 Ibid.
99 Hiscock (1999), p. 178. Hiscock names exponents of each view in footnotes 22 and 23 to this passage.
100 This is particularly in *The Symbol at Your Door* (Hiscock 2007), which is an extensive study applying Platonic or sacred geometry to medieval architecture.
101 Heyman (1995), pp. 4–5; 141. It is subject to certain conditions and exigencies.
102 See Vitruvius, *De architectura*, trans. Morgan (1914), 1.2.5–9.
103 Boethius, *De institutione arithmetica*, trans. Masi (1983a), 2.34, p. 159.
104 von Simson (1962), p. 198. Focillon (1963), p. 110; and Masi (1983b), p. 160, also read much into Villard's sketchbook without providing substantiation.
105 Villard de Honnecourt, ed. Bowrie (1959), Plates C.35–C.38.
106 Ewing (1965), dissertation, p. 86.
107 von Simson (1962), p. 199. For discussion of quadrature see Hiscock (1999), pp. 182–91.
108 Villard de Honnecourt, ed. Bowrie (1959), C.23, Pl. 41. See also Hiscock (1999), pp. 178–93.
109 See Hiscock (1999), p. 257, where he analyses the generation of the plan from the crossing in twelve out of eighteen examples.
110 *De arca Noe mystica*, Hugh of St-Victor (1962), 1. See my discussion in 'History and Everlastingness in Hugh of St Victor's Figures of Noah's Ark', Lewis (2003), p. 219.
111 Second Milan conference of the cathedral council, January 1401. See Ackerman (1949), p. 100.
112 Astrology in the Middle Ages was more scientifically respectable than it later came to be. To Grosseteste, for instance, it was an application of astronomy, though possibly problematical.
113 Dante, *Paradiso*, 22. 151, trans. Sinclair (1939), p. 325. See also 27. 76–85.
114 See Pseudo-Dionysius, *De caelesti hierarchia*, 6.2.
115 Pseudo-Dionysius, *De caelesti hierarchia*, 7.1, ed. Shrine of Wisdom (1935), pp. 46–7.
116 Pseudo-Dionysius, *De divina hierarchia*, 1.2, trans Luibheid (1987), p. 197.

156 Instruction: the quadrivium

117 Ibid., p. 196 (my emphasis).
118 Thomas Aquinas, *Summa theologiae*, 1a, q.66, 3, trans. Wallace (1967), *Vol. 10: Cosmogony*, p. 45.
119 Wallace (1967), in *St Thomas Aquinas: Summa Theologiae, Vol. 10: Cosmogony*, Appendix 4, p. 190.
120 Dante, *Paradiso* 27. 106–14, trans. Sinclair (1939), p. 393.
121 Plato, *Timaeus*, I, 37d, trans. Warrington (1965), p. 31.
122 Ibid., I, 40a, p. 34.
123 *Phaedrus*, 3.247, trans. Hamilton (1973), p. 52.
124 Ibid.
125 This theme is expanded by Pieper (1965) in *Love and Inspiration*.
126 Martianus Capella, *De nuptiis*, 2.202, 203, trans. Stahl, Johnson and Burge (1977), pp. 60–1. See **p. 66** above for the text of the last ellipsis.
127 Ibid., pp. 61–2.
128 Pseudo-Enoch, *I Enoch*, 72.3, trans. Charles (1982), in *The Book of Enoch*, p. 96. Books 72–82 comprise the 'Astronomy'.
129 Van Pelt (1983), p. 4. Van Pelt asserts that 'the history of post-antique European architectural philosophy starts not with Alberti, but with Philo'.
130 Ibid., p. 14. Josephus (37–c. 100AD) also saw the tabernacle as a symbol of the cosmos. See Josephus (1838), 3.6, 3.7, p. 91.
131 Philo Judaeus, *De specialibus Legibus*, 1.88. Cited by van Pelt (1983), p. 5.
132 Bernardus Silvestris, *Megacosmos* 13, trans. Wetherbee (1973), p. 121.
133 Henry of Avranches, *The Metrical Life of St Hugh, bishop of Lincoln*, 919–21, trans. Garton (1986), p. 57: '*Corpus terram sortitur, homo nubes, spiritus astra*'. Here 'man' (*homo*) may be intended to convey the sense of the mind or soul. See **p. 82** above, and note **p. 190** below for other lines cited.
134 Guthrie (1967), p. 51 (my emphasis). Plato, in *Timaeus*, II, 52d–53a, described in similar terms chaos in space, and the separation of like and unlike constituents. Compare also Martianus Capella, **p. 134** above.
135 Thomas Aquinas, *Commentary on the* Metaphysics *of Aristotle*, 3.1, trans. Rowan (1961), p. 192, n. 478.
136 Sayers in *Inferno*, trans. Sayers (1949), p. 147, f.n. to 12.42.
137 Dante Alighieri, *Inferno*, 12.41–44, trans. Anderson (1932), p. 60.
138 Augustine, *De civitate Dei*, 11.28, trans. Dyson (1998), p. 487.
139 Augustine, *Confessiones*, 13.9. trans. Pine-Coffin (1961), p. 317. See also above, **p. 127, f.n. 54.**
140 Matthew 22.37.

5 The mirror of contemplation
Life in nature

In love with things

A further part of the mental equipment for architects was a regard for things in nature, things in their particularity, and material itself. It was very different in their perception compared with our egocentric relation to nature. Phrases such as 'all things' and 'the nature of things' have been used in foregoing chapters with some frequency, though not as loosely as might be thought. Medieval minds at many levels were in love with 'things' (*res*), not least things 'in nature', the multitude of real existences. An indication of this from theology is the prominence of *Hexaëmeron* commentaries on the 'six days of creation' in which the natures of all created things are explained.[1] Love for things directed the mind to love the Maker. The subject was for contemplation. This chapter shows that nature, temporal and perpetual, was looked into by thinkers and artists as a mirror of the mind and purposes of God—not that they sought to work out their theology from observing nature; only that nature reflected the patterns of divine things in seemingly endless particularity open to observation and contemplation.

We may start with a threefold delineation of nature by Hugh of St-Victor. First is that which is not itself nature, but is eternal without beginning or end, subsisting only from itself. 'Such alone is the Begetter and Artificer of nature.'[2] The One without whom nature would not exist, sustains it. Second, nature comprises things which are perpetual, having a beginning but terminated by no end. Hugh includes more than the merely physical universe. It refers to all intelligent beings, angels and rational human souls; also, 'all the bodies of the superlunary world, which, from their knowing no change, have also been called divine'.[3] Nature is profound in its connectedness, understood in terms of likenesses on a metaphysical level, but then with deep implications for corporeal things:

> Through its being an image and likeness, this second being contained all things that were in the First—ideas and causes and likenesses and forms, the dispositions and foreseeings of all future things which were to be made. And when the corporeal things to be made were actually

made, they were made to the likeness of those things made in this second being, just as the latter was made in the likeness of the unmade things in the First.[4]

Third in Hugh's delineation are corporeal, temporal, things, which have both beginning and end. He gives prominence to how things come to be—the making of things. It is 'by the movement of an artifacting fire which descends with a certain power to beget all sensible objects'.[5] Calling this working of nature 'artifacting fire' seems to empower the human arts. Calcidius (c. 321), commenting on Plato's *Timaeus*, saw that, 'All things that exist are the work of God, or the work of nature, or the work of a human artisan [*hominis artificis*] imitating nature'.[6] Hugh drew on that, and the first chapter of *Didascalicon* is 'On the Origin of the Arts'.

On the composition of things Hugh again refers to *Timaeus* to affirm that nature comprises on the one hand the elements, on the other, all the things that are made from them.[7] In this mode the human soul is likewise composed, and being also mixed it thus comprehends 'the invisible causes of things', and it 'picks up the visible forms of actual objects' through sense impressions.[8] This is a double power, rather than an ambiguity or tension; and with this twofold faculty the human mind not only has the facility to ascend to invisible things, it goes out to sensible things:

> It circles about, drawing to itself the likenesses of things; and thus it is that one and the same mind, having the capacity for all things, is fitted together out of every substance and nature by the fact that it represents within itself their imaged likeness.[9]

Nature does not here mean a world over against the human soul. Rather the soul has the power to grasp the similitude of all things and all natures because its composition is analogous to theirs. From this in part derives its capacity for *participation* in all things.[10] We will want to probe the working of the artificer's mind, seeing that the 'likenesses of things' are imaged in the soul by this inherent 'capacity for all things'. Hugh well typifies the theology concerning the Creator and nature as it had developed by the twelfth century.

In *On the Sacraments* he asserts that both visible and invisible things are mirrored in the soul, evoking admiration and love—

> that it might grasp visible things without through the flesh, and invisible things within through reason [...]. The works of God were shown to the rational creature, so that it might admire Him within and without, and through admiration advance to love.[11]

Contemplation is from a middle position between things higher and lower. It is not a passive state, but is active in receiving wisdom from above and ministering to things below. A person was drawn towards objects—

within for invisible things, without for visible [...] that he might go in
and contemplate, and might go out and contemplate; that he might have
wisdom within, the works of wisdom without, that he might contemplate both [...] to go by cognition, to be refreshed by love.[12]

Cognition and love accompany contemplation. The proper inclination of
all nature which coinheres in the Creator's life is the giving back of love
and enjoying his works. Humans are made in the image and likeness of
God, and Hugh drew some fine distinctions between these reflections, such
as: 'image according to reason, likeness according to love'; 'image according to knowledge, likeness according to substance'; thus, 'image pertains
to figure, likeness to nature'.[13] Artists and artificers participating in the life
of the Creator, exhibited not only his image but also the likeness—love,
substance and nature. While keeping in mind the integration of all things,
this chapter first considers nature in earthly life, then the nature of supramundane things.

The Source, Support and End

In all medieval sources concerning the nature of things we can scarcely avoid
the focus which is given to God's nature and works. Indeed Chapter 2 has
initiated the subject. The sensitive drawing from the Anglo-Saxon Psalter
of *c.* 1020 suggests the eternal love within the Trinity, prior to everything
(Figure 2.4). The intimate ineffable scene is contemplated by angels. The
motif of a surrounding aureole, a presentation of glory, here has the pointed
form of a vesica.[14] Far more often we find scenes of God in glory outwardly
relating to the creation, his right hand raised in the act of blessing, or with
arms extended in liberality (Figures 5.2; 5.10). God is, with full theological justification, shown to be Jesus Christ, for by the Wisdom which is the
divine Mind, by the Son in whom the divine love ever flows, the world was
made and is sustained.[15]

Typically Christ holds in his left hand the book signifying that he is the
Word. The Word is the eternal, creative and self-revealing Mind. He is
the source, the author, compassing the end from the beginning. Often in
these archetypal scenes Christ's title, 'Alpha and Omega', is explicit in the
symbols inscribed on the book or on the background.[16] He may be seated
upon a rainbow representing his covenant with the earth and every living
creature.[17] The four symbolic living creatures are frequently juxtaposed, and
censing angels and seraphim of love may be shown. The gestures of Christ's
hands are authoritative and demonstrative. The signification is found first in
the affirmation of the six days of creation, 'And God saw everything that he
had made, and behold, it was very good', compounded with the command
of the fifth, sixth and seventh days, 'And God blessed . . .'. If we think of the
benedictions as *mere* affirmations of a desirable state of affairs we miss the
imperative force—they declare a fecund world. On the fifth day God made

the fish and fowl and blessed them: 'Be fruitful and multiply'. On the sixth day God made the beasts and creeping things of the earth; then humans, male and female, whom he blessed thus: 'Be fruitful and multiply and fill the earth, and subdue it; and have dominion over the fish of the sea and over the birds of the air and over every living thing that moves upon the earth'.[18] All this, the beginnings, the creatorial fiats, the order of things, and their support, was embedded in symbols of enduring vitality in art throughout the Middle Ages.

As to the end of things and goal of creation, Christ is portrayed in revealed majesty, as himself the end of each thing, the consummation. Between the two scenes, the Beginning and the End, is all creation, and all that we know. At the ascent to the fourth heaven of paradise Dante directs contemplation to the ordering of minds and all things by Love:

> Looking upon His Son with the love which the One and the Other eternally breathe forth, the primal and ineffable Power made everything that revolves through the mind or through space with such order that he who contemplates it cannot but taste of Him.[19]

In early medieval work, in illumination, fresco, mosaic and sculpture, the Maker in pre-incarnate glory was a subject more common than later. The frescoes covering the late eleventh-century chapel of Saint-Gilles, Montoire-sur-le-Loir, embody the diagram of Christ in Majesty composed in three locations; the sense is of the worshippers' passionate love of God. The Judge in majesty is a theme appearing increasingly from about the beginning of the twelfth century. A tympanum especially above a main door, usually the west door on the principal axis, was an important site for this subject in bas-relief. Among many well-known examples is the sculpture by Gislebertus, around 1130, at St-Lazare cathedral, Autun.

Between the subjects of first and last things are others associating deity and nature. On the façade of Angoulême cathedral is Christ in ascension energy, with angels participating (Figure 5.1). It is drawn from the theme of the opening vision which overcame St John on Patmos, of the Eternal in the midst of the new order joining heaven and earth. The four symbolic figures, which we conveniently describe in temporal and (uncertainly) spatial terms, could be conflated, and indeed often were. Thus the four creatures of Ezekiel's vision were made into the emblems of the four Evangelists, and were obviously identifiable with the four living creatures of the Apocalypse. As a rule the halo of the Deity was shown quartered by the Cross, signifying that, even before the Incarnation, the creative Wisdom is he who is the God-Man. The great symbol of his Passion, the Cross, was shown in many contexts, even Christ in Session. For instance, at San Zeno in Verona he surmounts his Cross, which appears as a tree, alluding not only to the rood but also to the Tree of Life.[20] Sometimes there are brought in representations of nature such as the zodiac and the seasons without any incongruity, indicative of belief that all was redeemed and sustained by Christ.

Contemplation: life in nature 161

Figure 5.1 Angoulême, France. Cathedral church of St-Pierre. The ascension of Christ, in a vesica, amidst foliage and angels (in the arch above and panel below), and the four symbolic creatures. Sculpture 1125–50.

One way or another such understanding of Christ was incorporated in prominent positions in the cathedrals and churches, most often exactly on one of the principal axes defining the building—embodying and declaring it in the church. The exposition of the incarnation, passion, resurrection and ascension of the Firstborn of all creation (*Primogenitus omnis creaturae*) has always affirmed God's glory seen in relation to creaturely nature. The imagination of the high Middle Ages brought in all nature under this theology, and engaged art and architecture more cogently than it had before.

The Creator of earthly nature

It is more than we can do to survey the antecedent medieval treatment of the things of nature as works of the Creator's wisdom and love. One point to recollect, however, is that the power to create, *ex nihilo*, was attributed to God alone. Thus Peter Lombard (*c.* 1100–60) wrote:

> Properly speaking, to create is to make something from nothing [...] a man or an angel is said to make some things, but not to create them; and he is called a maker or an artificer, but not a creator. For this name is properly suitable only for God, who makes some things from nothing and others from something.[21]

Augustine gave God's creativity close thought. He taught that all created works of nature were made 'with the true artist's skill, which here is the Wisdom of God'; that he worked in love with perfect foreknowledge; and that he enjoyed his works as good.[22] This had some correspondence with the origin and 'the pattern' which Plato had described in *Timaeus*.[23] But going further, Augustine found hints of the whole Trinity being involved in the act of creation and reflected in created nature.[24] Thinking about goodness in nature, he insisted on the value of things, and their hierarchies because, made by God: 'There is a scale of value stretching from earthly to heavenly realities, from the visible to the invisible; and the inequalities between these goods makes possible the existence of them all'.[25] So may humble even seemingly 'profane' work participate in the order of things. Each is glad to be in its place; each displays or reflects, in its own way, a facet of transitive goodness to people who love wisdom, and a facet of the Maker who gives it purpose.

The theological assertion of the Christocentric unity, the 'whole Christ', opens Grosseteste's *Hexaëmeron*. Expounding the work of the fifth day of creation, when God said, 'Let the waters bring forth abundantly', he introduced this superior meaning: 'This water consists entirely in the unity of love, and in the unity of the One that is the subject of theology, on which we remarked at the beginning'.[26] Then he ascribed the place of the disciplined senses to the 'creeping things' of humility, self-examination, even fretful activity; and also to the 'flying things' of love that seeks higher things, the burning desire for heaven, and composed contemplation.[27] The intimate relation of the sensuous and the spiritual was emphatically love. Bonaventure, in a chapter entitled 'Concerning the whole man placed in paradise', wrote:

> The first Principle created this perceptible world as a means of self-revelation so that, like a mirror of God or a divine footprint, it might lead man to love and praise his Creator. Accordingly there are two books, one written within, and that is God's eternal Art and Wisdom; the other written without, and that is the perceptible world.[28]

The assertion of divine self-revelation and intention (that creatures should be drawn to love the Creator) was axiomatic in theology, but to complete the method it required a discursive reading of the perceptible world. The theme is developed in detail in his treatise *The Mind's Road to God*. Our two previous chapters asserted connectivity between theology and architecture; here is an outworking of that as both embraced the created world.

The purpose and fecundity of created life was assured by the creative Word, blessing all things. In Genesis the original command and blessing of fruitfulness was renewed thrice.[29] In Abram's day the priest Melchisedek, made 'by the power of an indestructible life', blessed the patriarch who 'looked for the city which has foundations, whose builder and maker is God'. Thus: 'Blessed be Abram by God Most High, *maker of heaven and earth*'.[30] The import of it became explicit in Moses' blessing: 'Blessed of the Lord be [Joseph's] land, for the precious things of heaven [. . .] and for the precious fruits brought forth by the sun, and for the precious things put forth by the moon [. . .] and for the precious things of the earth and the fulness thereof'.[31] The phrase evidently became the climax to collective worship in the sanctuary: 'The Lord *that made heaven and earth* bless thee out of Zion'.[32] Thus the image of God seated amidst the stars, his hand raised in blessing, is a great assertion of creatorial intention. The fullness and fruitfulness of all creation, its partaking of divine life, was an early and common subject portrayed in book illuminations and incorporated in architecture, especially in Romanesque tympana.

If theology pointed to involvement in the life of God spiritually, and the goodness and beauty of nature physically, then part of the vision for cathedrals and churches might have been that they participate in the whole creation, from the first blessing to the consummation. We find them filled with manifold depictions and symbols of created life, images derived from that world-view. All things were deemed to coinhere in God, and we may reasonably deduce that this was signified when even common creatures and unbeautiful forms were brought into churches. The verities of theology, church and monastery were the frame of reference for temporal nature.

To be more specific, in architecture figures of spiritual and earthly nature were located on significant axes and intersections, in foci and elevations. The hierarchies may be seen to join on these coordinates between the mundane and spiritual worlds. Thus depictions in tympana and archivolts, column capitals, arch spandrels, vault bosses, rose windows and traceries, carried the beauty and fecundity of nature. A portal elaborated with archivolts was an apt place to represent angels and saints, birds and beasts, flowers, fruit and leaves, the signs of the heavenly bodies, the occupations of earthly seasons, and human arts, in serried ranks surrounding a theophany. More abstractly, derivation and development of forms were conveyed in structural lines and nodes, in proportion, shape, rhythm and symmetry (Figure 3.12). We can construe that these are rudiments of a grammar according with nature, a dialectic of ordering in nature and humans, and a rhetoric conveying life and purpose.

In his study of Romanesque sculpture, M. F. Hearn surveys the development of tympana in particular, relating it tellingly to theological aspects. In summary he sees the great portals of twelfth-century France evolving through three 'generations'.[33] The first generation he characterises as 'Theophany in the portal', one group centred in Burgundy, another in Languedoc, naming Vézelay and Moissac as originals.[34] The second generation he characterises as 'Theology made manifest', naming St-Denis (c. 1137), St-Gilles-du-Gard (late 1140s) and Chartres (c. 1145).[35] The third he denotes 'spiritual truth in physical beauty', and, focussing on Senlis (c. 1170), seeing this as indicative of the transition from Romanesque to Gothic style—'the emergence of a new artistic era'.[36] Discussing the influence of 'new developments in aesthetics', he says,

> While the figures of Romanesque sculpture are frankly inorganic in nature, the new style introduced the illusion of organic life. The representation of a holy mystery in such an illusionistic manner could be considered appropriate only after a radical change in the philosophy of the nature of images.[37]

This change, as Hearn defines it, flowed into the wider new vision and was effectual in this way:

> The Gothic style signals the return of natural beauty in art in much the same sense that it was cultivated by the ancients, but initially without any direct influence from antique art. Although its development was pursued as a virtual rather than an actual imitation of nature, the role of sculpture was to create images that reflect in the mirror of the physical world the higher truths of the spiritual world.[38]

So in 'the philosophy of the nature of images' henceforth the matter of *beauty* seen in nature would be charged with the role of effectively transmitting divine things. His survey and analysis of Romanesque sculpture is illuminating, and one feels that this final point should shed light on the first steps of Gothic art. But he says, 'From this point, the style of monumental sculpture became a purely artistic consideration, bound up in the concept of beauty and distinct from the formulation of the subject matter'.[39] This is not a comment on style narrowly, but implicates the subject matter, 'the higher truths'. But when style (which is only one part of rhetoric) is given undue importance judgement can be coloured. It detracts from the less visible roles of dialectic and of theology in informing the vision and the work. To deal with it deductively if possible is necessary.

As Hearn shows in the Romanesque, the appearances of Christ in glory are incorporated into churches with meaningful architectural associations. The structure of motifs—their centrality, geometry and iconography—illustrates the directive role of the theological ideas. Antecedents survive

Contemplation: life in nature 165

from the sixth century in Ravenna in the apse of San Vitale, and across the summit of the apsidal arch in Sant' Apollinare in Classe, which are outstanding in their fusion of the spiritual world and earthly creation. In the rhetoric of figures speaking of glory, the vesica surrounding Christ was a common motif in art from the eighth century. It pre-dated pointed arches—though this is not to suggest derivation. The pointed arch seems a natural sign of the superior world while yet standing on a horizontal base, the earth's surface (Figure 3.13). But if an opening is also pointed at the base it appears to have no rest on the earth, and its use would appear as even a natural symbol of the supra-mundane. In architectural design the motif seems to have appeared in the last quarter of the eleventh century. Early architectural appearances of the vesica are on the west façade gable of Notre-Dame-la-Grande, Poitiers, and the south transept of Dore Abbey, Herefordshire, but it was not widely used.

Examples of the theme of the Creator Christ presiding over nature were widespread and explicit from the twelfth century. All show careful

Figure 5.2 Florence, Italy. San Miniato al Monte church. Building mostly complete by 1207. The apse mosaic is of Christ with St Mary and St Mennas (Miniato), completed 1297 (restored 1860).

correspondence to the geometry of the specific places, and every element of the iconography reinforces the glory. In later Gothic art such themes were less prominent; but persisted rather more in Italian art, where there were many early models, particularly in mosaics. In San Miniato al Monte in Florence the symbols are incorporated, along with representations of nature (Figure 5.2). Schemes on this theme are also quite common in small vernacular churches throughout Europe.

How can we evaluate this key iconographic art that ostensibly penetrates the 'truths of the spiritual world'? We cannot, Owen Barfield says, re-enter the 'original participation'. 'It *is* a lost world [but] its spiritual wealth can be and indeed [. . .] *must* be regained'.[40] We might grasp the graphic and architectonic representations of perceptible things as they made vital connections to meaning and spiritual wealth. The links were rendered visible. And we need the connections to such truths in textual sources so that by both means we may glimpse direct and mediated medieval perceptions of the world and the nature of things. Barfield writes:

> The world was more like a garment men wore about them than a stage on which they moved. In such a world the convention of perspective was unnecessary. To such a world other conventions of visual reproduction, such as the nimbus and the halo, were appropriate as to ours they are not. It was as if the observers were themselves *in* the picture. Compared with us, they felt themselves and the objects around them and the words that expressed those objects, immersed together in something like a clear lake of—what shall we say?—of 'meaning' if you choose. [...] Aquinas's *verbum intellectus* was *tanquam speculum, in quo res cernitur*—'like a mirror in which the object is discerned'.[41]

Particularly useful here is the assertion that medieval perception of visible things, rendered into visual representations, was in itself immersion in the actual scene and in meaning—direct participation and truth reflected.

Reflection of nature in architecture

Through most of the Middle Ages art had but slight concern to portray the natural world as pictorial or spatial landscape; yet it did employ the wealth of the floral and arboreal world, birds and beasts, as models in endless decorative schemes. Representation delighted in the appearances of the manifold works of nature, and the question arises whether it was simply for their own sake, or whether it was for the making of associations between things temporal and divine—whether nature was a mirror of contemplation of God. It might have been a subconscious participation of all things in unity, or an imaginative use of natural symbols, or an intentional use of formal devices. The intellectual culture and the substratum of affective motivation that we have found thus far suggest that the perceptions and uses of the natural

Contemplation: life in nature 167

world were bound up in a unity of meaning. Again, written and pictorial sources are quite rich in various tropes of the relation of the natural world to the spiritual.

Mirror of nature

Written sources so far have told that to see all things in nature was to see as in a mirror the art and glory of the Maker, and be moved through love of nature to admire the Maker. Dante made the art itself the subject of contemplation: 'Here we contemplate the art which so much love adorns, and we discern the good by reason of which the world below again becomes the world above'.[42] The nature of 'seeing' was contemplation using imagination and reason according to Richard of St-Victor who detailed six levels. The first goes not above imagination, the second calls in reason to examine things seen and imaged. The third, drawing on similitudes of visible things, rises up to invisible things as by speculation. Finding rational principles in created things, 'reason uses, as it were, an instrument and gazes, for example, into a mirror'.[43] In Bristol cathedral a unity of vision and execution shows attention to principles of reason in the columns, shafts and vault ribs, while the sensed artifice of emulating a forest sustains a strong similitude to nature and makes a mirror of reflection (Figure 5.3).

Henry of Avranches, looking into the mirror of nature, contemplated the clustered column shafts in Lincoln cathedral about which he was writing:

> As for the slender shafts themselves, which thus surround the columns, they look like (maidens) in a round dance. Their outer surface, more polished than the growing fingernail, reflects a sparkling brilliance to the view: for nature has there painted so many different forms that, if art by long persistence laboured to get the likeness exact, it could hardly equal the reality. Thus precise jointing together sets there in becoming rank a thousand shafts which, stiff, precious and shining, enduringly maintain the whole structure of the church, endow it with riches, make it bright with their gleam.[44]

The dancers around the tree are the column shafts; the tree column is signified by the crockets. There is a subtle appeal to mind and sense in his description which lies in the vying of nature and art to outdo each other; it was a note running through a preceding account of the process of grinding and polishing. Here is nature being made a mirror in the crafting of the cathedral. The polisher's skill revealed nature's inimitable beauty endowing the building with brilliance. The mason's precision made the geometry and stability impressive to the intellect. The effect of this is multiplied by the shafts on columns and in minor arcades through every part of Lincoln cathedral, even transposed freely to the exterior. On the third level of contemplation Richard cited the text, 'The invisible things of God from the

168 *Contemplation: life in nature*

Figure 5.3 Bristol, England. Cathedral church of the Holy Trinity. Nave with aisles of same height. The rebuilt nave replicates the choir built 1298–1330.

creation of the world have been seen, being understood by means of those things which have been made'.[45] The 'rational principles' of nature are able to be grasped.

Forest and meadow of contemplation

Bernard frequently used spatial imagery in describing the soul's movements, such as this which is given virtually as a principle, at least for his monks: 'All of us make an effort to go upward, we all tend to the top. It is above to which we all aspire; we all make an effort to reach the heights'.[46] In the language of contemplation the vertical juxtaposition of here and there, lower and higher, earth and heaven, and movement between, is pervasive. Bernard said, 'For to will, according to blessed Gregory, is mentally to go there'.[47] In the abbey's church the locational reference in yet another sermon would hardly have failed to connect with the building: the eyes follow, and the mind ascends.

> The beloved has no choice but to endure this state until the hour when she lays down the body's weary weight, and raised aloft on the wings of desire, freely traverses the meadows of contemplation, and in spirit follows the One she loves without restraint wherever he goes.[48]

As the soul traverses the meadows, the mind in love would rise to the realm of the vaulted roof, and know an affinity with the beauty culminating there. Many church vaulting designs evoke Bernard's imagery. The church of St Mary-on-the-Sands, Wrocław (Figure 3.4) is full of free movement and the church of St Dorothy (Figure 4.11), also in Wrocław, has the lightness of wings. These are both hall churches, where aisle vaulting contiguous with the nave vaults gives lofty expansiveness.

The psychology of the vertical architectural line was natural and emphatic, and exploited with such artifice as to be a hallmark of Gothic. The columns or shafts rising upwards outdistance physical reach; only the eye can follow, and the mind. Columns comprise the greatest assemblage of vertical elements, and the more slender they appear to be the greater the illusion of their uplifting movement rather than the load above driving downwards. They thrust upwards with life like trees. Ascending adjacent lines curve and intersect forming pointed arches. The mind, perceiving the linear elements ascend with such kinetic force, wonders where and how they can be resolved. It sees them at a remote height spread out, making arboreal canopies, fabricating a non-terrestrial realm. The concentrated parallel lines of energy are distributed into a field of a different form of energy where weight and mass seem of no account. The choirs of Gloucester cathedral and Bristol cathedral exemplify the formal resolution by ramification (from *ramus*, branch) (Figure 5.3; Figure 5.4). We see that there are virtually no horizontal elements. It all conveys the power of intention.

Bernard, speaking of contemplatives who 'are taken up and descend', said, 'Our branches are our desires'.[49] It is part of a greater tree analogy which continues, 'We extend [the branches] toward the south if [our desires] are spiritual and toward to north if they are carnal'. This south-north moral attribution was commonly sensed in church buildings, deriving literally from the directional light (as was the east-west imagery), showing the architecture capable of bearing moral and spiritual application.

Innovations in vaulting were sometimes more aesthetic than structural. Notably in England, Spain and northern Europe, elaboration by tierceron and lierne ribs and fan and net vaults bestowed intricacy, delicacy and lightness. In Gloucester cathedral's choir the interlaced ramification of the roof grows out of walls covered in screen tracery as if great trellises. The pattern extends through the whole fabric following a highly unifying concept.

Figure 5.4 Gloucester, England. Cathedral church of the Holy Trinity. Choir clerestory and vaulting. Note the angel bosses which are more numerous towards the east end. 1337–77.

The visual lightening of walls by variegation and chiaroscuro skilfully employs effects found everywhere in nature. Such art according with nature was believable for the sake of supernal vision. Explicit arboreal motifs sometimes run through a whole church, interior and exterior, frequently in conjunction with geometric patterning, with degrees of abstraction, stylization and sophistication. Instances of such in wall and vault paintings can still be seen (original or restored), many in lesser churches, but also in large ones, as in Stargard cathedral and St Marien, Lubeck. Exteriors in manifold ways—in gables, buttresses, pinnacles, friezes and motifs—display this decoratively and structurally, with imagination and invention as if emulating nature in variety and richness. Without acute vision such things could not have simply materialised. If the artificer's work was reflecting the world, it was also inducting it into God's building. Concomitant with contemplation was coinherence.

The mystical vine

The metaphor of God's favoured people as a vine has its roots in Hebrew scriptures.[50] A transference to the Church was made from the beginning of Christianity, authorised indeed by Jesus' parables of the vineyard.[51] Achard of St-Victor (d. 1170) spoke of 'love which is the fecundity of the vine'.[52] A well-known elaborate use of the figure is in the twelfth-century apse mosaic of San Clemente, Rome. The Cross is the centre, and richness of life flows through the vine. The subscript provides the explicit link between the theology and the building through a similitude—the vine depicted signifies the Church: 'We have likened the Church to this vine [. . .] the Cross causes it to bloom'.

Bonaventure begins a homily, *The Mystical Vine*, with Christ saying, 'I am the true vine'.[53] He sees the pruning, the tilling, and the training of the vine as applying to the life and sufferings of Christ, rather than to his disciples. It is an exposition of the character and the passion of Christ under this figure. In order to evoke the picture of the crucifixion he writes, 'It is proper for a vine to be bound to a pole. What better thing could serve for a pole than the pillar to which our Lord was bound? Thus Christ was bound to a pillar as a vine to a pole'.[54] The stem of the vine he likens to the body of Christ, for, having no noble form, it speaks of the humiliation and disfigurement of Jesus. But the leaves of the vine, he says, are, 'finer than those of any other tree. But no leaves could be more admired than the words of our true Vine'. This is a preamble to the study of Christ's words from the cross.

> But the leaves of the vine are generally more appreciated in those places where the vine is fastened up to some wooden structure [...]. Observe how like the cross the wooden structure is, upon which vines are usually fastened up. So that the vine may be stretched out aloft, the wood is fixed cross-wise. Could the likeness be greater?[55]

Bonaventure extends his simile by association of ideas to convince his hearers of the verisimilitude of natural image and depths of divine truth. The leaves—the words—are evergreen, he exclaims; while explaining that the Son of God was planted in the soil of human frailty. 'But then, in order to unite us to his divinity through union with his humanity he put forth leaves and blossom, and bore much fruit.'[56] Here earthly fecundity is taken as the apt display of humanity's renewal. The flowers of many kinds represent the virtues of Christ's character. He focuses on the rose: 'It is red with the blood of passion, and glowing with the fire of charity'.[57] The rose as a symbol of the wounds of Christ is described in detail, with exhortations to appreciate its ardour and beauty; each of the petals of love is a drop of Christ's blood. Might not, then, a devout soul contemplating vine and floral patterns decorating parts

172   *Contemplation: life in nature*

of the church be meant to think of the mystical Vine of love, seeing in the leaves evergreen words, in each rose his wounds, in the redness his blood? High around the perimeter of Chorin Abbey is a continuous frieze of roses. In a spiralling vine motif worked on a column or frieze 'the true Vine' was probably close in the artist's mind swaying between the natural models and the devotional metaphor. There is nothing unlikely or difficult in that. In the convent church of Altenberg-en-der-Lahn such a frieze runs around the chancel. A vine bas-relief sculpture is on the columns of the west porch of Wrocław cathedral. The encoding in the art is corroborated by the specific association of the cross as Christ's Tree, budding, flowering, amidst a vine. The subject appears in manuscript illustrations and many media, but most powerfully in rood screen crucifixes, as in the cathedral at Schwerin.

The garden of charity

Bonaventure's meditation on the Cross as the Tree of passion is not an isolated treatment of the theme. Bernard had the Bride of the Song of Solomon, personifying the Church, contemplating this subject. The Tree transforms the earth which becomes the trysting-place of Christ and the Church:

> She sees [...] the Author of life and glory transfixed with nails [...]. Contemplating this the sword of love pierces through her own soul also [...]. The fruits which the Spouse gathers from the Tree of Life in the midst of the garden of her Beloved, are pomegranates borrowing their taste from the Bread of heaven, and their colour from the Blood of Christ. [...] Now the Church beholds [the earth] laughing with flowers and restored by the grace of a new benediction. [...] She refreshes herself with the fruits of His Passion which she gathers from the Tree of the Cross, and with the flowers of His Resurrection whose fragrance invites the frequent visits of her Spouse.[58]

It was conceptually a spiritual place, but it was contracted to earthly experience in every particular mnemonic place. Bonaventure, ending his homily, invited the soul to 'mount up to the garden of charity [...]. Approach this Paradise [...] that you may experience his embrace, when he invites himself to your house, and you to his'.[59] He had spoken of love earlier, but now he opens the eyes of the soul to see that love is its true environment, its rediscovery of the Garden. Love is the real theme. The divine Lover at the end shows the implications, in an adroit speech, commencing: 'I will have you conformed to the image of my deity, in which I created you. It was in order that I might fashion you that I myself was fashioned in the image of your humanity'.[60] The Spouse's love is a responsive love. In the west door tympanum of St Elisabeth, Marburg (*c.* 1283), Mary and the Child are set in a symbolic garden between the fruitful vine and the flowering climbing rose.

Response to such affective theology must have been an ardent motive in the invention of decorative schemes on walls, columns, vaults, arch soffits and

Contemplation: life in nature 173

Figure 5.5 St-Lizier, France. Cathedral church of St-Lizier. Nave vaults and murals with original masonry pattern and rose motif decor. Church built in the twelfth century. Vaulted in the fourteenth century.

window reveals, accounting God's goodwill and human felicity. Vernacular artists transformed surfaces by painted floral, arboreal and geometrical patterns eloquent with the passion of love. Again, a particularly poignant repetitive motif was the small, simple, rose, five-petalled, as at Notre-Dame church, Cunault. Often it marked the centre of each stone of a painted masonry design. It is used convincingly in the vaulting of St-Lizier cathedral (Figure 5.5). Masonry patterning has been mentioned and the presence of the rose notably increases the significance.[61] There are many textual allusions to the church's masonry, using metaphors of love, sufficient to warrant this as an emblem of the love between Christ and each member of the spiritual building.

174 Contemplation: life in nature

Living buildings

Not surprisingly in a culture living in close proximity to the natural world, a vernacular art of naturalistic forms enriched Romanesque buildings, such as in the sculpture of portals and column capitals. In Gothic vocabulary a new motif evolved, namely leaf or leaf-bud crockets, by which places were identified more conspicuously with earthly creation. More local motifs also developed.

As to the origin of the crocket device, there are first signs in graphic arts in the late ninth century, as in some canon table drawings (Figure 5.6). This example shows the leaf-buds before they became very stylised. Nascent forms emerged in the twelfth century, and around the end of that century the typical style appeared with full assurance in building sculpture. Across Europe, on gables, pinnacles and spires they enlivened silhouettes

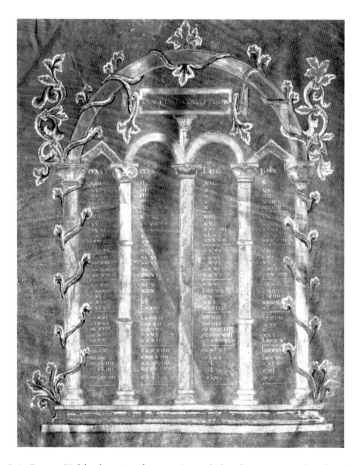

Figure 5.6 Canon Table drawing from a Gospels book. An example of probable generation of the crocket motif. Ninth century. (Paris, Bibliothèque Nationale, MS Lat.9383, Evangeliar, fol. 2^v.)

and evoked profuse sylvan images on exteriors and interiors (Figure 3.9; Figure 6.1; note Figure 5.11).

Around the same time Joachim of Fiore (*c.* 1132–1202) wrote his *Liber Concordie* and *Liber Figurarum*, illustrated with theological diagrams.[62] The particular significance which his stylised tree and flower forms carry cannot simply be transferred but they have architectural counterparts, and the intimation of life in the natural world representing life in the spiritual is here. Many of his diagrams are 'trees', having marvellous stems, ramification, foliage and fruit. In the 'Tree of the *Spiritus Sanctus*' the geometry could be compared with tierceron-rib vaults in Bristol cathedral (Figure 5.3). Another figure has geometrical branches with vine leaf-bud crockets in the same idiom as on architectural pinnacles, and fruit, apparently pomegranates—which commonly allude to the Church. The representations of organic nature were evidently instructive adumbrations, on some level, of Joachim's concepts of the operations of the Trinity through all human generations from the arcane root in Adam, to the Church, and fruition in the Spirit. Using similar images churches could be endowed with forms of living nature, which became ubiquitous and often exuberant. This case leads us to check some relations between a mental concept and an artefact.

Mind and hand of an artificer

In this chapter the subject has been orientated toward the work of the making of buildings. How makers saw their role in relation to God and their work may be gleaned from numerous and diverse sources and confirmed in their works. Augustine had called God the great Artificer, also Artist, Maker and Creator; artificers could emulate him and their art could imitate his.[63] God made the whole cosmos; their work could be a miniature in its likeness. God's universe was extensive and intensive; so too builders would make his dwelling-place on earth. Augustine said God's mode of working was—

> with the true artist's skill, which here is the Wisdom of God. It is not that God *discovered* that it was good, after it had been made. Far from it. Not one of those works would have been done, if he had not known it beforehand. It could not have come into being if he had not seen it already.[64]

For a church to be made in the mode of God's creation, designers would need to know and see beforehand what would be good. We have seen in dialectic and rhetoric that this is part of the process; and in the quadrivium how skill in judgement must be acquired. Though Augustine said 'beforehand' he immediately noted that,

> It is not with God as it is with us. […] He does not see things by turning his attention from one thing to another. […] And with him there is no difference between seeing with the eyes and 'seeing' with the mind, for he does not consist of mind and body.[65]

176 *Contemplation: life in nature*

For this reason contemplation has been emphasised: that the mind should see and attend to the whole work, being equipped to access every matter for consideration. Experience of the world of nature, and one's grasp of the intelligible nature of the world, to be conversant with it and hold it in oneself, was close and direct. From contemplative sight apprehending the works of earthly creation in their intrinsic goodness, consideration could turn to processes of emulative work. Then it could be translated by an artist.

In the conscious gestation of twelfth-century medieval arts, Hugh of St-Victor produced *Didascalicon* which was influential throughout Europe. He took Augustine's doctrine of terrestrial creation and applied it to endorse an artificer's working in nature, and as a manifesto for artists—the world as a model to imitate, the world which artists could hold up as a mirror of the wisdom of God. The imitation of nature was accepted and expanded in this way: 'The work of the artificer is to put together things disjoined or to disjoin those put together'.[66] This opens up some of the complexities of judgement, skill and power. Then, further, 'The human work, because it is not nature but only imitative of nature, is fitly called mechanical, that is adulterate, just as a skeleton key is called a "mechanical" key'.[67] Martin of Laon[68] had given the following application of 'adulterate' (from *moechus*):

> From 'moechus' we call 'mechanical art' any object which is clever and most delicate and which, in its making or operation, is beyond detection, so that beholders find their power of vision stolen from them when they cannot penetrate the ingenuity of the thing.[69]

Extreme skill and subtlety is the mechanism to draw the contemplator past the material work into the reality of the thing imitated.

A text which illustrates Hugh's statement and Martin's, is Henry of Avranches' description of the whole fabric of the new Lincoln cathedral as having a twofold form, and double meaning:

> These parts [...] import an allegory. On the outside the church is like a hard shell, but inside is formed a kernel; outside it is like wax, but inside it is a honeycomb.[70]

The first simile evokes, say, an acorn or chestnut, tough, protective on the outside, but refined and enfolding within. The apian simile suggests the monolithic external character and the harmonious arrangement and hierarchical purpose of internal order. These both describe forms according with designs so common in nature (Figure 5.7; Figure 5.8). Henry marvelled at the skill:

> The gripping mortar holds together the white stones, all cut true to the mark by the craftsman's hand. The wall, built by their heaping together, seems to distain this, appearing as though its close-laid parts were all one piece; it looks not artificial but a work of nature, not a thing united, but one.[71]

Contemplation: life in nature 177

Figure 5.7 Lincoln, England. Cathedral church of St Mary. West front. Romanesque lower arches, *c*. 1150. Gothic upper stories of arcading rebuilt 1220–30.

Figure 5.8 Lincoln, England. Cathedral church of St Mary. View from west end of nave to east end of sanctuary. Begun 1193, completed 1320.

He paid highest tribute—resemblance to a work of nature; a thing which is joined beyond detection, having such integrity as seems beyond the design and execution of art.

This accords with what Hugh had written a century earlier concerning the adepts in the arts. We read in *Didascalicon* of the intention and activity of artificers in relation to nature: 'In the design by which they imitate, they express the form of their exemplar, which is nature'.[72] It was a complex and challenging prescription. He illustrated the matter himself:

> The founder who casts a statue has gazed upon man as his model. The builder who has constructed a house has taken into consideration a mountain [...] as the ridges of mountains retain no water, even so does a house require to be framed into a high peak that it may safely discharge the weight of pouring rains. [...] From this the infinite varieties of painting, weaving, carving, and founding have arisen, so that we look with wonder not at nature alone but at the artificer as well.[73]

Thus an influential theologian reckoned that artificers knew what they were doing because they 'gazed' and 'took into consideration'. Their peculiar skill which Hugh perceived was that of design. Imitation was both more and less than copying—it was a matter of comprehending the essentials by contemplation of the model; then the design could appropriately interpret the very form. The medieval artificer was not to gaze interiorly at his own soul, to express *himself* or his emotions. His subject connected with all nature; nature which incidentally yet intimately included himself, for the human soul has a 'capacity for all things'. To design was to engage with life.

The mind can apprehend all created things because it exists in the same mode, and finds in itself an analogue of all nature. The cathedral could be a microcosm of the world because it was conceived as 'existing in the same mode' as nature. We accept this especially where we perceive a conscious and conspicuous analogy set up, by imitation, designed to reflect and partake in the divine handiwork. All nature could be contained in the church. *We* study the physical architecture as an antiquated mode working with a restricted range of structural, formal and decorative means. But the form-givers and artists engrossed *within* it were exercising the powers of intellectual and imaginative vision at the highest level. The sensitive perception that interpreted the visible world was essentially the power of the mind that contemplated the invisible world. There could be comprehension of both worlds, because the pattern of both is in human nature. Yet this is the range of human noetic power which of itself is limited in knowledge of God:

> The knowledge of God that can be gathered from the human mind does not transcend the genus of the knowledge gathered from sensible things; since even the soul knows what it itself is through understanding the natures of sensible things. Consequently, even in this way God is not known in a higher manner than the cause is known from its effect.[74]

Even in the highest reach of God being known from his creation, lower things serve in the same office as human things. To know the truth of both is to apprehend the essential life of nature: all things are 'true in their nature according as they are likened to that supreme nature'.[75]

Yet we can go further. Hugh of St-Victor in expounding the process of knowing made a particular point of the role of the human mind: it reflects to one's contemplation that process which is a reflection of the divine process, that of conceptualisation and transmission:

> Just as a man, when he has conceived something in his mind, draws an example of it externally, so that what was known only to him may be seen plainly by others [...]; so, too, God, wishing to show his invisible Wisdom, drew its example in the mind of the rational creature, and next, by making the corporeal creature, showed the rational creature an external example of what it itself contained within.[76]

The new point here is the initiative of God in giving to the rational creature the insight by which to understand the mental process, even showing how to use this wisdom. Seeing this model gives sharp clarity to the mind-hand synergy which is Hugh's real subject. Strategically in view is the *artist's* mind—conceiving 'something' he has an inner compulsion to bring it into existence, to communicate it, which requires the hand to make an external 'example'.

Deeper still, the hidden movement of the artist's mind is contemplation of God and love of Wisdom, until there is conformity to God. Such is the focus and aim of Book Two of *Didascalicon* prefacing the description of the arts:

> This, then, is what the arts are concerned with, this is what they intend, namely, to restore within us the divine likeness, a likeness which to us is a form but to God is his nature. The more we are conformed to the divine nature, the more do we possess Wisdom, for then there begins to shine forth again in us what has forever existed in the divine Idea or Pattern, coming and going in us but standing changeless in God.[77]

As this likeness increases so does the artist participate in, and the work mirror, the loved Idea and Pattern. Even thus ideally artificers were handling things seen and unseen. In another strand of theology there is further insight into the invisible activity of the mind.

Angelic contemplation

Attention to medieval theology's interest in angels may assist our appreciation of connections made between spirit and matter. Angels were fully accepted in the consciousness as real beings, actual in time and space, present in the world, sometimes particular in appearance and place. The importance this gives to the evidence adduced in this chapter must be allowed. If we

180   *Contemplation: life in nature*

recognise angels as of some higher order than earthly creatures, we learn that their nature and life was spiritual, and they were deemed to be exemplars in contemplation and love of God. We have followed the soul as it 'goes out to sensible things'; through participation in nature it could grasp the pattern of creation. Now we consider how reason 'ascends to invisible things'; it is an exploration of the hierarchies acting with intelligence throughout creation.

In *City of God* Augustine wrote of contemplation of the Trinity revealed in its works, unsuppressible in creativity. He attributed to the angels clearer knowledge than humans have, through their being knowingly in the presence of the Father, the Word and the Spirit. 'They have better knowledge of the created world *there*, in God's wisdom, *in the art by which it was made*, than in the created world itself.'[78] He develops this as a principle: grasping a thing's formal cause is to understand it beyond knowing it as an image or object.

> There is a great difference between knowing something in the form according to which it was made, and knowing it as it is in itself. For example, straight lines and accurate geometrical figures are known in one way when conceived by the intellect, and in another when drawn in the dust [...] And so it is with all other things.[79]

It assists our subject that Augustine offered this apt example. The principle can validly be applied to a whole building seen conceptually in its cause, which is 'in the art by which it is made'; it is elevated above the experiential. To have this kind of knowledge by contemplation is to gain access to meaning:

> The angels see the immutable and abiding causes and reasons according to which they were made; and in another way in themselves. In the former, they know them more clearly; in the latter, their knowledge is more obscure, and merely of the works themselves rather than their design. Yet when these works are referred to the praise and veneration of the Creator Himself, it is as if dawn has broken in the minds of those who contemplate them.[80]

The whole community of holy angels was identified as the City of which God is the centre: 'We are speaking of the City of God which is not on pilgrimage in this mortal life, but is eternally immortal in heaven, consisting of the holy angels who cleave to God'.[81]

In the Trinity all causes and reasons are found. The Father is generative love; the Word is form-giving creator; the Spirit vivifies spiritual creatures. Later, in scholastic theology Thomas explained that angels, being closest to God, are spiritual substances whose forms are 'so perfect that they are self-subsistent and self-complete, requiring no sub-structure of matter'.[82] But the form of the human being is in the conjunction of spirit and body. So disconcerting and difficult this is, the 'weight' of matter often limits the power to act, and is blamed for people being far from God and spiritually impotent.

> In as much, then, as it surpasses the actual being of corporeal matter, having of itself the power to subsist and to act, the human soul is a spiritual substance; but inasmuch as it is touched upon by matter and shares its own actual being with matter, it is the form of the body.[83]

The idea of nature can scarcely be investigated in medieval writings without attention to form; and it extends into the process of becoming according to nature, or making by art. Ideal forms are in things, 'informing' their nature. Or an ideal form of a thing is in the mind of a maker, who by art shapes and contracts it into particular material, making it actual. Augustine gave legitimation to *form* as having reference to material form, sensibly apprehended. He delineated two sorts of form. It is an application of the concept of form which superseded the ancient philosophy and which passed on into the Christian Middle Ages:

> There is one kind of form which is imposed from without upon every item of corporeal matter whatsoever: for example, the form given by potters and smiths and that class of artists who paint and mould shapes which resemble the bodies of animals. But there is another and internal kind of form, which is not itself made, but which produces, as their efficient cause, not only natural corporeal forms but also the very souls of living creatures, and which springs from the secret and hidden choice of a living and intelligent nature. Form in the first of these two senses can be attributed to every craftsman.[84]

Form of this kind is described here in a way still perceived in the modern world. In the Middle Ages the second was recognised as caused by the spiritual act of the Spirit of God moving and self-imparting, 'God alone' creating and shaping all that is:

> The second belongs to God alone, who alone is artist, maker and creator. He needed no material from the world, nor help from angels, when he made the world itself, and created the angels.[85]

On one level form is contracted in something material and individual; on a higher level it inheres in that which is spiritual and intelligible: implicitly the lower is an adumbration of the higher. Thomas says, 'Now it must be borne in mind that the more perfect a form is, the more does it surpass corporeal matter'.[86] It is noticeable how frequently in scholastic angelology ideas concerning form are brought in; for angels, invisible and incorporeal, are the antithesis of formlessness. A concomitant notion is that in order to reflect more fully the perfections of God there must be diversity of forms. From that flows the necessity of order underlying the gradations of hierarchy, and disclosures of perfection leading back to the source:

> The reason for the order of things is derived from the diversity of forms. Indeed since it is in accord with its form that a thing has being, and since anything, in so far as it has being, approaches the likeness of God Who is His own simple being, it must be that form is nothing else than a divine likeness that is participated in things.[87]

In a hierarchy of forms descending from spiritual to corporeal, we look for some connections or parallels between divine works and human works: spiritual form may be the referent of material form. We have just seen the two media of knowledge of a thing, the higher apprehending the origin. That being so there is, it seems, potency in matter that may access the highest and perfect reality by the action of some agent, such as love. With reassuring clarity and without technical terms Thomas repeats in at least four places the metaphysical epigram which offers a pragmatic connection: 'The highest point of the lowest always touches the lowest point of the highest'.[88] There is a defining actuality and accuracy in the point of contact. It is a spatial image which invites a literal transfer to architecture—very clearly in towers whose tops seem to be dialectical transitions from material to immaterial, and in spires making literal points of contact of the visible and invisible. Before the twelfth century towers were sometimes capped with pyramidal forms; then the development of high daringly slender spires might be a rhetorical expression of a theology of contemplation (Figure 6.1).

The highest and lowest are the opposites which define the limits of the hierarchical order of everything. Pseudo-Dionysius was prominent in expounding the concept of hierarchies. He said:

> The goal of a hierarchy is to enable beings to be as like as possible to God and to be at one with him. A hierarchy has God as its leader of all understanding and action. It is forever looking directly at the comeliness of God. A hierarchy bears in itself the mark of God. Hierarchy causes its members to be images of God in all respects, to be clear and spotless mirrors reflecting the glow of primordial light and indeed of God himself.[89]

The whole realm of angels who remained in love reflected God, but were known to mortals by little more than their titles: angels, archangels, virtues, powers, principalities, dominations, thrones, cherubim and seraphim. In the Middle Ages it hardly had to be argued that every hierarchy is 'under God'. We touched on this—that it is natural for angels to love God; that hierarchies derive from the divine Hierarch; that they are integral in the ordering of loves. All are inter-related, held together by love.

In architecture a hierarchical mode was not exempted simply because it ordered material things—as if nothing more. The distinctions remain, however, between angelic creation and earthly creation, between spiritual and corporeal; and the aim is to find a point at which spiritual and material realities were clarified and unified in the art and architecture.

Visualisation

By contrast with angelic beings, earthly things are virtually 'formless matter'. Augustine wrote: 'From nothing, then, you created heaven and earth, distinct from one another; the one close to yourself, the other close to being nothing; the one surpassed only by yourself, the other little more than nothing'.[90] He concluded that true understanding of the nature of things is through contemplative knowledge of God, applying the principle of angelic knowledge to humans.[91] Angels have substance and form without corporeity and matter; so they are scarcely knowable unless intellectually and spiritually, and the power to visualise them must be essentially on that level. Yet the powers of angelic minds may indicate how humans may see and know God. Visualisation of a sort is implied in all the theology and psychology of 'seeing'.

When Pseudo-Dionysius addressed this in *The Celestial Hierarchy*, he faced the problem of how 'heavenly and godlike intelligences' can possibly be visualised. He had in mind not only positive images of bodiless forms, such as the Tetramorph, but also negative types and 'manifestations of dissimilar shapes'—intentionally base and opposite images.[92] He was very clear that all visualisations being images, and art being the medium itself, are but means to an end. So he said, 'not for the sake of art, but as a concession to the nature of our own mind'.[93] Nor could one use images as one pleased for they had divine purposes to serve. The question concerns 'creating types for the typeless, for giving shape to what is actually without shape'. He explained our need:

> We lack the ability to be directly raised up to conceptual contemplations. We need our own upliftings that come naturally to us and which can raise before us the permitted forms of the marvelous and unformed sights.[94]

Images may be based on likeness or unlikeness, similarity or dissimilarity; but wherever they lie on such a scale every symbol is *both* similar *and* dissimilar to the reality it represents. His reasons for preferring those that are most incongruous point up an understanding underlying sacred art which would have persisted, though with declining force, to the end of the Middle Ages:

> A manifestation through dissimilar shapes is more correctly to be applied to the invisible. [...] I doubt that anyone would refuse to acknowledge that incongruities are more suitable for lifting our minds

up into the domain of the spiritual than similarities are. [...] Indeed the sheer crassness of the signs is a goad so that even the materially inclined cannot accept that it could be permitted or true that the celestial and divine sights could be conveyed by such shameful things.[95]

So art could have conventions by which to convey invisible, spiritual nature. This was explicitly treated by Eriugena in thinking about temporal similitudes used in relation to God. Metaphorical images 'tend to come from three bases, namely likeness, contrariety, difference'.[96] Concerning those based on *contrariety*, he wrote, 'So great is their power to express meaning that by a sort of privilege of their excellence they are rightly called by the Greeks *entimemata*, that is, concepts of the mind'.[97] The reasoning mind could see the dialectical logic in the contrariety, and thence intelligible meaning. Images of contrariety had like power in art.

Theology well recognised the issues of divine-human similarity and dissimilarity. This was enunciated in the *Acts of the Fourth Lateran Council, 2*, in 1215: 'Wherefore between Creator and creature no so-great similarity is able to be marked but that between them there should be a greater dissimilarity marked out'.[98] It was taken that devices might be useful and allowable by which transcendent realities could be signified by both highest and lowest creatures. Gerhart Ladner says that analogy involved, 'a universe of symbols in which, with the sole exception of God, everything could signify something else. [. . .] Above all, material things signified spiritual things or even God himself'.[99] On the other hand, spiritual creatures, angels who participate in the life of God, if contemplated as mirrors held closest to ineffable deity, may open a visualisation of spiritual realities. The imagination of artists was assisted by Scripture where it gives indications of their physical appearings.

The dissimilarity trope has a bearing on aspects of sculpture especially. Some historians touch on the diverse images of animals, strange creatures, grotesque faces and distorted humans in corbel-tables, gargoyles and the like, reckoning that they are purely decorative; or rather unsatisfactorily speculating on symbolic significance of secular rather than religious intent, concluding that they elude interpretation. Such a widespread feature of Romanesque sculpture, perpetuated in the Gothic period, warrants more radical explanation. There are several characteristics to observe: first, obviously they are not images of inanimate things, but signify the animal kingdom, whether birds, beasts, human or hybrid; they can be imputed with sensitivity and potency, and apt symbolism on that level. Second, as images of good or evil there is little consistency, and textual narrative is absent or tenuous. A majority appear benign, albeit not attractive; many simply ugly, frightful, shameful or stupid; fewer appear malign. Thus moral attributions are opaque and didactic power is diffuse. A third consideration is their setting, which is generally in exterior high places, but significantly they are not definitely excluded from church interiors; and they are not

Figure 5.9 Regensburg, Germany. Cathedral church of St Peter. Detail of south transept sculpture above principal window. Late thirteenth century (or before 1310).

necessarily segregated from angels or humans. The Regensburg detail shows Gothic characteristics rather more sophisticated than the very common Romanesque corbel table sculptures (Figure 5.9).

If there was a Christian use based on common theological notions of hierarchy and participation, the explanation surely had to do with *congruity*. It applied in the contraction of spiritual form to corporeal, in nature shadowing divinity, in dissimilarity touching similarity. Bonaventure articulated the thoughts of Augustine discussed above:

> It is necessary that there be something near to God and similar to him; and also at the other extreme, that there be something near to nothingness, and this also in some way like God, obviously not entirely nor perfectly, because it has in it the very least of good. It can be said, nevertheless, that even in its low condition, considering what it is, and its part in the whole gradation, it is ordered best.[100]

Congruity helps the mind to grasp the meaning. But not gratuitously things incongruous and unsightly are contemplated, rather they hint at opposite splendours which would be unbearable, at perfection which would crush

186 Contemplation: life in nature

the intellect. Pseudo-Dionysius had said, 'Forms, even those drawn from the lowliest matter, can be used, not unfittingly, with regard to heavenly beings'.[101] He taught that by contrariety the similarities must be used as dissimilarities, to avoid one-to-one correspondence with immaterial archetypes. He identified 'dissimilar' images as ranging from the sun to the cornerstone, from a lion to a worm. In this way what is holy has been kept separate—

> from defilement by anything in the realm of the imperfect or the profane. The [exponents] therefore honor the dissimilar shape so that the divine things remain inaccessible to the profane and so that all those with a real wish to see the sacred imagery may not dwell on the types as true. So true negations and the unlike comparisons with their last echoes offer due homage to the divine things.[102]

If creatures portrayed in art exercise a 'rule' proper to them in architectural contexts, their rhetoric demonstrates their function and meaning. Considering the three characteristics seen in their iconography—their constitution, state and situation—they have due participation in spiritual form, they are impressionable and passible in their corporeality, and they are antithetical to angels. Because of congruity working in them in these features, these most unlikely creatures are apt types of universal antitypes of all created living beings; and the antitypes govern them. The types are established hierarchically, contracted materially, and endorsed visibly by art and architecture. Peering faces under parapets, and grotesque gargoyles, express the great contrast with the most sublime spiritual beings, asserting the vast divide between material appearances and invisible forms. Within church naves and choirs, in vaults and spandrels, the presence of angels was often visualised in schemes which seem to be counterparts of exterior schemes. To recognise the whole range of incongruities at work within the idea of *congruence* best accounts for the role of naturalistic and fantastic animal representations in capitals, corbels and bosses. Finding the lowliest creatures and the noblest angels incorporated in the building a person is awed by the contrast, and is led on to contemplate the incomprehensible superiority of God to the angels.

That images of earthly creatures could represent intelligent beings of highest degree is evidenced in the four creatures surrounding God. According to context, these living creatures may signify direct vision of God, the revealed nature of Christ, and testimonial utterances. They are winged, indicating their spiritual nature and divine office, but their appearances are as a lion, an ox, an eagle *and* a man.[103] The symbols make a coherence between angels, beasts and man. They were clearly deemed right images in the sanctuary itself, in St-Julien, Brioude, in San Fermo Maggiore, Verona, and countless places (Figure 5.10). Through familiarity, and Scriptural usage, we take for granted their incongruous proximity to the glory of God. The symbols were intensely focussed and focussed contemplation.

In a remarkably effective architectural application an illustration from the *Bible historiée* of Jean de Papeleu suggests how the form of a cathedral

Contemplation: life in nature 187

Figure 5.10 Brioude, France. Church of St-Julien. The sanctuary vault fresco. Christ and the Tetramorph; seraphim above; angels surrounding. Wavy lines signify the heavenly realm. Twelfth century.

was visualised by the artist, and understood by the patron and readers (Figure 5.11). The church is filled by the enthroned Christ; from here he blesses the world. It is a spiritual place, as signified by the cloud motifs, and by the appearance of the normally invisible angelic beings and the seraphim of love in all the hierarchical places of the building. With the genius of Gothic art for conflating images it reads as an interior, in cross-section, while being a composition showing typical exterior components. It makes the structure congruent with the meaning, the architecture a coherent exposition of the spiritual order.

188 *Contemplation: life in nature*

Figure 5.11 Frontispiece of the *Bible historiée* of Jean de Papeleu. Christ seated within a church, blessing the world, with attendant angels and seraphim. 1317. (Paris, Bibliothèque Nationale, Bibliothèque de l'Arsénal, MS 5059, fol. 1.)

Representation

The existence of intangible realities was asserted by the countless depictions of angels in art. They represented the proposition that spiritual realities by privation 'coming down', and material by being conformable 'reaching up', could—in ways theology and metaphysics speculated on—touch, connect and communicate. The theory leads us to deduce that sculptural and pictorial images of angels were visually explicit affirmations of this. It runs everywhere through the *loci* of architecture. Painters, sculptors and illuminators easily treated the subject of angels; but how architects engaged it is harder to determine. The *Bible historiée* drawing evidently indicates a conscious literal association of architectural place and spiritual occupants.

Some primary literary sources underlie a discussion of artefacts. An important Biblical prototype was Solomon's temple. In the sanctuary, over the ark, the cherubims' wings touched; the outer tips touched the walls; thus they spanned the width. Carved on the walls and doors were cherubim, palm trees and flowers.[104] Medieval pictorial art sometimes translated the typology explicitly, with the locational associations in the sanctuary: for instance, cherubim protecting the mercy seat with outspread wings, and seraphs above the throne in the shekinah-filled temple. There were apt interpretations such as cherubim flanking the crucifix on the rood screen at Halberstadt cathedral, and angels swinging censers epitomising the priest censing the church.

Honorius of Autun, sometime before 1130, produced a manual of theological symbolism for churches. From its traditional origins he justified the legitimacy of representational art thus:

> The tradition of carving images began in the Law, when Moses made two cherubim of gold at the Lord's command. The painting of churches took its rise from Solomon, who caused divers paintings to be made in the temple of the Lord.[105]

It is worth noticing that it was specifically spiritual beings, the cherubim, whose representations were sanctioned. But any theological symbol given in Scripture was deemed translatable into visual form without changing its character or essential value.

William Durandus (1230–96) was aware of the significance of locational arrangement; and each *locus* was significant because of the architectonic setting, which had reference to the unity and continuum of place, time and hierarchy, experienced directly:

> Of pictures and images some are above the church, as the cock and the eagle: some without the church, namely, in the air in front of the church, as the ox and the cow: others within, as images, and statues, and various kinds of painting and sculpture: and these be represented either in garments, or on walls, or in stained glass.[106]

Durandus described the depiction of the four living creatures of Ezekiel's vision, and drew out in some detail the transposition by which they symbolise the Evangelists. Yet, in explaining the eagle of John, for instance, he is not concerned to distinguish natural symbolism and received theological symbol:

> John has the figure of the Eagle: because, soaring to the utmost height, he says, 'In the beginning was the word.' This also represents Christ, 'Whose youth is renewed like the eagle's': because, rising from the dead, He ascends into Heaven. Here, however it is not portrayed as by the side, but as above [the figure of Christ], since it denotes the Ascension, and the word pronounced of God.[107]

If the position of the eagle seems obvious it is a reminder that much symbolism depends upon associations which are so direct and intuitive that they usually escape attention.

Henry of Avranches grasped a tropological meaning of the vaults of Lincoln cathedral (Figure 5.8). He saw them in relation to the rest of the fabric, the world, indeed the universe:

> The foundation is buried in the womb of the earth but walls and roof appear, and with proud daring the wall rushes towards the clouds, the roof towards the stars. The skill of the craftsmen fitly matches the cost of the materials, for the vault spreading wide its wings like the feathered birds and as if in flight, strikes the clouds, though resting on its solid columns.[108]

In much Old Testament imagery, and in the development of Christian art, the wings of birds have been a natural symbol for the power of movement and operation, indeed the chief symbol for the spiritual creature. Thus wings were ascribed to the angelic orders, particularly following Isaiah's vision of the seraphim, and also to elect beasts. So when Henry described the vaults as wings as of birds flying in the clouds, the purely architectural-structural form became a trope of clear meaning: to denote the spiritual world of beings with the ability to ascend to heavenly things. Indeed the 'roof towards the stars' in a later line became 'the spirit has the stars'. The vaults of St Hugh's rebuilt choir are asymmetrical and seem illogical. Christopher Wilson admits (as do others) that explanations and derivations elude discovery, but he does not doubt the intentionality of the design.[109] The illusion of movement is in them—movement towards the altar—and perhaps Henry's 'wings *as if in flight*' was a critique more perceptive than we realise. How far such abstract representations of forms worked in the conscious thoughts of designers can scarcely be known.[110] William Durandus and Henry of Avranches made a certain amount explicit and we may suppose some circulation and influence of their writings.

Beyond that it is not implausible to see the many interpretations in churches as products of this mentality. Reims cathedral is an instructive case, having an extensive scheme of angels and creatures on the exterior of the east end, and on the north and south sides to almost the same pattern. Each buttress provides places, in ascending order, for a figure of a person or angel, a gargoyle, and in a high aedicule a large angel with outstretched wings protruding. At the top of the flying-buttress arch is an angel, above which a gargoyle. At each radiating chapel around the chevet other places and figures have been added to the scheme. In drawings made at the time of visiting Reims cathedral Villard de Honnecourt recorded a number of exterior elevations, and added the comment, 'On the tops of the pillars, there should be angels, and, in front, flying buttresses'.[111] His cross-section drawing (above the aisles) shows the buttress aedicules and the miniature canopy for each topmost angel. The drawing of the apsidal chapel exterior shows angels in the spandrels. Evidently this was to him a notable feature as a model for future work, for he annotates it, 'If those at Cambrai are done properly they will look like this'.[112] We take for granted the power the sculpture acquires by being on the generating lines of the structure radiating from the centre of the sanctuary, and by denoting the hierarchical ordering of the places. The sculpture's power to signify what the theology contemplated depends upon the integration with the architecture. Arthur Gardner perceived the artistic importance:

> It forms actually a part of the building it adorns, and the way in which each figure fits its niche and harmonises with its surroundings will always excite our admiration. Take a statue from its proper position and it loses half its value, but in its own place it is inimitable.[113]

A well-known example is the oxen which occupy conspicuous high places in the west towers of Laon cathedral, and Gardner's assertion is clearly true (Figure 4.12). And as well as the historical story a tropological sense is inevitable. They are exemplars of dissimilarity, rather like the Tetramorph. Then the corollary is that such incorporation of the art in the rationale of the building effectively makes the place representational also, and the expansive architecture itself as capable of heuristic purpose.

Can the architecture represent theological ideas where iconography is absent altogether? Where figural sculpture is absent there is, nevertheless, another level of intention indicated by associations which derive their force from the architecture. For instance, at high levels, at the transition where towers take their separate identities, galleries were often built, of no functional necessity, and often not for statuary. Early Gothic versions were arcaded screens, open where feasible, with slender colonnettes, and sometimes with refined tracery. This, set against the sky and girding the towers, speaks with a plausible rhetoric of the higher realm, this the threshold of the transcendent. The west front of Laon cathedral at the transition to the towers has double-storied aedicules foiling the buttresses and helping to visually free the towers in vertical movement, while horizontally they are linked by a congenial arcade. At Mantes cathedral, the façade above the third stage dissolves into an aery arcade, a complete stage enveloping the bases of the towers with an undulating screen (Figure 5.12). From the literary-theological sources we may credibly deduce that these are visions and affirmations of heavenly places. The height speaks of noble rank in the hierarchy between mundane and spiritual worlds.

The sense of the arcade as an accessible, habitable place entails the notion of participation in some order or milieu. In the language of architecture, congruent noetic-mystical concepts might be thus represented and focussed. Where ideas patently correspond, or even sub-consciously connect, abstraction and imagery are media of exchange increasing understanding. Thus façades at the large scale are a representation of the nature, form and narrative of the church.

Similar correspondences may be found between written sources, schemes of representational art, and the architecture. Medieval perception evidently knew a literalness in visualisation and representation which we do not easily grasp. Barfield's insight of immersion in meaning should be recalled.

Figure 5.12 Mantes, France. Cathedral church of Notre-Dame. West front with the towers girt by an elevated arcaded gallery. 1215–50.

He critiques modern versus medieval sense of the literal, the symbolic and representations. 'A representation experienced as such is neither literal nor symbolical; or, alternatively, it is both at the same time.'[114] He writes:

> Yet the essence of symbolism is [...] that things or events themselves, are apprehended as representations. [...] *Our* 'symbolical' therefore is an approximation to, or a variant of, *their* 'literal'. Even when they got down to the bedrock of literal, they still experienced that rock as a representation. [...] To understand how the word 'literal' has changed its meaning is to understand the heart of the matter. [...] It is only by

reconstructing in imagination, and not just in theory, the nature of the representations they confronted that we can hope really to understand the mode of their thinking.[115]

This may be appreciated in a remarkable example in the upper church of San Francesco, Assisi, where the angelic presence in frescos is transposed to the architecture which partakes in the literalness of the whole representation. The embrasures of the apse and transept have an elevated shallow loggia, surmounted by a fresco-work arcade—a subtle merging of plastic and pictorial media. On the mural behind the colonnade are full-length angels, not matched to the arches, not corresponding, but the whole literalness generates remarkable congruence. Also it is a use of the device of *diatyposis*. Above in fresco, with great verisimilitude, are half-length angels, each in an arch, appearing as above a parapet, as representations indeed. John White here appreciates the 'real presence'—this is what *we* find it difficult to give credence to:

> The intention is unmistakable, and in transept and choir alike there is an astonishing sense of the equation of real and painted space, of actual and painted architecture. The real presence of angelic apparitions is suggested.[116]

These, in contrast to the great cycles of the frescos filling the nave, are representational rather than narrative, theological rather than historical.

To us angels are natural symbols by intuition and convention—symbols merely. But in the medieval mind they were more. They were incorporated in the unworldly regions of high arcades and vaults, pointing to life highest and closest to God. Using natural *locus* signification Gloucester cathedral's choir vault bosses have flights of angels ascending from each side and centred on the figure of Christ high over the altar (Figure 5.4). In the sanctuary arch of St Laurentius, Erwitte, tall angels, one above another, ascend to the apex from both sides. There are numerous notable instances of arcade spandrels, with their repetition, perfect shape and location, displaying angels particularly in choirs and sanctuaries.

What this amounts to is that means were discovered whereby the church building and place outwardly and inwardly represented the spiritual world. These examples show what was being conveyed and how it was done in a world of created intelligential nature; beings far below and dissimilar from the Maker referring to inconceivable deity, and beings deemed most similar and nearest to the Source reflecting its splendour. The non-material was represented in the material by architecture working in both modes.

Operatio

The nine-fold hierarchical arrangement of the angels alludes to order in the entire spiritual world, and the assertion that God is the supreme focus of

194 *Contemplation: life in nature*

thought and operation, apprehended morally in obedience, mystically in ascent. Where the same focus is in hierarchical architecture it will mirror the intention and functioning of the life of the spirit. The architecture and scheme of the mosaic of the octagonal vault in the San Giovanni Baptistry, Florence, is for contemplation of this spiritual world. But this is the baptistry, and for a catechumen it is a vision of the life of obedience and service.

Of the soul transcending nature, Bonaventure wrote *The Journey of the Mind to God*. Two middle stages, 'through which we enter into the contemplation of God within us as in mirrors of created images, are like the two middle wings of the Seraph spread out for flight'.[117] The seraph of love hovers over the images. Rising through all stages, one comes to see all the angelic operations:

> Our spirit is made hierarchical in order to mount upward [...]. These correspond level by level to the nine choirs of angels. [...] Having attained these, the soul, entering into itself, enters the heavenly Jerusalem, where beholding the choirs of angels, it sees in them God, who dwells in them and performs all their operations. [...] From all this, God is seen as *all in all* (I Cor. 15:28) when we contemplate him in our minds, where he dwells through the gifts of the most abundant charity.[118]

He applied this affective scenario as involving interior but practical work: 'Our soul is marked with nine levels when within it the following are arranged in orderly fashion: announcing, declaring, leading, ordering, strengthening, commanding, receiving, revealing, anointing'.[119] In these terms the angelic orders modelled corresponding activities in the life of the soul. Furthermore, we may construe from the visual significations in churches that the building was similarly 'marked', meaning that the spiritual *modus operandi* was essentially the same in the material mode.

In a sermon, 'The Loves of the Angels', Bernard portrayed the character, endowment and activity of each of the nine orders, showing how each loves God in a distinctive way and on account of various attributes of God. They were made thus and thus to love. 'The Cherubim are moved to love because the Lord is a God of knowledge.' 'The Seraphim love him because he is love.'[120] Such, and others, are the activities of creative work. In all the angels divine attributes motivate and operate; it is a model for earthly work by humans.

Leaving the subject of angels we can consider the radical purpose and meaning of the creation and life of all things. Grosseteste, in his *Hexaëmeron*, traversed the significations which depend much on the nisus towards higher things. That involves the inclination and acting of love, *operatio*:

> The living and moving soul is understanding, loving and working, or faith acting through love [...] 'life' is truly ascribed to love (*dileccionem*), 'motion' to acting (*operacionem*). But when a faithful soul acts well out of love, it is developed into a completed kind (*formatam speciem producta est*).[121]

Contemplation: life in nature 195

Human creatures have life and form through love, and things take form through love's work. The rebuilding of the choir of St-Denis abbey is a clear twelfth-century application of such theology. The work was done because the protagonist was moved by clear vision. Abbot Suger described the consecration of the church, when the hierarchs, king and nobles saw themselves as participating in a celestial ceremony.[122] He claimed that the splendid show was born of gratitude, honouring God, not glorifying himself. The manner of this was by seeking whole perfection, even as Christ 'fused our nature with His into one admirable individuality'. The incarnation joined God not with angels but with humans. Yet, more strongly he emphasised how low *our* nature stands, and how unworthy in virtue, even in the spiritual re-forming of our substance to be akin to the angels.[123] He recognised the persistence of the human and material condition. Peter Kidson is generally sceptical of Suger's overlay of theology, and even more so of Panofsky's Pseudo-Dionysian interpretations, and caution is necessary.[124] As to the depth of Suger's theology it is easy to minimise it supposing that his abbatial concerns and admiration of visible things obscured keen spiritual insight. However, his writing is of one who felt that doctrine and art can be integrated; that what is visualised may be represented; who achieved it in this work. The commencement of *De consecratione* should not be overlooked, for the doctrine and coinherence is here:

> The admirable power of one unique and supreme reason equalizes by proper composition the disparity between things human and Divine; and what seems mutually to conflict by inferiority of origin and contrariety of nature is conjoined by the single, delightful concordance of one superior, well-tempered harmony. Those indeed who crave to be glorified by a participation in this supreme and eternal reason often devote their attention to this continual controversy of the similar and dissimilar, and to the trial and sentence of the litigant parties, sitting on the throne of the acute mind as though on a tribunal.[125] With the aid of loving-kindness [*charitate ministrante*] [they are] preferring that which is spiritual to that which is corporeal [...]. Thus, through communion with supreme reason and eternal bliss, they rejoice [...] in being deservedly united with the Glorious Consciousness.[126]

The concordance in nature of that disparity had been explained by Pseudo-Dionysius as perfectly exemplified in the place and function of angels. Before working an angel first participates in the things above, receiving, as a mirror, the image of God, 'purely enlightening within itself as far as possible the goodness of the silence in the inner sanctuaries'.[127] For humans, the participation, even of acute minds, is not without the *charitate ministrante*. Suger's enthusiasm in participation lifted his effusions above mere platitudes. He seemed to feel himself possessed of an insight on this matter for he returned to it again in closing his account:

196   *Contemplation: life in nature*

By this sacramental unction with the most holy Chrism and by the susception of the most holy Eucharist, you uniformly conjoin the material with the immaterial, the corporeal with the spiritual, the human with the divine, and sacramentally reform the purer ones to their original condition. By these and similar visible blessings, you invisibly restore and miraculously transform the present [state]. [...] May you powerfully and mercifully make us and the nature of the angels, heaven and earth, into one state.[128]

The literal and symbolic representations themselves could fuse. The active exchange between spiritual and material realms is conveyed in Malmesbury Abbey's porch lunettes, strategically integrated with the building, in the place between the outer world and the inner. The apostles appear as recipients of vision or unction from the angel on assignment. Bonaventure wrote of a dual aspect of angels—as recipients from 'above', and dispensers to those 'below'. This was the essence of their work of charity which is *operatio* (Figure 2.5). On the one hand an angel is 'a clear and most brilliant mirror; for grace coming down upon it conserves, adorns and completes its nature [*naturam conservat, naturam decorat, naturam consummat*]'.[129] On the other hand angels, like suns, look below to dispense what they receive. In so doing they can remove the causes of ugliness. Angels may seem to be miraculous in all their operations, but Thomas perceived that if they 'make use of natural things in order to produce definite effects, they use them as instruments'.[130] Humans use natural things as instruments, but find works of purely spiritual power to be beyond their natural capacities. Thomas, discussing such potential in work, said, 'The works of clever artisans appear wondrous because it is not evident to other people how they are produced'.[131] As in angels so in artisans the means is 'grace coming down'—operative love, conserving, adorning and completing. They can be God's agents in the world, and their work become a mirror directed above and below. From contemplation of all things in nature, and gathering up all the earlier subjects, a definitive integration is the next aim in directing and concluding our research.

Notes

1 A succinct summary of Genesis creation commentaries, from patristic writers to Thomas Aquinas, is given by William Wallace: see Thomas Aquinas, *Summa Theologiae, Vol. 10: Cosmogony*, Wallace (1967), Appendices 7–9.
2 Hugh of St-Victor, *Didascalicon*, 1.6, trans. Taylor (1961), p. 52.
3 Ibid., p. 53.
4 Hugh of St-Victor, *De sacramentis Christianae fidei*, 1.5.3, trans. in *Didascalicon*, Taylor (1961), Notes, p. 187.
5 Hugh of St-Victor, *Didascalicon*, 1.6, trans. Taylor (1961), p. 53.
6 Cited by Chenu (1997), p. 41. See *Didascalicon*, 1.9, trans. Taylor (1961), p. 55.
7 Plato, *Timaeus*, I, 32b–33b. Similarly Boethius had drawn on this from *Timaeus*, I, in *De consolatione*, 3.9, vs. 6–21.

8 Hugh of St-Victor, *Didascalicon*, 1.1, trans. Taylor (1961), p. 46.
9 Ibid. Jerome Taylor asserts (p. 27) that Hugh followed Remigius of Auxerre's commentary on Boethius, seeing this as the human soul not Plato's world-soul.
10 For instance, Augustine in *De civitate Dei*, 11.9–10.
11 Hugh of St-Victor, *De sacramentis Christianae fidei*, 1.6.5, trans. Defarrari (1951), p. 97.
12 Ibid.
13 Ibid., 1.6.2, p. 95. See Genesis 1.27; 5.1–2.
14 This is an early example of a pointed vesica (*vesica pisces*). It appears from the early tenth century, for instance in the *Æthelstan Psalter* of Winchester. The aureole or mandorla was the earlier form, sometimes circular, often oval, or of composite shape.
15 Proverbs 8.22–31; John 1.1–4; Colossians 1.16–17.
16 Revelation 1.8, 17; 21.6.
17 Genesis 9.16; also Revelation 4.3.
18 Genesis 1.22 and 1.28.
19 Dante, *Paradiso*, 10. 1–6. trans. Singleton (1975), p. 107.
20 This is one of the scenes on the bronze west doors, of the second quarter of the twelfth century.
21 Peter Lombard, *Sententiae*, 2, 1.2, trans. Silano (2008), pp. 3–4.
22 Augustine, *De civitate Dei*, 11.21, trans. Bettenson (1972), p. 451.
23 See, Plato, *Timaeus*, Prelude, 28a–b, 29a.
24 See, Augustine, *De civitate Dei*, 11.24, 26. C.f. Dorothy L. Sayers (1959), *The Mind of the Maker*, pp. 32, 52, 104. It concerns also contemplation of the things made.
25 Augustine, *De civitate Dei*, 11.22, trans. Bettenson (1972), pp. 453–54.
26 Grosseteste, *Hexaëmeron*, 6.12.5, trans. Wright (2017). Refer 1.1.1 for the fundamental context.
27 Ibid., 6.13.1, p. 198.
28 Bonaventure, *Breviloquium*, 2, 11.2, trans. de Vinck (1963–66), Vol. 2, p. 101.
29 Genesis 8.22; 8.17; 9.1,7.
30 Hebrews 7.16; 11.10; Genesis 14.19 (my emphasis).
31 Deuteronomy 33.13–16, AV.
32 Psalm 134.3, AV (my emphasis).
33 See Hearn (1981), Chapter 5.
34 Ibid., p. 169. Others are Beaulieu and Autun, Conques and Angoulême.
35 Ibid., p. 191.
36 Ibid., p. 215.
37 Ibid., p. 221.
38 Ibid., p. 223.
39 Ibid.
40 Barfield (1988), p. 85. This is a perceptive study of the metaphysical concept of 'participation', and references the Middle Ages.
41 Ibid., pp. 94–5. Barfield cites Thomas from *De natura verbi intellectus*.
42 Dante Alighieri, *Paradiso*, 9. 106–08, trans. Singleton (1975), p. 101.
43 Richard of St-Victor, *Benjamin maior*, 1.6 and 1.7, trans. Zinn (1979), pp. 161–2; p. 164. The fourth to sixth stages are mentioned in **p. 203** below.
44 Henry of Avranches, *Metrical Life*, 882–96, trans. Dimock, in Harvey (1972), p. 237.
45 Romans 1.20, in Richard of St-Victor, *Benjamin maior*, 2.12.
46 *Sermones de diversis*, 33.1, trans. Michael Casey, in Bernard of Clairvaux, *Sancti Bernardi Opera*, Vol. 6.1, ed. Leclercq, Talbot and Rochais (1972), p. 222.

198 Contemplation: life in nature

47 Ibid., 72.4. Gregory is cited from *Moralia in Job*, 15.53. Dom Cuthbert Butler translates it: 'Merely to love things above is already to mount on high'.
48 Bernard of Clairvaux, *Sermones super Cantica canticorum*, 32.2, trans. Walsh and Edmonds (1971–80), II, p. 135. '[. . .] *per campos contemplationis, et mente sequens expedita dilectum quocumque ierit.*' SBO, Vol.1, p. 227.
49 Bernard of Clairvaux, *Sententiae*, 2.187, trans. Sweitek (2000), p. 178, in f.n. 33.
50 For instance, Psalm 80.8–11; Isaiah 5.1–7.
51 Matthew 20.1–6 and 21.33–41.
52 Achard of St-Victor, *Sermo 10*, 'On Cultivating the Lord's Vineyard,' in *Works*, trans. Feiss (2001), pp. 78.
53 Bonaventure, *Vitis mystica*, Prologue, trans. Friar of S.S.F. (1955), p. 13. The text is John 15.1, 5.
54 Ibid., 4, p. 24.
55 Ibid., 6, p. 34.
56 Ibid., 14, p. 46.
57 Ibid., 15, p. 46. The five petals of the rose denote the five wounds of Christ. On the significance of red in the tabernacle's curtains, Bede said: 'Scarlet, because it has the appearance of fire, is most rightly compared to the ardent love of the saints', *De tabernaculo*, 2, 2, trans. Holder (1994), p. 50.
58 Bernard of Clairvaux, *De diligendo Deo*, 3.7, trans. van Allen (1959), pp. 23–4.
59 Bonaventure, *Vitis mystica*, 24, trans. a Friar of S.S.F. (1955), p. 60.
60 Ibid., 24, p. 63.
61 See **p. 78** above. It is discussed again on **p. 224–25**.
62 The figures and translated excerpts are in Joachim of Fiore, *The* Figurae *of Joachim of Fiore*, eds Reeves and Hirsch-Reich (1972).
63 See Augustine, *De civitate Dei*, 11.22; 12.4.
64 Ibid., 11.21, trans. Bettenson (1972), p. 451.
65 Ibid., p. 452.
66 Ibid. According to Jerome Taylor this sentence is also adapted from Calcidius's commentary.
67 Ibid., pp. 55–56.
68 Presumed to be Martianus Hiberniensis (819–75), who was at Laon, a contemporary of Eriugena. Hugh is believed to have known Martin's writings.
69 Quoted in Hugh of St-Victor, *Didascalicon*, trans. Taylor (1961), p. 191, n. 64. The association of *machina* and *moechus* may be Martin's own, based on meanings of *machina* being an 'artificial contrivance', 'device', 'stratagem' (or 'trick'). A *machinator* was an 'engineer', 'inventor', 'contriver'; *mechanicus* similarly.
70 Henry of Avranches, *Vita Sancti Hugonis*, 910–13, trans. Garton (1986), p. 57.
71 Ibid., 864–70, trans. Dimock, in *Mediaeval Architect*, ed. Harvey (1972), p. 237.
72 Hugh of St-Victor, *Didascalicon*, 1.4, trans. Taylor (1961), p.51.
73 Ibid., 1.9, p. 56. C.f. Basil, *Hexaëmeron*, 10.16–17, cited in Grosseteste, *Hexaëmeron*, 8, 8.1, trans. by Martin (1996), p. 234. See **p. 55** above.
74 Thomas, *Summa contra gentiles*, 3, 47.8, trans. Pegis (1948), p. 463.
75 Ibid., 3, 47.6, p. 462.
76 Hugh of St-Victor, 'Concerning the three subsistences of things', in *Didascalicon*, Appendix C, trans. Taylor (1961), p. 156.
77 Hugh of St-Victor, *Didascalicon*, 2.1, trans. by Taylor (1961), p. 61.
78 Augustine, *De civitate Dei*, 11.29, trans. Bettenson (1972), p. 464 (my emphasis).
79 Ibid., trans. Dyson (1998), p. 489. Compare with the illustration and application given by Martianus Capella, **p. 134** above.
80 Ibid., pp. 464–65.

81 Ibid., 11.28, p. 463.
82 Thomas, *Summa contra gentiles*, 3. 97.6, trans. Bourke (1975), vol. 2, p. 68.
83 Thomas, *De spiritualibus creaturis*, 2.a, trans. Fitzpatrick (1949), p. 36. The line of demarcation here is the same as Hugh of St-Victor used in distinguishing *perpetual nature* and *temporal nature*. See **p. 157** above.
84 Augustine, *De civitate Dei*, 12.26, trans. Dyson (1998), p. 536.
85 Ibid., trans. Bettenson (1972), p. 505.
86 Thomas, *De spiritualibus creaturis*, 2.a, trans. Fitzpatrick (1949), p. 36.
87 Thomas, *Summa contra gentiles*, 3. 97.3, trans. Bourke (1975), vol. 2, p. 67. He cites Aristotle's statement in *Physics*, I. 9, that form is 'something godlike and desirable'.
88 Thomas, *De spiritualibus creaturis*, 2.a, trans. Fitzpatrick (1949), p. 36. Also in *Summa contra gentiles*: 2. 68.6; ibid., quoting Pseudo-Dionysius (*De divinis nominibus*); and 2. 91.4.
89 Pseudo-Dionysius, *De caelesti hierarchia*, 3.2, trans. Luibheid (1987), p. 154.
90 Augustine, *Confessiones*, 12.7, trans. Pine-Coffin (1961), p. 285; so also 12.8.
91 See Augustine, *De civitate Dei*, 11.29.
92 See Pseudo-Dionysius, *De caelesti hierarchia*, 2.1–5.
93 Ibid., 2.1, trans. by Luibheid (1987), in *Pseudo-Dionysius*, p. 148.
94 Ibid., 2.2, p. 149.
95 Ibid., 2.3, p. 150.
96 Eriugena, *De divina praedestinatione*, 9.2, trans. Brennan (1998), p. 60.
97 Ibid., 9.3, pp. 60–1.
98 Text in Ladner (1983), vol. 1, p. 242, f.n. 11: '[. . .] *quia inter creatorem et creaturam non potest tanta similitudo notari quin inter eos maior sit dissimilitudo notanda*' (my translation).
99 Ladner (1983), vol. 1, p. 243.
100 Bonaventure, *Commentary on the Sentences*, 2.1.1.1, trans. in Spargo (1953), p. 52.
101 Pseudo-Dionysius, *De caelesti hierarchia*, 2.4, trans. Luibheid (1987), p. 151.
102 Ibid., p. 152. See comment in Barfield (1988), p. 75.
103 William Durandus described their iconographical features in *Rationale divinorum officiorum*, 1.3.9. See Holt (1957), p. 125. The three Biblical sources are referred to above, **p. 160**.
104 I Kings 6.29, 32, 35.
105 Honorius of Autun, *De gemma animae*, trans. Mortet (1972), p. 226.
106 Durandus, *Rationale divinorum officiorum*, 1.3.5, in Holt (1957), p. 123.
107 Ibid., 1.3.9, p. 125. (English spelling modernised.)
108 Henry of Avranches, *Metrical Life*, 859–65, ed. Dimock, in Harvey (1972), p. 237. *Alas* 'wings' also means 'aisles'. Note **p. 150** above for other lines cited.
109 See Wilson (1990), p. 165. Compare also the aisles of St-Mary-on-the-Sands, Wrocław (Figure 3.4).
110 See Heslop (1990), 'The Iconography of the Angel Choir at Lincoln Cathedral', for a good analysis. However, our point follows the visualising process in a designer.
111 Villard MS *c*. LXII, fol.31^v (*c*. 1220–30). Text in *The Sketchbook of Villard de Honnecourt*, ed. Bowrie (1959), p. 100.
112 Villard MS *c*. LXI, fol.30, ibid., p. 94.
113 Gardner (1938), p. 6. He connects this with its being building-stone sculpture.
114 Barfield (1988), p. 75.
115 Ibid., p. 87 (author's emphasis).
116 White (1993), p. 187. Compare with instances of *diatyposis* in **p. 103** above.
117 Bonaventure, *Itinerarium mentis ad Deum*, 4.7, trans. Cousins (1978), p. 92.

118 Ibid., 4.4, p. 90.
119 Ibid., p. 92. C.f. Dante, *Paradiso* 28. 127–9.
120 Bernard, *Sermones super Cantica canticorum*, 19.6, trans. Walsh and Edmonds (1971–80), I, p. 144.
121 Grosseteste, *Hexaëmeron*, 6.16.1, trans. Wright (2017).
122 See, Suger, *De consecratione*, 6, trans. Panofsky (1979), p. 107.
123 See, Suger, *De administratione*, 33, trans. Panofsky (1979), p. 67. Anselme Dimier (1999), in Chapter 7, critiques Suger's abbey project in wider context.
124 See Kidson (1987).
125 He affirms the value of this 'controversy'. Kidson sees as tenuous Suger's references to Pseudo-Dionysius. He seems to overlook this of 'the similar and dissimilar'.
126 Suger, *De consecratione*, 1, trans. Panofsky (1979), p. 83.
127 Pseudo-Dionysius, *De divinus nominibus*, 4.22, trans. Luibheid (1987), p. 89.
128 Suger, *De consecratione*, 7.3–18, trans. Panofsky (1979), p. 121.
129 See, Bonaventure, *Commentary on the Sentences*, 2.9. *Opera Omnia*, 2. p. 239.
130 Thomas, *Summa contra gentiles*, 3, 103.8, trans. Bourke (1975), vol. 2, p. 88.
131 Ibid., 3, 103.9, p. 89.

6 Building in love

Consideration

To the extent possible within the limits of this book we have tried to appreciate the scope and enter into the mode of thinking and reasoning in the Middle Ages, to gain insight into processes of exercising and composing the mind, *cogitatio*, and ordering the affections, *affectus*. From texts on the liberal arts, likewise within constraints, we have deduced a heuretic of applications and outworkings of love in works of artists, architects and artificers emulating the creative Mind, their perception advancing from thinking, *cogitatio*, to seeing, *aspectus*. James Ginther, discussing Robert Grosseteste's epistemology, focuses on the 'continual use of the terms *aspectus mentis* and *affectus mentis* to describe the human mind'.[1] He equates the first with 'the mind's eye', and referring to the mind's powers notes its judging role:

> The gaze of the mind, embraces both a receptive and a discursive capacity. The mind not only sees, it also judges. In Aristotelian terms it embraces sense data via the faculty of the imagination [...] and through division and judgement it verifies the truth of the object. Grosseteste goes further and even incorporates the intelligence (*intelligentia*) as part of the mind's gaze, the highest mental capacity which is necessary for obtaining wisdom.[2]

Intelligence seeking illumination presses things back to the vital causes. The searching consideration of Ezekiel in the end saw the final cause (Figure 2.1). Illumination is itself a subject which received much attention and was grounded in a philosophy and science of light by Grosseteste, a key exponent. It warrants fuller explanation and application to the church architecture than is possible here. But a relevant perception was that there was actual connection—which to us is merely metaphorical—between material light and spiritual light, enabling knowledge and insight:

Spiritually, light is created, in the church as in any soul, when that rational cognition rises to the contemplation of the Trinity through the intelligence, stripped of images (*fantasmatibus*); or [it rises] to the regarding (*speculacionem*) of intellectual and immaterial creatures, through the intellect.[3]

In an admirable treatise which Bernard wrote to Pope Eugenius III he distinguished contemplation from consideration: 'Contemplation may be defined as the soul's true unerring intuition, or as the unhesitating apprehension of truth. But consideration is thought earnestly directed to research, or the application of the mind to the search for truth'.[4] He emphasised how close they are and asserted the need for consideration.

Figure 6.1 St-Savin-sur-Gartempe, France. Church of St-Savin. Romanesque west tower with Gothic spire, octagonal, as is usual. In form the corner spirelets belong equally to tower and spire. Twelfth and thirteenth century.

We have seen radical kinds of connection made in medieval thought and learning: for instance, proportion in Thomas's philosophy, similitude in the Victorines, and abstraction in Bonaventure's aesthetics, all (albeit caricatured thus) had a role in bringing lower and higher entities into relation. Proportion, similitude, abstraction and illumination indeed—all media of connection—are everywhere in buildings, patently in churches in the Middle Ages. So far the nub of connection of architecture and theology might be the attention of the mind on its objects, and we can see an instance of this in which the built form expresses the mind's contemplation and illumination.

A tower tends naturally to evoke an imaginary ascent of vision—and of the mind—not only *to* its top but *from* its top. Notional vertical extension began to take physical expression around the early-twelfth century in the development of spires.[5] The rationale of spires involved more than their acting as conspicuous landmarks. A spire was surely a natural symbol of the upwards reach to a superior world. The very point of a spire was an innately felt connection with the invisible and divine. The St-Savin spire by its pure form and slenderness expresses extreme aspiration (Figure 6.1). This example also enables us to visualise the tower without a spire, as was common enough; and in such cases to speculate whether spires of invisible presence might have been imagined (Figure 4.12). Spires often had series of small ascending dormer windows suggestive of high vision. The theology tells more. Chapter 5 mentioned Richard of St-Victor's exposition of ascending stages of contemplation.[6] His fourth stage goes above imagination to a grasp of invisible things which reason can access. The fifth stage is contemplation of things which cannot be reached by reason, yet are not beyond reason to grasp—'that which is perceived by the fine point of the understanding'. The sixth stage is understanding in the mind beyond reason.[7] The first two stages use imagination; the middle two employ reason; the highest two reach understanding.[8]

Richard says 'the loftiness of divine showings may be an open disclosure of love'.[9] He dwells at some length on love for God as the consummation in 'contemplation of the creative essence and its supereminence'.[10] It is a tangential reference to God's creativity, but in two related places he mentions human creativity. The first instance is in the fourth stage of contemplation: the mind can create, as if, as it were, another creator.[11] The second instance is in the interaction of the fifth and sixth stages with the fourth: a human by virtue of being in the image of the Creator, can 'form some unique creatures [. . .] without pre-existing material and from nothing, as it were'.[12] He brings in the creative imagination explicitly in order that from the similitude with divine creativity we may better grasp the latter. The real matter of these highest contemplations concerns superior things; and it is not by the imagination that the soul rises up, but by 'the irradiation of divine light'.[13] The highest rationale is the work of love and wonder.[14]

In the intellectual culture of the Middle Ages we have seen three essential kinds of access to truth: comprehension, instruction, contemplation. On a wide spectrum we have seen associations of architecture and the skills and art of the making of churches, with noetic, mystical and affective theology. It is asserted that there were radical connections then such as we now value little, or even understand. We have seen the architecture and art speaking in their own language. We have read theology explaining and advocating the journey to God, communally and individually. The task remaining is to interpret how the two strands ran together—the mind in architecture and the mind in theology—and how the third strand, reiterated throughout, bound them. The insight to recover from this is that love was embedded in the whole building work. If we can make the connection we will be doing no more than the medieval thinkers and artificers did.

The demonstration has required the implications of theology's persuasions to be weighed, and works of architecture to be scrutinised for their intelligible aspirations. This reading and rethinking has demanded the kind of attention and judgement signalled in Chapter 1. The results, we can argue, comprise a better than *prima facie* case; this has been the merit of the deductive methodology. We have used three epistemological mirrors, but the demonstration of the thesis requires a synthesis. This can be done by applying four subjects of emerging importance and uniting power across the two fields of study. The first two subjects are *judgement* and *intuition*; they are salient in the constructive arts, in disciplines where they are activities of mind, heart and hand; but they also have a critical interface with affective theology. The second two, grounded in theology, are *incarnation* and *trinity*. Thinking in terms of *incarnation* we may find the point where the highest meets the lowest and see medieval churches to be works participating in nature and deity. The concept of *trinity* reveals the profound form of love, and integration by love, indeed the 'architecture' of minds in love translatable to phenomenal architecture.

Judgement

The subject of judgement was explicitly raised in Chapter 3 in 'Dialectic' where reasoning requires its skilful use, and in 'Rhetoric' where appraisal is made by the recipient of a communication. Then in Chapter 4, in 'Music', Augustine explained the application universally to places, times and bodies, albeit not without limits and hazards, so that there is a further level of judging of a judgement. There was an imperative that judgement be ultimately derived from God.

Discussing the reach of knowledge, Thomas Aquinas stated that, 'A sure judgement about a thing is formed chiefly from its cause, and so the order of judgements should be according to the order of causes'.[15] This assures us of some perspicuity as we have sought to understand works of architecture according to proximate causes in the minds of their makers. The works are to be known in their essential cause; the fundamental *Wherefore?* That requires mental rigour. They may be studied superficially; but Thomas's general principle seems applicable—there is a knowledge that intimacy with the works and with God produces, akin to love:

> To know in themselves the very things we believe, by a kind of union with them, belongs to the gift of wisdom. Therefore the gift of wisdom corresponds more to charity which unites man's mind to God.[16]

This is an articulation of the place and process of the kind of judgement that gives access to understanding—an architectural wisdom.

For application consider how in treating dialectic and rhetoric Hugh of St-Victor and John of Salisbury both associated invention and judgement. Dialectic and rhetoric clearly operate in architecture, and as invention proceeds bringing in things to be incorporated, so must judgement be engaged by the architect. Then the artefact is, inevitably, a communication. The architecture is the language, so accordingly the effects of the process are actually in the work, with degrees of clarity. Assessment was integral with the making process, and its range was the whole of the mandating theology. The subjects spanned all nature, hierarchies, participations, life, death, earth and heaven. These things were believed, honoured and declared.

It was instructive for architecture to learn how music deals with modulated multitude, thus movements in ratios, thus rhythm and metre, amplitude and altitude. This, as Augustine taught, requires judgement on a number of levels—sensory, rational, affective. It is very pertinent to our conclusion that it was reckoned to be by virtue of its judgements that music has special and affective power. We could see how it was by its finding unity, concord and perfection. Thomas said, 'The gift of knowledge is both speculative and practical'; so it applies to an artificer's own knowledge and judgement of his work.[17] Here is theory and practice directly transferable to judgement in and of architecture.

In *The Consolation of Philosophy* Boethius prefaced the penultimate verse with this: 'For since every judgement is an action of the one who judges, it is necessary that each should perform its work by its own power and not another's'. The verse refers to images of things in the 'active mind' as it judges things above and below and within. The question is:

> Whence comes to minds this concept strong
> Which thus discerns and sees all things?
> What power can individuals see,
> First analyse that which it sees,
> Then synthesize analysis
> And by alternate paths progress?[18]

The verse concludes with judgement's active power, *actus iudicantis*, mingling images received with 'forms it hides within'. Then, seeing that beings on different levels—from animals, to humans, to the divine—have increasing powers of discernment, he shows that the 'higher' can properly judge in matters concerning those 'below' them. Quite properly the senses and imagination yield to reason. Looking above, the power of human reasoning 'can judge the mind of God', and therefore should both 'bow before divine wisdom', and raise itself up 'to the heights of that supreme intelligence'.[19] The final sentence of the book once had powerful application: 'A great necessity is laid upon you [. . .] to be good, since you live in the sight of a judge who sees all things'.[20] This philosophy identified two strands of active judgement in medieval apprehension; and architectural application can be direct. First, each person has their own power of judgement to exercise in relation to their own work and that below which serves it. Second, judgement should rise above its immediate subject to evaluate the work's relation to God in the light of God. Clearly at this level of validation judgement was unconcerned with fashion-led 'style'.

The emphasis in *The Consolation* and in John of Salisbury's *Metalogicon*, on *active* judgement, was important, for it implied an empowering of the will. It was necessary for the ordering of work, practically, with discipline and proper rigour. We also saw it as belonging to all as participants, not just to an elite. Every individual involved in every part of the making of a church, busily working at their own level, judges what they are doing by their own power of judgement. A hierarchy of judgement is operating throughout; and just as tasks and skills are arranged in hierarchies, as well as unisons, so one exercises judgement of works 'below', or simpler, and acquires understanding of those 'above' as needful for one's own exercise. The work goes ahead with great power when each is in their right role and exercising good judgement. Here is an active ingredient affecting the quality and harmony of every part large and small. If each worker, artificer, architect judges truly that work for which they are responsible, the whole building will be full of judgement. On one hand each will do their work in accordance with nature, referring to traditions and direct sense of materials and techniques. On the other hand, regarding themselves as working under the judging mind of God, they will see the necessity laid upon them to do their best work. If one loves God with ordered love it is that person's own active judgements as to the task that embed their love inseparably in the building. Their judgements actually inhere in the work and accordingly their love, stamping *its* nature (not the individual's identity) on the work. By all working in harmony, the building is replete with judgement and love. It is itself the demonstration. The whole, full of the learning of love, breathes the spirit of life.

In all these respects medieval cathedrals and lesser churches formed one continuum, distinct from more monumental, sophisticated, anthropocentric architecture of following centuries in Europe, even to the present day. In the Middle Ages (until the late-Gothic decline) style appears accidental to the language of expression, and incidental to judgement of things of greater importance. Style is a human construct not intrinsic in the life of nature or the spirit. What, then, judged in terms of the art, gave such power to the cathedrals and abbey churches? How could such a phenomenon of clarity and congruity and glory have arisen? What culture enabled it? The discipline of the logical arts and the skills of the mathematical arts equipped the mind, the power of comprehension and judgement, and we saw too how the arts conceived superior patterns and purposes. Panofsky found formal affinities between Gothic cathedral architecture and scholastic theological *Summae* at a high level of ratiocination.[21] He compared parallel contemporaneous workings of reason in fields difficult to connect directly. He limited himself, however, by not adducing the views held by theologians and architects themselves of the logical art they were employing; and without justifying his stance he set aside theological content:

> When asking in what manner the mental habit induced by Early and High Scholasticism may have affected the formation of Early and High Gothic architecture, we shall do well to disregard the notional content of the doctrine and to concentrate [...] upon its *modus operandi*.[22]

To go further, we can appraise the art in the power of its content. Many medieval theologians reckoned that the work of an artificer has integrity and purpose when the maker, even while self-examining and self-judging, is not self-centred, but works at a higher level of intention. Builders of churches were shown the divine love and activity as model and pattern for their work—the conditions of *potentia* in work, and the process in its coming into *actus*. If inspired it would be good. As to 'content', minds and hearts skilled in comprehension, instructed in knowledge, participating in nature, interpreted the nature and causes of all things with judgement. The result of the process of reasoning, ordering, brooding, inventing, composing, and much else, was that the work was given its nature, *naturised*, by art tutored in love for the divine Exemplar. Theology affirming this role of love authorises us to judge the churches as artefacts made as acts of love.

If an art loses continuity with its traditions and immediacy of contact with the artefacts themselves, conscious judgement tends to develop a metalanguage and theoretical canon. Yet, we can infer from the paucity of evidence for such, that medieval architecture and art was not judged and transmitted that way.[23] The theoretical canon relating to it was embedded in the whole of theology, philosophy, metaphysics and science. Insofar as we can judge works with an understanding of their causes we discern that high rationality and conscious judgement operated widely. Two examples may illustrate this. In Hereford cathedral's north transept the near-triangular arches indicate a formal-visual and practical-rational experiment, not the product of a metalanguage, but an original vision of clarity and lightness (Figure 6.2). In Coutances cathedral's apse the paired columns articulate the integrated form of choir and ambulatory, the inner and outer columns respectively enunciating the design rationale (Figure 6.3). The judgement involved shows not only experimental knowledge and perceptive sensitivity to the expression; it effects, so far as possible, the translation of the material to the spiritual as its *modus vivendi*. Bonaventure said the judgement is twofold: first, a process of pruning (*deputando*), taking away the contingent things of time, place and mutability; second, by abstraction (*abstrahendo*), seeing the essential form that remains.[24] And contemplation ultimately goes by 'pruning' and 'abstraction' beyond all images to an inner simplicity and immediacy of recognition. In aesthetic evaluation too (beyond

Figure 6.2 Hereford, England. Cathedral church of St Mary. The east side of the north transept, *c.* 1260.

the scope of this study) such judgement has priority and authority, appraising the goodness and beauty of an artefact according to criteria of virtue.

Intuition

While we think to see affective *theology* influencing the architecture, we can also see unmediated love itself operating in the building process. As to theology somehow informing cathedrals, Bernard McGinn signalled that it might be 'conscious or unconscious', which implies that it might work on

Building in love 209

Figure 6.3 Coutances, France. Cathedral church of Notre-Dame. Ambulatory clerestory and vaulting. The paired columns relate to the choir (left) and ambulatory (right). Mid-thirteenth century.

two levels, and even concurrently.[25] The *conscious or unconscious* informing mind corresponds to *judgement and intuition* in the mind's processing. The judging and the intuition can be concomitant. Evidence has reiterated that they were not in conflict, indeed each played its part in the other. The practise of judging was clearly part of the direct, hands-on building process.

Two aspects of a culture of particular relevance to architecture are *tradition* and *directness*. Where they are a channel by which knowledge and wisdom is accessed by artificers and translated in their work they are defining elements of a vernacular process. It seems extraordinary that without

210 *Building in love*

apparent contradiction this process could work in tandem with extremely complex exercises of architecture, as also with rigorously intellectual disciplines. It can best be explained by recognising that the catalyst was love. As to tradition the continuity was like that maintained by theologians when they called innovation *renovatio*.[26] And in every direct involvement in the making process it seemed angelic *operatio* was at hand.

Vernacular tradition and directness seems to work more by intuition than by intellectual reasoning. Using the word 'intuition' here may be debatable; but it has the emphasis (common to both medieval and modern usage) on the immediacy of apprehension in accessing direct knowledge of something. It may be immediate apprehension by the mind simply, or by sense very directly. The Latin root of intuition is *intueor*: to look or gaze upon, mentally to consider, to contemplate. Angels were deemed to know and see with such immediacy that knowledge and vision were identical. Richard of St-Victor, describing the highest stages of contemplation, used the word more strictly referring to ultimate spiritual sight.

To concur with van Pelt's caution that 'architectural historicism cannot deal with the phenomenon of vernacular building', and to keep the appraisal of architecture open-ended, we have treated medieval church architecture in its underlying causes and constituents, rather than using historicist analysis. Gathering up much scattered evidence we can see that such apparently sophisticated achievements as Gothic cathedrals belonged to or constituted a vernacular architecture, albeit of an extraordinary order. We must consider relevant essential traits of vernacular building, and ask whether the genre permits or necessarily precludes works of the highest achievement. And we must still respect the historical context. In its origins the Gothic developed directly *out of* its Romanesque antecedents, in a transition in which the emergence of the Gothic (at least in its early phase) did little violence to its predecessor. It was firmly attached to a tradition which was the stock from which new efforts and experiments sprang and continued to draw life. The churches of that Romanesque period were themselves vernacular artefacts. Then too the process, not depending on a canon of theory or design, was remarkably direct, involving people of all ranks and diverse roles, in monastic communities especially.

The term 'vernacular' is commonly used of language, and this reminds us of the unselfconscious level of the grammar of architecture operating even where there was a high development of the logical arts. Dialectic working at different levels of consciousness could hardly have been a premeditated exercise, but it seems everywhere apparent. Even in rhetoric Geoffrey of Vinsauf advocated using 'speech native to the craft', to be directly comprehended. For medieval authorial insight into vernacular art the works of Dante are unparalleled. Before producing his great poem of the ascent of love to Love, he wrote something like a *speculum* of love (love for Lady Philosophy, however ambiguously), *The New Life* (*La Vita Nuova*) in the Tuscan dialect. Later he produced his exposition of it, *The Banquet*

(*Convivio*) in a broader Italian vernacular. In *De vulgari eloquentia*, in Latin, he advocated the adoption of the vernacular, and justified its use for such high purpose as *The Banquet* where love of Wisdom was set forth.[27] He viewed the vernacular language as the nobler ('as being natural to us') than 'grammar' ('secondary speech') which springs from it. He saw that 'the whole world makes use of it though it has been divided into forms differing in pronunciation and vocabulary'.[28] When he came to write the *Commedia* he used vernacular Italian. So he purposely demonstrated that the vernacular language was perfectly apt in the highest art, and, *because* of its natural connections to the whole world and the hearts of people, was most suitable to the themes of love of the highest order. This so well demonstrating what was achievable, it is not implausible to regard a cathedral as a work of vernacular architecture taken to a similarly high pitch of expression and even of the same theme.

Within a culture's mentality and values, as a given determining any particular work, there was what Linda Seidel calls 'a prevailing set of concepts' which preceded 'interplay between such generic form and individual manifestation'. She states:

> Combination of preexistent elements in a work takes precedence over either the specifics of a particular piece or the part played by an individual in its formation. Tradition, rather than an author's individuality, constitutes the referent of a work. And the idea of audience 'collaboration,' not just in the enjoyment but in the creation of the work, is acknowledged.[29]

Seidel's reference is to the audience of a work of medieval literature, while her application is to Aquitainian Romanesque churches, saying, 'These structures should be considered as essentially "communal" creations, poetically elaborated around and interacting with a core of traditional, familiar elements'.[30] The intuitive transmission of tradition and direct participation in vernacular art had its communication arts—its grammar, dialectic and rhetoric.

We saw that intuition had a place in medieval number theory, and in the judging mind—in the apprehension by *ratio*, for instance—even across the arts of the quadrivium; while in vernacular art intuitive understanding of number, proportion, harmony and hierarchy, was natural in the culture. Intuition was a grasp of the quiddity, seeing how to judge, knowing how to act. It involved an inner force of initiative and realisation. John of Salisbury wrote:

> Nature has endowed the soul with a certain force, which either constitutes or at least evokes the initial [and fundamental] activity of the soul in its investigations. Natural talent is said to be 'immanent' inasmuch as it has need of nothing else as a prerequisite, but precedes and aids all subsequent [abilities].[31]

212   *Building in love*

We can be more specific in relation to the making of buildings. Tradition provides the precedents, but continuity is essential because discontinuities make for failure. In Gothic experimentation there were givens which continued to be the basis for invention; but formal abstract analytical design process was evidently rudimentary. Arcane knowledge and masonic arts probably received but slight attention from schoolmen and theologians, or even architects. More forcefully, the buildings themselves were grammar books, dialectical discussions, authoritative rhetoric. Architecture could only be understood in its artefacts, as in the reading of computus. Jacques Heyman asserts that there was little of use for theoretical design that was embodied and passed on in rule books, though, importantly, the rules themselves were essentially correct.

> Architects working to these rules had, no doubt, an intuitive understanding of forces and resulting stresses, but this would not have taken a form that would be of use in design, and there is no trace in the records, over the two or three millennia for which they exist, of any ideas of this sort. Instead, it is likely that the design process would have proceeded by trial and error, by recording past experience and venturing, more or less timidly, into the unknown.[32]

Tradition directed that it was the shape of the structure, as Heyman says, that governed stability. The 'design process' which he identifies depended on direct involvement of the artificer with the artefact. The technical mastery was astonishing. He notes, 'The standards of lining, levelling and plumbing employed in the construction of Gothic cathedrals were outstanding'.[33] That was important for structural integrity, and admired in itself; more than that, it sustained associations with higher perfections. If sometimes imperfections of appearance were seemingly accepted with a relaxed pragmatism, that does not appear to apply to workmanship. Seeing the sheer size and complexity it seems astonishing that such an informal process as imitation and correction engaging intuitive judgement can have the power to produce such results.

To look again at the way in which the nave design of Girona cathedral was decided we may see that the dialectic of the process and scrutiny leading to the individuals' judgements, devolved in the end upon their intuitive evaluations, particularly of the second and third questions.[34] How successful achievement was regarded and measured in the Middle Ages was a different matter from the criteria of the subsequent classical Renaissance. The foregoing chapters have shown that there was a fundamental sphere of participation, experience and empathy more essential than adherence to a formulated aesthetic.

These hallmarks of the vernacular making process, tradition and directness, were analysed by Christopher Alexander, and a crucially important point in his study is that it is an *unselfconscious* process. Not, perhaps, unconscious, nor even always subconscious, but un*self*conscious. On the face of it this might not seem true of medieval cathedral architecture, yet we can see in the foregoing discussion in this chapter that engagement with tradition, and direct hands-on involvement, provided conditions most conducive to the artist and artisan being self-disregarding. The artificer needed to be able to judge within himself with objectivity, that is, to disregard himself. William of St-Thierry could see the issue, and put it in these terms to a monastery's abbot, 'Let it be [the monks] who do their own building'. Seeing their natural, unconcerned way of working, and the results, he continued,

> No skill on the part of hired craftsmen will be so successful as their own lack of concern in producing an expression of poverty, the beauty of holy simplicity and the traditional sobriety of the Fathers.[35]

In the monk's intuitive inventing and making, the preoccupation with the art and the reality to which the artefact referred drew his attention away from himself. As spiritual intelligences, angels modelled highest powers of intuition, and, far from being introspective, they are continually looking above themselves and below.

It might seem that the medieval culture of learning brought adepts to a high pitch of selfconsciousness. However, in the spiritual life of devotion that selfconsciousness was the knowledge of the self before God, which drew it away from self-centredness. Alexander (albeit not specifically addressing medieval culture) produced this working definition: 'I shall call a culture unselfconscious if its form-making is learned informally, through imitation and correction. And I shall call a culture selfconscious if its form-making is taught academically, according to explicit rules'.[36] In a selfconscious culture the rules are tools and techniques by which form-making is separated at several removes from the work on the building site. But we have been aware that the business of building was transmitted and learned informally.

In Chapter 5 another aspect emerged which could distinguish vernacular architecture from sophisticated, monumental, architecture in this way: that the artificer worked *according to nature*; it is the big theme of participation. By it the soul can grasp the world of nature, and the nature of things. We saw it involving contemplation, and the artificer emulating the Maker of all. One could imitate nature which is the model, and participate in the process and order believed to be divinely patterned. Small simple churches we may easily grant were vernacular buildings. But such participation in nature also characterised complex cathedrals. Great and lesser churches shared in common the continuity of the whole tradition, an effectively direct mode of their making, and a belonging in nature's works. The amazing work of artifice which is Lincoln cathedral was praised by Henry of Avranches for appearing to the mind and imagination to be not an artificial work but a work of nature.[37] Of course the artifice was understood, but the result was appraised on another level by which it was fitted into the universe.

214 *Building in love*

All this implied a pattern above all spiritual and articulated in the ordering of the affections. Relating it to architecture, the entire concept and arrangement of the medieval abbey, down to the cell and a chink of sunlight, corresponded to the pattern, was a construct of the pattern. So too the church itself and cathedral; they were visible diagrams, reflections, of the greater forms which theology and liturgy patterned. According to theology the ordering of love was the process that must run through all. That this was even running through the design process was possible when artificers cared about patterns of nature and similarities of forms, and identified or intuitively knew a greater model integrating theology and building.

Thus even in the conscious process there was the subconscious inclination of the lower towards the higher, and influence of the higher on the lower. In the 'pruning' which Bonaventure enunciated, judgement did not dispense with theological knowledge, and 'abstraction' did not mean a drawing away of a subject from its theological parameters. A deep discipline was the involvement of the makers and whole monastic community directly with the content and meaning, however it might be expressed outwardly. The content and embodied knowledge belonged to them. To see abbey churches, and all medieval churches, as vernacular buildings made by hearts in love, is the counterpoise to admiring how they can sustain attention as intellectual demonstrations by minds in love. The result was not affectation and pretentiousness, but patent integrity. Clear illustrations are in the east ends. The sanctuary was of highest importance yet intuition of order and virtue restrained extravagance. Thus we evaluate the clarity of form and consideration in the chevet of Vignogoul abbey church (Figure 6.4), and the balance of strength and lightness of the chevet of Mantes cathedral (Figure 4.6). Transcendent content and meaning was intuitively interpreted, immanent in nature, instinct with love.

Incarnation and nature

Alexander, discussing architecture, wrote: 'There is a deep and important underlying structural correspondence between the pattern of a problem and the process of designing a physical form which answers that problem'.[38] This has a parallel—or referent—in theology. The pattern of the problem is that God, having made humans in his own image, had to remake them; to answer that problem he devised precisely the 'physical form' of the Incarnation of God. Likewise when an architect sought a design in which to make an image in nature remade under God, it was in fact in the manner of the Incarnation.

In order for Thomas to probe the Incarnation of Christ he had to consider 'what is nature'. He noted that the word comes from nativity; and that 'this word *nature* was taken to signify the principle of this begetting [...]. Now this principle is either form or matter. Hence sometimes form is called nature, and sometimes matter'.[39] It is the goal of generation in the

Figure 6.4 Vignogoul, France. Cistercian abbey church. East apse. The sanctuary has a seven-part vault, expressed in the gables. Built *c.* 1211–1259.

thing generated that is the essence of the species. This essence is called the nature. *Nature* 'signifies the essence, or the *what-it-is*, or the quiddity of the species'.[40] Then, as to how two natures, divine and human, could come together, Thomas explained (with illustrations of heaping stones together, or arranging stones and beams to make a house) that it was not by composition, order, or figure—the two would remain discrete—it could not be by confusion nor by commensuration. The form of such would be 'not a nature, but an art, as the form of a house'.[41] In application to the church building: composition, order, figure, go so far, but not far enough for use of the term incarnation. Nor could the union of the Incarnation come about as by combination (as a mixture is made up of its elements), for that would involve the deity in change. Nor in the mystery of the Incarnation could the union be as of things imperfect, for the Divine and the human each have specific perfection of nature—incorporeal and corporeal—which must remain such. Nor is it even in art. If in order to discern the fullest nature of the physical church we try to probe the act of bringing it into being, it must be with reference to the divine act of union in the Incarnation—beyond composition, order, figure, combination, or art.

216 *Building in love*

Thomas asserted a twofold unity: *of nature*—'inasmuch as the soul is united to the body and formally perfects it, so that one nature springs from the two as from act and potentiality or from matter and form'; and *of person*—'inasmuch as there is an individual subsisting in flesh and soul; and herein lies the likeness, for the one Christ subsists in the Divine and human natures'.[42] Theologians could say that the flesh, form and matter, could be deified:

> As Damascene says, the Divine Nature is said to be incarnate because It is united to flesh personally, and not that It is changed into flesh. So likewise the flesh is said to be deified [...] not by change, but by union with the Word, its natural properties still remaining [...].[43]

Even thus a church is consecrated. Because of the Incarnation the natural corporeal properties of everything united so to God are retained and re-centred with full effect. Recall, in Chapter 2, Athanasius declaring that God was 'meeting their senses, so to speak, half way'. That passage continues:

> When the minds of men had fallen finally to the level of sensible things, the Word submitted to appear in a body, in order that He, as Man, might centre their senses on Himself [...] The Self-revealing of the Word is in every dimension—above, in creation; below, in the Incarnation; in the depth, in Hades; in the breadth, throughout the world.[44]

The Incarnation of Christ is a mystery and paradox. Athanasius described it so, and saw ramifications in 'every dimension', in relation to all things:

> The Word was not hedged in by His body [...]. His body was for Him not a limitation, but an instrument, so that He was both in it and in all things, and outside all things, resting in the Father alone. [...] His being in everything does not mean that He shares the nature of everything, only that He gives all things their being and sustains them in it.[45]

When Hugh of St-Victor, in *On the Sacraments*, described the restoration of creation it was centred in 'the Incarnation of the Word with all his sacraments from the beginning of the world to the end'.[46] The Incarnation was a sacrament really because it was an instrument; and, in this theology, the sacramental character of things in which the Word is, involves their being instrumental to the same end of restoration. Human works, by the same instrumentality of incarnation, may be part of the whole restoration of 'all things' to God. For they pertain to the life of the corporeal as the higher comes into the lower even through the human senses. Architects assayed to embody this. Such restoration, such incarnation, such sacrament, in nature, in matter, in the senses, is expressed in the apse of St-Bertrand-de-Comminges cathedral—for if not all this to what purpose is it? (Figure 6.5). The simple wall and vaulting structure is assuredly material; while the traceries of the

Figure 6.5 St-Bertrand-de-Comminges, France. Cathedral church of Ste. Marie. Apse clerestory. The choir and nave are aisleless. Completed 1350.

windows, and the small distant quatrefoils above mediate the numinous. The whole form is like the union of body and spirit.

Thomas and Athanasius in the foregoing passages each related the Incarnation to the reality of nature, the actuality of hierarchies, and coinherence in God. Bonaventure quite similarly, but emphasising the experiential path, set out the process of 'retracing the arts to theology'. At each step he considers three postulates:

> The eternal generation and incarnation of Christ,
> the pattern of human life, and
> the union of the soul with God.[47]

In the illuminations of knowledge a first step is the 'illumination of *sense perception.*' Under the three postulates are corresponding perceptions (*cognoscendi*): 'the *medium* of perception, the *exercise* of perception, and the *delight* of perception.'[48] As to the medium Bonaventure explains:

> We shall see there the Word begotten from all eternity and incarnate in time. No sense object can stimulate the cognitive faculty except by

means of a similitude which proceeds from the object as a child proceeds from its parent. And this procession by generation, whether in reality or in terms of exemplarity, is necessary for each of the senses.[49]

Here the operation of incarnation of the divine in sensible things is spelled out; and it is meaningless if disconnected from Christ's incarnation. The *exercise* of perception is in grasping the patterns of the divine in things (*res*). The *delight* of perception—the sensory taken into the union—is well illustrated in Abbot Suger's praise of the new choir of St-Denis abbey at its consecration.[50]

William of St-Thierry describes the actual sensory embodiment of the spiritual in material things and places—the medium, the exercise, the delight. His *Epistle* is directed to monks seeking to practice the inward and outward disciplines of love for God. The main image throughout is the monk's cell. In relation to outward experience, the physical place in the world, it is the monk's literal cell. As a metaphor for inner experience, it is the interior chamber of the man. Such is the congruity between the two places the cell has virtually one identity and definition; the architecture and the ascesis share one form. To those two places William joins a third: to be in the cell is to be in heaven:

> The cell (*cella*) and heaven (*celum*) are akin to one another: the resemblance between the words *celum* and *cella* is borne out by the devotion they both involve. [...] the same occupation characterizes both the one and the other. What is this? Leisure devoted to God, the enjoyment of God.[51]

The linguistic association leads him to link the cell and heaven; but the actual connection he makes is the devotion he ascribes equally to both; it is the necessary condition. The radical reason he gives brings affective theology into the definition of the places:

> God's holy angels regard cells as heaven and take the same delight in cells as they do in heaven. For when heavenly pursuits are continually practiced in the cell, heaven is brought into close proximity to the cell by the reality which underlies them both alike, by the loving devotion common to both, and by the similarity of the effects they produce.[52]

In the shared identity of the cell and heaven the love is the point, the incarnation of divine love. Here now are three places in one: the cell, the heart, and heaven—total participation including the sensory perceptions. They could be called physical, psychological, spiritual. The cell is a place of discipline, devotion, and converse with heaven. There are two questions in this to follow up: whether this trope can extend from the cell to the church as a place (thus, *church*, heart, heaven); and how, according with the rudimentary model of this cell, such a place, a church, is made.

On the first question are these aspects: corresponding to the physical cell meeting the monk's need is the physical church ministering to the needs of the community—be it abbey church, parish church or cathedral. Then, an equivalence with the monk's inner life is that the church is congenial to the experience of the senses, mind and heart in the corporate worship. Another aspect, matching the small cell's identification with infinite heaven, is the affiliation of the church in the monastery with the spiritual Church in heaven. Quite explicitly these parallels are confirmed when William appraises the cell thus: 'Indeed as a church is a place holy to God, so the cell is the sanctuary of God's servant. For both in a church and in a cell the things of God are practiced [. . .]'.[53] He notes the affinity in the matter of sacraments in their respective places: the private, spiritual, continual ones celebrated in the cell; the corporate, visible, liturgical ones in the church. The sacraments serve, 'although not yet with the same untarnished magnificence or the same security that marks eternity'—not yet on a consummate level which the incarnation predicates.[54] To the senses a small cell was like a contraction of the abbey church. The pattern was that in these affiliations of the cell, the church and present heaven, they *together* constituted one reality—each true, but none fully itself in isolation. The cell was not without the church, or the church without the cell, or either without heaven.

Returning to Bonaventure, the second step in the illuminations of knowledge is the 'illumination of *the mechanical arts.*' It depends on the same conditions, and holds pertinent lessons:

> In the same way divine wisdom may be found in the illumination of the *mechanical arts*, the sole purpose of which is the *production of artifacts*. In this illumination we can see the same three truths; namely, the *generation and incarnation of the Word*, the *pattern of human life*, and the *union of the soul with God*; And this is true if we consider the *production*, the *effect*, and the *fruit* of a work [*egressum, effectum* et *fructum*]; or if we consider the *skill of the artist*, the *quality of the effect produced*, and the *usefulness of the product that results.*'[55]

Here the first postulate, 'the generation and incarnation of the Word' is the basis of the artist's skill in generating and bringing forth the work (what we call creativity). The second, 'the pattern of human life' is in the quality and true effect of a work. The third postulate, 'the union of the soul with God', is aligned with the real purpose and usefulness of the production, drawn into the union which 'takes place through charity'.

The illumination of the mechanical arts producing artefacts must, of course, include buildings; a retracing of architecture to theology. Yet for anything to become actual the human instrument needed to be illuminated and united with the incarnate Maker and creative Word. Nothing could warrant an intrusion of an architect's ego. It is as with Mary: 'That which is conceived in her is of the Holy Spirit'.[56] This, we might say, is Bonaventure's underlying script.

Intention

William of St-Thierry had specific things to say about how the cell was made, and what it was to be like. It may seem a small part of the *Epistle* until its practical and pivotal role is appreciated. He says the worldly-wise misuse intelligence, inventiveness and skill, 'to satisfy their curiosity, their pleasure and their pride, while [devoted men] render service with them as necessity demands, finding their joy elsewhere'.[57] These things discovered and made are to be means not ends. William's approval of art and skill is guarded, but nonetheless he allows some place for it. When he later commented on some cells made too lavishly, and by hired artisans, we can detect the perennial tension between an expansive exercise of art, and parsimonious simplicity—both deemed to be for the glory of God. He asked, 'Why do not the sons of grace rather build for themselves free of cost?'[58] He cited God's instruction for the building of the Tabernacle: 'See that you make everything according to the model that was shown to you on the mountain'.[59] So he asked:

> Is it right that the place where God dwells with men should be made by men of the world? Let it be themselves, they to whom is shown in the heights of their spirit the model of the true beauty of God's house, let it be themselves who do their own building. Let it be themselves, they who are bidden by their preoccupation with interior things to scorn and disregard all outward things, let it be themselves who do their own building.[60]

In this view it mattered very much *who* was making the place to be the sanctuary of God. It was they whose 'joy is elsewhere' who could build in joy with heightened appreciation; they who had ascended the mountain and seen the archetype *there*, who could build the ectype below. Like Moses receiving the model, they have received the model of God's house in its spiritual and interior meaning. Again, a slight inconsistency may lie unstated in the unacknowledged role of embellishment and perfection in the Tabernacle's making. However, he astutely observes a possible accord and congruity when the context is rightly 'arranged'; and he is referring to the material building:

> For what is within us is benefited in no slight degree by what is around us, when it is arranged to accord with our minds and in its own way to correspond with the ideals we have set before us.[61]

Strong ideals, the mind's intentions, frequently prompt an ordering of the physical environment. To William, the ideal, common to the cell and to heaven, was love, so that this became the highest defining feature of the physical cell, the *locus* of love, the essential intention in its making as it was in the making of the inner chamber of the monk's heart.

Building in love 221

William knew the need for the reason to be ordered like the ordered life of the cell, and the work of contemplation to need the cell's seclusion, a hidden sanctuary. This was the pattern of reason and love:

> When reason as it progresses mounts on high to become love, and grace comes down to meet the one who so loves and desires, it often happens that reason and love, which produce those two states, become one thing. No longer can they be treated or thought of separately.[62]

In a person's mental and spiritual inclination the unity of love inducts the mind into an intimacy with God, seeing God's intentions and aligning with the objects of divine creativity. The subject is still not far from architecture. This chapter has been showing the vital roles of consideration by the mind, judgement and intuition. They give clarity, but strong intention is required for the production of any creative work.

William refers human intention to the creative Artificer—that, when from an impulse and inclination in the artificer a thing is comprehended, ordered, made, shaped, and executed in harmony with its ideal form and real object, it is in accord with the true art of God:

> For he is the almighty Artificer who creates man's good will in regard to God, inclines God to be merciful to man, shapes man's desire, gives strength, ensures the prosperity of undertakings, conducts all things powerfully and disposes everything sweetly.[63]

In humans the process works in respect of things 'below' in the love by which all things are done and made in a God-breathed way; like the Spirit brooding over creation and bringing forth intentionally man in his image. In relation to things 'above', intentionality is born of responsive love, willing to participate and serve. Thus intention is not merely a general ideal and indefinable. There is to be specific intent. Then to build their own cells and their own church, monks had knowledge resources, skills and spiritual assistance.

A manuscript illustration depicts an individual's part in the process exactly: hierarchy, unity, participation and intention are here (Figure 6.6). The roles are described by Thomas (citing Pseudo-Dionysius) thus: 'Love moves those, whom it unites, to a mutual relationship: it turns the inferior to the superior to be perfected thereby; it moves the superior to watch over the inferior'.[64] The two figures here seemingly represent one monk. Even while labouring with intention he is praying—a simultaneous attention to God with inner intent.[65] He is wonderfully assisted by an angel who helps carry the weight of the stone, and gently guides the judgement of the monk. Understanding passes between them. Each figure has the red spot on the cheek denoting love for God and between angel and man. The blush spot is of frequent occurrence, in contexts that suggest quite precise applications.[66]

222   *Building in love*

Figure 6.6 Manuscript illumination. Yates Thompson 26, British Library. The monk is shown in two roles—active and contemplative. Note the cheek blush spots; the mortar is also red. Late thirteenth century.

The meaning of it can be traced back to Origen where he commented on the Song of Songs:

> [The Bridegroom] next describes the beauty of the Bride in terms of spiritual love [...]. He praises her face, and is kindled to admiration by her rosy cheeks. [...] So let us likewise take the cheeks as revealing the beauty of the soul.[67]

Bernard of Clairvaux's commentary on the Song of Songs text goes further. After describing the blood-red colouring on the pearly skin he shows the spiritual import:

> The mind's intention is the soul's face. The quality of the work is evaluated from the intention, just as the body's beauty from the face. We may see in this flush on the cheek an unassuming disposition in which virtue and beauty thrive and grace increases. [...] The intention which we have referred to as the face of the soul must have two elements: matter and purpose, what you intend and why. It is from these that we judge the beauty or deformity of the soul.[68]

This text surely justifies a deduction that the blush spots in this illumination are meant to show that the building work depicted is to be evaluated from the mind's intention directed purposefully by love. Bernard remarks on an 'unassuming disposition', and this echoes the unselfcentred process of vernacular architecture. In it 'virtue and beauty thrive and grace increases', the angel indicating the assistance of higher *operatio*.

As the worker's purpose is carried forward the function of the artefact, as well as its form, becomes apparent. We see the whole ambit and effect of communal life, from a single cell, the cloister, the chapter house, to the church where supremely all in harmony were joined. Grosseteste was Bishop of Lincoln. In a sermon which he may have given there is this imagery:

> As many heavy things when bound together descend the quicker, and many light things when united ascend with greater velocity, inasmuch as the inclination of each of the separate things has a general effect upon the combined aggregate, so many individuals joined together by the bond of love and prayer, are moved upwards more easily and more swiftly as the prayer of each one of them has its influence upon that of each of the others. For as polished objects when placed close together, and illuminated by the power of the sun, in proportion to their number, shine with greater brightness on account of the multitude of the reflection of the light rays, so too the more souls that are illuminated by the rays of the Sun of Righteousness, the more they shine by reason of the reflection of their mutual love.[69]

We may well believe that he was pointing out the clustered polished shafts of Lincoln's choir and chancel (Figure 5.8. Compare Figure 4.5). His lesson is that in the church individual loves are multiplied by reflection from the Source, to the increase of the sum of love by the process of mutual exchange. The motif is throughout the cathedral. The building's configurations suggest such multiplying of love and the functioning of coinherence as translatable to architectural intention.

Form deriving from intention is in love and art working together. The percept is remarkably frequent and precise in numerous medieval sources that make the church building in the form of the spiritual Church. The construction of Solomon's temple provided Bede (c. 673–735) with the picture of the accurately prepared stones being—

> fitted together with the glue and bands of mutual charity so that they can never be dissolved, to form heavenly dwellings according to the pattern, bound together in the sight of their Maker and King. For when *the multitude of believers* is made *of one heart and soul* in this life, and *all things* are *common to them*, is it not as if living stones are being squared to form the building of the future house of the Lord [...] and are joined to one another with the bond of love that is divine, and at the same time properly their own?[70]

To Bede the historical building in its pattern, preparation and construction really mirrored the spiritual building. Unconsciously or consciously all the intention of the work had a spiritual goal. Bernard saw significance in the dressing of the stone: 'It is dressed above, with the love of heavenly things; below with the dismissal of earthly things'.[71] Honorius of Autun saw the material stone and the mortar as illustration of mutual love in the church: 'The stones are held together with mortar, and the faithful linked by the bond of love'.[72] Durandus analysed the constituent ingredients of the mortar thus:

> The cement, without which there can be no stability of the walls, is made of lime, sand, and water. The lime is fervent charity, which joins itself to the sand [...]. Now the lime and the sand are bound together in the wall by an admixture of water. But water is an emblem of the Spirit. And as without cement the stones cannot cohere, so neither can men be built up in the heavenly Jerusalem without charity, which the Holy Spirit works them. All the stones are polished and squared,—that is, holy and pure, and are built by the hands of the Great Workman into an abiding place in the Church.[73]

The force of this imagery is that love was the uniting agent throughout the entire building, like the particles and conjunctions of grammar making words into coherent speech. The stones signified all individuals co-inhering in life and holiness.[74] The joints of the masonry pictured in the monk's building operation are coloured red, purposely we might suppose (Figure 6.6). The outward beauty of the work is like the blush that cannot conceal the intention, the motivation of spiritual love. We deduce a connection with texts we have read: the bonding mortar is love.

The masonry pattern and mortar colour corresponds to the decoration of many churches, small and great. We are accustomed to unpainted, undecorated interiors of medieval churches; but interior masonry was generally deemed to be unfinished unless rendered, perhaps plastered, and painted.

(Alternatively, the aim was that the cutting and jointing of the stonework should be so near perfect that the whole effect would seem like 'a work of nature'.) On rendered surfaces of walls, columns, and vaults, a masonry pattern was often painted as an intentional foil, showing that the image of precise and perfect stonework was admired, or even significant (Figures 3.5; Figure 5.5). That this was a conscious intention is confirmed by a further device often found in the centre of each stone—a flower motif, usually red, often five-petalled, a rose.[75] The significance is inescapable—all the members of the church, past and future and the present community, are as stones bonded together constituting the building permanent in love and unity. In the church of Les Jacobins, Toulouse, it is repeated on every stone in rows alternating with an AvE motif and the Marian monogram. In the middle of each perpend is a small painted knot signifying the bond between the stones. As well as being a symbol of love, the rose was a symbol, often, of Mary, reminding us of the Incarnation. The rose motif was used in other ways and patterns, such as part of the beautifully significant consecration crosses in the monastery church of Limburg-an-der-Lahn. Being decorative devices, free of construction constraints, such figures reveal the makers' perceptions. We look at the artefacts (even with the insights of architectural historians) and wonder what was in the minds of the makers. Then we read what the contemporary theologians wrote, and we understand something of the intentions and the purpose.

Trinity and integration

To begin to draw things together we return to Chapter 2, particularly where we saw the model of love in deity, and in that the clarity of an intrinsic pattern of love: two things united by love constitute a trinity. Augustine gave an instance so intricate that it can scarcely be observed: the union of the mind itself with its knowledge is love.[76] Love between a lover and the beloved is constituted by themselves uniquely. Then while love is the very quiddity of trinity it defines indefeasible unity. Further, the pattern is transferable, love being the constant in endless trinities integrated, and love being compounded.

Diverse things, conceptual, substantive, sensory, and so on, can be connected logically by syllogisms, but there is deeper integrating judgement, also intuition, and intention. This is the gist of the account Ginther gives of Grosseteste's *Dictum* 118 which commences, 'Every syllogistic science is constructed like a net in the manner of triangular figures'.[77] The sciences comprise nets of triangles of syllogistic form; but theology alone makes a net of triangles of such form, and also of *function*, as draws humanity up to restored nature in God. This is integration.

Ramon Llull, in *Ars brevis* (1308), developed a syllogistic tool and technique, *ars*, not for logical deduction but to aid discovery of connections. It was for use by a maker of anything searching for correspondences between ideas and concrete things; showing how they were connected; aiming at judgement and integration. Each of Llull's Four Figures is based on triangulations, each Figure is a device for eliciting the meaning in the conjunction, contraction or abstraction of two things in the third, their 'middle term'. Three of his Figures encompass by circles everything in their categories, indicative of their integrating purpose; two of them show the triangulations of manifold subjects, the connections conspicuous. They build up a complex whole, a pattern out of chaos, as an aggregation and arrangement of basic triadic 'entities', each as small and particular as concerns artists may have with their art, makers with their material. He describes the form, emphasising the connective part:

> There is the middle of mensuration, which refers to the act existing between the doer and the doable, like loving between the lover and the lovable. And then there is the middle between extremes, like a line between two points.[78]

Connecting these very entities he alludes to their unique purpose: they are, 'like the two points that terminate a line, or like the lover and beloved in relation to loving'.[79] Making a single line has the essential character of an act of love, can be an act of love. Thus he juxtaposes elements of geometry and the ineffables of love. The dialectic works in both. The same pattern is in both. They can be built up as far as the mind can go—Llull offers each 'angle' (or, each entity) of each triangle as 'a ladder by which the intellect can ascend and descend'.[80] It was for comprehension of all entities.

We have several times discussed the percept that where there are two entities there is a third being that which is both conjoined; this is axiomatic and authoritative. It was the starting point in discussing how mathematics apprehended the universe: the Same, the Diverse and their Composite.[81] Grosseteste applied it explicitly to the firmament of light: form, matter and composition, saying that 'composition' takes 'informed matter' and 'materialized form' to make 'a third constituent distinct from matter and form'.[82] William of St-Thierry's picture of the enclosed life was heaven, the cell and their conjoining love in the heart of the monk. The picture of the communal life was heaven, the abbey church and their composing love.[83] While love is not an additional and optional third—it is the very substance of the two known together as one entity—it should not escape notice that the interconnections are acts, and they are profoundly known only in the context of the whole.

The theology is that the three-and-one God is the origin and model of love. The point that was emphasised was the generative, active character of divine love and all love of passionate expression. Here is a medieval understanding of real connections which, seen in the material church, can help to explain its essential nature, indeed its vital design. The whole reality will only be partly apprehended in the visible artefact, the extrinsic aspect only; but that will correspond to an intrinsic reality. The theological diagram shown in Chapter 2 can be applied to represent the mystical reality and the architectural case.

First here is a diagram of the trinitary scheme of heaven, the cell and their composite which is the very thing in which heaven and the cell coinhere and are composed: William of St-Thierry identified this explicitly as love.

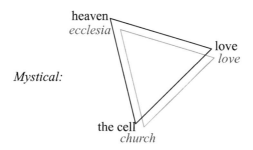

'Heaven' is shorthand for all that pertains to the spaceless, timeless realm of God; but if it implies a *locus* it is not necessarily incongruous. The physical cell represents the inner life of each enclosed person. Love is in the exchange between cell and heaven. Love is 'the cell in heaven' and 'heaven in the cell'. Here are the two common relational tropes we have seen throughout, namely hierarchy and participation, both of which were accounted necessary in and wholly fulfilled in love, which is mutual exchange. Without love hierarchy and participation are problematical. Love makes heaven and the cell a trinity; and in its unity is a complete integration. William set up the heaven–cell relation as an illustration of love in the *church* where it must be the currency and language of exchange. Hence another trinity can clearly be seen: the universal ecclesia, and every particular church, and their uniting love. The mystical ecclesia is the archetype, the ideal for the church as an earthly entity: the earthly church is the ectype, the copy.

In this chapter the hermeneutical mirror is the Incarnation and the Trinity, reflecting the trinitary pattern everywhere. In the churches illustrated, buildings made with evident understanding, of numinous clarity, theological rationale is integrated with the material building; in this is their art. Corresponding to the spiritual diagram there is an architectural application. In the correspondence, equating the diagrams, love is the art.

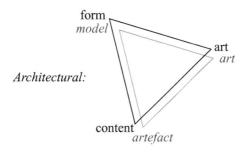

228 *Building in love*

Here the joining of form and content is vital in the constitution, the congruity, and the composition: to make form and content one is the art. If we consider an artificer shaping an artefact in accord with a model, the activity is, again, art.

Art unites the concept in the mind and the material under the hand. Llull, in his scheme *Ars*, called the conjoining not only art, but also the process of work for the making of things.

'Form' pertains to the architectural subject. Alexander gives a serviceable meaning: 'The crucial quality of shape, no matter of what kind, lies in its organization, and when we think of it this way we call it form'.[84] This is our unconscious usage and is obvious. In human forming of things it alludes to intention; and intention alludes to meaning. 'Content' of the architectural subject is all that is brought to the place, put into it, done in it. In the content meaning is contracted. Brigitte Bedos-Rezak writes: 'While positing the form-content dyad as an inseparable entity, I consider its elements, one signifying, the other meaning, as having independent histories and contingent modes of interaction'. As interaction she posits 'social process', but this seems too contingent to rise to the potential of theocentric intention and meaning in art.[85]

In the diagram's matching triad, the art produces entire agreement between the model in the artificer's mind for a particular building, and the artefact, the physical entity itself. Art involves the operation of conjoining and composing. It integrates by providentially translating form to artefact, it brings what is potential into act.[86] Germane to art is an intrinsic–extrinsic dialectic. The intrinsic view is an entity's whole inner reality, perhaps concealed, but clarified and known inwardly. The extrinsic view is an entity's whole phenomenal existence, accessible to the senses, generally conspicuous, comprehensible. The two aspects pertain to one art. The spiritual and the architectural expositions coincide.

To grasp the implications we can overlay the two diagrams and see that the four elements of each indeed correspond: heaven/form; ecclesia/model; cell/content; church/artefact. The identifications are recognisable in the consistent evidence of the foregoing chapters in which inner reality is transposed to the outer, and the outer reflects the inner. The deductive method has involved a search in medieval theology and learning, and translation into architectural praxis.

In the mirror of comprehension we detect the grammar, dialectic and rhetoric of these arts articulating the pattern of human love for God in medieval churches and cathedrals. The grammar of Coutances cathedral's west front carries signs and conventions of concentrated intention (Figure 3.2). Interiorly the semi-circular form of the apse is generated by the dialectic between the sanctuary and ambulatory, the ambit of love for God and people (Figure 6.3). Extreme verticality is the rhetoric of the west towers, expressing desire and aspiration for God (Figure 1.2). The elevated central arcade is like the very language of love.

Then in the mirror of instruction the conspicuously high degree of ratiocination, in measure, hierarchy, figuration and harmony, produced material artefacts of extraordinary power and conceptual clarity. They witness to theocentricity in creative intellects at work. In the first three stages of the west front of Mantes cathedral is arithmetical measure; the arcaded fourth stage and towers belong to astronomy (Figure 5.12). The east chevet is a geometrical figuration of the spiritual function and rationale. The interior arcading of the chevet, abstract and pure in form, is the music of movement and performance (Figure 4.6).

The mirror of all nature and created life, human and angelic, reflected divine energy, focussed by consideration in the mind, the life and energy infused by contemplation into the art and architecture. When Bernard enjoined consideration it was for deeper participation in all things. It ran throughout church buildings. In the very fabric of Lincoln cathedral and its exterior associations with the world (Figure 5.7), in its interior places with intimations of heaven (Figure 5.8), the spiritual church involved the material.

In this oneness in which exchange and integration occurred as it were naturally, the architecture possessed great power. The point of the trinitary concept is that the triads are axiomatic, not theoretical; they bear consideration and application, not needing proof. Accordingly the architecture phenomenally corresponded to the theology and ecclesiology. The phenomenon then can be described further.

The *church*, belonging to a monastery, college, cathedral or parish, is primarily the adherents; and as material *artefact* it is the building—say, the material cause.

Heaven, as said above, stands for the spaceless, timeless presence of God; and the theocentric culture tried to realise the *form* appropriate to it—say, the formal cause.

The *cell* represents the monastic place into which is contracted all heaven, and the picture easily extends to the cloister and chapter house, and the organisation of the enclosed life. The practical experience comprised the *content* which shaped the monk, even in the work—the efficient cause.

The *ecclesia* has its locus in heaven, the new and perfected work of God. Such meaning is evident in representational art where a model of a church is held by the bishop, king, Mary, saint or apostle and love for the church is signified.[87] It is, indeed, the *model*—it is like the final cause of the church.

The theological union of Lover and Beloved in Love was mirrored by the spiritual integration of heaven and the cell by love, and by the architectural integration of the model and artefact by art. There was theology and love in the architecture and its art. The overriding point which the study shows is that love, and art, meant love and art 'because of' God.

In this study the significance of the concept of the Trinity is that it shows the radical nature of love—it is the very reality, the unity, the spirit, which defines the joining of entities such as lover and beloved, and heaven and earth. And as it defines the joining of creator and creature, we realise that

230   *Building in love*

the love is also generative in its nature. Divine love is all act; human love is potential. Yet it is the very thing that really *joins* the artificer and artefact. Where the pattern of love is effectual and operative, it is incarnational. Between God the Artificer and the Incarnation was this connection as given by Athanasius:

> He, the Mighty One, the Artificer of all, Himself prepared this body in the virgin as a temple for Himself, and took it for His very own, as the instrument through which He was known and in which He dwelt.[88]

For this study the implication of the Incarnation is particularly that it was the Artificer's instrument in the remaking of things; the creative Mind becoming flesh, the Spirit overshadowing the body with life. It was for a purpose. It was to be the pattern of nature being made new. Dante spoke of being 'transhumanised' (*trasumanar*) by love producing a radical change in human experience; seeming to even change one's nature.[89] The *Commedia* embodies the pattern, encapsulated in this:

> Gazing upon his Son with the Love which the
>   one and the other eternally breathes forth, the
>   primal and ineffable Worth,
>
> made whatsoever circleth through mind or space
>   with so great order that whoso looketh on it
>   may not be without some taste of him.
>
> [...] amorously there begin to gaze upon that
>   Master's art, who within himself so loveth it,
>   that never doth he part his eye from it.[90]

The first tercet expresses love in the Trinity. The second asserts that one cannot see the pattern and frame of things of mind and space unless there is 'some taste' of God. Then the master craftsman's art is contemplated and loved; it is the Trinity always in act and work. Dante's art well indicates the range and power of the minds of great medieval thinkers (he was indeed a theologian deserving of recognition). Such concepts are profound and poetic expression at the highest human reach. The architecture achieved a no less astonishing integration and exposition.

Junction between heaven and earth

When Dante, as protagonist in the *Commedia*, is led by Beatrice to survey Paradise (to the limit of human grasp), his mind is still baffled by many questions. Even while progressively resolving these for him Beatrice has to convert his love from being enamoured by her beauty to being at the end filled with ardour for God. Paul Claudel has the glorified Beatrice, no longer beside him but having returned to the empyrean, pointing out to Dante, 'If I had not been one side and the other at the same time, wouldst thou have made thyself the engineer of this junction between heaven and earth?'[91] Beatrice's role was dual and crucial; Dante *the poet* made himself the engineer of the junction of his loves, and of the long process leading to this resolution. In our survey we have had the guidance of medieval thinkers and theologians who have been speaking, as it were, from the mundane and material side, and from the heavenly, spiritual side, at the same time. If we put ourselves inside the story, the challenge handed down to us is to transfer our love (doubtless disordered) from marvelling at the appearance of the churches and cathedrals, to love (however unpractised) the Love who is their cause; this is how we will be able understand these works. Our subject concerns the architecture of medieval churches and, drawing on those guides, we have seen how the makers, similarly guided, engineered 'this junction between heaven and earth'.

The church building achievements of the Middle Ages, so remarkable for not having had a canon of art or architectural theory, were intellectually informed by theology, and full of processes of judgement; they evidence a highly integrated architecture ordered, above all, to God. We have to recognise in the theology the striving for truth and precision in the mind, in order to grasp its ramifications. Only people working in love are able to emulate the love in the mind of God the Maker. It prompts us to adjust our own approach to judging medieval architecture.

The real work of a human artificer is incarnational when the idea of making a vessel representing God coming in flesh, becomes actual in a body. It is especially the mode of the material church: it is the here and now, the labour, the pain and the joy. Churches were not the accomplishments of individuals, and many involved never saw the work completed. Pertinent to this, Abbot Suger's explanation, in *De consecratione*, of his vision for the St-Denis abbey church, has been regarded sceptically because of his exuberance and satisfaction for the work brought to completion. While the architecture was highly rationally informed and conceived, it was nevertheless also radically vernacular in character and unselfcentred. Participation in nature and organisation of cultural hierarchies were key modes of operation. Vernacular process also brought together intuition and judgement using the head, hand and heart, the process being a continuum from genesis and design to building and enjoyment. Alexander concludes his *Notes on the Synthesis of Form*: 'I believe that our feeling for architectural form can never reach a comparable order of development, until we too have first learned a comparable feeling for the process of design'.[92] This study has aimed at sharpening our 'feeling for architectural form', but the process, we have found, is the engineering of the junction of two things.

In present attitudes there often seems to be an assumed disjunction between disciplines which apparently work in different modes, theology

232 *Building in love*

being noetic and other-worldly, architecture being more pragmatic and this-worldly; while aetiology is too rigorous. The difficulty becomes evident when we try to grasp ideation and intention in visual and constructive arts as operating within a mentality different to our own. This is the reason for using the deductive method—which has also been less susceptible to unconscious modern interpretations.

The foci of church architecture and theology have not been too narrow, for architecture has embraced the visual arts of painting, sculpture, decoration, and the tectonic art of construction, and philosophy, metaphysics and science have been brought in. The ease with which this has been permitted by the sources attests to the integration in each discipline, albeit with difference and diversity in the works. Justification, if needed, of the dominance in the study of these two disciplines is in the old view that theology was pre-eminent in learning and wisdom, and architecture over the visual and constructive arts. Though those priorities are now taken to be untenable, and their privileges withdrawn, the core reasons for such ordering actually remain.

From the commencement, the nature of connections between the two fields has had to be watched. Despite caveats, such as to be wary of generalisations, the most important conclusions from the evidence are conservative. The deductive argument from theological and literary sources is not itself a proof of the case in its outworking—but it constitutes a fresh and radical approach to the artefacts, explaining the reality and integrity which is evidenced in them, and tracing the makers' intentions and motivation to their origins. The premiss has been that where written sources cast light on the work of artificers they must be recognised. The source materials are rich and diverse, and there are a multitude of interwoven issues, to be read with understanding; but seeming digressions have led home. The case articulated may seem obvious, yet it has been a blind-spot in modern scholarship.

The attention to tools of thought and image-making from contemporary sources has, for this study, rendered of peripheral importance some academic preoccupations such as historicist method, socio-political context and patronage, monumentalist focus, style comparison, aesthetic beauty, plastic space and even symbolism. That the works studied were products of contemporary minds gives them authority to witness to and confirm what was important. Deeper than questions of style and proximate influences, the perception of works made in high ratiocination yet in vernacular modes has emerged as a credible and useful explanation of their power and vitality.[93]

The diverse sources of theology referred to have spanned eleven centuries, perhaps raising the question whether there were shifts in perception on the subject of love for God. But the core verities founded in Scripture and the early authorities persisted and it is these that underpinned medieval theology. The more telling shift was away from love for God as the constant referent—that from 'the Enlightenment' that emphasis was displaced increasingly by an anthropocentric mentality; this was reflected in architecture and the arts. It is what our present-day mentality is built upon, which is the real impediment in regaining an understanding of medieval church architecture.

A corresponding question might be raised whether the shifts in architectural styles over the long Middle Ages, or across the geographical areas, invalidate the propositions made concerning the essential common nature of the works. It is one of the remarkable features that within the general coherence of the architectural idiom there is such diversity and ingenuity that all churches and cathedrals are distinctively individual and distinguishable. But it is the witness to the outworking of theology in architecture that is of more consequence than historic differences between Romanesque and Gothic eras, or stylistic developments in either. We can respect the genius of medieval theology. We might pause to imagine how amazing the great cathedrals and abbeys must have appeared in their time, and how elevated their spiritual mode.

In their full extent the theological and architectural identifications studied make it clear that the love that acted to unite spiritually, and the art which directed the process in the architecture, were two complementary affirmations of extraordinary power. The theological, spiritual and architectural views are integrated in the diagrams which are one. The art of the architecture was love. It depends upon the identifications being true, and the real security of that is in the culture's own witness. The study has identified love for God as working on both sides of the junction of theology and architecture.

The concluding question must be whether this study is relevant in our world. In terms of truth in the theology it does serve to show how the incontrovertible priority of love for God can still inform and direct human work and creativity. In relation to goodness in architecture, it asserts the indispensable working of love in all persons in the entire process, acting in two ways—towards the spiritual source, and upon the material work and artefact. The junction between heaven and earth needs to be perceived with the clarity of the Middle Ages, before it can again be articulated and configured with authority and integrity.

Notes

1 Ginther (2003), p. 246.
2 Ibid., p. 248.
3 Grosseteste, *Hexaëmeron*, 2.9.1, trans. Wright (2017).
4 Bernard, *De consideratione*, 2.2.5. trans. Lewis (1908), p. 41.
5 Early spires in France are St-Leu-d'Esserent, Le Dorat and St-Marcel, Cluny. The south spire of Chartres is an early cathedral example.
6 See **p. XXX** above; the first three stages.
7 Richard of St-Victor, *Benjamin maior*, 1.6, trans. Zinn (1979), pp. 162–4.
8 See van 't Spijker (2004), p. 150.
9 Richard of St-Victor, *Benjamin maior*, 4.16, trans. Zinn (1979), p. 288.
10 Ibid., 4.9, p. 273.

234 Building in love

11 Ibid., 3.21: '*quasi alius quidam creator*', van 't Spijker (2004), p. 152.
12 Ibid., 4.20: '*quasi sui generis creaturas quoties voluerit sine praeiacenti materia et velut ex nihilo formare*', ibid.
13 Richard of St-Victor, *Benjamin maior*, 1.6, ibid., p. 163.
14 See particularly Richard of St-Victor, *Benjamin maior*, 4.11 and 12.
15 Thomas, *Summa theologica*, 2a 2ae, q.9, 2, trans. Dominican Fathers (1915–28), vol. 9, p. 114.
16 Ibid., q.9, 2, ad.1, p. 115.
17 Ibid., q.9, 3, ad, p. 116.
18 Boethius, *De consolatione*, 5.4, trans. Watts (1969), p. 160.
19 Ibid., 5.5., p. 162.
20 Ibid., 5.6., p. 169.
21 See Panofsky (1968), passim.
22 Ibid., p. 27.
23 See Croddy (1999), pp. 264, 271. He finds no appurtenant metalanguage external to the artefacts of Romanesque or Gothic architecture.
24 Bonaventure, *Itinerarium* 2.6, trans. Cousins (1978), p. 72.
25 See **p. 21** above.
26 McGinn (1995), p. 45, notes *renovatio* in a similar context.
27 Italian dialects had been used in the thirteenth century by such as Francis of Assisi and Jacopone da Todi, in religious poetry, but without linguistic analysis.
28 See Dante Alighieri, *De vulgari eloquentia*, 1.1, trans. Howell and Wicksteed (1940), p. 4. He pictures the confusion in the building of the Tower of Babel as the inability of the various groups of workers—architects, masons, quarrymen, and all—to communicate, because their language became peculiar to their operations and trades. See ibid., 1.7, p. 19.
29 Seidel (1981), p. 19.
30 Ibid.
31 John of Salisbury, *Metalogicon*, 1.11, trans. McGarry (1955), p. 34 (translator's brackets).
32 Heyman (1995), p. 141.
33 Ibid., p. 139.
34 Refer **pp. 88–9** above.
35 William of St-Thierry, *Epistola*, 1.150, trans. Berkeley (1976), p. 60.
36 Alexander (1964), p. 36.
37 See **pp. 167, 176** above.
38 Alexander (1964), p. 132.
39 Thomas, *Summa theologica*, 3, q.2, a.1, ad., trans. Dominican Fathers (1915–28), vol. 15, p. 24.
40 Ibid., p. 25.
41 Ibid.
42 Ibid., ad.2., p. 27.
43 Ibid., ad.3., p. 27. This is the Syrian John of Damascus (*c.* 675–749).
44 Athanasius, *De incarnatione Verbi Dei*, 16, trans. A Religious of C.S.M.V. (1944), p. 44. Refer **p. 52** above.
45 Ibid., 17, pp. 45–6.
46 Hugh of St-Victor, *De sacramentis* 1, Prolog. 1, trans. Deferrari (1951), p. 1. Compare *Quid vere diligendum est*, 3.7, **p. 53** above.
47 Bonaventure, *De reductione*, 5, trans. Healey (1955), Vol. I, p. 27.
48 Ibid., 8, p. 29.
49 Ibid., 8, trans. Hayes (1996), p. 47.
50 See **pp. 195–96** above.
51 William of St-Thierry, *Epistola*, 1.31, trans. Berkeley (1976), p. 20.

52 Ibid., 1.32, p. 21.
53 Ibid., 1.35–36, p. 22.
54 Ibid. William's meaning may be that the truth in which the sacraments participate will then appear as open, unconditioned reality.
55 Bonaventure, *De reductione*, 11, trans. Hayes (1996), p. 49 (translator's italics).
56 Matthew 1.20.
57 William of St-Thierry, *Epistola*, 1.59, trans. Berkeley (1976), p. 32.
58 Ibid., 1.149, p. 60.
59 Exodus 25.40. William cites this in 1.149.
60 William of St-Thierry, *Epistola*, 1.150, trans. Berkeley (1976), p. 60.
61 Ibid., 1.153, p. 61. Compare all this with Hugh of St-Victor's illustration of learning in *Didascalicon*. See **p. 82** above.
62 Ibid., 2.196, p. 78.
63 Ibid., 2.265, p. 96. Compare with Wisdom of Solomon, 7.27 and 8.1: 'And being but one [Wisdom] can do all things: and remaining in herself, she maketh all things new. [...] Wisdom reacheth from one end to another mightily: and sweetly doth she order all things'.
64 Thomas, *Summa theologica*, 2a 2ae, q.31, a.1, ad.1, trans. Dominican Fathers (1915–28), Vol. 9, p. 399. The citation is *De divinis nominibus*, 4.12. See also **p. 56** above.
65 C.f. *Sirach* 38.34: '[...] they keep stable the fabric of the world, and their prayer is in the practice of their trade'.
66 Examples can be found increasingly from the ninth century in manuscript depictions, and in eleventh-century frescos of Christ in glory (e.g. in Sant' Angelo in Formis, and St-Gilles, Montiore-sur-Loir). These all pre-date conventional use in secular art.
67 Origen, *Cantica canticorum*, trans. by Lawson (1957), p. 282. The text is Song, 1.10 (Vulgate 1.9).
68 Bernard, *Sermones super Cantica canticorum*, 40.2, 2, trans. Walsh and Edmonds (1971–80), II, pp. 199–200. Alan of Lille in *Elucidatio*, trans. Turner (1995), p. 305, likewise interprets Song 1.10 as the cheek's blush.
69 Cited in Stevenson (1899), p. 36. Stephenson gives the source as Brown's *Fasciculus*, 2.
70 Bede, *De tabernaculo*, 2.1, trans. Holder (1994), p.45 (author's italics).
71 Bernard, *Sententiae*, 2.188, trans. Swietek (2000), p. 179.
72 Honorius of Autun, *De gemma animae*, trans. Mortet (1972), p. 226.
73 William Durandus, *Rationale divinorum officiorum*, trans. Frisch, see Frisch (1971), p. 35. (English spelling modernised.)
74 The imagery is in Biblical texts such as Ephesians 2.21–22, and I Peter 2.5.
75 This motif was referred to in 'The Garden of Charity', **p. 173** above; the masonry pattern in 'Grammar', **p. 78** above.
76 See **p. 48** above.
77 See Ginther (2003), pp. 240–1.
78 Llull, *Ars brevis*, 2.2, trans. Bonner (1993), p. 303. This echoes Bonaventure's saying that between apices 'a relation of a procession (*emanatio*) has the character of a line'. See **p. 51** above.
79 Ibid. Compare with Worringer's percept of the making of lines, **p. 75** above.
80 Ibid., 2.3, p. 304.
81 See **pp. 112–13** above, citing Plato's *Timaeus*.
82 Robert Grosseteste, *De luce*, trans Riedl (1942), p. 27.
83 See **p. 218** above.
84 Alexander (1964), p. 134. See also **p. 181** above for Augustine on kinds of form.
85 Bedos-Rezak (1995), p. 237.

236 *Building in love*

86 For discussion on intentionality in form and conscious design see Bedos-Rezak (1995); but this holistic design theory seems not to resonate with the medieval spirit and *modus operandi*.
87 Persons holding models of churches are not always donors. See Klinkenberg (2009).
88 Athanasius, *De incarnatione Verbi Dei*, trans. a Religious of C.S.M.V. (1944), p. 34.
89 Dante, *Paradiso* 1.70.
90 Dante, *Paradiso* 10. 1–6; 10–12., trans. Wicksteed (1899), p. 117. 'Love', being the Holy Spirit, breathes from Father and Son.
91 Claudel, *Feuilles de Saints* (Paris: Gallimard, 1925, p. 187), see Beaumont (trans.) (1954), p. 14.
92 Alexander (1964), p. 134. It concludes the Epilogue where Alexander illustrates 'the action of the unselfconscious form-producing system'. The commencement of the Epilogue is cited on **p. 214** above.
93 The secondary and contingent place of style is clearly illustrated by the general failure of the Gothic Revival movement because direction no longer came from the same affective theology.

Bibliography

Primary sources

Achard of St-Victor, *Sermones, De unione spiritus et corporis, De unitate*, trans. Hugh Feiss (2001) in *Achard of Saint Victor: Works*, CS 165, Kalamazoo, MI: Cistercian.

Aelred of Rievaulx, *De speculo caritatis*, ed. A. Hoste and C. H. Talbot (1971), CCCM 1, Turnhout: Brepols; trans. Elizabeth Connor (1990), in *The Mirror of Charity*, CF 17, Kalamazoo, MI: Cistercian.

Alan of Lille, *Elucidatio super Cantica canticorum*, trans. Denys Turner (1995), in *Eros and Allegory: Medieval Exegesis of the Song of Songs*, CS 156, Kalamazoo: Cistercian, pp. 291–307.

Alberti, *The Ten Books of Architecture* (Florence: 1485), trans. G. Leoni (1755), London; facsimile edn, 1986, New York.

Alcuin, *De dialectica*, J.-P. Migne, *Patrologia latina* 101.952, trans. Wilbur S. Howell (1965), in *The Rhetoric of Alcuin and Charlemagne*, New York, NY: Russell & Russell.

Athanasius, *De incarnatione Verbi Dei*, trans. A Religious of C.S.M.V. (1944), in *The Incarnation of the Word of God: Being the Treatise of St. Athanasius*, London: Geoffrey Bles.

Aristotle, *Nicomachean Ethics*, trans. J. A. K. Thomson (1955) in *The Ethics of Aristotle*, Harmondsworth: Penguin.

—— *Sophistici Elenchi*, ed. W. D. Ross (1928–31), in *The Works of Aristotle Translated into English*, 11 vols, Oxford: Clarendon Press.

—— *Topica*, ed. and trans. W. D. Ross (1928–31), in *The Works of Aristotle Translated into English*, 11 vols, Oxford: Clarendon Press.

Augustine, Bishop of Hippo, *Confessiones*, trans. Albert C. Outler (1955), in *Augustine: Confessions and Enchiridion*, LCC 7, London: SCM; trans. R. S. Pine-Coffin (1961), in *Confessions*, Harmondsworth: Penguin.

—— *De civitate Dei*, CCSL 47–48, eds B. Dombart and A. Kalb (1955), Turnhout: Brepols; trans. R. W. Dyson, Cambridge University Press (1998) in *Augustine, The City of God against the Pagans*, Cambridge: Cambridge University Press; trans. Henry Bettenson (1972), in *City of God*, Harmondsworth: Penguin.

—— *De doctrina christiana*, CCSL 32, ed. J. Martin (1962) Turnhout: Brepols.

—— *De libero arbitrio*, trans. John H. S. Burleigh (1953), in *Augustine: Earlier Writings*, LCC 6, Philadelphia, PA: Westminster, pp. 113–217.

—— *De musica*, trans. Robert C. Taliaferro (1947), in *The Fathers of the Church: Saint Augustine*, FC 4, Washington, DC: The Catholic University of America Press.

—— *De quantitate animae*, trans. John J. McMahon (1947), in *The Fathers of the Church: Saint Augustine*, FC 4, Washington, DC: The Catholic University of America Press.

—— *De Trinitate*, trans. John Burnaby (1955), in *Augustine: Later Works*, LCC 8, London: SCM.

—— *De vera religione*, trans. J. H. S. Burleigh (1953), in *Augustine: Earlier Writings*, LCC 6, Philadelphia, PA: Westminster.

—— *Enchiridion* (*On Faith, Hope, and Love*), trans. Albert C. Outler (1955), in *Augustine: Confessions and Enchiridion*, LCC 7, London: SCM.

Bede, *De tabernaculo*, ed. D. Hurst (1969), in *Opera exegetica*, 2, CCSL 119A, Turnhout: Brepols; trans. Arthur G. Holder (1994), in *Bede: On the Tabernacle*, TTH 18, Liverpool: Liverpool University Press.

—— *De templo*, ed. D. Hurst (1969), in *Opera exegetica*, 2, CCSL 119A, Turnhout: Brepols; trans. Seán Connolly (1995), in *Bede: On the Temple*, TTH 21, Liverpool: Liverpool University Press.

Bernard of Clairvaux, *De consideratione*, trans. George Lewis (1908), in *On Consideration*, Oxford: Clarendon.

—— *De diligendo Deo*, trans. Edmund G. Gardner (1916), in *The Book of Saint Bernard on the Love of God*, London: Dent; trans. Harman van Allen (1959), in *On Loving God and Selections from Sermons*, ed. Hugh Martin, London: SPCK; trans. Emero Stiegman (1995) in *On Loving God by Bernard of Clairvaux with an Analytical Commentary*, CF 13B, Kalamazoo, MI: Cistercian, first pub. 1973.

—— *Epistola 11, Ad Cartusiensis*, SBO 7, trans. S. J. Eales (1904), in *The Works of St Bernard, Vol. 1, The Letters*, London: Burns and Oates, pp. 52–60.

—— *Sancti Bernardi Opera*, SBO 1–7, ed. J. Leclercq (1957), C. H. Talbot (1970), and H. Rochais (1972), Rome: Editiones Cistercienses.

—— *Sententiae*, SBO 6.1, trans. Francis R. Swietek (2000), in *The Parables and The Sentences*, CF 55, Kalamazoo, MI: Cistercian.

—— *Sermones super Cantica canticorum*, trans. Kilian Walsh and Irene M. Edmonds (1971–80), in *On the Song of Songs*, Sermons 1–86, CF 4, 7, 31, 40, Kalamazoo, MI: Cistercian.

Bernardus Silvestris, *Megacosmos* and *Microcosmos*, trans. Winthrop Wetherbee (1973), in *The Cosmographia of Bernardus Silvestris*, New York: Columbia University Press.

Boethius, *De consolatione philosophiae*, ed. L. Bieler (1957), CCSL 94, Turnhout: Brepols; trans. V. E. Watts (1969) in *Boethius: The Consolation of Philosophy*, Harmondsworth: Penguin.

—— *De institutione arithmetica*, trans. Michael Masi (1983a), in *Boethian Number Theory: A Translation of the De Institutione Arithmetica*, Amsterdam: Rodopi.

Bonaventure, *Commentary on the Sentences* (1882–1902), in *Opera Omnia*, 2, Quaracchi: Ex Typographia Collegii S. Bonaventurae, pp. 235–57.

—— *De reductione artium ad theologiam*, trans. Sister Emma Therese Healy (1955); trans. Zachary Hayes (1996), in *Works of Saint Bonaventure, Volume I*, Saint Bonaventure, NY: Franciscan Institute.

—— *In Sententiarum*, trans. Denys Turner (1995), in *Eros and Allegory: Medieval Exegesis of the Song of Songs*, CS 156, Kalamazoo, MI: Cistercian.

—— *Itinerarium mentis ad Deum*, trans. George Boas (1953), in *Saint Bonaventura: The Mind's Road to God*, Indianapolis, IN: Bobbs-Merrill; trans Ewart Cousins (1978), in *The Soul's Journey into God*, New York, NY: Paulist.

—— *The Works of Bonaventure*, Vol. 1: *The Journey of the Mind to God (Itinerarium mentis ad Deum)*, *The Triple Way or Love Enkindled (De triplici via, seu incendium amoris)*, Vol. 2: *Breviloquium*; Vol. 3: *On the Reduction of the Arts to Theology (De reductione artium ad theologiam)*, trans. José de Vinck (1963–66), Paterson, NJ: St Anthony Guild Press.

—— *Vitis mystica*, trans. A Friar of S.S.F. (1955), in *The Mystical Vine*, Fleur de Lys Series 5, London: Mowbray.

Boncompagno da Signa, *Rhetorica novissima*, trans. Sean Gallagher (2002), in Mary Carruthers and Jan Ziolkowski, eds, *The Medieval Craft of Memory: An Anthology of Texts and Pictures*, Philadelphia, PA: University of Pennsylvania Press.

Bradwardine, Thomas, *Tractatus de continuo*, trans. George Molland (1989), in *Geometria speculativa*, Stuttgart: Franz Steiner.

Cicero, *De inventione: De optimo genere oratorum: Topica*, trans. H. M. Hubbell (1949), Cambridge, MA: Harvard University Press, pp. 20–21.

Dante Alighieri, *Convivio*, trans. P. H. Wicksteed (1931), in *The Convivio of Dante Alighieri*, Temple Classics, London: Dent.

—— *De vulgari eloquentia*, trans. A. G. Ferrers Howell and P. H. Wicksteed (1940), in *A Translation of the Latin Works of Dante Alighieri*, Temple Classics, London: Dent.

—— *Inferno*, trans. Melville B. Anderson (1932), in *The Divine Comedy of Dante Alighieri*, London: Oxford University Press.

—— *Inferno*, trans. Dorothy L. Sayers (1949), in *The Divine Comedy of Dante Alighieri, 1: Hell*, Harmondsworth: Penguin.

—— *Paradiso*, trans. Melville B. Anderson (1932), in *The Divine Comedy of Dante Alighieri*, London: Oxford University Press.

—— *Paradiso*, trans. Dorothy L. Sayers and Barbara Reynolds (1962), in *The Divine Comedy of Dante Alighieri, 3: Paradise*, Harmondsworth: Penguin.

—— *Paradiso*, trans. Charles S. Singleton (1975), in *The Divine Comedy, Paradiso: 1. Italian Text and Translation, 2. Commentary*, Bollingen Series LXXX, Princeton, NJ: Princeton University Press.

—— *Paradiso*, trans. John D. Sinclair (1939), in *The Divine Comedy of Dante Alighieri, 3. Paradiso*, New York, NY: Oxford University Press.

—— *Paradiso*, trans. P. H. Wicksteed (1899) in *The Paradiso of Dante Alighieri*, Temple Classics, London: Dent.

—— *Purgatorio*, trans. Dorothy L. Sayers (1955), in *The Divine Comedy of Dante Alighieri, 2: Purgatory*, Harmondsworth: Penguin.

Durandus, William, *Rationale divinorum officiorum*, ed. Elisabeth G. Holt (1957), excerpts in *A Documentary History of Art: Volume I*, Garden City, NY: Doubleday.

Eriugena, John Scottus, *De divina praedestinatione*, trans. Mary Brennan (1998), in *John Scottus, Eriugena: Treatise on Divine Predestination*, Notre Dame, IN: University of Notre Dame Press.

—— *De divisione naturae*, trans. George B. Burch (1955), in Anne Fremantle, *The Age of Belief: The Medieval Philosophers*, New York, NY: New American Library.

240 Bibliography

Faventinus, Marcus Cetius, *De diversis fabricis architectonicae*, trans. Hugh Plommer (1973), in *Vitruvius and Later Roman Building Manuals*, London: Cambridge University Press.

Filarete (Antonio di Piero Averlino) *Treatise on Architecture*, trans. John R. Spencer (1965), 2 vols, New Haven, CT: Yale University Press.

Geoffrey of Vinsauf, *Poetria nova*, trans. Jane Baltzell Kopp (1971), in *Three Medieval Rhetorical Arts*, ed. James J. Murphy, Berkeley, CA: University of California Press; trans. Margaret F. Nims (1967), in *Poetria Nova of Geoffrey of Vinsauf*, Toronto: Pontifical Institute of Mediaeval Studies.

Grosseteste, Robert, *De luce seu inchoatione formarum*, trans. Clare C. Riedl (1942), in *On Light, or the Beginning of Forms*, MPTT 1, Milwaukee, WI: Marquette University Press.

—— *Hexaëmeron*, trans. C. F. J. Martin (1996), in *Robert Grosseteste: On the Six Days of Creation*, ABMA VI(2), Oxford: Oxford University Press.

—— *Hexaëmeron*, excerpts trans. Michael J. Wright (2017), Auckland: University of Auckland (unpublished).

—— *Le Château d'amour*, trans. Evelyn A. Mackie (2003), in 'Robert Grosseteste's Anglo-Norman Treatise on the Loss and Restoration of Creation, commonly known as *Le chateau d'amour*: An English Prose Translation,' in *Robert Grosseteste and the Beginnings of a British Theological Tradition*, ed. Maura O'Carroll, Rome: Istituto Storico Dei Cappuccini, pp. 151–79.

Henry of Avranches, *Vita Sancti Hugonis*, ed. J. F. Dimock (1860), in *Metrical Life of St Hugh, bishop of Lincoln*, Lincoln: n.pub.; trans J. F. Dimock, excerpt 833–965 in *The Mediaeval Architect*, ed. John Harvey (1972), London: Wayland; trans. Charles Garton (1986), in *The Metrical Life of Saint Hugh of Lincoln*, Lincoln: Honywood.

Honorius of Autun, *De gemma animae*, trans. Victor Mortet (1972), excerpt in *The Mediaeval Architect*, ed. John Harvey, London: Wayland, pp. 225–7.

Hugh of St-Victor, *De arca Noe morali*, and *De arca Noe mystica*, trans. A Religious of C.M.S.V. (1962), intro. Aelred Squire, in *Hugh of St Victor: Selected Spiritual Writings*, London: Faber and Faber.

—— *De sacramentis Christianae fidei*, trans. Roy J. Deferrari (1951), in *Hugh of Saint Victor: On the Sacraments of the Christian Faith (*De Sacramentis*)*, Mediaeval Academy Publication 58, Cambridge, MA: Mediaeval Academy of America.

—— *Didascalicon (Eruditio Didascalica)*, trans. Jerome Taylor (1961), in *The Didascalicon of Hugh of St Victor*, New York, NY: Columbia University Press.

—— *Quid vere diligendum est*, trans. Vanessa Butterfield (2011), in *On Love*, ed. Hugh Feiss, VTT 2, Turnhout: Brepols.

Isidore of Seville, *Etymologiae*, trans. Faith Wallis (1990), q.v.

Jacopone da Todi, *Laude*, trans. George T. Peck (1980), excerpts in *The Fool of God: Jacopone da Todi*, Alabama City, AL: University of Alabama Press, pp. 153–86.

Jacques de Liège, *Speculum musicae*, trans. Kay B. Slocum (1993), excerpts in *Medieval Numerology*, ed. Robert L. Surles, Garland Medieval Casebooks 7, New York: Garland, pp. 11–37.

Joachim of Fiore, *Liber Figurarum*, in *The* Figurae *of Joachim of Fiore*, ed. Marjorie Reeves and Beatrice Hirsch-Reich (1972), excerpts and figures, Oxford: Clarendon Press.

John of Salisbury, *Metalogicon*, trans. Daniel McGarry (1955), in *The Metalogicon of John of Salisbury: A Twelfth-Century Defense of the Verbal and Logical Arts of the Trivium*, Berkeley, CA: University of California Press; trans. J. B. Hall (2013), in *John of Salisbury, Metalogicon*, CCT 12, Turnhout: Brepols.

Josephus, Flavius, *The Antiquities of the Jews*, trans. William Whiston (1838), in *The Works of Flavius Josephus*, Edinburgh: Peter Brown.

Llull, Ramon, *Ars brevis*, trans. Anthony Bonner (1993) in *Doctor Illuminatus: A Ramon Llull Reader*, Princeton, NJ: Princeton University Press.

—— *Liber amici et amati*, trans. Eve Bonner (1993), in *Doctor Illuminatus: A Ramon Llull Reader*, Princeton, NJ: Princeton University Press; ed. and trans. Mark D. Johnston (1995) in *Ramon Llull: The Book of the Lover and the Beloved*, Warminster: Aris & Phillips.

Martianus Capella, *De nuptiis Philologiae et Mercurii*, trans. W. H. Stahl, R. Johnson and E. L. Burge (1977), in *Martianus Capella and the Seven Liberal Arts, Vol. II: The Marriage of Philology and Mercury*, New York, NY: Columbia University Press.

Origen, *Cantica canticorum*, trans. R. P. Lawson (1957), in *The Song of Songs Commentary and Homilies*, ACW 26, Westminster, MD: Newman; London: Longmans, Green.

Peter of Celle, *De disciplina claustrali, The School of the Cloister*, trans. Hugh Feiss (1987), in *Peter of Celle: Selected Works*, CS 100, Kalamazoo, MI: Cistercian.

Peter Lombard, *Sententiae*, trans. Giulio Silano (2008), in *The* Sentences, *Book 2: On Creation*; MST 43, Toronto: Pontifical Institute of Mediaeval Studies.

Plato, *Phaedrus*, trans. Walter Hamilton (1973), in *Plato: Phaedrus and Letters VII and VIII*, Harmondsworth: Penguin.

—— *Timaeus*, trans. H. D. P. Lee (1965), in *Plato: Timaeus and Critias*, Harmondsworth: Penguin; trans. John Warrington (1965), in *Plato: Timaeus*, Everyman's Library, 493, London: Dent.

Pseudo-Dionysius, *De divinis nominibus, De mystica theologia, De caelesti hierarchia, De divina hierarchia*, trans. Colm Luibheid (1987), in *Pseudo-Dionysius: The Complete Works*, CWS, London: SPCK.

—— *Mystical Theology and the Celestial Hierarchies of Dionysius the Areopagite*, editors of The Shrine of Wisdom (1935), Fintry: The Shrine of Wisdom.

Pseudo-Enoch, *I Enoch*, trans. R. H. Charles (1982), in *The Book of Enoch*, first pub. 1912; 2nd edn. 1917; repub. London: SPCK.

Richard of St-Victor, *Benjamin minor, Benjamin maior, De Trinitate*, trans. Grover A. Zinn, Jr. (1979), in *Richard of St. Victor: The Twelve Patriarchs, The Mystical Ark, Book Three of the Trinity*, CWS, London: SPCK.

—— *De quatuor gradibus violentae caritatis*, 6., trans. Andrew B. Kraebel (2011), in Hugh Feiss, ed., *On Love*. VTT 2, Turnhout: Brepols.

Robert of Basevorn, *Forma praedicandi* (*The Form of Preaching*), trans. Leopold Krul (1971), in *Three Medieval Rhetorical Arts*, ed. J. J. Murphy, Berkeley, CA: University of California Press.

Suger, Abbot, *Liber de rebus in administratione sua gestis, Libellus alter de consecratione ecclesiae Sancti Dionysii, Ordinatio*, trans. Erwin Panofsky (1979), in *Abbot Suger on the Abbey Church of St.-Denis and its Art Treasures*, first pub. 1946, 2nd edn. ed. Gerda Panofsky-Soergel, Princeton, NJ: Princeton University Press.

242 Bibliography

Thomas Aquinas, *Commentary on the* Metaphysics *of Aristotle*, trans. John P. Rowan (1961), Library of Living Catholic Thought, Vol. 1, Chicago, IL: Henry Regnery.
—— *De caritate*, trans. Lottie H. Kendzierski (1960), in *On Charity (De caritate)*, MPTT 10, Milwaukee, WI: Marquette University Press.
—— *De spiritualibus creaturis*, trans. Mary C. Fitzpatrick (1949), in *On Spiritual Creatures*, MPTT 5, Milwaukee, WI: Marquette University Press.
—— *Summa contra gentiles*, in *Summa Contra Gentiles, Book 1: God*, trans. Anton C. Pegis (1975); *Book 2: Creation*, trans. James F. Anderson (1975); *Book 3: Providence, Part I* and *Part II*, trans. V. J. Bourke (1975), 2 vols. First pub. 1955, 1956, repr., Notre Dame, IN: University of Notre Dame Press; trans. Anton C. Pegis (1948), selection in *Introduction to Saint Thomas Aquinas*, New York, NY: Random House.
—— *Summa theologica*, trans. Fathers of the English Dominican Province, 22 vols (1915–28), London: Burns, Oates and Washbourne; trans. Anton C. Pegis (1948), selection in *Introduction to Saint Thomas Aquinas* (New York, NY: Random House; trans. J. Crehan (1964), in *Thomas Aquinas: Selected Writings*, ed. M. C. D'Arcy, London: Dent.
—— *Summa theologiae*, various translators, Blackfriars Series, 60 vols (1963–81); *Volume 10 Cosmogony*, trans. William A. Wallace (1967), with appendices, London: Eyre & Spottiswoode.
Thomas of Perseigne, *Commentarium in Cantica canticorum*, trans. Denys Turner (1995), in *Eros and Allegory: Medieval Exegesis of the Song of Songs*, CS 156, Kalamazoo, MI: Cistercian, pp. 309–15.
Villard de Honnecourt, *The Sketchbook of Villard de Honnecourt*, ed. Theodore Bowrie (1959), Bloomington, IN: Indiana University Press.
Vitruvius Pollio, *De architectura*, trans. M. H. Morgan (1914), in *Vitruvius: The Ten Books on Architecture*, Cambridge, MA: Harvard University Press.
William of St-Thierry, *Brevis commentatio*, trans. Denys Turner (1995), in *Eros and Allegory: Medieval Exegesis of the Song of Songs*, CS 156, Kalamazoo, MI: Cistercian, pp. 275–90.
—— *De natura et dignitate amoris*, trans. Geoffrey Webb and Adrian Walker (1956), in *On the Nature and Dignity of Love*, Fleur de Lys Series 10, London: Mowbray.
—— *Epistola ad fratres de Monte-Dei*, trans. Theodore Berkeley (1976) in *The Works of William of St Thierry, 4: The Golden Epistle*, CF 12, Kalamazoo, MI: Cistercian.

Secondary sources

Ackerman, James S. (1949) '"Ars Sine Scientia Nihil Est": Gothic Theory of Architecture at the Cathedral of Milan', *Art Bulletin*, 31, 84–211.
Adams, Henry (1913) *Mont-Saint-Michel and Chartres*, London: Constable, rev. edn. [n.d.].
Alexander, Christopher (1964) *Notes on the Synthesis of Form*, Cambridge, MA: Harvard University Press.
Barfield, Owen (1988) *Saving the Appearances: A Study in Idolatry*, Hanover, NH: Wesleyan University Press.

Bargellini, Piero (1954) *The Cloisters of Santa Maria Novella and the Spanish Chapel*, trans. H. M. R. Cox, Florence: Arnaud.

Beaujouan, Guy (1982) 'The Transformation of the Quadrivium', in *Renaissance and Renewal in the Twelfth Century*, eds Robert L. Benson and Giles Constable, Cambridge, MA: Harvard University Press; Oxford: Clarendon Press. pp. 463–87.

Bedos-Rezak, Brigitte (1995) 'Form as Social Progress', in *Artistic Integration in Gothic Buildings*, eds Virginia Chieffo Raguin, Kathryn Brush and Peter Draper, Toronto: University of Toronto Press, pp. 236–48.

Belting, Hans (1994) *Likeness and Presence: A History of the Image before the Era of Art*, Chicago, IL: Chicago University Press.

Beaumont, Ernest (1954) *The Theme of Beatrice in the Plays of Claudel*, London: Rockliff.

van den Berg, Dirk J. (2004) 'What is an image and what is image power?' in *South African Journal of Art History*, 19, 155–77.

Binding, Günther (2002) *High Gothic: The Age of the Great Cathedrals*, trans. Ingrid Taylor, Cologne: Taschen.

Bonner, Anthony (1993) *Doctor Illuminatus: A Ramon Llull Reader*, Princeton, NJ: Princeton University Press.

Bony, Jean (1954) *French Cathedrals*, London: Thames and Hudson.

Burckhardt, Titus (1995) *Chartres and the Birth of the Cathedral*, trans. William Stoddart, first pub. 1962, Urs Graf-Verlag; Ipswich: Golgonooza.

Camargo, Martin (1983) 'Rhetoric', in *The Seven Liberal Arts in the Middle Ages*, ed., David L. Wagner, Bloomington, IN: Indiana University Press, pp. 96–124.

Cambron, Glauco (1969) *Dante's Craft: Studies in Language and Style*, Minneapolis, MN: University of Minnesota Press.

Carruthers, Mary J. (1993) 'The Poet as Master Builder: Composition and Locational Memory in the Middle Ages,' *New Literary History*, 24, 881–904.

—— (1998) *The Craft of Thought: Meditation, Rhetoric, and the Making of Images, 400–1200*, Cambridge: Cambridge University Press.

Caviness, Madeleine Harrison (1995) 'Artistic Integration in Gothic Buildings: A Post-Modern Construct?' in *Artistic Integration in Gothic Buildings*, eds Virginia Chieffo Raguin, Kathryn Brush and Peter Draper, Toronto: University of Toronto Press, pp. 249–61.

—— (1990), *Sumptuous Arts at the Royal Abbeys in Reims and Braine:* Ornatus elegantiae, varietate stupendes, Princeton, NJ: Princeton University Press.

Chenu, M.-D. (1997) *Nature, Man, and Society in the Twelfth Century*, trans. Jerome Taylor and Lester K. Little, Toronto: Toronto University Press.

Chesterton, G. K. (1904) *The Napoleon of Notting Hill*, London: John Lane The Bodley Head.

—— (1933) *St Thomas Aquinas*, London: Hodder and Stoughton.

Cook, G. H. (1955) *Old S. Paul's Cathedral: A Lost Glory of Mediaeval London*, London: Phoenix.

Cowan, Painton (1979) *Rose Windows*, London: Thames and Hudson.

Croddy, Stephen (1999) 'Gothic Architecture and Scholastic Philosophy', *British Journal of Aesthetics*, 39: 3, 263–72.

Crossley, Paul (1988) 'Medieval Architecture and Meaning: the Limits of Iconography', *Burlington Magazine*, 130, 116–21.

Dales, Richard C. (1957) 'Robert Grosseteste's *Commentarius in octo libros Physicorum Aristotelis*', *Medievalia et humanistica*, 11, pp. 10–33.
Dimier, Anselme (1999) *Stones Laid Before the Lord: A History of Monastic Architecture*, trans. by Gilchrist Lavigne, CS 152. Paris: Arthème Fayard, 1964; Kalamazoo, MI: Cistercian.
Doig, Allan (2008) *Liturgy and Architecture: From the Early Church to the Middle Ages*, Aldershot: Ashgate.
Dronke, Peter (1997) *Dante's Second Love: the Originality and the Contexts of the Convivio*, Occasional Papers, 2, Exeter: Society for Italian Studies.
Dvořáková, Vlasta, Josef Krása, Anežka Merhautová and Karel Stejskal (1964) *Gothic Mural Painting in Bohemia and Moravia 1300–1378*, London: Oxford University Press.
Evans, John D. G. (1977) *Aristotle's Concept of Dialectic*, Cambridge: Cambridge University Press.
Ewing, Wayne A. (1965) '*Speculum Ecclesiae*: A Study of Correlations Drawn between Medieval Theology and the Gothic Cathedrals', PhD dissertation, Yale University, Ann Arbor, MI: University Microfilms.
Farley, Edward (2001) *Faith and Beauty: A Theological Aesthetic*, Aldershot: Ashgate.
Feiss, Hugh (Ed.) (2011) *On Love: A Selection of Works of Hugh, Adam, Achard, Richard, and Godfrey of St Victor*, VTT 2, Turnhout: Brepols.
Fernie, Eric and Paul Crossley (Eds) (1990) *Medieval Architecture and its Intellectual Context: Studies in Honour of Peter Kidson*, London: Hambledon.
Focillon, Henri (1963) *The Art of the West: I, Romanesque Art, II, Gothic Art*, trans. by Donald King, London: Phaidon.
Frankl, Paul (2000) *Gothic Architecture*, trans. Dieter Pevsner, first pub. 1962, rev. Paul Crossley, New Haven, MA: Yale University Press.
Frisch, Teresa G. (1971) *Gothic Art, 1140–c. 1450: Sources and Documents*, Englewood Cliffs, NJ: Prentice-Hall.
Gardner, Arthur (1938) *An Introduction to French Church Architecture*, London: Cambridge University Press.
—— (1915), *French Sculpture of the Thirteenth Century*, The Medici Portfolios, No.1, London: Philip Lee Warner.
Ginther, James R. (2003) 'Robert Grosseteste and the Theologian's Task', in *Robert Grosseteste and the Beginnings of a British Theological Tradition*, ed. Maura O'Carroll, Bibliotheca Seraphico-Capuccina, 69, Rome: Istituto Storico Dei Cappuccini, pp. 239–63.
Guthrie, W. K. C. (1967) *The Greek Philosophers: From Thales to Aristotle*, London: Methuen.
de Hamel, Christopher (1994) *A History of Illustrated Manuscripts*, London: Phaidon.
Harman, Alec (1973) *Man and his Music. The Story of Musical Experience in The West: 1, Mediaeval and Early Renaissance Music*, London: Barrie & Rockliff.
Harvey, John (1972) *The Mediaeval Architect*, London: Wayland.
Hearn, M. F. (1981) *Romanesque Sculpture: The Revival of Monumental Stone Sculpture in the Eleventh and Twelfth Centuries*, London: Phaidon; Ithaca: Cornell University Press.
Henderson, George (1968) *Chartres*, Harmondsworth: Penguin.

Heslop, T. A. (1990) 'The Iconography of the Angel Choir at Lincoln Cathedral', in *Medieval Architecture and its Intellectual Context*, eds Eric Fernie and Paul Crossley, London: Hambledon, pp. 151–58.
Heyman, Jacques (1995) *The Stone Skeleton: Structural Engineering of Masonry Architecture*, Cambridge: Cambridge University Press.
Hiscock, Nigel (1999) *The Wise Master Builder: Platonic Geometry in Plans of Medieval Abbeys and Cathedrals*, Aldershot: Ashgate.
—— (2007) *The Symbol at Your Door: Number and Geometry in Religious Architecture of the Greek and Latin Middle Ages*, Aldershot: Ashgate.
Holt, Elisabeth Gilmore (Ed.) (1957) *A Documentary History of Art, Volume I: The Middle Ages and Renaissance*, Garden City, NY: Doubleday.
Hou, Dennis (2008) 'The Infinity of God in the Biblical Theology of Denys the Areopagite,' *International Journal of Systematic Theology*, 10:3, 249–66.
Huntsman, Jeffrey (1983) 'Grammar', in David L. Wagner, ed., *The Seven Liberal Arts in the Middle Ages*, Bloomington, IN: Indiana University Press, pp. 58–95.
Karp, Theodore (1983) 'Music', in *The Seven Liberal Arts in the Middle Ages*, ed. David L. Wagner, Bloomington, IN: Indiana University Press, pp. 169–95.
Kessler, Herbert (2004) *Seeing Medieval Art*, Peterborough: Broadview.
Kidson, Peter (1987) 'Panofsky, Suger and St Denis', *Journal of the Warburg and Courtauld Institutes*, 50, pp. 1–17.
Klinkenberg, Emanuel S. (2009) *Compressed Meanings: The Donor's Model in Medieval Art to around 1300*, Turnhout: Brepols.
Kraebel, Andrew B. (2011) Introduction to Richard of St-Victor, *De quatuor gradibus*, in *On Love*, ed. Hugh Feiss, VTT 2, Turnhout: Brepols, pp. 263–73.
Kren, Claudia (1983) 'Astronomy', in *Seven Liberal Arts in the Middle Ages*, ed. David L. Wagner, Bloomington, IN: Indiana University Press, pp. 218–47.
Ladner, Gerhart B. (1983) *Images and Ideas in the Middle Ages*, 2 vols, Rome: Edizione di Storia e Letteratura.
Leclercq, Jean (1979) *Monks in Love in Twelfth Century France: Psycho-Historical Essays*, Oxford: Clarendon Press.
—— (1982) *The Love of Learning and the Desire for God: A Study of Monastic Culture*, trans. Catherine Misrahi, Fordham University Press.
Lewis, John A. H. (2003), 'History and Everlastingness in Hugh of St Victor's Figures of Noah's Ark', in eds Gerhard Jaritz and Gerson Moreno-Riaño, *Time and Eternity: The Medieval Discourse*, International Medieval Research Series 9, Turnhout: Brepols, pp. 203–22.
—— (2005) 'Presentation of verbal and visual images in the Middle Ages, and applications in medieval architecture,' *South African Journal of Art History*, 20.1, 116–30.
—— (2007) 'Medieval perception of space and place in the architecture of Gothic churches', *South African Journal of Art History*, 22.1, 73–90.
Louth, Andrew (1989) *Denys the Areopagite*, Wilton: Morehouse-Barlow.
McGarry, Daniel (1955) —refer John of Salisbury, *Metalogicon*.
McGinn, Bernard (1995) 'From Admirable Tabernacle to the House of God: Some Theological Reflections on Medieval Architectural Integration', in *Artistic Integration in Gothic Buildings*, eds Virginia Chieffo Raguin, Kathryn Brush and Peter Draper, Toronto: Toronto University Press, pp. 41–56.

McInerny, Ralph (1983) 'Beyond the Liberal Arts', in *Seven Liberal Arts in the Middle Ages*, ed. Wagner, Bloomington, IN: Indiana University Press, pp. 248–72.

Mackie, Evelyn A. (2003) 'Robert Grosseteste's Anglo-Norman Treatise on the Loss and Restoration of Creation, commonly known as *Le chateau d'amour*: An English Prose Translation', in *Robert Grosseteste and the Beginnings of a British Theological Tradition*, ed. Maura O'Carroll, Rome: Istituto Storico Dei Cappuccini, pp. 151–79.

Magee, John (1989) *Boethius on Signification and Mind*, Philosophia Antiqua Series 52, Leiden: Brill.

Mâle, Émile (1961) *The Gothic Image: Religious Art in France of the Thirteenth Century*, trans. Dora Nussey, London: Collins; first pub. in trans., London: Dent, 1913.

Marenbon, John (1983) *Early Medieval Philosophy (480–1150): An Introduction*, London: Routledge & Kegan Paul.

Maritain, Jacques (1934) 'St. Augustine and St. Thomas Aquinas', in *A Monument to Saint Augustine: Ten Essays on the Saint*, trans. Fr. Leonard, London: Sheed & Ward, pp. 199–223.

Marriage, Margaret and Ernest (1909) *The Sculptures of Chartres Cathedral*, London: Cambridge University Press.

Masi, Michael (1983a) see Boethius.

—— (1983b) 'Arithmetic,' in *The Seven Liberal Arts in the Middle Ages*, ed. David L. Wagner, Bloomington, IN: Indiana University Press, pp. 147–68.

Maurer, Armand A. (1982) *Medieval Philosophy*, Toronto: Pontifical Institute of Mediaeval Studies.

Morrison, Karl F. (1990) *History as a Visual Art in the Twelfth-Century Renaissance*, Princeton, NJ: Princeton University Press.

—— (1983) 'Incentives for Studying the Liberal Arts', in *The Seven Liberal Arts in the Middle Ages*, ed. David L. Wagner, Bloomington, IN: Indiana University Press, pp. 32–57.

Mueller, Ian (2005) 'Mathematics and the Divine in Plato', in *Mathematics and the Divine: A Historical Study*, eds T. Koetsier and L. Bergmans, Amsterdam: Elsevier, pp. 99–121.

O'Meara, D. J. (2005) 'Geometry and the Divine in Proclus', in *Mathematics and the Divine: A Historical Study*, ed. T. Koetsier and L. Bergmans, Amsterdam: Elsevier, pp. 131–45.

O'Rourke, Fran (1992) *Pseudo-Dionysius and the Metaphysics of Aquinas*, Notre Dame, IN: University of Notre Dame Press.

Panofsky, Erwin (1979) *Abbot Suger on the Abbey Church of St.-Denis and its Art Treasures*, 2nd edn., ed. Gerda Panofsky-Soergel, Princeton, NJ: Princeton University Press; first pub. 1946.

—— (1968) *Gothic Architecture and Scholasticism*, Cleveland, OH: World; first pub. 1951.

Peck, George T. (1980) *The Fool of God: Jacopone da Todi*, Alabama City, AL: University of Alabama Press.

van Pelt, Robert Jan (1983) 'Philo of Alexandria and the Architecture of the Cosmos', *AA Files* 4 (Annals of the Architectural Association, School of Architecture, London), 3–15.

—— and Carroll William Westfall (1993) *Architectural Principles in the Age of Historicism*, New Haven, CT, and London: Yale University Press.

Pieper, Josef (1965) *Love and Inspiration: A Study of Plato's* Phaedrus, trans. Richard and Clara Winston, London: Faber and Faber.

Poole, Reginald Lane (1932) *Illustrations of the History of Medieval Thought and Learning*, London: SPCK; first pub. 1880.

Price, Betsy B. (1992) *Medieval Thought: An Introduction*, Oxford: Blackwell; Cambridge, MA: Blackwell.

Radding, Charles and William W. Clark (1992) *Medieval Architecture, Medieval Learning: Builders and Masters in the Age of Romanesque and Gothic*. New Haven, CT: Yale University Press.

Reeves, Marjorie and Beatrice Hirsch-Reich (1972) *The* Figurae *of Joachim of Fiore*, Oxford: Clarendon Press.

Rousselot, Pierre (2001) *The Problem of Love in the Middle Ages*, intro. and trans. Alan Vincelette, Milwaukee, WI: Marquette University Press; first pub. in French, 1902.

Sauerländer, Willibald (1995) 'Integration: A Closed or Open Proposal', in *Artistic Integration in Gothic Buildings*, eds Virginia Chieffo Raguin, Kathryn Brush and Peter Draper, Toronto: Toronto University Press, pp. 3–18.

Sayers, Dorothy L. (1959) *The Mind of the Maker*, London: Methuen.

Seidel, Linda (1981) *Songs of Glory: The Romanesque Façades of Aquitaine*, Chicago, IL: University of Chicago Press.

Shelby, Lon R. (1977) *Gothic Design Techniques: the Fifteenth-Century Design Booklets of Mathes Roriczer and Hans Schuttermayer*, Carbondale, IL: Southern Illinois University Press.

von Simson, Otto (1962) *The Gothic Cathedral: Origins of Gothic Architecture and the Medieval Concept of Order*, Bollingen Series, XLVIII, New York: Pantheon.

Slocum, Kay B. (1993) '*Speculum musicae*: Jacques de Liège and the Art of Musical Number', in *Medieval Numerology: A Book of Essays*, ed. Robert L. Surles, New York: Garland, pp. 11–37.

Spargo E. J. M. (1953) *The Category of the Aesthetic in the Philosophy of Saint Bonaventure*, Philosophy Series 11, New York: Franciscan Institute of Saint Bonaventure.

van 't Spijker, Ineke (2004) *Fictions of the Inner Life: Religious Literature and Formation of the Self in the Eleventh and Twelfth Centuries*, Turnhout: Brepols.

Stevenson, Francis S. (1899) *Robert Grosseteste, Bishop of Lincoln: A Contribution to the Religious, Political and Intellectual History of the Thirteenth Century*, London: Macmillan.

Stump, Eleonore (1983) 'Dialectic', in *The Seven Liberal Arts in the Middle Ages*, ed. David L. Wagner, Bloomington, IN: Indiana University Press, pp. 125–46.

Surles, Robert L. (Ed.) (1993) *Medieval Numerology: A Book of Essays*, New York: Garland.

Taliaferro, Robert —refer Augustine, *De musica*.

Turner, Denys (1995) *Eros and Allegory: Medieval Exegesis of the Song of Songs*, CS 156, Kalamazoo, MI: Cistercian.

Wagner, David L. (Ed.) (1983) *The Seven Liberal Arts in the Middle Ages*, Bloomington, IN: Indiana University Press.

Wallis, Faith (1990) 'Images of Order in the Medieval Computus', in *Ideas of Order in the Middle Ages*, ed. Warren Ginsberg, Binghamton: CEMERS (ACTA v.15), pp. 45–68.

—— (2005) '"Number Mystique" in Early Medieval Computus Texts,' in *Mathematics and the Divine: A Historical Study*, eds T. Koetsier and L. Bergmans, Amsterdam: Elsevier, pp. 179–99.

Ward, Colin (1986) *Chartres: The Making of a Miracle*, London: Folio Society.

Watson, Francis (1997) *Text and Truth: Redefining Biblical Theology*, Grand Rapids, MI: Eerdmans.

Watson, Gerard (1986) 'Imagination and Religion in Classical Thought', in *Religious Imagination*, ed. James P. Mackey, Edinburgh: Edinburgh University Press, pp. 29–54.

Weitzmann, Kurt (1977) *Late Antique and Early Christian Book Illumination*, New York: George Braziller.

White, John (1993) *Art and Architecture in Italy 1250–1400*, New Haven, MA: Yale University Press; first pub. 1966.

Whitehead, Christiania (2003) *Castles of the Mind: A Study of Medieval Architectural Allegory*, Cardiff: University of Wales Press.

Wilson, Christopher (1990) *The Gothic Cathedral: The Architecture of the Great Church 1130–1530*, London: Thames and Hudson.

Worringer, Wilhelm (1964) *Form in Gothic*, trans. Herbert Read, London: Alec Tiranti; first pub. 1927.

Yates, Frances A. (1982) *Llull and Bruno: Collected Essays, Volume 1*, London: Routledge & Kegan Paul.

Zinn (1979) —refer Richard of St-Victor.

Index

Scripture text references in bold.

Abbo of Fleury 118, 153 n14
Abelard, Peter 83, 109 n66
abstract, abstraction 21, 78, 83–4, 87, 103, 112, 114, 124, 130, 136, 139, 170, 190, 203, 207–8, 214, 226
Achard of St-Victor 171
act, actuality 35, 68, 78, 96, 123, 130, 133, 181, 194, 216; actuality of the body 32; artefacts as acts of love 55–6, 207; connections as acts 51, 226; love is in act 27, 44, 48, 53, 230; mode of God's acts 40, 42–3, 52
Acts of the Fourth Lateran Council 184
Adam 68, 96, 175
Aelred of Rievaulx 31–2
affectus 57, 63, 201
Alan of Lille 61 n.105, 67, 235 n68
Alberti, Leon Battista 5
Albertus Magnus 69
Alcuin, 89–90
Alexander, Christopher 212–13, 214, 228, 231
Altenberg-en-der-Lahn, St Mary Convent church 172
Amalarius of Metz 24 n2
Amiens cathedral, St-Firmin: bas-relief of Ezekiel 39
amor 29, 30, 32, 33, 35, 47; *amor dei intellectualis* 107
Andrea di Bonaiuto 70, 72
angels 7, 14, 48, 55, 104, 157, 159–60, 181, 190; angelic contemplation 179–87, 210, 213; angelic orders 143–4, 182; as City of God 180; re monastic cells 218; operations 196; participation in divine things 195; visualising of angels 183, 186, *187*, *188*, 193

Angoulême cathedral 160, *161*
Anticlaudianus (Alan of Lille) 67
Aquitaine Romanesque churches 211
De arca Noe morali (Hugh of St-Victor) 110 n103
De arca Noe mystica (Hugh of St-Victor) 141
arch, arcade 73, 75, 79–80, 81, 99, 123, 165, 167, 193, 207; chancel arch 80, 193; choir arcade *86*; nave arcade *85*; screens between towers 191, *192*, 228, *18*; triforium arcade 127
De architectura (Vitruvius) 5, 140
architectural history 2; historicism 4, 8, 210; history of origins 19, 210
architecture: excluded as liberal art 64; grammar, dialectic, rhetoric of 210–11; as language of communication 205; named by Hugh of St-Victor 65; named by Thomas Aquinas 70; named by William of St-Thierry 34; rethinking of 15–18, 21, 232; taking form of love 204; triangular *Architectural* figure 227; vernacular 210
Aristotle 27, 54, 64, 67, 80, 81–2, 145, 151; prior and posterior representations 84
arithmetic 114, **118–24**, 152, 229; Lady Arithmetic 120
ark of Noah 5, 141; *see also* Hugh of St-Victor
ark of the Tabernacle 97, 188; *see also* Richard of St-Victor
arrangement 113, 138, 145, 214
Ars brevis (Llull) 225–6
ars dictaminis, ars poetriae, ars predicandi, in rhetoric 91

250 Index

art and artefacts: buildings 212–13; divine art 53, 55; as evidence 11, 16–17
artificer: 'artifacting fire' 158; clever 196; judging his own work 205; method 178, 213
ascension 17, 45, 132, 158, 160, *161*, 168–9, 189, 203
ascesis 36, 132, 218
aspectus 57, 201
Assisi, San Francesco upper church 193
astronomy 114, **143–52**, 229
Athanasius 52, 216–17, 230
Augustine of Hippo 5–6, 11–12, 20, 27, 28, 40, 63–4, 136, 151, 162, 175, 225; on angels 180; on arts and culture 65, 89; on form 41–2, 116, 181; knowledge as a machine 101; on love of 'God, neighbour, self' 31; love in the Trinity 47–8, 51; on 'measure, number, weight' 13–14, 36–7, 53; on music 124–8, 204–5; on number six 13–14, 122; on understanding the nature of things 183; 'universal commonwealth' 113; wisdom and number 113–14, 120
Autun cathedral, St-Lazare 11, 160
Averlino, Antonio di Piero (Filarete) 5–6
axis, axes 35, 94, 141, 160, 161, 163

Barfield, Owen 166, 191–2
Bargellini, Piero 70–1
Basil 55
beatitude 39–40, 60 n82; beatitudes personified 67
Beatrice Portinari (in Dante) 35, 38, 230–1
Beaujouan, Guy 118, 122
beauty 14, 29, 90, 100, 114, 116, 126, 127, 146, 164, 167, 169, 208, 213; of the Bride 222–3; in geometrical figures 136, 142; *see also* ugliness
Beauvais cathedral, St-Pierre 140
Bede 153 n14, 118, 198 n57, 224
Bedos-Rezak, Brigitte 228
Benjamin maior (Richard of St-Victor) 97, 132, 203
Bernard of Chartres 68, 72
Bernard of Clairvaux 8–10, 30, 102, 168–9; on angels 55; on consideration 202, 229; four degrees of love 32; love in Trinity 48; measure of love 40; on Song of Songs 44–6, 223–4
Bernardus Silvestris 150
Beverley minster, St John Evangelist 123, 127
Bible historiée of Jean de Papeleu 187–8, *188*
Binding, Günther 3
blush spot, rosy cheek 221, 222–4, *222*
body 32, 33, 84, 127, 150, 151, 155 n93; form of the body 181; geometrical 135–6, 140; of glory 32, 40, 144; incarnational 52, 230; instrumental 46, 230; metaphor for the church 150; physical church 82; weight 46, 169
Boethius 28, 64, 68–9, 81, 91, 103–4, 106; 114, 119–20, 129, 136, 140, 196 n7, 205–6
Boffy, Guillaume 89
Bonaventure 37, 51, 112, 124, 185, 194; on angels 196; on creation as mirror 162–3; gradations of things 185; illumination of mechanical arts 219; mystical vine 171; on number 129; on steps to God 217; twofold judgement 207
Boncompagno da Signa 100, 110 n83
bond, binding 48, 120, 134, 223–5
Bradwardine, Thomas 138
Braine Abbey, St-Yved 114
Breviloquium (Bonaventure) 162
Brevis commentatio (William of St-Thierry) 50
Bristol cathedral, Holy Trinity 167, *168*, 169, 175
Brioude, St-Julien church 186, *187*
building: builder and stonemason illustration 56; building language 73–4; direct process 209, 220; full of judgement 206; house building analogy 92; mnemonic building 101; universe metaphor 147
Burckhardt, Titus 12

De caelesti hierarchia (Pseudo-Dionysius) 58 n7, 143, 183
Calcidius 41, 44, 60 n71, 158, 198 n66
Camargo, Martin 91
Cambron, Glauco 107
canon tables 73, 123, 174, *174*
Cantica canticorum, Prologue (Origen) 30, 31, 58 n7, 222

Cantica canticorum (Bernard of Clairvaux) 40, 44, 46, 55, 223
caritas 29, 30, 33, 34, 47
De caritate (Thomas Aquinas) 27, 37, 39, 43, 44, 46–7, 56, 58 n6
De caritate (William of St-Thierry) 58 n6
Carruthers, Mary 71, 101
Cassiodorus 91
Castle Acre priory 123
Castle of Virtue of Love 5, 14
cause(s) 13–14, 67–8, 70–1, 107, 118, 122, 157–8, 178, 180, 201, 204; four causes 39, 77, 229; in Empedocles 150; in Plato 137
Caviness, Madeline 5
cell 21, 100, 214, 218–21
central crossing of church 35, 93, 121, 133, 140–2
chaos *see* disorder
chapter house 70–1, 115, *119*
charity: edifice of 28; form of the virtues 37; of 'God, neighbour, self' 31, 32; habit of charity 27; as 'number of love' 123; which unites to God 205
Charlemagne 89
Chartres cathedral, Notre Dame 65, 164; north and west porches iconography 67–8
cherubim 182, 188–9, 194
Chesterton, G. K. 1, 24
choir 93, 121, 124, 133, 193
Chorin Cistercian abbey church 172
Christ *see* Jesus Christ
Church, ecclesia 28, 44, 52, 82, 103, 143–4, 171–2, 175, 187, *188*, 219, 224, 227
church building(s) 114; anagogical parts 150; arithmetical diagram analogous 121; as incarnation, restoration, sacramental 53; intrinsic content 16; as microcosm 148–9, 178; present state 17–18, 118; sequential plan arrangement 34, 93; as 'signum' 52
Cicero 67, 90, 92
circle 92, 113, 114, 136
City of God 65, heavenly Jerusalem 194, 224
De civitate Dei (Augustine) 13, 31, 65, 122, 151
clarity 16, 113, 118, 142, 144, 206

Clark, William 139
Claudel, Paul 231
cloister 34, 36, 71–2
cogitatio 57, 63, 201–2
coherence 1, 21, 87, 101, 120, 138, 186, 224
coinhere 158, 163, 171, 195, 217, 223–4
Cologne, St Maria im Kapitol 93
Commentarium in Cantica canticorum (Thomas of Perseigne) 61 n105
Commentarius in Metaphysicorum Aristotlis (Thomas Aquinas) 151
Commentarius in octo libros Physicorum Aristotelis (Grosseteste) 155 n93
composition, composite 57, 84, 116, 118, 120, 134, 151, 195, 228; composing love 226; geometrically composed 138; musical 130
comprehension **63–107**, 63–5, 67, 73, 77–8, 80–1, 90, 92, 96, 99, 102, 104–05, 146, 178, 228
computus **116–18**, 124, 138, 212; 'images of order' 117–18
Confessiones (Augustine) 5, 27–8, 151
congruity: in architecture 16, 188, 191, 206; congruent geometry 123; in Girona cathedral design 88–9; in monastic cell 218, 220; in modes in grammar 78; in rhetorical *collatio* 96; in sculptural schemes 186, 193; in Trinity 48; *see also* incongruity
conjunction *see* connection, *also* joining
connection: between artificer and artefact 128; in Christ 114; of dichotomies in astronomy 143–4; evidential, methodological 3, 8, **18–24**, 34, 93, 166, 225–6; 'highest touches lowest' motif 145, 182, 188, 203, 216; in light 201; obtained in quadrivium 152; simile and metaphor in *collatio* 96
conscious attention 107, 124, 130, 190; conscious and unconscious 209, 213–14; sub-conscious 146, 166
consideration 84, **201–4**, 221, 229
De consideratione (Bernard of Clairvaux) 202
De consecratione (Abbot Suger) 195, 231
De consolatione philosophiae (Boethius) 58 n7, 114, 205–6

contemplation 34, 36, 41, 72, 84, 97, 100, 101, **157–96**, 203, 207; in astronomy 144, 146, 152; contemplative life personified 67; 'meadows of contemplation' 169; in music 132; of nature 157–96; of the Trinity 202
content *see* intrinsic content
contrariety 20, 183–4, 186, 195
Convivio (Dante) 210–11
correlation 21, 92; *see also* parallels
Cosmographia: Megacosmos and *Microcosmos* (Bernardus Silvestris) 150
cosmos 113, 134, 146–47, 149–50; cosmic temple 148
Coutances cathedral, Notre-Dame 17, *18*, *74*, *75*, 87, *90*, *95*, *97*, 207, *209*, 228
creation 54, 55, 68, 160, 176; six days 122, 159
creative art, creativity 24, 28, 40, 132, 150, 219; divine and human 203, 221; *ex nihilo* 162, 183, 203; number in creator's mind 120, 123
creatures 162, 205; Laon towers' oxen 191; placement around a church 189; symbolic 189, 190; *see also* Tetramorph
crockets 167, 174–75
Croddy, Stephen 139
Crossley, Paul 22
crucifixion of Christ: cross 143, 189; cross as Tree of Life 160; in Vine analogy 171
Cunault, Notre-Dame church 173

Dante Alighieri 35, 38, 56, 73, 103, 105–6, 107, 143, 146, 152; *Commedia* 211, 230; *Convivio 2.6* 62 n134; *2.13*, *2.16* 111 n136; *Inferno 12.41–4* 151; *Purgatorio 10. 32–33*; *94–96* 103; *Paradiso 1.70* 230; *9.106–8* 166; *10.1–6* 160, 230; *22.151* 143; *27.109–11* 35; *28.127–9* 56; 'transhumanised' 230; on vernacular 210–11
decoration 18, 71, 136, 166; arch motif 79; dispensed with 131; painted masonry pattern 78, 79, 173, 224–5; painted panels in brickwork 78; paintings in the Temple 189, 220

deductive method 7–8, 204, 228, 232; use of texts 11, 15–16, 18–19, 114, 152
dialectic 66–7, 80–90, 163, 175, 204–5, 226; architectural 71, 78, 210, 212; dialectical logic 184; intrinsic-extrinsic 228
De dialectica (Alcuin) 89
diatyposis, diacrisis, in rhetoric 103, 193
dichotomy: in artificer 42; in form 41, 176; material-spiritual 58, 144; sensible and superior 113, 168; in the soul 28, 46; things below and above 205–6
Dictum 118 (Grosseteste) 225
Didiscalicon (Hugh of St-Victor) 65, 82–3, 123, 133, 158, 176, 178–9
dilectio 30, 33
De diligendo Deo (Bernard of Clairvaux) 32, 40, 48, 58 n6
De disciplina claustrali (Peter of Celle) 72
disorder, chaos 52–3, 116, 134, 137, 151, 226, 231
dispositio, in rhetoric 90, 93–7
dissimilarity: between human and divine 195; sun and cornerstone example 186; *see also* similarity
De divina hierarchia (Pseudo-Dionysius) 143–4
De divina praedestinatione (Eriugena) 14, 46
De divinus nominibus (Pseudo-Dionysius) 56, 153 n13, 153 n28, 235 n64
De divisione naturae (Eriugena) 68
Doig, Allan: Foreword 15–16; 24 n3
Dore Abbey church 165
Dronke, Peter 26 n56
duality: dual reality 103; motif 41, 42, 45, 47; operations 196; of towers 87
Durandus, William, 189–90, 224

Earth: picture of threshing floor 143; shadow 143
efficient cause 55, 77–8, 181, 229; motive cause, love and strife 150
elements (fire, earth, air, water) 134, 150, 151
elocutio, in rhetoric 90, 97–100
Elucidatio (Alan of Lille) 61 n105, 235 n68

Empedocles 150–1, 154 n81
empyrean 66, 144, 147, 231
end, goal 19, 33, 39, 46, 55, 113, 116, 134, 160, 182, 214
Enoch 1 (Pseudo-Enoch) 'The Book of Astronomy' 147
Epistola ad fratres de Monte-Dei (William of St-Thierry) 21, 32–4, 49, 57, 213, 218–21
Epistola 11, Ad Cartusiensis (Bernard of Clairvaux) 59 n27
Eriugena, John Scottus 14, 20, 28, 46, 67–8, 184
eros 28–9, 34, 57
Erwitte, St Laurentius 193
Etymologiae (Isidore of Seville) 116
Eugenius III, Pope 202
evidence 11–14, 16, 28, 82; *see also* sources
Ewing, Wayne 141
exchange, mutual exchange 48, 81, 84, 191, 196, 223, 227
Exeter cathedral, St Peter 70, 81
extrinsic content 19, 21, 96, 211, 226
Ezekiel: temple 5, 38, 39; four living creatures 160; seeing the final cause 201

Farley, Edward 5
Faventinus 5–6
figures: of diction and thought in rhetoric 97, 103; in Llull's art 226; in mathematics 115; in Plato's geometry 134; *see also* geometry
final cause 39, 46, 201, 229
Florence, San Giovanni Baptistry 194; Santa Maria Novella chapter house fresco 70, 80, 90; San Miniato al Monte church 138, *165*, 166
form(s) 19, 41–4, 57, 68, 78, 83–4, 112, 115, 124, 130, 154 n43, 157, 180, 186, 205, 228, 231; form of angels 180; of art and love 223; diversity of forms 182; form of human beings 180, 195; form-making 213; forms of theology and liturgy 214; geometrical 133, 141, 225; of Incarnation 214; perfect form 181–3; two kinds of form 181; united with matter 216
form and content 16, 104, 211, 223, 228
formal cause 39, 55, 77, 180, 229
formal principle 27, 42, 214; 'form follows function' 133
Forma praedicandi (Robert of Basevorn) 102
foundations: building metaphor 190; dialectical 81–2; numbers 120; premisses 28; spiritual 70, 82
four living creatures, four Evangelists *see* Tetramorph
Frankl, Paul 139

Gardner, Arthur 191
gargoyle(s) 184, 186, 190
Gaudì, Antoni xv
De gemmae animae (Honorius of Autun) 9, 82, 224
De Genesi ad litteram (Augustine) 20
Geoffrey of Vinsauf 91, 92–3, 98–100, 210
Geometriva speculativa (Thomas Bradwardine) 138
geometry 89, 114, 124, **133–42**, 152, 229; figures, evaluation and demonstration 136, 180; line, simile of love 226; triangular figures 225
Ginther, James 52, 201, 225
Girona cathedral, Santa Maria 87–9, *88*, 95, 212
Gislebertus 160
Gloucester cathedral, Holy Trinity 92, 169, 193
goal *see* end
God 182: Alpha and Omega 120; Architect 53; Artificer 52–3, 157, 175, 221, 230; Artist 36, 53, 175, 181; Begetter 157; Cause 53; Creator 43, 46, 53–4, 116, 175, 181; Exemplar 37, 53–4, 130, 207; Father 147; First Principle 162; Glorious Consciousness 195; Idea, Pattern 179; Intellect 113; Maker 129, 157, 175, 231; Mind 146, 159; Musician 132; Wisdom 159; unmoved Mover 145; Workman 224
Goethe xv
Gothic xv, 4, 20, 22, 72, 75, 79, 91, 97, 124, 139, 164, 174, 210
grammar 66–7, 72–80, 163, 210, 212, 224
Gregory the Great 101, 169, 198 n47
Grosseteste, Robert 162, 194, 201, 226; citing Basil 55; *Le Château d'amour* 14–15, 37; on light and seeing 57;

on number 123; sermon 223; on the Trinity 51; wisdom and number, citing Augustine 113–14
Guthrie, William 150–51

Halberstadt cathedral, St Stephen and St Sextus 189
hand(s) of artificer 42, 92, 96, 99; mind and hand of artificer 175–9, 228
harmony 118, 120–2, 125–6, 131, 132, 195, 206
heaven(s) 21, 97, 134, 144, 149, 162, 168, 218–19, 227, 229
Henry of Avranches 5, 82, 103, 150, 167, 176, 190, 213
Hereford cathedral, St Mary 99, 207, *208*
Hearn, M. F. 164
Hexaëmeron commentaries 53, 157
Hexaëmeron (Basil) 55
Hexaëmeron (Grosseteste) 51, 54, 55, 57, 113, 123, 162, 194, 202
Heyman, Jacques, 140, 212
hierarchy, hierarch 34, **53–8**, 150, 182, 184, 194, 221, 227; angelic 180, 193; in architecture 183, 191; in astronomy 143; in Christ 217; of forms 182; 'highest touches lowest' motif 145, 182; in judging 206; musical 130; of nature 163
higher–lower *see* connections
Hiscock, Nigel 13, 122
Holy Spirit 43, 132, 175, 219, 224; in fresco 70; as Love in the Trinity 48–9; as will 51
Honorius of Autun 9–10, 189, 224
Hugh of Libergier 93
Hugh of St-Victor 72, 123, 143, 176, 179; on arts 65, 178; ark of salvation (of Noah) 53, 141; dialectic and building process 82–3, 205; on geometry 133; Incarnation as sacrament 216; on nature 157–8
Huntsman, Jeffrey 76

iconography 16, 67–8, 164, 166
idea(s) 68, 79, 83, 84, 86, 97, 157, 191; Idea in the mind of God 104; in music 130
ideal form 181, 195
illumination 217, 219, 223 *see also* light
images: base and opposite 183; image of God 43, 195; graphic 73; mental 20, 64, 68, 103, 194, 205; monastic 118; without images 202
imagination 17, 41, 42, 44, 57, 68, 100, 103–4, 178, 193, 201, 203, 205
imitation 63, 121, 164, 176, 178; painted masonry pattern 78, *79*; 87
Incarnation 15, **51–3**, 160, **214–19**, 227, 230; the 'glue' of theology 52; imaged 67; instrumental 52, 204; as restoration 53
De incarnatione Verbi Dei (Athanasius) 52, 216, 230
inclination 43, 44–6, 127, 159, 194, 214, 221, 223
incongruity 183, 193
inductive method 8, 16, 18–19, 139, 140; inference 20, 81
infinite, infinity 115, 123–5, 203, 219
innovation, *renovatio*, 210
De institutione arithmetica (Boethius) 114, 119–22, 140, 154 n67
instrument 46, 52–3, 57, 167, 196, 216, 230
integration: of all things 159, 225; of time, performance, context 21–4; 58, 191, 195, 227
intention **220–25**
De interpretatione (Aristotle) 64
intrinsic content 16, 17, 19, 21, 84, 96, 207, 214, 216, 226; intrinsic principle 27, 82
intuition, *intuitus* 8, 104, 112, 118, 119, 202, 204, **208–14**, 211
invention, *inventio* 15, 17, 34, 76, 78, 83, 87, 90–3, 100–1, 205, 220
De inventione (Cicero) 90, 92, 97
Isaiah: quoted by Jesus 113, vision of seraphim 190
Isidore of Seville 116, 153 n14
Itinerarium mentis ad Deum (Bonaventure) 129, 163, 194, 207

Jacopone da Todi 47
Jacques de Liège 129–30
Jerome 30, 97
Jesus Christ: Alpha and Omega 159; Author of Life 172; Creator 165; depicted in the church *187, 188*; Divine Nature 216; Firstborn of Creation 161; God-Man 160; harrowing of hell 151; Judge 160; Majesty 160; Maker 167, 218–19; quoting Isaiah 113; reasoning in the

Temple 81; 'a reckoning in Christ' 114; Source, Support and End 159; Sun of Righteousness 223; the Word 159, 216, 219; words, parables and eloquence 90
Joachim of Fiore 175
John of Damascus 216, 234 n43
John of Salisbury 68, 73, 83–4, 87, 103, 205–6, 211–12
joining, junction 96, 160, 176, 178, 196, 228–9; junction between heaven and earth **230–3**
Josephus on Tabernacle as symbol 156 n130
judgement 8, 16–17, 42, 56, 66, 80, 81, 87, 164, 175; in synthesis 201, **204–8**, 231; in dialectic 83; in rhetoric 90, 100, 103, 104; in music 130; *judicial numbers* 126; judging of judgement 126, 204; building full of judgement 206; by pruning and abstraction 207; concomitant with intuition 209, 213–14, 221, 225
Jupiter (Jove), and Juno 143, 147

Karp, Theodore 131–2
Kidson, Peter 195
kiss: in the Trinity 49–50, 61 n105; application in the soul 50
Kraebel, Andrew 34

Ladner, Gerhart 184
Laon cathedral, Notre Dame 68–9, 94, *121*, 123, 149, *149*, 191
Laude 88 (Jacopone da Todi) 47
Le Château d'amour (Grosseteste) 14–15, 58 n6
Leclerq, Jean 31
Le Mans cathedral, St-Julien 124, 136, *137*, 140
Leonardo Bruni xv
Lewis, John 61 n117, 109 n73; 111 n121; 155 n92 n110
liberal arts: application 8, 63, 114; associated with cloister 72; curriculum 6–7; metaphor of chariot and horses 67; personified 66–7, 69, 70, 114
Liber amici et amati (Llull) 57, 58 n6
Liber Concordie, Liber Figurarum (Joachim of Fiore) 175
Liber de rebus in administratione sua gestis (Abbot Suger) 26 n68

De libero arbitrio (Augustine) 41–2, 58 n7, 153 n7, n17
light 42, 57, 136, 144, 147, 169, 201, 203, 226; 'chink of sunlight' 214; reflected from polished objects 223
Limburg-en-der-Lahn, St Sebastian convent church 225
Lincoln cathedral, St Mary 73, 103, 150, 167, 190, 213, 223, 229; chapter house 115, *115*; kernel and honeycomb images 176, *177*
line(s): between extremes in Llull's Art 226; boundary line 92; expressive 75, 169; *gramma* 73; graphic 51, 84–6, 87, 123, 134–6, 163, 180; measuring line–taut cord 82, 92; multiplied mouldings 80; spider's thread 136
liturgy 3, 24 n3, 57, 214, 219; liturgical music 125, 132–3; performance 23
Llull, Ramon: the Art, *ars*, 21, 225–6, 228; mystical theology 57
locus see place
logic 64–5, 72, 80–2, 87, 89, 90, 123
London, Old St Paul's cathedral, chapter house 71
Louth, Andrew 56
Lübeck, St Marienkirche 78, 170
Lucca church of San Frediano: east-front mosaic 45, *45*
De luce (Grosseteste) 226
lunar table AEIOV 118

McGinn, Bernard 23–4, 208
machine, for lifting up 101, 198 n69 *see also* 'mechanical art'
McInerny, Ralph 89
macrocosm and microcosm 145–46, 178
Magdeburg cathedral, St Maurice and St Catherine 75, *76*, 99
Magee, John 68, 103–4
making, maker 15, 40, 52, 96, 130, 150, 151, 158; with *operatio* 210; range and art of making process 180, 205, 228
Mâle, Emile xv, xvi, 20
Malmesbury Abbey, St Peter and St Paul 196
man: animal, rational, spiritual 33–4; in *Microcosmos* allegory 150
Mantes cathedral, Notre Dame 90, 131, *131*, 191, *192*, 214, 229

256 *Index*

Marburg, St Elisabeth church 172
Marenbon, John 81
Maritain, Jacques 37
Mars, planet 143
Martianus Capella 64, 66, 100, 102, 134; *see also De nuptiis*
Martin of Laon 176, 198 n68
Masi, Michael 120
masonry 78, 87, 167, 173, 176, 224–5; *see also* decoration
master-builder, craftsman 83, 101, 117, 213
mathematics 112–13, 115
matter, material 68, 75, 77, 83–4, 87, 94, 96, 103, 115–16, 124, 140, 154 n43, 181, 194, 196; deified 216; lowliest matter 186; material cause 229; potency in matter 182; translation to spiritual 207; united with form 216
mean (between extremes), middle; 100–1, 158, 196; in Llull's figures 226
meaning, 2, 16, 19, 42, 52, 63–4, 66–7; 75, 79–80, 84, 99, 102, 113, 118, 140, 142, 180, 214, 228; congruity gives 185, 187; 'like a lake' 166
'measure, form, inclination' (or 'measure, number, weight') 13, 36–47, 53, 115
measure 38, 80, 93, 123, 125, 146, 229; the great measure *ordinatio* 117; measure the unmeasurable 116–17; measuring-rod 38; rational 40, 89
'mechanical art', 'adulterate' 176
medium: agent 43, 57–8, 136; material 65, 79, 145; of perception 217; visual 68
Megacosmos and *Microcosmos see Cosmographia*
memory, *memoria* 90, 100–2, 138; memory in music 126–7, 132
mental concepts, *entimemata* 20, 64, 175, 179; mental process 63, 179, 204
Mercury 66, 80, 82, 143, 146
Metalogicon (John of Salisbury) 83–4, 211
metaphor, *translata* 20
Metaphysics (Aristotle) 151
Metz cathedral, St Étienne 144, *145*
Middle Ages, medieval: culture 203; time-frame 4, 81

Milan cathedral, Santa Maria Maggiore 141, *142*, 147; 2nd conference of cathedral Council (1401) 142
mind: divine Mind 68–9, 81, 157, 160, 169, 179; of a maker 118, 147, 149, 152, 158, 172, 175, 181, 201
mirror, *speculum* 19–20, 77, 100, 102, 162, 182, 196, 204, 229
model 41, 55, 77, 114, 116–17, 118, 134, 137, 140, 142, 144, 146, 148–9, 166, 172, 176, 178–9, 207, 213; of love 15, 28; ratiocination 38; triadic 8, 50–1
model, physical model: cell 218; church 92–3, 229; Tabernacle 220
modern assumptions 87, 89, 138–40, 232–3
Moissac Abbey 78, *79*, 164
monastery 118, 219; community 28, 210, 213–14; experience 34, 57; paradoxes 28; study 91
Montiore-sur-Loire, St-Gilles chapel 235 n66
Moon 73, 116, 143, 147, 163
Morienval Abbey, Notre-Dame *10*, 11
Morris, William xv
Morrison, Karl 24 n4, 63–4
mortar, cement, glue 224 *see also* masonry, *and* stone metaphors
Moses 5, 163, 220
music 114, **124–33**, 152, 204–5, 229
De musica (Augustine) 6, 124–8; 154 n60
De musica (Boethius) 114
mystical theology 57; *Mystical* triangular figure 227; mystical vine *see* vine

Narbonne cathedral, St Just 88
De natura et dignitate amoris (William of St-Thierry) 60 n64
nature 103, 114, 157–8, 166, 170, 206; nature and art 167, 174, 176, 178; nature of humans 195; personified 150; work according to nature 213; of a work *naturised* 207
nave 34, 85, 87–9, 93, 121, 124, 133, 169, *177*
neoplatonism: astronomy 143; influence 28–9, 57; philosophy 13
Nicomachean Ethics (Aristotle) 26 n49, 27

number, numbering: number and form 42; number symbolism 129, 188; number theory, philosophical, mystical 120, 146; science and use 41–2, 112, 114, 116; 'spiritual' power 128
numbers: 'number of love' 122; numbers one to four 125; number six 13–14, 122, 153 n37; perfect numbers 122; 16 symbolic lamps 42, *43*
De nuptiis Philologiae et Mercurii (Martianus Capella) 64, 66–7, 72, 90, 92, 97, 134–5, 146–7

oculus 89, 95
O'Meara, Dominic 113
operation(s), *Operatio* 116, 133, **193–6**; action and work of love 55, 194, 210, 223; medallion *54*, *55*
order 11, 87, 113–14, 115, 122, 139, 149, 151: architecture ordered to God 231; in arithmetic 120; body ordered by spirit 32; computus order 116–17; hierarchical order 182, 193; internal ordering 127, 160; in love 37, 46–7, 214; of reason 221; sabbath order 31–2; of virtue 47; of work 206
ordinatio see measure
Origen 28, 31
origin, source 19, 31, 40, 116, 120, 134, 182, 193, 226
ornament: in rhetoric 90, 97, 99
O'Rourke, Fran 54

Panofsky, Erwin xvi, 38, 118, 195, 206–7
paradoxes 44, 96; *see also* dichotomy
parallels 21, 83, 90, 96, 126, 175, 182
Paris cathedral, Notre-Dame 124
participation 23, 40, 53, 67, 104, 107, 120, 124, 143, 158, 166, 184, 186, 191, 194–5, 227; collaboration 211; relation to vernacular 213
Paschal table 116
passio 29–30, passion 143
pattern: in building 131, 213–14, 224, 226; in computus 118; of love 34, 207; of human life 217; in music 132; in numbers 120, 123; of trinity, of mind 48, 50

personification **66–70**; of Dialectic 80; of heavenly bodies 146; of liberal arts 66–7; of Rhetoric 90; of Wisdom 69
Peterborough cathedral, St Peter 80, 87, 90, 95, 104, *106*, 138
Peter Lombard 162
Peter of Celle 72
Phaedrus (Plato) 30, 146
phantasias 127
phenomena 64, 77, 104, 112, 144, 206
Philibert de l'Orme xv
Philo of Alexandria (Judaeus) 147–9
philology 66, **70–2**, 146–7
philosophy: influence of Greek 11–12, 113; re judgement 205–6; Lady Philosophy 69, 105, 114, 210; philosophical grammar 76–7
physics 89; Physis (natural science) 150
Pieper, Josef 29–30
place(s) 46, 116, 118, 123, 126–7, 138–9, 144, 147, 151, 155 n93, 166, 189, 218, 220
plan setting out 115, 121, 140–1
Plato 11, 28, 29, 113, 134, 137, 162; 'idea' in *Timaeus* 68, 112; 'necessity' in *Timaeus* 134, 137; 'receptacle' in *Timaeus* 137; origin of Time 146; 'surface of the universe' 146; theory of Forms 41; theory of origins 54
Platonism: Christian adoption 13, Platonic geometry, symbolism 13, 140
plenary 81, 138; plenum 145; work full of love 206
pleroma 21; 'all things' 123, 129, 138, 157–8, 163, 194, 213, 216
Plotinus 11, 28, 41
Poetria nova (Geoffrey of Vinsauf) 91, 98
point, geometrical 84, 85, 92, 135–6, 138; metaphysical 120, 203
Poitiers, Notre-Dame-la-Grande, 165
Porphyry 11, 41, 68; simile of colouring in a drawing 68
potentia, potential 207, 216, 228; human love is potential 230
Prenzlau cathedral, St Mary 78, 136 (Front cover image)
Primum Mobile 143–4, 146
prior and *posterior* representations 84–6
Proclus 28, 113

258   *Index*

productive work: by love 44, 55; by wisdom 129
progression: in love **31–6**; in music 125–6, 133; spatial in the church 36, 133
pronouncement, inner 104; 'pronouncing' sound 125
pronuntiatio, in rhetoric 90, 102–7
propinquity 46, 185
proportion 40, 47, 58, 79, 83, 89, 116, 121–2; 125–6, 130, 134, 149, 203; structural 140, 163
prototypical buildings 5, 102, 188
Psalter Anglo-Saxon, of Trinity 49, *49, 50*, 159
Psalter of Isobel of France, Psalm 27 *42, 43*
Pseudo-Dionysius 11, 28, 54, 56, 116 n13, 129, 143, 183, 186, 195, 221
Pugin, A. N. W. xv
Pythagoras 129

quadrivium 64, 67, 73, **112–52**, 211, 229
De quantitate animae (Augustine) 136
De quatuor gradibus violentae caritatis (Richard of St-Victor) 34–6, 58 n6
Queen Mary *Psalter* 81
quiddity 104, 211, 215, 225
Quid vere diligendum est (Hugh of St-Victor) 53
Quodlibetum (Thomas Aquinas) 44

Radding, Charles 139
ramification 169; in 'every dimension' 216
ratio 124–5, 127–8, 130, 141
ratiocination 38, 66, 93, 119, 124, 207, 228
rationale 40, 82, 141, 152, 203, 207, 227
Rationale divinorum officiorum (William Durandus) 189, 224
Ravenna, San Vitale basilica 165
reason, rationality 158–9, 167, 180: re charity 37; re form 42; in judging music 127, 130; pattern of reason and love 221; in *Timaeus* 113, 137
De reductione artium ad theologiam (Bonaventure) 217–19
Regensburg cathedral, St Peter 185, *185*

Reims cathedral, Notre-Dame 81, 190; St-Nicaise abbey church 93; St-Remi abbey 136
Remaclus, Bishop 55
Remigius of Auxerre 197 n9
Renaissance 5, 79, 212
representation(s) 33, 55, 64, 79, 103, 160, 166, **188–93**
restoration: of all things 53, 216, 225
rhetoric 66–7, 78, **90–107**, 163, 175, 204–5, 210, 212
Rhetorica ad Herennium 97–8
Rhetorica novissima (Boncompagno da Signa) 110 n83
Richard de Fournival 71
Richard of St-Victor: *Benjamin maior* 97; on contemplation 132, 210; four degrees of violent love 34–6; six levels of contemplation 167, 203
Robert of Basevorn 102
Romanesque 75, 79, 87, 91, 97, 139, 174, 210; tympana 163, 164
Rome xv; Roman Empire's greatness 13
Rome, San Clemente basilica 171
rose, symbolic: motif of love 172–3, 225; red as the blood of Christ 171
rose window 21, 136; Braine wheel window 114; Laon 69, 94; Sens 144
Ruskin, John xv

sabbath 31
sacrament(s) 53, 216, 219
De sacramentis Christianae fidei (Hugh of St-Victor) 53, 158, 216
De sacramentis numerorum (William of Auberive) 122
sacred geometry 118, 140
St Alban's Bible 73, 123
St-Bertrand-de-Comminges cathedral, Ste. Marie 99, 216, *217*
St-Denis Abbey 12, 22, 23, 66, 102, 108 n9, 164, 195, 218, 231
St-Germer-de-Fly abbey 66, 108 n9
St-Gilles-du-Gard, abbey church 164
Saint-Gilles, Montoire-sur-le-Loir 160
St John: measuring the Temple 38; New Jerusalem 5; Patmos vision 160
St-Lizier cathedral, St-Lizier 78, 173, *173*
St Mary Virgin 93, 219: AvE motif, and rose symbol 225; image of castle 14–15; as *sedes sapientiae* 67; representing Wisdom 69

St Paul 36, 40, 64
St-Savin-sur-Gartempe, St Savin church 96, *202*
Salisbury cathedral, St Mary 70, *105*
sanctuary 35–6, 80, 93, 133, 144, 147, 163, 186, 188–9, 193, 214, 220, 228
Sant' Angelo in Formis church 235 n66
Sant' Apollinare in Classe abbey church 165
Saturn 143–4
Sauerländer, Willibald 22–3
Sayers, Dorothy L. 151, 197 n24
scheme, *schemata* 56, 67, 72–3, 82–3, 87, 90, 92, 101, 166, 186, 194
scholastic(s) 36, 57, 81, 91, 118, 207
Schwerin cathedral, St Mary and St John the Baptist 172
sculpture, statues, bas-relief 55, 67, 81, 103, 160, 164; context and setting 184, 191; corbel-tables and gargoyles 184–5; crockets 174
Seidel, Linda 211
Senlis cathedral, Notre-Dame 164
Sens cathedral, St-Etienne 66, 108 n9, 144
sense perception 104, 130, 133, 136; apprehension 210; senses 33, 41–2, 52, 63, 66–7, 68, 71, 72, 81, 101, 125, 132–3, 138, 158, 162, 205, 216; sensible world 113, 178, 216
In Sententarium (Bonaventure) 51
Sententiae (Bernard of Clairvaux) 224
Sententiae (Peter Lombard) 162
seraphim 56, 143–4, 159, 187, *187*, 188, *188*, 190, 194
sermo humilis 91
Sermo 10 (Achard of St-Victor) 171
Sermo 337 (Augustine) 12
Sermones de diversis (Bernard of Clairvaux) 9, 197 n46
Sermones super Cantica canticorum (Bernard of Clairvaux) 9, 58 n6; 200 n120, 223
similarity: similitude (*similitudo*) 20, 184–5, 203, 218; and dissimilarity 183, 185, 191, 193, 195
situs, situation 145, 147
skill 34, 63–4, 72, 83, 99, 102–3, 107, 162, 176, 190, 219–20
Slocum, Kay 129–30
Soest, St Patroclus church 97, 135, *135*
Soissons cathedral, St Gervais and St Protais 122

Solomon's temple 5, 188–9, 224
Song of Songs: exposition 28–30, 50, 89–90; the Bride as the Church 172; paradoxes 44; in art 45
sources of evidence 4–5, 118, 166, 191; lack of design records 212; lack of texts 5–6, 64, 82, 184; no canon in computus theory 117
Southwell Minster, St Mary 85–6, *85*, *86*, 124
space 35, 46, 50, 65, 137–9, 145
De specialibus Legibus (Philo Judaeus) 149
speculative knowledge 112, 130, 132, 150–1
De speculo caritatis (Aelred of Rievaulx) 31, 58 n6
Speculum musicae (Jacques de Liège) 129–30
stability, permanence 113–14, 116, 120, 140, 167, 212
Stargard cathedral, Blessed Virgin Mary, 170
Stavelot Abbey, retable medallion *54*, 55, 61 n123
stone 103, 144, 221; *see also* masonry
stone metaphors: Bede's metaphor 224; as members of the Church 173, 225; Thomas's metaphor 27
structure: of building elements 77, 80, 131; spiritual structure analogy 83; stability and integrity 88–9, 140, 212; 'structure of charity' 101
style 12, 16, 23, 87, 91, 98, 139, 164, 206, 232: in *elocutio* 97, 99
De substantia dilectionis (Hugh of St-Victor) 58 n6
Suger, Abbot 5, 12, 23, 102, 108 n14, 195, 200 n123, n125, 218, 231
Summa contra gentiles (Thomas Aquinas) 23, 55, 64, 66, 133, 178–9
Summa theologica (Thomas Aquinas) 17 (n49), 38, 40, 70, 123, 144, 204–5, 214–16, 221
Sun 143, 147, 163
surface 75, 84–6, 145; *epiphaneia* 135–6, 138; surface of the universe 146
syllogism 8, 20–21, 225
symbol, symbolism 12–13, 16, 20, 26 n56, 50, 66, 159, 163, 165–6, 171, 183–4, 186, 189, 192; graphic, geometric symbols 73, 79–80, 140;

natural symbol 33, 80, 203; number symbolism 118, 120, 122, 129
symmetry 83, 87, 121–22, 126, 132, 136, 140, 142, 163
Symposium (Plato) 28

Tabernacle: as cosmic building 148; of Moses 5, 220
De tabernaculo (Bede) 224
Taliaferro, Robert 125
Taylor, Jerome 197 n9, 198 n66
Ten Books of Architecture (Alberti) 5
Tetramorph 141, 159, 160, 183, 186, *187*, 189
texts *see* sources
theology: affective 57, 208; affirmative 3, 15, 23, 51; content 31, 38, 52, 82, 89, 93, 157, 163, 164; role of 27–9, 37, 113, 204; *Theological* triangular diagram 50
third entity 50, 134, 204, 218
Thomas Aquinas: 23, 24, 27, 54, 56, 123–4, 133, 180, 205; on agent causes 55, 204; *On Charity* 37, 39, 42–4, 47; on Empedocles 151; on the Empyrean 144; re expression 64; in fresco 70; on incarnation 53, 214, 216; on measure, limit (*modus*) 38, 40; on mutuality 221; on Wisdom text 115
Thomas of Perseigne 61 n105
Timaeus (Plato) 60 n71, 68, 112–13, 134, 137,146, 156 n134, 158, 162, 226
time, temporality 22–3, 46, 116, 118, 126–7
Topica (Aristotle) 84
Toulouse, Les Jacobins church *98*, *99*, 225
towers and spires 17, 81, 96–7, *98*, *99*, 122, 135; crossing tower 141; development 182; dual towers 87; signification 202–3; Tower of Wisdom 5; towers and galleries 191
tradition 206–7, 210, 213; directness 209–10; precedents 212; trial and error 212
tracery 94, 95, 99, 144, *145*, 169, 216
Tractatus de continuo (Thomas Bradwardine) 138
transcendence 41, 144, 147, 149, 214
transept(s) 121, 140, 142
tree analogy 169, 175; *see also* ramification

triadic model, trinitary pattern 8, 47–8, 50–1, 58, 225–7, 229
triangular figures: *Theological* 50; *Mystical* 227; *Architectural* 227
De trinitate (Augustine) 40, 48, 51, 225
De Trinitate (Thomas Aquinas) 58 n6
Trinity **47–51**, 159, 162, 175, 180; manifest form of love 204, 225; in music 130; Trinity and integration **225–30**
De triplici via, seu incendium amoris (Bonaventure) 58 n6
trivium **63–107**, 64, 67, 72–3, 228
Troyes, church of St-Urbain 90, 93–5, *94*, *95*
Turner, Denys 28–9, 30

ugliness 196; unbeautiful 163
union with God 34, 36, 50, 195, 205, as through Incarnation 215, 217
unity 162: application in soul 50, 221; in geometry 134; in incarnation 215–16 of material and immaterial 21, 196; in music 125, 127, 205; of objects of love 56, 225; in trinity 48–9, 227
universals 81, 83, 109 n66
universe 76, 112–13, 125–6, 134, 137, 143–4, 145–8, 150–1, 175, 190, 213
unselfsconscious(ness) 209–10, 212, 223 *see also* conscious attention
upward movement 80, 203, 206 *see also* ascension

van den Berg, Dirk 104, 108 n4
De vanitate mundi (Hugh of St-Victor) 143
van Pelt, Robert Jan 4, 147–8, 210
van 't Spijker, Ineke 57
vaulting 77–8, 79, 86, 88, 100, 147, 169, 216; angels portrayed 193; emulating forest 167, 175; as wings 190
Venus, planet 90, 105–6, 143
De vera religione (Augustine) 154 n60
vernacular: in art 100, 173–4; in building 99, 166, 209–10, 223, 231; language 66; in texts 6
Verona, San Zeno church 160; San Fermo Maggiore church 186
verticality 17, 76, 99, 168–9, 203, 228; vertical axis 35, 122, 142
vesica 50, 159, *161*, 165

Vézelay, Sainte-Madeleine 164
Victorius of Aquitaine 116
Vignogoul Abbey church 214, *215*
Villard de Honnecourt 5, 140–1, 190
Vincent of Beauvais 20
vine metaphor 171–2
Viollet-le-Duc xv, 22
virtue 40, 47, 146, 195, 208, 223; of numbers 120
virtues 44; cardinal four 65; charity their form 37; cardinal virtues personified 67, 70
vision of God 32, 35, 42, 170, 186, 203
visual language 66, 72–5, 79; seeing 'unformed sights' 183, 203; visualisation 183–8, 191, 195; visual pattern 118; visual representations 166, 188
La Vita Nuova (Dante) 210
Vita Sancti Hugonis (Henry of Avranches) 82, 103, 150
Vitis mystica (Bonaventure) 171–2
Vitruvius 5
von Simson, Otto xvi, 12, 139, 140–1
Vulgate, Latin in Song of Songs 30
De vulgari eloquentia (Dante) 211

Wallace, William 145, 196 n1
Wallis, Faith 116–18
Watson, Gerard 41, 44
Wells cathedral, St Andrew 70; chapter house 87, 92, *119*, 120
Westfall, Carroll 16, 19
west front of church, west door 17, 93–4, *95*, 104, *105*, *106*, 160, 165, 172, *177*, 191, 228–9
White, John 193
will 13–14, 33–4, 206; charity a form of willing 51
William of Auberive 122
William of St-Thierry 21, 44, 60 n64, 126; animal, rational, spiritual kinds of person 32–3; *aspectus* and *affectus* 57; cell-church-heaven 219–20, 226–7; creative work 221; love in the Trinity 48–50; re monks building 213, 218
Wilson, Christopher 190
Winchester, New Minster 122; St Cross chapel 123, 127, *128*
windows 99, 100, 144, 147; illustrations and metaphors 9–10; of north transept 68; *see also* rose window

wisdom 37, 41, 72, 158–9, 179, 201, 204; Wisdom of God 69, 162, 175; Wisdom's house of seven pillars 70; Wisdom and number 113–14
Wisdom of Solomon text: in wide use 13; in Augustine 13–14
work of architect, artificer, artist 37, 42, 53, 55–6, 58, 74, 96, 114, 123–4, 175–6, 178, 194, 204, 223 *see also* operation
Worringer, Wilhelm 75
Wren, Christopher xv
Wrocław, cathedral, St John the Baptist 172; church of St Dorothy 136, 147, *148*, 169; church of St Mary-on-the-Sands 77, 78, 169

Zechariah 38
Zenobi de' Guasconi 70
Zinn, Grover 132
zodiac 67, 146, 149, 161

Scripture references

Genesis **1. 22, 28**: 160, 197 n18; **1. 26**: 26 n.56, 51; **1.27**: 197 n13; **2. 7**: 96; **5. 1–2**: 197 n13; **6. 14–22**: 5 (n16); **8. 17, 22**: 163, 197 n29; **9. 1, 7**: 162, 197 n29; **9. 16**: 197 n17, n29; **14. 19**: 163, 197 n30
Exodus **25. 40**: 235 n59; **26: 5**(n12)
Deuteronomy **33. 13–16**: 163, 197 n31
I Kings **6. 29, 32, 35**: 199 n104
II Chronicles **3: 5** (n13)
Psalm **27. 1**: 42–43; **80. 8–11**: 198 n50; **134. 3**: 163, 197 n32
Proverbs **8. 22–31**: 197 n15; **9. 1**: 70 (n23)
Ecclesiastes **8. 16**: 114
Song of Songs **1. 4**: 44; **1.10**: 235 n67, n68; **2. 4, 2. 5**: 30, 47; **3. 10**: 30; **5. 8**: 30; **8. 7**: 30
Wisdom of Solomon **7. 7–8**: 70; **7.27**: 235 n63; **8. 1**: 41, 235 n63; **11. 20**: 13–14, 36, 44; **11. 22, 24, 26**: 13
Sirach **38. 34**: 221 (n64)
Isaiah **5. 1–7**: 198 n50; **54. 10–13**: 113
Ezekiel **1, 8, 10**: 26 n.56; **40–42**: 5 (n14)
Zechariah **2. 1–5**: 38
Matthew **1. 20**: 219 n56; **20. 1–6**: 198 n51; **21. 33–41**: 198 n51; **22. 37**: 152

John **1. 1–4**: 197 n15; **6. 45**: 113; **15. 1, 5**: 198 n53
Acts **17. 24**: 117 n21
Romans **1. 20**: 168
I Corinthians **3. 10**: 70; **8. 1**: 28 n5, 111 n113; **13. 7**: 36; **15. 28**: 194
II Corinthians **5. 1**: 117 n21
Ephesians **2. 21–22**: 235 n74; **4. 13, 16**: 40
Colossians **1. 16–17**: 197 n15
Hebrews **3. 3–4**: 60 n74; **7. 16**: 163, 197 n30; **9. 11**: 117 n21; **11. 10**: 163
I Peter **2. 5**: 235 n74
I John **4. 8, 16**: *see* 48 n103
Revelation **1. 8, 17**: 197 n16; **4. 3**: 197 n17; **11. 1–2**: 38; **11. 19**: 197 n30; **21. 6**: 197 n16; **21. 10–22. 5**: 5 (n15)